The First Urban Christians

THE
FIRST URBAN
CHRISTIANS

*The Social World of the
Apostle Paul*

WAYNE A. MEEKS

YALE UNIVERSITY PRESS

NEW HAVEN AND LONDON

Published with assistance from the foundation established in memory of Amasa Stone Mather of the Class of 1907, Yale College.

Designed by James J. Johnson
and set in Sabon Roman type.
Printed in the United States of America by
The Vail-Ballou Press, Binghamton, N.Y.

Library of Congress Cataloging in Publication Data

Meeks, Wayne A.
　The first urban Christians.

　Bibliography: p.
　Includes index.
　1.　Sociology, Christian—Early church, ca. 30–600.
2.　Paul, the Apostle, Saint.　I.　Title.
BR166.M44　1983　　　270.1　　82–8447
ISBN 0–300–03244–7 (pbk.)　　　AACR2

14　13

TO HANS W. FREI
colleague, mentor, friend

CONTENTS

PREFACE

In my first year of teaching, certain students at Dartmouth College let me know that the splendid constructions of modern New Testament scholarship, which I was eager to impart after seven years of professional and graduate schools, were not really intelligible to them. By the end of the semester, some of the students' questions had become my own; I have spent eighteen years trying to answer them. If this book achieves any clarity, those students and their successors at Indiana University and Yale University deserve the first thanks.

I do not mean that I have abandoned the methods and results of New Testament criticism. On the contrary, I believe that those methods and results, viewed from a perspective different from the usual, can provide materials for a genuine social history of some parts of the early Christian movement. It is such a social history that I have undertaken here.

Had I attempted to acknowledge my entire debt to previous scholarship, the reference apparatus would have become gargantuan. I have tried to keep the text clear of such distractions, and the endnotes mention only the most important secondary works and those upon which I am immediately dependent. The specialist will know many others that are germane; the general reader who wishes to find more can do so through the ones I have cited. At the beginning of the notes I have explained my method of citation. Translations from ancient and modern languages are my own unless otherwise specified.

Research for this book was made possible by leaves from Yale University in 1975–76 and 1980, supported respectively by fellowships from the National Endowment for the Humanities and the John Simon Guggenheim Memorial Foundation. I am grateful to all three institutions.

Conversations with many colleagues at Yale and elsewhere have given focus and reason to this project. Especially helpful were discussions in the working group on the Social World of Early Christianity of the American Academy of Religion and the Society of Biblical Literature and in two summer seminars for college teachers, sponsored at Yale in 1977 and 1979 by the National Endowment for the Humanities. My colleague Abraham J. Malherbe and my wife, Martha F. Meeks, read the whole manuscript and made many valuable suggestions for improvement. Ramsay MacMullen did the same for chapter 1. My wife also researched and drew the map. For this generous help and for much else I thank them.

The expert and superbly efficient staff of the Yale University Press, especially editor Charles Grench, and the copyeditor Ann Hawthorne, whose precision is awe-inspiring, have made the book far more readable than the manuscript was. For preparation of the indexes I am grateful to Mr. David Kuck and to the A. Whitney Griswold Fund for the Humanities.

Easter 1982

The First Urban Christians

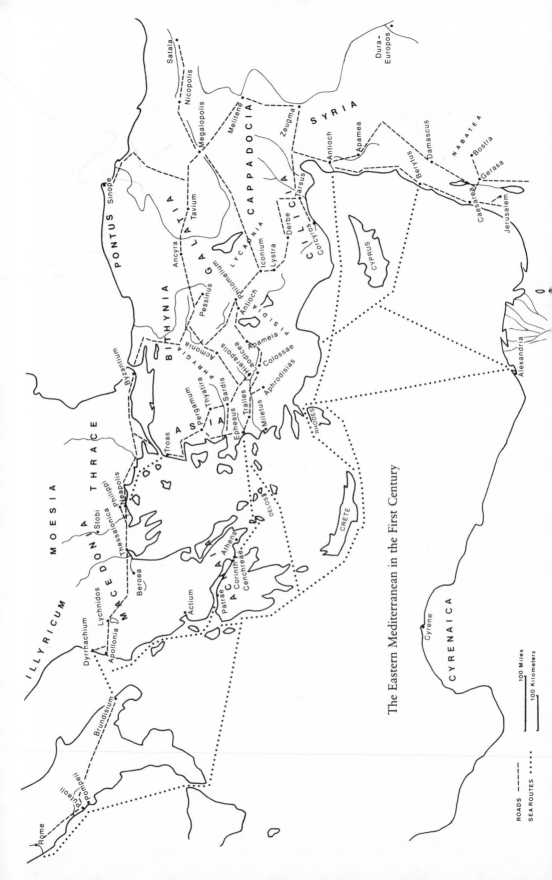

The Eastern Mediterranean in the First Century

ROADS ------
SEA ROUTES ••••••

100 Miles
100 Kilometers

ILLYRICUM
MOESIA
THRACE
MACEDONIA
ACHAEA
CYRENAICA

PONTUS
BITHYNIA
GALATIA
CAPPADOCIA
LYCAONIA
PHRYGIA
ASIA
CILICIA
SYRIA
NABATEA
CYPRUS
CRETE
RHODES
DELOS

Rome
Puteoli
Pompeii
Brundisium
Dyrrhachium
Apollonia
Lychnidos
Stobi
Thessalonica
Philippi
Neapolis
Beroea
Actium
Patrae
Athens
Corinth
Cenchreae
Byzantium
Troas
Pergamum
Thyatira
Sardis
Tralles
Ephesus
Miletus
Aphrodisias
Colossae
Laodicea
Hierapolis
Apameia
Acmonia
Antioch
Pessinus
Ancyra
Tavium
Philomelium
Iconium
Lystra
Derbe
Sinope
Satala
Nicopolis
Megalopolis
Melitene
Zeugma
Corycios
Tarsus
Antioch
Apamea
Damascus
Bostra
Gerasa
Berytus
Caesarea
Jerusalem
Dura-Europos
Alexandria
Cyrene

INTRODUCTION

In the early decades of the Roman Empire, a new sect of Judaism appeared and spread rapidly, though not in great numbers, through the cities of the East. It did not stand out among the many "Oriental" cults being carried from place to place by immigrants and traders. Few people of importance paid attention to it. Its origins were unnoticed by writers of the day. Yet it was to become a new religion, separate from, even hostile to, the Jewish communities that gave it birth. In a few centuries it would become not only the dominant religion of the Roman Empire but unique in its imperial sponsorship.

The origins of Christianity have excited deep curiosity since the second century. In modern times no ancient phenomenon has been the subject of such intensive research. Yet its beginnings and earliest growth remain in many respects mysterious. There are a number of reasons for this. The sources are few and consist almost exclusively of the internal literature produced by the sect for its own purposes. They confront the interpreter with complex literary, linguistic, and historical puzzles. Further, these documents have themselves had a unique history, for some were suppressed in the later struggles of the Christian movement to achieve and preserve a unified "catholic" and "orthodox" self-definition, while others became part of the movement's new canon of scripture. To employ the latter as historical sources, we must try to disentangle them from the dense web of traditions in which they are embedded, traditions that are integral with the cultural identity of the West and with the personal faith of many.

WHY A SOCIAL DESCRIPTION OF EARLY CHRISTIANITY?

Yet these factors do not altogether explain the air of unreality that pervades much of the recent scholarly literature about the New Testament and early Christianity. A clear symptom of the malaise is the isolation of New Testament study from other kinds of historical scholarship—not only from secular study of the Roman Empire, but even from church history.[1] Some New Testament students have begun to retreat from critical history into theological positivism. Others no longer claim to do history at all, but favor a purely

1

literary or literary-philosophical reading of the canonical texts. Moreover, those who do continue to regard themselves as historical critics fill the learned journals with articles that depict a strange world, one that seems composed exclusively of theological ideas or compact mythic complexes or purely individual "self-understandings." If we ask, "What was it like to become and be an ordinary Christian in the first century?" we receive only vague and stammering replies.

To be sure, ordinary Christians did not write our texts and rarely appear in them explicitly. Yet the texts were written in some sense *for* them, and were used in some ways by them. If we do not ever see their world, we cannot claim to understand early Christianity.

Since we do not meet ordinary early Christians as individuals, we must seek to recognize them through the collectivities to which they belonged and to glimpse their lives through the typical occasions mirrored in the texts. It is in the hope of accomplishing this that a number of historians of early Christianity have recently undertaken to describe the first Christian groups in ways that a sociologist or anthropologist might.[2] Without wishing to abandon previous accomplishments in philology, literary analysis, history of traditions, and theological insight, these scholars have sought in social history an antidote to the abstractions of the history of ideas and to the subjective individualism of existentialist hermeneutics.

To write social history, it is necessary to pay more attention than has become customary to the ordinary patterns of life in the immediate environment within which the Christian movement was born. It will not do to describe that environment in terms of vague generalities: "the Greek concept of immortality," "the Roman genius for organization," "the spirit of Hellenism," "the Jewish doctrine" of this or that, "the mystery religions," nor to be satisfied with reproducing the generalizations and idealizations that aristocratic writers of antiquity themselves repeated.[3] Rather, to the limit that the sources and our abilities permit, we must try to discern the texture of life in particular times and particular places. After that, the task of a social historian of early Christianity is to describe the life of the ordinary Christian within that environment—not just the ideas or the self-understanding of the leaders and writers. This is the double task undertaken in the following pages, for a discrete segment of the early Christian movement.

SOME OBJECTIONS

Not everyone welcomes the renewed attempts to describe the social history of early Christianity. A number of scholars, principally theologians, have warned that sociological interpretations of religious phenomena are inevitably reductionist. The questions that the social historian addresses to religious texts, for example, seek to extract from them something contrary to or at least different from their manifest content or "intention." This kind of approach often denies the religious phenomena any distinctive character of their own by treating them as the effects of nonreligious causes. In this fashion, say these objectors, the social scientist is wont to "explain" religion by explaining it away, to claim that religious beliefs are really projections of group consciousness or individual fantasies, or that faith in an all-powerful God is nothing more than compensation for a group's perceived deprivation of power, and so on. In offering such explanations the sociological interpreter imposes his own belief system on his evidence, implicitly or explicitly claiming to know more about the meaning of religious behavior than did the participants.

There are good reasons for these allegations. The two best-known attempts at thoroughgoing sociological interpretation of early Christianity have in fact been reductionist. One of these is the Marxist reading, beginning with Karl Kautsky's *The Foundations of Christianity;* the other is the Chicago school of New Testament studies in the early part of this century.[4] Marxists undertook to discover the roots of Christianity in the class struggle of ancient society. Religious beliefs and ideas were discounted as belonging to ideology, which not only is a secondary formation deriving from the underlying economic causes—at least in the crude popular versions of the Marxist critique—but also *conceals* its social roots by pretending to be autonomous. The Chicago school also, for rather different reasons, had little use for theological concepts. Shirley Jackson Case, for example, insisted that the "essence" of first-century Christianity was "its entire content," "since each phase of it arose in answer to some demand of the time."[5] Case explained the ideas, values, and practices of the early Christians simply as responses to "needs" manifest in the society of that time. Yet even these extreme interpretations, though undoubtedly reductionist, were not without value. More recent Marxist historians, adopting a much more complex conception of the dialectic between social structures and belief structures, have made important contributions to our understanding of ancient society, not least the social context of early Christianity.[6] The Chicago school, too, wrote an agenda for historians of early Christianity that remains impressive and unfulfilled. The naiveté of Case's functionalism must not be allowed to overshadow the subsequent advances of functionalist theory in secular sociology or to lead us to deny its interpretative power when more carefully used. In fact what is most surprising about Case and his Chicago associates is their apparent indifference to sociological theory and their failure to develop any specifically sociological modes of analysis.[7] Since that time social scientists themselves have become increasingly sensitive to the problems of conflict between participant and observer viewpoints, of "latent" and "manifest" function, of cross-cultural translation, and of the dialectic between cognitive and structural elements of culture. Some of the things the theologian dislikes most about the social sciences are no longer characteristic of those disciplines.

Moreover, the theological remover of specks from the social historian's eye must beware the log in his own. To assert that only theological interpretation of the canonical texts is legitimate is surely only another kind of reduc-

tionism. The claim that all such texts are really about theological ideas conceals several sorts of confusion, including the following. First, it fails to
distinguish among different contexts of meaning and among different uses of
the texts in question. What a text (or other phenomenon) "means" depends
at least in some important degree on what the interpreter wants to know. If
the interpreter wishes to discover patterns of language that can serve as
norms for behavior or for belief by members of a community that takes these
texts as scripture, then it may be appropriate to insist that the context is the
whole canon of scripture and that community's whole interpretative tradition. He may, if that tradition permits, ignore historical questions altogether.
Or he may insist that all he needs to know from the historian is what explicit
beliefs about God, Christ, salvation, and so on the early Christians held.
Whether he would thereby be shortsightedly cheating himself is a question of
theological, not historical, method. On the other hand, if the interpreter
wants, out of sheer curiosity, to know what the earliest Christians were like
and what they were doing when their first writings were composed—before
there *was* a canon of "the New Testament"—then to limit questions to those
concerning explicitly stated beliefs would be odd and misleading. In any case
there would be no reason to let the theologian legislate what questions the
interpreter is allowed to ask.

Second, theological reductionism conceals some model of what religion
is, a model which ought to be made explicit and opened to criticism. The
matter is made more difficult by the reluctance of some theologians, influenced by polemical assertions made in a special historical context by Karl
Barth and Dietrich Bonhoeffer, to use the word *religion* at all for normative
Christianity. (By this reluctance they exactly miss the point made by Barth
and Bonhoeffer, but that is another issue.) Nevertheless, it seems that critics
of this sort usually operate with one of two implicit models of religion: a
distinctive set of ideas, or a set of symbols that express an underlying state or
array of dispositions. We will return to this question later.

Third, the theological critics seem often to imply a reduction of language's meaning to its ostensive, locutionary force, its "manifest intention."
Yet when I use the word *God* in a sentence I may be doing any number of
things other than conveying information or recommending a belief about
God. I may be currying favor by showing that I am pious; I may be threaten-
ing my audience by means of a prophetic utterance; or I may be swearing and
thus only expressing anger or dismay. Now, it could be argued that my
speaking in this way presupposes that my speech community holds or once
held certain beliefs about God, without which my utterance would not have
the force it does. Hence those beliefs, too, would be part of a "thick description" of my communication—but only a part. We are certainly interested in
what the early Christians believed and what they said. But we are also interested in what else they did, including what they did by means of what they
said.

Not only theologians are suspicious of social history; a great many

philologians, working exegetes, and ordinary historians also have doubts. What they chiefly object to is the way in which the social historian fills in the many gaps that exist in the evidence from the past. The sociological interpreter is tempted to infer what *must* have happened and the conditions that *must* have obtained on the basis of certain assumed regularities in human behavior. To the extent that he yields to this temptation, he modernizes. He recreates the people of the past in his own image, for the supposed laws of behavior are based on observations in our own or other contemporary cultures that may differ in fundamental ways from those of antiquity. To avoid these dangers, the exegetical critic insists that the task of the historian is only to report the facts: what the texts say, what the monuments show. To an extent, this is a matter of taste. Some scholars are more comfortable with generalizations than others, perhaps less disturbed by the possibility that they may be wrong. Nevertheless, these are important warnings. There are good reasons to be chary of grand theory and unproven "laws." We ought to keep as closely as possible to the observed facts.

The difficulty is that without interpretation there are no facts. Every observation entails a point of view, a set of connections. The pure empiricist would drown in meaningless impressions. Even so simple a task as translating a sentence from an ancient language into our own requires some sense of the social matrices of both the original utterance and ourselves. When we take up dictionary and grammar to aid us, we err unless we understand that they only catalog the relics of language as a fluid, functioning social medium. If we translate without that awareness, we are only moving bones from one coffin to another. To collect facts without any theory too often means to substitute for theory our putative common sense. Making that substitution modernizes no less than does the scientist who follows his theory, for our common sense, too, is a cultural artifact. The advantage of an explicitly stated theory is that it can be falsified.

In writing social history, then, we cannot afford to ignore the theories that guide social scientists. But which of the competing schools of sociology or anthropology or social psychology shall we heed? At what level of our inquiry and on what scale are theoretical proposals useful? To what degree of overall coherence can we reasonably aspire, without endangering our appreciation of our objects' stubborn particularity? There is no comprehensive theory of social movements so commanding that we would be prudent to commit our method to its care. Even if there were, we should be suspicious of it. Christianity, even at the earliest moment we can get any clear picture of it, was already a complex movement taking form within several complex societies. What social theory is adequate to grasp the whole?

In this study the use of theory will be suggestive, rather than generative in the manner of experimental sciences. As Max Weber long ago pointed out, historical hypotheses do not admit of verification in the manner of scientific laws, and the controlled experiment is inevitably a misleading model for historical inquiry.[8] In asking about the social context and social forms of

early Christianity, we are not undertaking to discover or validate laws about
human behavior in general. We are seeking rather to understand a particular
set of phenomena in the second half of the first century, although *understand*
need not be taken in the special sense that Weber used. Our case is analogous
to Clifford Geertz's description of the social anthropologist's task as an
ethnographer, a describer of culture. The description is interpretative. What it
interprets is the "flow of discourse," from which it tries "to rescue the
'said' . . . from its perishing occasions and fix it in perusable terms."[9] For
that purpose theory is necessary, both to construct interpretation and to
criticize constructions, but it must "stay rather closer to the ground than
tends to be the case in sciences more able to give themselves over to imaginative abstraction."[10] As Peter Brown said in one of his elegant essays, the
historian's attitude toward the social sciences is like that of the African tribal
chief who described the neighboring tribe for the inquiring ethnographer,
"They are our enemies; we marry them."[11]

   In short, the application of social science in the following chapters is
eclectic. I take my theory piecemeal, as needed, where it fits. This pragmatic
approach will be distasteful to the purist; its effect will be many rough edges
and some inconsistencies. Nevertheless, given the present state of social theory and the primitive state of its use by students of early Christianity, eclecti-
cism seems the only honest and cautious way to proceed. I am encouraged by
Victor Turner's remarks about the way theory works for an anthropologist in
the field:

Although we take theories into the field with us, these become relevant only if and
when they illuminate social reality. Moreover, we tend to find very frequently that it is
not a theorist's whole system which so illuminates, but his scattered ideas, his flashes
of insight taken out of systemic context and applied to scattered data. . . . The intui-
tions, not the tissue of logic connecting them, are what tend to survive in the field
experience.[12]

   Still, although there is no comprehensive theory of human social behavior to guide us, there is a family of perspectives shared by a growing number
of social scientists and historians of religion that encompasses the general
point of view of this book. Society is viewed as a process, in which personal
identity and social forms are mutually and continuously created by interactions that occur by means of symbols. Culture, as Geertz puts it, consists of
"webs of significance."[13] Moreover, there is some real but complex relation
between social structure and symbolic structure, and religion is an integral
part of the cultural web. It is, however, neither necessary nor wise to decide in
advance just what role religion plays, for it plays many. Even Geertz's famous
diagram of sacred symbols synthesizing "world view" and "ethos" may be
misleading, for it tends to imply that religion's function is always integrative.[14] In fact, it may be disruptive or, paradoxically, integrative for a disruptive movement.

   Within this general context, this view of religion as a system of commu-

nication, as a subset within the multiple systems that make up the culture and
subcultures of a particular society, I assume the position of a "moderate
functionalist."[15] That is, the sort of questions to be asked about the early
Christian movement are those about how it worked. The comprehensive
question concerning the texts that are our primary sources is not merely what
each one says, but what it does. Of course, what language does, most of the
time, it does by saying something, but that is only part of the transaction. By
adopting a functionalist perspective in this moderate form, we can avoid the
reductionism that would result from smuggling in the whole of Durkheim's
theory of religion's functions. We will be able in principle to remain open to
the particularities of the unique groups we are interested in, and we need not
neglect the beliefs and concepts of those groups.[16]

As a result this kind of social description may, after all, be useful to the
theologians whose skepticism I mentioned earlier. This book deliberately
avoids theological categories as its interpretative framework. I hope it will
not on that account be viewed as antitheological. Yet it will be, so long as the
prevailing models of religion implicit in theological discourse are, as George
Lindbeck has recently observed, either "cognitivist-propositional" or "expe-
riential-expressive." Lindbeck himself, however, urges theologians to adopt a
"cultural-linguistic" model rather like that employed here.[17] If they did so,
theologians might find raw material in these explorations of Pauline Christianity.

PAULINE CHRISTIANITY

New Testament scholarship in this century has discovered great diversity in
early Christianity.[18] To heed Geertz's advice that our "thick description" be
"microscopic," we should choose one reasonably coherent and identifiable
segment of early Christianity. For several reasons the most satisfactory choice
comprises the extended missionary activity of Paul of Tarsus and a broad
circle of co-workers and the congregations they established in cities across the
northeastern quadrant of the Mediterranean basin. First of all, they are in-
trinsically fascinating. Second, they are the best-documented segment of the
early Christian movement. We have at least seven indubitable letters by the
principal figure (which in their received form may contain fragments of yet
other letters). These are the earliest of all extant Christian writings. Two
characteristics make these letters particularly useful for social-historical inquiry: each responds to some specific issue in the life of one of the local
churches or in the missionary strategy of the leaders; and they frequently
quote traditional material, which provides glimpses of rituals, rules, admonitions, and formulated beliefs common to the Pauline communities. In addition, the Acts of the Apostles contains an extended description of the Pauline
mission written within a few decades of Paul's death by someone who was
probably not an immediate member of the Pauline school.

From both the letters and Acts it is evident that Pauline Christianity was not the work of a single person, but of an extended group of associates. Furthermore, there are six letters in the canon of the New Testament that are purported to be by Paul but whose authorship modern scholars dispute. Two of these, the Letter to Colossians and the Letter to Ephesians, were most likely written by disciples of Paul. The same may be true of 2 Thessalonians. These pseudonymous letters provide evidence that the Pauline association was a self-conscious movement which accorded to Paul the position of "founder" or leading authority. It is likely that this distinctive movement within Christianity kept some identity for a time after the apostle's death, although the notorious difficulty in dating the letters just mentioned prevents their serving as evidence for this. Much more problematic is the evidence of the remaining canonical letters—the so-called Pastoral Epistles addressed to Timothy and Titus—and the various apocryphal writings attributed to Paul or written about him, such as the Acts of Paul, the spurious correspondence with Seneca, the several Apocalypses of Paul, and 3 Corinthians. Often the Pastorals and such works as the Acts of Paul and Thecla are regarded as products of a Pauline school that continued into the second century. It seems more likely, however, that they all represent a slow development in which the figure of Paul was adopted as a patron both in the great church and in "heretical" movements because of his general fame or, less often, because of specific aspects of his teaching.[19] They therefore cannot be used with any confidence, either as evidence of any sort of social continuity or as independent testimony to any traditions of the Pauline groups, so I do not employ them here as sources.

The third reason Pauline Christianity is an apt subject for our investigation is that it was entirely urban. In that respect it stood on the growing edge of the Christian movement, for it was in the cities of the Roman Empire that Christianity, though born in the village culture of Palestine, had its greatest successes until well after the time of Constantine.[20] This does not mean that Pauline Christianity was typical of all urban Christianity of the first century. There are many signs that it was distinctive in some respects, and we do not really know enough about the other contemporary forms of the movement to say with confidence how many basic characteristics were widely shared. There is merit, though, in trying to describe as carefully as possible the one we do know.

It has become customary among some scholars to speak of the "social world of early Christianity,"[21] and that term usefully describes the object of this inquiry. It has a double meaning, referring not only to the environment of the early Christian groups but also to the world as they perceived it and to which they gave form and significance through their special language and other meaningful actions. One is the world they shared with other people who lived in the Roman Empire; the other, the world they constructed.[22] We will begin with the outside view, the ecology of the Pauline groups, and work in toward the patterns of meaningful action by which their lives were shaped.

1

THE URBAN ENVIRONMENT OF PAULINE CHRISTIANITY

PAUL AND THE CITY

Paul was a city person. The city breathes through his language. Jesus' parables of sowers and weeds, sharecroppers, and mud-roofed cottages call forth smells of manure and earth, and the Aramaic of the Palestinian villages often echoes in the Greek. When Paul constructs a metaphor of olive trees or gardens, on the other hand, the Greek is fluent and evokes schoolroom more than farm; he seems more at home with the clichés of Greek rhetoric, drawn from gymnasium, stadium, or workshop.[1] Moreover, Paul was among those who depended on the city for their livelihood. He supported himself, at least partially, by work "with my own hands"—making tents, according to the book of Acts—and he several times reminded his churches of that fact with a kind of wry pride, either in self-defense or as an object lesson.[2] This life as an artisan distinguished him both from the workers of the farms, who, slave or free, were perhaps at the very bottom of the social pyramid in antiquity, and from the lucky few whose wealth and status depended on their agricultural estates. The urban handworkers included slave and free, and a fair range of status and means, from desperate poverty to a reasonably comfortable living, but all belonged thoroughly to the city. They shared neither the peasant's hostile fear of the city nor the aristocrat's self-confident power over both *polis* and *chōra*. When Paul rhetorically catalogs the places where he has suffered danger, he divides the world into city, wilderness, and sea (2 Cor. 11:26). His world does not include the *chōra,* the productive countryside; outside the city there is nothing—*erēmia.* The author of Acts hardly errs when he has Paul boast to the tribune, astonished that Paul knows Greek, that he is "a citizen of no mean city" (Acts 21:39, RSV).

If Paul's world consisted, practically speaking, only of the cities of the Roman Empire, then it is perhaps easier to understand the extraordinary claim he makes to the Christians in Rome. "From Jerusalem and as far round as Illyricum," he writes, "I have fully preached the gospel of Christ." The result was that "I no longer have any room for work in these regions" (Rom. 15:19b, 23a). Yet what he had done to "fill everything with the Gospel of Christ" (as Luther paraphrases)[3] was only to plant small cells of Christians in

9

scattered households in some of the strategically located cities of the north-east Mediterranean basin. Those cells were linked to one another and to Paul and his fellow workers by means of letters and official visits and by frequent contact through traveling Christians, and he had encouraged local persons of promise to establish new groups in nearby towns. We shall return later to the geographic pattern and the missionary method; the point to be made here is simply that the mission of the Pauline circle was conceived from start to finish as an urban movement.

An astute reader may object, remembering Paul's own reminiscence of his conversion in Gal. 1:15–17, that Paul's first reaction, upon receiving his strange revelation commissioning him to "preach [God's son] among the Gentiles," was to abandon the city and head for Arabia. "Arabia," however, is not the sandy wasteland of romantic imagination, but the Nabataean kingdom, which extended to the territory of Damascus and possibly even included Damascus.[4] We know this because it was the ethnarch of the Nabataean king Aretas IV who tried to have Paul arrested in Damascus (2 Cor. 11:32). It is evident that Paul had stirred up this official hostility not by meditating in the desert nor by wandering from village to village, but by preaching in flourishing Hellenistic cities such as Petra, Gerasa, Philadelphia, and Bostra, whose remains have recently been excavated.[5]

FROM VILLAGE TO CITY

This preoccupation with the cities was not peculiar to Paul. Before Paul's conversion the believers in Messiah Jesus had already carried their new sectarian message into the Jewish communities of the Greco-Roman cities. It was their success in Damascus that had aroused Paul's "zealot" attack on them and there that the strange reversal of his life occurred that we call his conversion (Gal. 1:13–17).[6] Even more important, the movement had been planted in the Jewish community of Antioch-on-the-Orontes, and in that city certain Cypriots and Cyrenaeans, among the "Hellenists" who had been forced out of Jerusalem, first passed outside the bounds of Judaism to seek gentile proselytes (Acts 11:19–26).[7] After Paul's three-year sortie into the Nabataean kingdom, which produced no lasting results, and his rather ignominious exit from Damascus (2 Cor. 11:32) and brief consultation with the leaders in Jerusalem (Gal. 1:18f.), Antioch became the center of his activities, perhaps for most of the twelve to fourteen years that he spent "in the regions of Syria and Cilicia" (Gal. 1:21; cf. 2:1–14 and Acts 11:25f.; 13:1).[8] Antioch, center of political, military, and commercial communication between Rome and the Persian frontier and between Palestine and Asia Minor, was one of the three or four most important cities of the empire and the home of a large and vigorous Jewish community. There developed the form of missionary practice and organization which we call Pauline Christianity, but which was probably characteristic of most of the urban expansion of the movement. There Paul served his apprenticeship, as the fellow worker of Barnabas and others.[9] Antioch was also the place where controversy between Jews and gentiles first erupted within the church, and the radical position which Paul took in that issue led eventually to his breaking not only with Peter but even with Barnabas (Gal. 2:11–14) and gave a distinctive theological cast to his own subsequent mission, which thenceforth moved steadily westward through Asia Minor into mainland Greece.

In those early years, then, within a decade of the crucifixion of Jesus, the village culture of Palestine had been left behind, and the Greco-Roman city became the dominant environment of the Christian movement. So it remained, from the dispersion of the "Hellenists" from Jerusalem until well after the time of Constantine.[10] The movement had crossed the most fundamental division in the society of the Roman Empire, that between rural people and city dwellers, and the results were to prove momentous.[11]

FROM POLIS TO EMPIRE

The cities of the Mediterranean world were at the leading edge of the great political and social changes that occurred during the six and a half centuries from Alexander to Constantine. Periclean Athens had already discovered the paradox that the polis, which gave to the Western world the ideal of direct democracy, could be transformed into an instrument of imperial ambition. The lessons of colonization and of manipulation of leagues of "free" cities were well learned by Philip. But it was his more famous son who made the city the vehicle of a new cultural vision; urbanization became the means of hellenization. Alexander's successors pursued the same policy. They founded or refounded cities, establishing there the Greek institutions of formally enrolled citizen body (*dēmos*), governing council (*boulē*), and a system of education for their children, centered in the gymnasium. Thus they could trade on the prestige which these institutions held among ambitious men of the East while securing the dependence of the new cities on the king as founder and benefactor.

Soon Italian armies followed Italian merchants to the cities of the Aegean, mainland Greece, and Asia Minor. The results at first were not auspicious for the flourishing of urban life. The greedy and ceaseless rivalry of the Seleucids and Ptolemies and the local kings who imitated them, like those of Pontus and Pergamum, had devastated city after city. Now the Romans injected into the unstable region the foreign extensions of their own civil wars. The victory of Octavian, however, which brought the Roman Republic to an end under the pretense of restoration and set in motion the methodical organization of an empire, yielded an era of unprecedented stability and opportunity for urban life, an era which would last a century.

"The Roman Empire," Rostovtzeff has written, "was to become a commonwealth of self-governing cities."[12] The *pax* of Augustus was more pragmatic than Alexander's dream of *homonoia*, but for Augustus's policy too the Hellenistic cities had a central role. Caesar and Antony had already discovered the usefulness of colonies: they compensated veterans, provided potential military strength in dangerous areas, and revived the eastern economy.[13] In addition to the veterans' colonies, Augustus also adopted the Hellenistic monarchs' practice of founding and refounding other cities, so that names like Sebastopolis and Sebasteia multiplied on maps of the East.[14] His successors, with varying degrees of vigor culminating in the special enthusiasm of the hellenophile Hadrian, pursued the policy of chartering cities throughout the growing expanse of Roman provinces.[15]

Perhaps even more important than the formal refounding of cities was the general climate of stability and security which the early principate created for urban people in the provinces. Local government was reinforced. Increasing recourse to the courts even tolerated local law, while the possibility of appeal to the provincial governor or to the emperor himself led to greater consistency in the exercise of justice. This led to more-widespread expectations, or at least hopes, even among inconspicuous persons, of actually obtaining justice.[16] Roads were built and maintained; the Mediterranean was nearly cleared of pirates. Free cities were permitted to issue their own coins. Taxes were stabilized, more equitably and efficiently collected, and even, in some cases, temporarily reduced. Greek institutions of local government and education were actively encouraged, as were benefactions to cities by their wealthier citizens.[17] Indeed, the ability to provide such benefactions became the principal means by which individuals and families gained prominence and social power.

The alliance between the Roman principate and the Greek cities of the eastern provinces also brought important, but subtle and complex, changes in the relationships among persons and classes. Bowersock has shown, for example, how adroitly Augustus used the system of patronage, which Caesar and Antony had already adapted for purposes of foreign relations, to build a network of personal dependency between the upper classes of the eastern cities and himself. In return for the loyalty of the local aristocrats and the formal honors which they voted him, the *princeps* not only gave them his protection but also materially advanced their careers and those of their sons. In choosing magistrates for the new provinces, Augustus sought men who themselves had a significant *clientela* in the East—large enough to give them weight, not so large as to make them dangerous.[18] Often these imperial officials were themselves Greeks—well-educated Greeks, rhetors and philosophers like those who had enjoyed the friendship and patronage of leading Romans during the late republic.[19] The Roman policy thus introduced certain opportunities for social and economic mobility in the Greek cities. To be sure, the connections were limited to the urban aristocracies, so that the opportunities were principally for some of the rich to become richer and more powerful. However, the Romans were also prepared to reward certain specific skills used for the benefit of the new order—skills of education and, more and more as time passed, of the military—and these were not entirely correlated with wealth and high status. Thus were introduced sources of change and, inevitably, of new tensions between groups.

In those areas where a strong local monarchy made it unnecessary or as yet inexpedient for Rome to organize a province, the native kings themselves became clients of the Roman *princeps.* Herod is a well-known and typical, if not entirely successful, example.[20] His foundation and enthusiastic rebuilding of Sebaste, Caesarea Maritima, and other towns in his own realm,[21] and his benefactions to Antioch and other foreign cities[22] illustrate how the client kings also helped promote Roman imperialism, Hellenism, and urbanization, and simultaneously their own ambitions.

THE PEOPLE OF THE CITY

As a consequence of Rome's entry into the East and her active interest in the cities, urban society became somewhat more complex than it had been even during the Hellenistic age. For a very long time groups of foreigners had gathered in each city: merchants and artisans following the armies or in search of better markets or better access to transportation, persons enslaved and displaced by war or piracy and now set free, political exiles, soldiers of fortune. These noncitizen residents, or metics (*metoikoi*), often retained some sense of ethnic identity by establishing local cults of their native gods or by forming a voluntary association, which also had at least the trappings of religion. One example was the Association of the Poseidoniasts of Berytus, who built an elegant clubhouse on Delos next to the famous Lion Terrace.[23] Of course the Roman settlers soon came to have a privileged position among these groups,[24] but their precise relationship to the others varied. Even in Roman colonies, such as the Pisidian colonies of Galatia that Barbara Levick has carefully analyzed, "No consistent pattern . . . can be discerned in the relations between Roman settlers and native populations; they were strictly *ad hoc,* and . . . they might be radically affected by reasons of discipline or expediency."[25] Two or even three organized bodies of residents might exist side by side, or Greek and Roman citizens might be wholly integrated. Among the resident aliens, alongside the Roman citizens and the citizens of the city, one group occupied a special position. The Jews were normally organized as a distinctive community, governed by its own laws and institutions, and often contended, sometimes successfully, for equality with the full citizens.

The different groups in the city and, within each group, persons of differing status were variously affected by the hegemony of Rome, and they reacted with various emotions and strategies to the effective presence of that power in their towns. Because Roman policy was to encourage the aristocracies, anti-Roman feeling was naturally more likely to be found among the lower classes than among the privileged. Matters, however, are never quite that simple.[26] Not everyone of the urban curial class would be equally successful in the newly important contest for Roman favor; not all would even have a taste for playing the game. Many among the lower classes found their condition decidedly improved under Roman rule, and some individuals and groups even found that the Romans had unwittingly introduced possibilities for that ambition almost undreamed of in antiquity, to rise above one's father's class. For example, Levick has traced the careers of two veterans of obscure, lower-class Italian origin who found in the colony of Antioch by Pisidia the opportunities that would bring their descendants into the Roman senate.[27] Such social climbing remained rare, but not so rare for those who migrated to the new cities—not only from Italy, but also from the East—as for those who remained at home. It could also happen that individual members of minorities that, as groups, were excluded from local power could, by shrewd cultivation of highly placed Roman patrons, build a career. Perhaps the most famous example is Tiberius Julius Alexander, scion of the best-known and probably wealthiest Jewish family of Alexandria and nephew of the great apologist for Judaism, Philo. His very names attest both the degree and method of his family's ambition. He would become procurator of Palestine and then prefect of Egypt, though abandoning Judaism along the way.[28] Moreover, the whole Jewish community in a city could cultivate the protection of the emperor, [29] sometimes in the face of local hostility. And perhaps a Jew, as a reward for some special service to the Roman army or administration, could even obtain the coveted *civitas Romana* without compromising his religious loyalty—as Paul's father did, if the report of Acts 22:28 is accurate.[30] A couple of centuries later it was fairly common for Jews to hold citizenship and even municipal office in the cities of western Asia Minor.[31]

CITY VERSUS COUNTRY

As the cities grew in number and power, their relations with the countryside became more and more ambivalent. Each depended upon the other, but by every measure of physical and social advantage the symbiosis was one-sided in favor of the city. Under the principate agriculture continued to be the base of the whole empire's economy, but ownership of productive land was increasingly concentrated in the hands of fewer and fewer proprietors—who lived in the city or its extension, their villas. The small, independent landowners living on their own land began to disappear,[32] reduced to tenancy or slavery, gone to the city to subsist as laborers, or recruited into the army. From thousands of tiny fragments of evidence, Ramsay MacMullen has described the way people experienced the results:

Economic ties between urban and rural centers are thus of the closest. They are not friendly. The two worlds regard each other as, on the one side, clumsy, brutish, ignorant, uncivilized; on the other side, as baffling, extortionate, arrogant. Peasants who move to a town feel overwhelmed by its manners and dangers and seek out relatives or previous emigrants from the same village to settle among. Rent- or tax-collectors who come out to the country face a hostile reception and can expect attempts to cheat and resist them, even by force. They respond with their own brutality.[33]

The cities were where power was. They were also the places where changes could occur. MacMullen emphasizes the conservatism of villages, their "central characteristic." "They and their population hovered so barely above subsistence level that no one dared risk a change."[34] If some extraordinary circumstance should compel a villager to seek change—a lucky inheritance, a religious vision, or even, rarely, the accumulation of a little real money through frugality, shrewdness, and hard work—it must be in the city that he would work out his new life.[35]

COSMOPOLIS

The conservatism of the villages preserved their diversity; changes in the city were in the direction of a common Greco-Roman culture. This was most obvious in language. Today a tourist may manage comfortably with English or German through most of the Pauline mission area, so long as he stays in the cities, but if he wants to communicate in the villages of the same countries, he must know several languages and even then may find his best efforts stymied by local pronunciation or idiom. Just so, Greek was the universal urban language of the eastern Roman provinces, but not far beyond the city walls. When the author of Acts wants to depict an encounter of Paul and Barnabas with people of a real backwater town, he has the locals shout their amazement in Lycaonian. Still, it was with Greek gods, Zeus and Hermes, that they identified the two miracle-workers; Lystra was after all a Roman colony.[36] It is no accident that all the documents of the New Testament and virtually all other extant writings from the first two centuries of Christianity were written in Greek. Yet, in the villages of Galilee, Aramaic was presumably still the dominant language. When Christianity in its new, urban forms eventually penetrated village cultures, the Greek documents had to be translated into the indigenous languages, including, ironically, Aramaic, now in the dialect spoken in the Syrian countryside.

Not only the language was shared. City folk used common forms in many areas of life. Inscriptions from all over the East use stereotyped phrases: city councils announced decrees, clubs honored their patrons, the bereaved commemorated their dead in like fashion from Alexandria to Thessalonica. Students from Athens to Antioch learned style from the same rhetorical handbooks. Styles of pottery and glassware, of furniture, of floor and wall decoration, of sculpture and painting also spread from city to city. Even today a visitor to the excavated remains can hardly fail to see that throughout the Mediterranean basin there was a common conception of the way a city should be laid out and what sorts of construction would enhance its elegance. To be sure, these similarities did not override important local differences. A sleepy traveler would not imagine for a moment that he had arrived in

Corinth instead of Tarsus, in Philippi instead of Pisidian Antioch. But in each of those cities he would have little difficulty recognizing the important temples, the government buildings, the agora or forum, the gymnasium and palaestra, the theater, the baths, and even the inns, taverns, and shops.

The city, then, was the place where the new civilization could be experienced, where novelties would first be encountered. It was the place where, if anywhere, change could be met and even sought out. It was where the empire was, and where the future began. To become a city dweller meant to be caught up in movement—not just the "Brownian movement," as MacMullen put it, of the farmer from his hamlet to the next or to the city to buy and sell or complain to the governor and then back again[37]—but the tides of migration, the risky travel of the merchant, and even the irregular movement of manners, attitudes, and status.

MOBILITY

"The guiding thread for every history of earliest Christianity," writes Martin Hengel, "is the irresistible expansion of the Christian faith in the Mediterranean region during the first 120 years."[38] That expansion was closely associated with personal mobility, both physical and social. The former is simpler and its importance more obvious.

From the schematic itineraries of the book of Acts alone, Ronald Hock has calculated that Paul traveled nearly ten thousand miles during his reported career, which put him on roads busy with "government officials, traders, pilgrims, the sick, letter-carriers, sightseers, runaway slaves, fugitives, prisoners, athletes, artisans, teachers, and students."[39] Besides Paul himself and the companions who traveled with him, we hear often of associates sent on special missions in Paul's stead—for example, Timothy to Thessalonica (1 Thess. 3:2–6); Timothy, Titus, and two now-unnamed "brothers" to Corinth (1 Cor. 4:17; 16:10; 2 Cor. 2:13; 7:6–16; 8:6, 16–24)—of delegates from the churches to Paul (Stephanas, Fortunatus, and Achaicus from Corinth, 1 Cor. 16:17; cf. 7:1; Epaphroditus from Philippi, Phil. 2:25; 4:18); of travelers who on the way bring greetings and news (members of Chloe's household, 1 Cor. 1:11). Particularly revealing is the final chapter of Paul's letter to the Roman Christians, which begins with a recommendation of Phoebe, an important member of the church at Cenchreae (one of Corinth's ports) and patroness of Paul and others, who now is on her way to the capital, evidently bearing Paul's letter.[40] There follow greetings to twenty-six individuals by name and to several groups—although Paul has never been to Rome. Probably some of these are Romans of whom Paul has only heard, not whom he has met personally—the members of the households of Aristobulus and Narcissus, for instance. But the majority have probably migrated from the eastern cities to Rome—like Epaenetus, "the first convert in Asia for Christ" (Rom. 16:5, RSV), and Prisca and Aquila, natives of Pontus who have lived and worked in Rome (Acts 18:2), Corinth, and Ephesus (Acts

18:1–3, 19–21; 1 Cor. 16:19) before making their way back again to Rome.[41]

Some of this travel was undertaken specifically for the Christian mission, but much of the mission was carried out by people who were traveling for other reasons. Both were possible, and not surprising to the writers of the New Testament, because the people of the Roman Empire traveled more extensively and more easily than had anyone before them—or would again until the nineteenth century.[42] Paul was able to achieve the near self-sufficiency of which he was so proud because it was not unusual for artisans to move from place to place, carrying their tools with them and seeking out, say, the leatherworkers' street or quarter of whatever town they came to.[43] For merchants such as Lydia the dealer in purple goods, who was from Thyatira (Asia Minor) but met Paul in Philippi (Macedonia) (Acts 16:14), travel was an occupational necessity—and hazard. Anxieties about travel and its dangers—brigandage and piracy, shipwreck, and hardships on the road—were among the fears that most often sent such people to astrologers or dream interpreters.[44] The anxieties were evidently not insuperable, however. The merchant whose tombstone attests that he had been to Rome from Phrygia seventy-two times was not unique.[45]

Roman power made possible this flourishing travel in two very practical ways: the Roman military presence undertook to keep brigandage on land and piracy on the sea at a minimum,[46] and the imperial government took responsibility for a road system throughout its regions. The "earliest official record of Roman rule in Asia" are milestones set up by Manius Aquilius, who organized the province after Rome inherited it from the last king of Pergamum.[47] By the time of Claudius, the emperor was taking charge, through his procurators, of road repair throughout the empire, even in senatorial provinces.[48] Many of these routes, of course, had been in use for centuries before the Roman expansion to the East, but now their importance and usefulness were magnified by Roman administrative planning and engineering prowess. The roads were one of the occasions for the praise of Rome by the second-century orator Aelius Aristides;[49] the modern traveler, who may see their remains from Britain to North Africa, may be less eloquent but hardly less impressed.[50]

Merely to outline the routes of two of the most important East-West highways will quickly illustrate their significance for the Pauline mission. Across Asia Minor the "common route" (*koinē hodos*) ran from Ephesus past Tralles, up the Maeander valley to Laodicea, to Apameia, Antioch by Pisidia, Philomelium, across Lycaonia to Iconium, down by Laranda and the Cilician Gates to Tarsus, then either to Antioch in Syria or across to Zeugma on the Euphrates.[51] Here, in reverse order, is a virtual catalog of the course of expansion of the Pauline groups from Antioch to the Aegean. Farther west, the major communication between Rome and the East was by the Via Egnatia. It began at the Adriatic coast of Greece in two branches, one from Dyrrhachium (modern Durrës, Albania), the other from Apollonia (modern

Pojan) some eighty kilometers to the south, meeting at Clodiana. Then it ran up the valley of the Genusos, crossing the river to Candavia, skirting the northern side of Lake Lychnitis to Lychnidos, across the mountains to Heraclea, Edessa, down the valley of the Ludias, across the Axius to Thessalonica, and on to Philippi. From there one could continue by land to Byzantium or take ship from Philippi's port Neapolis (modern Kavalla, Greece) across the Troad.[52] Two of the most important locations of Pauline groups, Thessalonica and Philippi, were key spots on the Egnatian road. "Indeed one may say without fear of exaggeration that the whole history of Philippi in the Roman epoch was directly connected with its situation on the Via Egnatia."[53]

The thriving maritime commerce was no less important for the early Christians' mobility. Except for the dangerous winter season from mid-November until the feast of the Ship of Isis in early March,[54] travel by sea was faster and cheaper than by land. Charlesworth estimates that an ancient ship could make one hundred miles in a day.[55] On land the state post instituted by Augustus, imitating a Persian model, made from twenty-five to thirty miles a day, including stops at *mutationes* for fresh horses.[56] Ordinary travelers, who had to haggle over rentals of mules, horses, or carriages, took much longer.[57] The vast majority, including most likely Paul and his associates, would walk, and that was slower still: perhaps fifteen or twenty miles a day at most.[58]

Much of the travel on these routes, apart from the military and administrative operations of the empire, was undertaken by individuals for purposes of trade or professional advancement. It is not surprising that the spread of foreign cults closely followed the spread of trade, or that Christianity repeated this already-established pattern. The southern route through Asia Minor, along which the Pauline congregations sprang up, "ran through country rich in opportunities for trading."[59]

The ways in which the movement of artisans and tradespersons could facilitate movements of religious cults were manifold. The way most familiar in the Hellenistic world has already been mentioned: foreign settlers in a city found neighbors from the same country and set up a shrine of their native gods. As their numbers and solidarity grew to the point that they could demand some civic recognition, their cult, by now usually housed in a proper Greek temple and assimilated in many other ways as well to their Greek urban environment, became part of the municipal religious establishment. The splendid sanctuaries of the Syrian and Egyptian gods that overlook the theater and harbor of the sacred island of Delos from the lower slopes of Mount Kynthos well illustrate the process, as do the somewhat less imposing sanctuaries similarly situated above the forum of the Roman colony of Philippi.[60] It is at least symbolically significant that the Isis sanctuary of Cenchreae—the very one in which Apuleius's hero Lucius was initiated, if the excavators are correct in their identification—was nestled among warehouses on the south dock.[61]

New cults also moved with migrants in quieter, less public ways: peddled along with their wares or gossiped in their workrooms. The best-known instance is the account Josephus gives of the conversion of the royal house of the little kingdom of Adiabene, in Mesopotamia, at the time of the Roman emperor Claudius. The crown prince Izates was living in exile, for his own protection, when "a certain Jewish merchant named Ananias visited the king's [Izates'] wives and taught them to worship God after the manner of the Jewish tradition. It was through their agency that he was brought to the notice of Izates, whom he similarly won over with the co-operation of the women."[62] Recalled to Adiabene to take the throne, Izates brought Ananias with him, now as his catechist (*didaskalos,* §46); there he found that his mother Helena "had likewise been instructed by another Jew and had been brought over to their laws" (§35). Izates' conversion was completed when another Jew, one Eleazar of Galilee, arrived with a much more rigorous interpretation of the Torah and persuaded the king to be circumcised (§§43–47). Josephus does not say whether Eleazar and the unnamed instructor of Helena were also merchants, but nothing suggests that they were professional missionaries. They combined their trade with the time-honored method of migrant philosophers and sophists, attaching themselves as teachers to a wealthy household;[63] in this case their teaching happened to be *ton theon sebein, hōs Ioudaiois patrion ēn:* "to worship God after the manner of Jewish tradition."

Another example of the spread of cults by means of individuals' travels suggests an intermediate process. Xenainetos of Opus was visiting Thessalonica sometime in the first century, not on private business, but on some municipal mission (*presbeia*). Apparently in response to a question he had asked (lost from the broken beginning of the inscription) the god Sarapis appeared to him in a dream. He commanded Xenainetos to take him and his sister Isis back to Opus and to present to Eurynomos, Xenainetos's political enemy, a letter that Xenainetos would find under his pillow. The envoy awoke, "amazed and perplexed." Falling asleep again, he had the same dream, and when he awoke this time, the promised letter was under his pillow. He obeyed the command of the god, and when Eurynomos saw the letter, proof of the miraculous story told by his former enemy, he agreed to the founding of the cult of Isis and Sarapis in Opus.[64]

It is more problematic to speak of social mobility in the Roman Empire, and more difficult to assess its importance for religious change. Only within the past few years have historians of antiquity undertaken seriously to describe the processes of economic and social change in relation to common people in the provincial cities, rather than the careers of the great political and literary figures. The more convincing of these social historians all warn that the perceptions and attitudes about change which we take for granted in modern industrial societies are in almost every case inappropriate to the conditions of Greco-Roman society. Neither the extreme individualism that is the presupposition of the lore and practice of personal advancement in industrial democracies nor the class structure essential to conventional Marxist analysis has a counterpart in the ancient Mediterranean world.[65] Once we look beyond the minuscule elite of Greco-Roman society, we see hardly any movement at all, nor, perhaps more important, do we find much expectation of movement. The late Cambridge dean of social historians, A. H. M. Jones, aptly summarized the situation:

> The society of the principate was, as I see it, stratified and stable. There was of course some movement from class to class. There was a steady trickle of decurions into the equestrian and senatorial orders, but it must have been very small; it must be remembered that the senate numbered only 600 persons and the total of equestrian posts was still well under 200 in the Severan period. A larger number of prosperous plebeians rose to the decurionate. Soldiers might rise to the equestrian order or even the senate. But on the whole the classes were hereditary. The rich landowning families served generation after generation on the city councils. Sons of soldiers followed their fathers in the legions and the *auxilia*. Peasant proprietors cultivated their ancestral holdings, and tenants likewise.[66]

Where movement of the nonelite did occur and has left traces in the stones and records of the ancient city, it worked in ways that are strange to us and in ways that are alien to our usual categories of class and status; not only that, their movement seems also to have muddled some of the ancient categories, producing uncertainties and tensions.

The army as a means of advancement, particularly for some few of the veterans settled in the new Roman colonies in the East, has already been mentioned. However, so far as our sources permit us to judge, this kind of career has little or no relevance for the first generations of Christians, although later on Christians in the army would constitute a problem both for the empire and for the church's leaders. More germane, as we shall see in the next chapter, are questions about the status and opportunities of artisans and tradespeople, of slaves and freedpersons, and of women.

The most fundamental change of status for a person of the lower classes was that from slavery to freedom—or vice versa. This does not mean that all free persons were better off than all slaves; far from it. There were slaves who owned slaves; who manipulated large sums of money in what were, in effect but not legally, their own businesses; who practiced highly skilled professions. And there were free laborers who starved. Nevertheless, slaves worked hard to obtain manumission, and often did.[67] The importance of the change of legal status, and of the means by which they obtained it, is displayed on their tombstones, as Marleen B. Flory has shown in her investigation of a huge number of epitaphs from three large *familiae* of Rome.[68] For example, a surgeon brags that "he paid 50,000 sesterces for his freedom."[69] The distinction in status between slave and free (or freed) could override others, such as the hierarchy of the sexes. Thus, when the name of a woman appears before that of her husband, Flory finds that it is generally because she has already been freed whereas her husband is still a slave. Similarly, the name of a son who is freeborn may be placed ahead of both father (slave) and mother (freed).[70] These slaves and former slaves evidently shared the deep sense of relative status that was also characteristic of Roman society at higher levels.[71] They displayed it by including in their epitaphs the occupational titles that elevated them above the mass of their *conservi: cubicularius, paedagogus, nutrix,* and the like.[72] To be sure, the degree of status awareness in Flory's sample may be exceptional, for these were exceptional households: one was that of the empress Livia. Besides, we lack a comparable study—or anything like comparable data—from the Greek East. Nevertheless, we may be safe in venturing two generalizations: in any household of any size there was an informal pecking order that was taken seriously, and the threshold between slave and free remained fundamental in a perception of one's place in society.

The freedperson occupied a peculiar niche in society, a transitional category between slave and free. The *libertus* or *liberta* was clearly superior to the slave but still obligated to the former owner, now patron, in numerous ways both legal and informal, and carried to the grave the more general stigma of servile origin. Yet freedpersons also had special opportunities. While slaves they had often learned specific skills that enabled them to pursue a business or profession on their own after emancipation; not many, of course, became as famous as the Stoic philosopher Epictetus. It was also common for wealthy householders to use slaves and freedmen as agents in all sorts of transactions, particularly those in which it was considered unseemly for a person of high standing to engage directly. A freedman might thus accumulate both considerable capital and skill in using it to make more money. Understandably, then, MacMullen finds that among those few people who by means of a craft or commercial activity managed to gain relative affluence, "freedmen stood out."[73] Furthermore, their sons, if born after their fathers' manumission, were *ingenui* and could escape the entirely temporary stigma of the *liberti* and add social honors to the wealth their fathers had won.[74]

I have focused briefly on the freedmen not because we know of particular persons in that category among the Pauline Christians (although we shall see that several very likely were), but because they provide an especially vivid instance of social transitions and the resulting dissonance of status indicators. Subsequent chapters will furnish evidence that such transitions and such dissonance may have been important in circles from which Pauline Christianity drew its members. There is, however, one particular group of slaves and freedmen who constituted probably the most mobile category that can be identified in Roman society, and among whom we know quite explicitly there were Christians of the Pauline circle. These were the members of the *familia caesaris,* the "household of Caesar."[75] As ordinary persons of wealth turned many business responsibilities over to their slaves and freedmen, so Augustus and his successors employed their *familiae* in the business of empire.[76] Claudius greatly extended the practice, and for most of a century, until Domitian, then Trajan and Hadrian, acted to reduce the power of the freedmen, the *familia caesaris* was virtually the civil service of the empire, in the provinces no less than in Rome.[77] This brought enormous power to some individual freedmen of the emperors and, to many members of the household, opportunities for advancement that constituted stages in a career analogous to the formal *cursus honorum* of the equestrians. Several recent intensive studies of the inscriptional evidence have documented the restless upward movement of the imperial slaves.[78] The clearest indicator of their enhanced social power is the tendency of slaveborn members of the household to marry freeborn wives—a kind of union rare in the rest of society. P. R. C. Weaver calculates that nearly two-thirds of the male members of the *familia caesaris,* counting slaves and freedmen together, married freeborn wives. In contrast, from a control group of some seven hundred inscriptions outside the *familia* Weaver estimates that no more than 10 percent of wives of ordinary slaves and no more than 15 percent of those of ordinary freedmen could have been *ingenuae.*[79]

The rise of the freedmen aroused deep resentment among many people who thought themselves their betters. Witness the venom that the mere sight of a statue of Pallas, freedman and financial secretary of Claudius, could provoke in Pliny the Younger half a century after Pallas's death. Pliny was so incensed at the honors voted Pallas by the senate that he wrote not one but two letters venting his spleen to his friend Montanus: "Honours were then to be so cheap, the honours which Pallas did not disdain; and yet people of good family could be found who were fired by ambition for distinctions which they saw granted to freedmen and promised to slaves."[80] By this time, the power of freedmen to rise above their station, particularly in the imperial establishment, had been sharply curbed. But complaints were common earlier; Philo, for example, described Helicon as "an abominable execrable slave, who had been foisted for ill into the imperial household" and blamed him for Caligula's hostility to the Jews.[81] And it was during the reign of Nero that Petronius wrote his satire of the freedman Trimalchio's dinner party. What the critics find so outrageous in the parvenus is their crossing of social boundaries. They have dared to claim the status to which their education, intelligence, skill, power, and wealth accord but which is forbidden by their birth, origin, and legal rank. It is not surprising that those who complain most vehemently have themselves suffered the pains and slights of status inconsistency.[82]

From the particular case of the *familia caesaris,* we come again to the more general phenomenon of status inconsistency. In every society the status of a person, family, or other group is determined by the composite of many different clues, status indicators. For example, Tony Reekmans has extracted from Juvenal's satires seven social categories, in each of which there is a traditional hierarchy of ranks: language and place of origin, formal *ordo,* personal liberty or servitude, wealth, occupation, age, and sex.[83] These categories, of course, apply directly only to Rome, but similar factors counted in the provinces. It is the "criss-crossing of categories" (Finley's apt phrase) that made Juvenal's satires amusing to upper-class Romans. Sociologists call it status inconsistency or status dissonance.[84] Depending on the number of categories in conflict, the relative importance of those categories in widely held attitudes, the distance traversed in each category from one level to the next, and so on, such criss-crossing produces feelings and reactions of varying power, both within the mobile person or group and in others, especially actual or potential competitors. We may plausibly suppose that such feelings would often find some form of religious expression or—contrariwise—that some kinds of religious symbols, beliefs, and attitudes would enhance, inhibit, or channel social mobility differently from others.

WOMEN IN THE GRECO-ROMAN CITY

Among those persons who crossed categories in order to better their lives, even at the cost of enduring some obloquy from neighborhood gossips and, presumably, considerable internal tensions within their families and within themselves, there were a great many women. Sarah Pomeroy looks at the phenomenon of marriage upward by imperial slaves and freedmen from the point of view of the women. Why would a freeborn woman marry an imperial slave or freedman? The reason might be that while in some social categories (liberty, extraction) she was his better, in others (money, influence, possibly education or profession) he could improve her position.[85] Outside the *familia caesaris* it was much more common for slaveborn women to marry free men than the reverse. Weaver found in his control group of seven hundred sepulchral inscriptions that freedwomen were usually manumitted at an earlier age than freedmen and quite often for purposes of marriage. In fact, 29 percent married their own patrons—one of the most common means for female slaves to gain freedom and improved status.[86]

Upwardly mobile women must have been constantly reminded that they were crossing boundaries that a good part of the society held sacred. The hierarchical pattern of the family, in which the male was always superior to the female, as surely as parents to children and masters to slaves, was deeply entrenched in law and custom and its erosion constantly deplored by the rhetorical moralists and the satirists.[87] Still, in practice there were more and more opportunities for some women to break through this pattern. The traditional *patria potestas* of Rome had become less absolute from the time of the late republic on; the Hellenistic queens of the East and of Egypt had set a pattern of "masculine" ambition and ruthlessness that women of the Julio-Claudian houses soon imitated. There were even theoretical justifications for considering women the equals of men. The Stoics had taken up the Cynic epigram attributed to Antisthenes, "Virtue is the same for man and for woman,"[88] and Cleanthes is said to have written a book on the topic,[89] although women remain conspicuously absent among the pupils of the earlier as of the later Stoics. Musonius Rufus did indeed write tracts urging that "women too should study philosophy" and that, except for vocational matters, daughters should "receive the same education as sons," but his aim was to make women better managers of their households, that is, in their traditional roles.[90]

For some women the traditional roles were too confining. Not surprisingly, the most conspicuous examples come from the upper classes, whose situations gave them greater freedom. Even Philo, a firm believer in the spiritual and mental inferiority of women, granted that the formidable empress Livia was an exception. The instruction (*paideia*) she received enabled her to "become male in her reasoning power."[91] Nor were opportunities altogether wanting for women of lower standing. Inscriptions show that women were active in commerce and manufacture and, like their male counterparts, used some of the money they made in ways that would win them recognition in their cities. Pomeroy observes that freedwomen from the eastern provinces often traded in luxury goods, "such as purple dye or perfumes"[92]—a fact to be remembered when we meet Lydia, "a seller of purple goods," in Acts.[93] In Pompeii a woman named Eumachia, who made her money in a brick-manufacturing concern, paid for one of the major buildings and donated it to a workmen's association. She held the title of *sacerdos publica*. Another woman there, Mamia, built the temple of the Genius of Augustus.[94] Women with estates and in business of all sorts are attested in Pompeii. Moreover, MacMullen points out that women appear more and more frequently as independent litigants, although the greatest activity begins just after the period of our primary concern.[95] Throughout Italy and in the Greek-speaking provinces, MacMullen finds a small but significant number of women mentioned on coins and inscriptions as benefactors and officials of cities and as recipients of municipal honors therefor.[96]

Like men, though not nearly so frequently, women joined clubs—usually the same clubs as the men, for apart from associations of priestesses there is little evidence for all-women's clubs.[97] In lists of members of Greek associations, women appear alongside men, usually in fairly small proportions, long before the Roman period. It is not easy to tell what the social significance of such membership was, however. In Attica most of the mixed groups were related to Artemis or an associated deity; outside Attica they were mostly family associations.[98] What may be more significant is that fairly often in imperial times women were asked to serve as founders or patrons of men's clubs. This might involve provision of a place of meeting, either in the patron's house or in a special building erected or obtained for the purpose, or an endowment for the other expenses of the association, including its banquets, sacrifices, and funeral expenses for members. MacMullen, drawing evidence only from Italy and the Latin-speaking provinces, estimates that "perhaps a tenth of the protectors and donors that *collegia* sought out were women."[99] Pomeroy sets the figure at half that.[100] And these were quite often not women of the aristocracy, but those, like Eumachia, who had made money from commerce.

Women were also active in religious matters, both in cults that were exclusively or primarily practiced by women and in state or municipal and private cults that appealed to men and women alike. Inscriptions commemorate priestesses in ancient cults of many kinds.[101] In the Hellenistic and Roman periods, women seem to have been especially attracted to the syncretic cults produced by the spread of eastern and Egyptian religions through the Mediterranean cities. Conservative historians and satirists frequently blamed the lush growth of these cults on the superstition and irresponsibility of emancipated women; Juvenal's sixth satire is the most vivid example. Plutarch urged that a husband use not only philosophy to protect his wife from such gullibility,[102] but also a strong hand, for "it is becoming for a wife to worship and to know only the gods that her husband believes in, and to shut the front door tight upon all queer rituals and outlandish superstitions. For with no god do stealthy and secret rites performed by a woman find any favor."[103]

There is probably some truth behind these complaints. As mentioned earlier, the wives and mother of King Izates of Adiabene played a considerable role in his conversion to Judaism, and Josephus tells a couple of stories of fraudulent proselytism of women in Rome—one to the Isis cult, one to Judaism—that resemble Juvenal's portrayal.[104] The cult of Isis had a special affinity for women; in an aretalogy she is made to say, "I am the one called the Deity by women."[105] However, the invective of the traditionalist critics certainly exaggerated the extent to which women were the primary devotees of the new cults.[106] Epigraphic evidence does not support the view that women were leaders in religious innovation.[107]

It is also difficult to tell whether the participation of women in the new cults represented any significant change in their ordinary social roles. True, Johannes Leipoldt's assertion that Isis was "patroness of the women's movement" has been widely accepted.[108] The prayer to Isis in *POxy.* 1380, lines 214–16, is often quoted: "You have made the power of women equal to that of men." But the Isis cult also emphasized the goddess as a model spouse, protector of marriage,[109] and defender of chastity.[110] Within the cult the equality of women was stressed, but even so the priests seem to have outnumbered the priestesses and perhaps outranked them in most cases.[111] What seems most likely is that some of the newer cults, especially in the years before they became part of the municipal establishments, allowed considerably more freedom for women to hold office alongside men than did the older state cults. This freedom in turn fueled the invective of opponents, who portrayed foreign superstitions as an insidious threat to the proper discipline of the household, and therefore to the fabric of the whole society.[112] No doubt as a cult became more visible and better established, drawing its adherents from higher strata of the city, it would feel pressure to counter such attacks by emphasizing its agreement with traditional values.[113] Whatever "women's movement" there may have been would be suppressed early.

CONNECTIONS

I have suggested in this chapter that the rapid spread of Christianity through the lands of the Mediterranean basin was facilitated in manifold ways by the urbanization that had begun there before Alexander and accelerated during the Hellenistic and Roman imperial times. We need now to look at the relationship on a smaller scale, to ask just where and how Christianity was introduced into the cities. Let us put the question as simply as possible: When Paul and Silas, Timothy, Titus, and the others arrived in a city in order to preach the gospel, where and how did they begin? How did they make connection with those who would listen?

The book of Acts, because it is narrative and thus provides settings for the many speeches it reports, offers more answers to these questions than do the letters. In Acts the Pauline missionaries almost unfailingly go first to the Jewish synagogue and find opportunities to speak and debate at the regular Sabbath services.[114] When they meet resistance there, or even if they do not (16:13–15; 18:2), they sometimes take up residence in the households of individuals: of Lydia in Philippi (16:15), of Jason in Thessalonica (17:5–9), of Priscilla and Aquila in Corinth (18:2–4), of Titius Justus, also in Corinth (18:7). So far as Acts informs us, these meetings are by chance. Lydia, a gentile worshipper of the Jewish God[115] and an alien merchant in Philippi, is at the "place of prayer" on the Sabbath. Priscilla and Aquila are "found" by Paul in some undisclosed place; they share his trade of tentmaking and take him into their workshop. Titius Justus, another gentile *theosebomenos,* lives next door to the synagogue. Of Jason we know nothing except that "he received them" and that his hospitality proved costly. Acts also has Paul and his companions on two occasions rent houses: the *scholē* of Tyrannus in Ephesus, which may be a sort of guildhall of a trade association (19:9f.),[116] and Paul's private lodgings while he awaited trial in Rome (28:16, 30).[117] Otherwise we see the missionaries speaking to crowds in public places, the agora and Areopagus of Athens (17:17, 19–34) or undesignated places (Lystra, 14:8–18; Philippi, 16:16–34; Ephesus, 19:11–20). Sometimes an official creates an occasion to speak, either because of his curiosity or because Paul and his companions are under arrest (Sergius Paulus, 13:7–12; the jailer in Philippi, 16:25–34; the mob at the entrance to the barracks in Jerusalem, 21:37–22:24; the tribune's hearing, 22:30–23:10; Felix in Caesarea, ch. 24; Festus, 25:6–12; Agrippa and Bernice, 25:13–26:29).

Unfortunately we cannot simply accept the Acts picture of the mission as a direct, factual account. The pattern of beginning always in synagogues accords ill with Paul's own declarations that he saw his mission as primarily or even exclusively to the gentiles (Gal. 1:16; 2:7–9; Rom. 1:5, 13–15; 11:13f.; 15:15–21). To be sure, these statements are not to be taken absolutely: his becoming "as a Jew to the Jews, in order to win Jews" (1 Cor. 9:20) is not merely rhetorical, for if he had never been in contact with synagogues he would not have "five times . . . received at the hands of the Jews the forty lashes less one" (2 Cor. 11:24). But his policy seems to have been very different from the way it is described in Acts. We must also ask whether the more public settings in Acts may not often reflect some of the author's subtle literary allusions, such as the several hints of Socrates in the encounters in the agora and Areopagus in Athens,[118] or sometimes simply the pattern of the author's day rather than of Paul's.[119]

The letters of Paul do contain some reminders of the way in which he first preached the gospel to the recipients. For the most part, the aspects he wants to call attention to are not the mundane details that would help to satisfy our curiosity, but there are a few hints worth noting. There is not a word about synagogues, apart from the floggings already mentioned. Individuals who are called the "firstfruits" in a given area—presumably the first converts there—are singled out: Epaenetus of Asia (Rom. 16:5); the household of Stephanas of Achaia (1 Cor. 16:15). Paul also mentions protectors and hosts: Phoebe (Rom. 16:2), Prisca and Aquila (Rom. 16:3–5), Gaius (Rom. 16:23), Philemon (Philem. 22), perhaps Rufus's mother (Rom. 16:13). Paul addresses assemblies (*ekklēsiai*) in people's homes (1 Cor. 16:19; Rom. 16:5; Philem. 2; Col. 4:15). Some special hospitality was also involved when Paul first entered the province of Galatia, for whatever he means by the enigmatic reminder that "it was because of an illness of the flesh that I originally preached the gospel to you" (Gal. 4:13), he uses it as proof of a bond of friendship thus established between the Galatian Christians and himself.[120] We learn, too, that Paul regarded his work as an artisan not only as a source of support but also as in some way characterizing his evangelizing activity: "You remember, brothers, our work and toil. It was while we were laboring night and day, in order not to burden any of you, that we proclaimed to you the gospel of God" (1 Thess. 2:9).[121]

The thanksgiving period of the first Thessalonian letter also contains a glimpse of the way in which the active missionary travel of people like Paul was reinforced by a sort of "contagion" (as later pagan opponents would describe it) from new converts in an area. The Thessalonian Christians' "imitation" of both Paul "and the Lord," for which he congratulates them, consists in their having "received the word in much affliction with joy of the Holy Spirit," with the result that they became "a model [*typos*] for all the believers both in Macedonia and in Achaia" (1:6f.). How did this happen? The "word of the Lord" has "reverberated" from the Thessalonians "not only in Macedonia and Achaia, but in every place" (vs. 8a). That does not mean, as might first appear, that the Christians from Thessalonica have traveled about preaching. Rather, people in the other places are able to describe Paul's arrival in Thessalonica and the conversions that followed (vss. 8b–10). It is not Paul, Timothy, and Silvanus who have bragged about the Macedonians to the Corinthians and others (though Paul could do so: 2 Cor. 9:2), for "as a result we had no need to say anything" (vs. 8c). So the report must have been carried by other people who, for whatever reason, have traveled to neighboring towns and even as far away as Corinth. A further clue is found in 2 Cor. 11:9 and Phil. 4:15f. The Christians in nearby Philippi had sent money to help Paul in his mission first in Thessalonica, then in Corinth, for "the brethren who came from Macedonia" to bring help in Corinth were evidently the Philippian messengers. It is likely that they were also the ones who told the story of how things had gone in Thessalonica, thus reinforcing Paul's initial preaching in Corinth.

From Acts and the letters we thus get pictures of the Pauline missionaries' ways of making contact that in some ways diverge but in others support and supplement each other. Acts mainly depicts Paul and his companions speaking in public or quasi-public places and impressing masses of people, both positively and negatively, by miracles and rhetoric, and then taking advantage of the patronage of officials and well-to-do householders for extended teaching. They look, in short, like traveling sophists or philosophers—extraordinarily successful ones, with a retinue and rich patrons. E. A. Judge, who in his early essays on New Testament problems took the Acts narratives at face value, describes the Pauline "school" in just these terms.[122] From the letters, although they by no means contradict all aspects of the Acts picture, we receive on the whole the impression of a less grand and public mission, of communication more along the natural networks of relationship in each city and between cities. The families and houses of certain individuals seem to have been starting points, and connections of work and trade seem to have been important. In these last two respects the narratives of Acts and the clues in the letters are fully in accord. If we knew more about the small-scale texture of life in the neighborhoods of ancient cities, we would be in a better position to make sense of the few clues found in the New Testament documents. Unfortunately, some of the things we should most like to know the ancient writers considered too obvious or too vulgar to mention. Until recently classical archaeologists have understandably found the recovery of famous monuments and the lifting of mosaics more rewarding than systematic excavations of residential or industrial quarters, and political and military historians of antiquity have greatly outnumbered the social historians. We thus have no comprehensive, detailed picture of life in a first-century provincial town into which we could fit our few early-Christian puzzle pieces. We have only a scattergram of random facts and fragmentary descriptions, to which we can add a few dots.

One thing we do know about is size. The cities where Pauline Christianity took shape were very small compared with our postindustrial and post-population-explosion megalopolises. Antioch-on-the-Orontes, for example, was one of the giants in the first century, yet a person could easily walk the circumference in an afternoon. The modern town Antakya is somewhat less than half the area of the ancient city. A generous estimate of the modern population would be 75,000, and the town seems, to Western eyes, fairly crowded. Yet estimates of the ancient city at its peak, based on guesses of ancient writers, range as high as six times that number.[123] Even a more modest estimate, perhaps a quarter of a million, yields a high density in a relatively small area. The scale of a Philippi or a Beroea or even a Corinth would be a good bit smaller, but the density probably as high. MacMullen estimates that the average population density in cities of the Roman Empire may have approached two hundred per acre—an equivalent found in modern Western cities only in industrial slums. Further, given that much of the space—one-fourth, by MacMullen's calculations—was devoted to public areas, "the bulk of the population had typically to put up with most uncomfortable crowding at home, made tolerable by the attractive spaciousness of public facilities."[124]

It follows that privacy was rare. Much of life was lived on the streets and sidewalks, squares and porticoes—even more than in Mediterranean cities today. Not much that happened in a neighborhood would escape the eyes of the neighbors. News or rumor would travel rapidly; riots could flare up in a moment. Philo tells how Herod Agrippa's attempt to slip quietly into Alexandria occasioned instead a public lampoon of the Jewish king, leading on to a pogrom.[125] In the Acts of the Apostles we have the familiar story of the silversmiths of Ephesus, who feared damage to their business from the iconoclasm of Paul's converts, filling the theater with a rally for Artemis (19:23–41). But reactions to news were obviously not always violent; curiosity was as active as suspicion. A peddler of copper pans or magic amulets, of horoscopes or a revelation, could count on the word's getting around—once he had made his initial contacts.

How would those contacts be made? Acts gives a tiny glimpse of one way Paul and Silas (Silvanus) found an audience; whether it comes from a source close to the event or is the author's skillfully constructed vignette makes little difference for our purposes here.[126] In Philippi the missionaries went on the Sabbath "outside the gate to the riverside, where we supposed there was a place of prayer" (Acts 16:13, RSV). Later the same author reports that in Corinth Paul "found a Jew named Aquila," who with his wife Priscilla (Prisca) ran a tentmaking shop (18:2f.). When a stranger arrived in a city, then, it is taken for granted that he knew, or could easily learn, where to find immigrants and temporary residents from his own country or *ethnos* and practitioners of his own trade. Nothing could be more natural, for these were the two most important factors in the formation and identification of neighborhoods. In Antioch the Kerateion, in the southeastern quadrant of the city, was "the traditional Jewish quarter,"[127] although Jews lived elsewhere as well. Philo says that two of the five formal divisions of Alexandria were called Jewish.[128] Jews in Rome were concentrated in the Transtiberinum (modern Trastevere).[129] Kindred crafts and trades also tended to gather in the same areas, which often took their names from the fact: Linenweavers' Quarter, Leatherworkers' Street, Portico of the Perfumers.[130] From what we have seen of Paul's emphasis on his "working with my own hands," an emphasis that was still remembered at the time Acts was written, we will not go far wrong in supposing that his contact with fellow artisans and their customers often provided the first contacts in a city.[131] Hock's suggestion that the workshop itself may have been a locus of much of Paul's missionary preaching and teaching is not implausible.[132]

Below the level of the ethnic quarter and the neighborhood of similar trades came the individual household. Our sources give us good reason to think that it was the basic unit in the establishment of Christianity in the city, as it was, indeed, the basic unit of the city itself. In a subsequent chapter we shall consider the effects on the structure of the Pauline congregations of the fact that they ordinarily met in private homes and included as their nuclei the households of certain converts. At this point it is sufficient to remember that the *oikos* (or *oikia*; Latin *domus* or *familia*)[133] mentioned when the New Testament reports the conversion of someone "with all his house" is broader than our concept of the nuclear family. Cicero, for example, spoke of duty, as was customary in both Greek and Roman moral philosophy, in hierarchical order: first to country, then to parents, "next come children and the whole family [*domus*], who look to us alone for support and can have no other protection; finally, our kinsmen. . . ."[134] "Family" is defined not first by kinship but by the relationship of dependence and subordination. The head of a substantial household was thus responsible for—and expected a degree of obedience from—not only his immediate family but also his slaves, former slaves who were now clients, hired laborers, and sometimes business associates or tenants.[135] The floor plans of some of the houses that have been excavated in Pompeii or on Delos can be read as a kind of physical diagram of some of these relationships: private rooms and offices for the head of the house; a section of the house probably for the women and children; apartments for slaves; rented rooms; on the street side a shop or two, perhaps a tavern or even a hotel, sometimes connecting with the atrium; and, centrally located, a dining room in which the *paterfamilias* might enjoy the company of his equals and friends from other households, or entertain his *clientela,* or do both at once (with each assigned his fitting place).[136]

To be part of a household was thus to be part of a larger network of relations, of two sorts. Within the household, a vertical but not quite uni-linear chain connected unequal roles, from slave to paterfamilias, in the most intimate strand, but also included bonds between client and patron and a number of analogous but less formal relations of protection and subordination. Between this household and others there were links of kinship and of friendship, which also often entailed obligations and expectations.[137] These connections, however, were not necessarily always formal. Both along and between these lines there were often strong ties of feeling and voluntary loyalty. Among the most lucid demonstrations of one level of such affective ties are the sentiments expressed in epitaphs erected by slaves and freedmen for fellow members of the same household. Flory's investigation of such epitaphs from three large *familiae* found that they distinguished this relationship from friendship; it came closest to feelings of kinship.[138] It is apparent that such feelings and attitudes could be expressed in various ways, including common religious practices. It was ordinarily assumed that the subordinate members of a household, particularly the servile ones, would share the religion(s) of the master. This expectation would of course be more relevant to some kinds of cultic activities, such as the *lares* of the traditional Roman household, than to others, such as city cults in which the head of the household might occasionally have obligations. And unity would be more enforce-able in a smaller household than in a larger one. There is some evidence that it became more common in imperial times for different members of a household to go their own religious ways.[139] One of Paul's letters (1 Cor. 7:12–16) addresses this issue.

One additional form of social relationship was very important in the Greek and Roman cities: the voluntary association. Clubs, under a great variety of names, had been known in Greek cities since the fifth century, in Rome from somewhat later. In imperial times they proliferated in both East and West, despite periodic efforts by the government to suppress them.[140] It seems to have been possible for almost anyone to "gather" (synagein is the word often used)[141] a group of friends, relatives, neighbors, or working associates, draw up a constitution, find a meeting place, and declare themselves the Association (thiasos, synodos, eranos, or the like) of N. The group was usually not large: most often it contained from a dozen to thirty or forty, rarely more than a hundred members.

In large households, masters sometimes encouraged the formation of a club and provided a meeting place for it, like the burial society that met in the house of Sergia Paullina in Rome, attested by a well-known inscription.[142] Sometimes the household could become the basis of a cultic association, as in the famous instance of Pompeia Agrippinilla, who established a Dionysiac thiasos in Tusculum in the early second century of our era. The hierarchy of the cult association's officers largely reproduced that of the household, with Agrippinilla as priestess at the head.[143]

However small, a club must have officers, with titles the grander the better, often imitating the titles of municipal officials. Roman collegia generally had a group of presidents, called magistri; a Greek club usually had a single leader, variously named. The treasurer (tamias, quaestor) was next in importance, having to account for entrance fees and dues and to pay the regular expenses of banquets and festivals, honors for patrons and others, and, in many cases, for the funerals of members. Besides these, there were priests and priestesses, logistai, grammateis, epistatai, epimeletai, archontes, curatores, prytaneis, hegemones, brabeutai, and so on, and on. Evidently, besides conviviality the clubs offered the chance for people who had no chance to participate in the politics of the city itself to feel important in their own miniature republics.

Trade and professional associations were especially important in Rome. Before the Roman Empire they had not been common in the East, apart from the special case of the "Dionysiac artists," a guild of actors, scene painters, and other specialists associated with theater. In the period we are concerned with, however, the organization of other artisans and of merchants spread through the Greek cities as well.[144] Although it is now common to call these groups guilds, their purpose is not to be confused with those of medieval guilds, much less with those of modern trade unions.[145] "So far as the evidence of the inscriptions goes the guilds seem to have been purely social bodies, unconcerned with the business activities of their members."[146] Only in the later empire did the government sometimes intervene and manipulate the trade associations in attempts to regulate some aspects of commerce.

Earlier, the Builders and Carpenters (*fabri, tignuarii*), the Patchwork-Rug-makers (*centonarii*), the Porters (*phortēgoi*), the Purple-Dyers of Eighteenth Street (in Thessalonica)[147] met, as did their counterparts of many other names, to eat a meal perhaps a bit better than the usual, to drink some rather good wine supplied by the member whose turn it was, to celebrate the birth-day of the founder or patron or the feast of Poseidon or Hermes or Isis or Silvanus, and to draw up rules to ensure that all members would have a decent burial when their times came. The *ekklēsia* that gathered with the tentmakers Prisca, Aquila, and Paul in Corinth or Ephesus might well have seemed to the neighbors a club of the same sort.

It is more difficult to determine the structure of the larger associations of foreign merchants and artisans that formed in most cities, especially the great commercial centers. The colonies of Italian merchants on Delos and Rhodes are the best known.[148] It has been debated, for example, whether the free-born and freed Italians of Delos, who called themselves Hermaists, Poseidoniasts, and Apolloniasts, were organized into three separate cultic associations, or whether they were organized into one very large association which elected *magistri* (*magistreis Mirquri Apollonis Neptuni*) to be in charge of the cults of their three principal patron deities. The latter now seems more likely, which means that the whole Italian colony was organized as a club or *conventus*, though it had grown, in the two centuries before Christ, far beyond the bounds of the private associations we have been considering.[149] In an at least partly analogous way, the Jews in some cities were organized in the fashion of a *collegium*, with their single deity, officers and rules, private funds, and patrons.

URBAN JUDAISM AND PAULINE CHRISTIANITY

It is now generally acknowledged that no one can understand the peculiar form of early Christianity we call Pauline without first gaining some under-standing of contemporaneous Judaism. But what kind of Judaism? As surely as modern scholarship has forced us to recognize that Christianity, even in its earliest decades, was already a complex of movements in several directions, so also discoveries and investigations in this century have revealed great diversity and rapid changes within Judaism in the early Roman Empire. A century ago, a handful of imaginative scholars guessed the importance of an obscure sect called Essenes by Philo, Josephus, and Pliny, but none would have dared suppose that we would one day possess a substantial part of the library of a major settlement of them or a closely related group. Before the excavations in Dura-Europos in 1932 most people would have thought the notion preposterous that third-century Jews in a Roman garrison town would have covered the walls of their synagogue with narrative paintings. Until much more recently than that, collections of rabbinic texts have been as-sembled and mined for "the rabbinic view" of this or that, as if from Hillel to Saadia Gaon "rabbinic Judaism" had been one monolithic and static whole.

There has been no dearth of attempts to set Paul against the background of various kinds of Judaism. Now he appears as a "rabbi," again as a representative of "Jewish apocalyptic"; perhaps he stands closest to "Jewish mysticism," or even to "Jewish gnosticism." Or his peculiar concerns are simply the result of his having been reared in "Hellenistic Judaism." The failure of any of these schemas to win allegiance as *the* context within which the text of Paul's letters makes sense should alert us to the fact that these categories do not add up to an adequate taxonomy of first-century Judaism. Anyone who does serious, close exegesis of the texts must have documents from all these categories and from others besides. Paul himself is the clearest proof of their inadequacy. He writes in fluent Greek; his Bible is the Septuagint; he is certainly a "Hellenistic Jew." He is convinced that the present, evil age is soon coming to an end; in the meantime he urges the children of light not to be like the children of darkness—surely this is "Jewish apocalyptic." He has been caught up into the third heaven and seen ineffable things—surely, if ever, one can speak of "Jewish mysticism" here?—yet he calls himself "in terms of the Law, a Pharisee."

The conventional categories suffer from vagueness, anachronism, and inappropriate definition. Vagueness is most obvious in the case of "Hellenistic Judaism." Does this mean all Jews who spoke Greek in the Hellenistic and Roman periods? Or does it mean people who shared other aspects of Greek urban culture, including certain metaphysical beliefs, some standards of literary and artistic style, a certain ethos? "Rabbinic Judaism" is the category most infected by anachronism. The Temple's destruction in A.D. 70 and the even more profound aftershocks of Bar Kochba's failure in the years 132–135 transformed the life and institutions of Judea and Galilee in ways that we can only dimly reconstruct. The earliest documents we have of "rabbinic Judaism" were compiled in the circle around the Patriarch at the end of the second century. They and later sources undoubtedly contain traditional material of much earlier provenance, but only by the most painstaking—and often subjective—form critical studies can we guess which parts are really early or what changes they have undergone in transmission and editing. We will do well to avoid using the term *rabbi* or *rabbinic* of any phenomenon earlier than the academy founded at Yavneh (Jamnia) by Yohanan ben Zakkai, and we will be on safer ground to restrict these terms to second-century and later developments.[150] Finally, all these categories have usually been defined as if the phenomena they referred to had been theological systems, to be described by listing their constitutive beliefs in propositional form and displaying their logical connections and implications. Whether that is ever the best means for obtaining primary understanding of a religious movement need not be debated here. For anyone interested in a social description of early Judaism and early Christianity, it is not a very helpful method.

Most scholars who have written on the subject of Paul and Judaism have been interested in tracing Paul's upbringing and pre-Christian affiliations and in understanding the sources and implications of his theological ideas, the

Jewish practices he rejected, and his modes of argument. These are fascinating questions, and they cannot be totally ignored here, but they are not the focus of this book. Rather, the major question is what, if any, were the connections between the Christian communities founded by Paul and his co-workers and the varieties of Judaism in the Greco-Roman world. The Judaism that is directly relevant to our attempt to describe Pauline Christianity (whatever the case with Paul as an individual) is not the Judaism of Galilean or Mesopotamian villages, but the Judaism of the Roman provincial cities. Therefore, one concern here is whether the Jewish immigrants between the times of Alexander and Claudius had found ways of adapting to the cities which served as models and channels for the Pauline Christians.

In the first century some five to six million Jews were living in Diaspora, that is, more or less permanently settled outside Palestine. The Diaspora had begun at least as early as the deportations of the Babylonian exile, in the sixth century, and had been fed by subsequent dislocations through successive conquests of the homeland, but even more by voluntary emigration in search of better economic opportunities than the limited space and wealth of Palestine could afford. Consequently there was a substantial Jewish population in virtually every town of any size in the lands bordering the Mediterranean. Estimates run from 10 to 15 percent of the total population of a city—in the case of Alexandria, perhaps even higher.[151] Like other immigrant groups in the cities, the Jews naturally joined together to continue familiar religious practices, to enjoy the society of relatives and others of common heritage, to settle internal disagreements, and to exert joint pressure to obtain rights and privileges from the larger community. Some aspects of their religious beliefs and practices, however, set them apart from the other immigrant cults that were becoming so common, and created special problems in their relations with dominant groups in the local society, on the one hand, and with the Roman imperial authorities on the other.

Josephus has preserved a number of documents that shed light on these relations. Two dealing with the Jews of Sardis are particularly interesting. In 49 B.C. Lucius Antonius,[152] proquaestor and propraetor of the province of Asia, responded to an appeal from Sardian Jews in a decree addressed to the magistrates, council, and *dēmos* of Sardis: "Jewish citizens of ours have come to me and pointed out that from the earliest times they have had an association [*synodos*] of their own in accordance with their native laws [*kata tous patrious nomous*] and a place [*topos*] of their own, in which they decide their affairs and controversies with one another."[153] Evidently the city authorities had in some way threatened the rights enjoyed by the Jews, which the Roman official now directs to be maintained as earlier.[154] Some time later the city council and *dēmos* of Sardis issued a decree confirming the right of "the Jewish citizens living in our city" to "come together and have a communal life [*politeuesthai*] and adjudicate suits among themselves, and that a place be given them in which they may gather together with their wives and children and offer their ancestral prayers and sacrifices to God. . . ."[155] The magistrates are to set aside a place "for them to build and inhabit," and the market officials are to make provision for "suitable food" to be available for the Jews.

The subsequent history of the Jews in Sardis was apparently extraordinarily happy. In the second or early third century they were given for their "place" a remodeled basilica, of huge size and elegant decoration, part of the monumental Roman gymnasium complex on the main street of the city,[156] which they kept until the city itself was destroyed, long after the empire had become officially Christian.[157] The controversy in the time of Julius Caesar, which seems to have been settled quickly and amicably, nevertheless hints at some of the perennial tensions that affected urban Jewish communities.

Lucius Antonius, presumably echoing the language of the Jewish petition, called their community a *synodos,* one of the most common and general terms for a club, guild, or association.[158] For legal purposes the Romans classified the Jewish groups in each city as collegia; when Caesar ordered all collegia disbanded except certain long-established groups, the synagogues were among those explicitly exempted.[159] In several respects the identification was a natural one, for the organization of the Jewish community shared a number of traits with clubs, guilds, and cultic associations. The members gathered in a particular place, which served both cultic and social functions.[160] They depended on benefactions of patrons, including non-Jewish sympathizers as well as wealthy members of the congregation, whom they rewarded by inscriptions, special seats in the assembly room, and honorary titles like "Father" or "Mother of the Synagogue."[161] The community provided for the burial of its dead.[162] It had officers with titles that imitated those of the polis.[163]

On the other hand, as Smallwood points out, the functions of the synagogues were wider than those of the collegia and in some respects quite different.[164] Perhaps most important, "membership was automatic for a Jew by right of birth, without question of admission or enrollment; on the other hand, membership was exclusive to Jews and proselytes, while other *collegia* were corporations with voluntary, open membership."[165] The differences are underlined by the political role which the Jewish associations played. In most cities there seems to have been some central body that could speak for the Jews in negotiations with the city magistrates or with Roman officials. In Alexandria, the one city for which evidence for internal organization of the Jewish community is relatively good, this consisted of a *gerousia,* a council of elders, who represented the Jews of the whole city, probably through officers (*archontes*) chosen by each congregation.[166] Some similar organization probably existed in Antioch, for we hear there of a single *archōn* of the Jews, in the first century A.D., and of an *archōn tōn archontōn* ("magistrate of the magistrates") in the fourth century.[167] Whether that was the rule in all cities where there was more than one synagogue is debatable.[168]

Whatever the details of local organization, which probably varied somewhat from one town to the next, the Jews in those cities where their numbers constituted a large segment of the population formed a virtual city within the city, for which one Greek term was *politeuma*.[169] This was a recognized, semiautonomous body of residents in a city who, though not citizens, shared some specified rights with citizens. As we have seen, such an arrangement was not unusual in the Hellenistic cities, to accommodate significant groups of immigrants, like the Italians or Syrians on Delos, or the natives of an older city refounded as a Roman colony.[170]

The relations between the *politeuma* and the *dēmos,* the body of full citizens, were subject to various interpretations and often the focal point of controversy. Josephus likes to use the term *citizens* (*politai*) to refer to Jews resident in a city. For example, he says that those "resident in Antioch" were called Antiochenes[171]—but the very term *residents* (*katoikountes*) normally signifies resident aliens, not citizens. The same ambiguity occurs in the two documents from Sardis already quoted, in which the Jews are called *politai*. In the decree of Lucius Antonius the text is uncertain, for most manuscripts read "our [Roman] citizens," but one reads "your [Sardian] citizens."[172] The decree of the city, as Josephus reports it, contains the same self-contradiction as his note about the Antiochenes, referring to the Jews simultaneously as *katoikountes* and *politai*.[173] The nub of the problem is stated concisely in the complaint made thirty-five years later by certain Ionians (Greek citizens of western Asia Minor, probably in Ephesus): "if the Jews were to be their fellows [*syngeneis*], they should worship the Ionians' gods."[174] The Jews sought at every opportunity to acquire rights identical with those of citizens, but at the same time they insisted on guarantees that they would not have to violate their religious laws, notably sabbath observance, dietary rules, and avoidance of "idolatry." They could not participate in the civic cults and still remain Jews.

The competition which, in a society of limited goods, inevitably developed among the various *politeumata* and lesser groups of the city entailed for the Jews some peculiar ambivalences. On the one hand, they showed themselves adept and vigorous in pursuing the opportunities which Hellenistic and Roman urbanization created for mobile people. Their strict monotheism, their "imageless" worship, the strong cohesion of their communities won admiration among many of their pagan neighbors, leading some to become outright proselytes, others to become sympathizers or even formal adherents to the synagogue.[175] Yet these same qualities, added to the size and wealth of many of the Jewish communities, provoked others of their neighbors to resentment and jealousy. One story that made the rounds was a vicious parody of the Exodus, according to which the people whom Moses organized into a nation were lepers who had been expelled from Egypt. That, it was said, explained why the Jews were antisocial, refusing "to share a table with any other race."[176]

From their side, the Jews knew that their very identity depended upon their maintaining some distinct boundaries between themselves and "the nations." Yet they also found themselves under strong pressures to conform to the dominant culture of the cities for reasons of expediency. Moreover, many of them experienced a powerful attraction to the values of that culture, which in so many respects seemed harmonious with their own ethos and their biblical traditions. The dilemma can be sensed on almost every page of Philo. He writes an elegant, rhetorical Greek; it is doubtful whether he knew any more Hebrew than he might have found in some handbook interpreting biblical names.[177] Greek was the language of all the Jewish diaspora communities within the Roman Empire from which evidence has survived. Furthermore, while what he wrote was a series of elaborate commentaries and paraphrases on the books of the Pentateuch, a large part of what he finds in the biblical narratives and laws is identical with much that one might hear from the pagan moralists and philosophers who were teaching in the schools of Alexandria.[178] "He read Plato in terms of Moses, and Moses in terms of Plato, to the point that he was convinced that each had said essentially the same things."[179] At the same time, Philo saw the importance of the Jews' preserving their distinctive identity. When he came to Balaam's oracle, which said of Israel:

> Behold, a people will dwell [katoikēsei] alone
> and among the nations it will not be reckoned,[180]

he explained: "not because their dwelling-place is set apart and their land severed from others, but because in virtue of the distinction of their peculiar customs they do not mix with others to depart from the ways of their fathers."[181] Philo was appalled that some Jews who, like himself, took the rituals and festivals to be "symbols of things of the mind," on that account neglected the physical performance of the required actions. Such people, said he, acted as if they were "living by themselves, alone in a desert, or had become disembodied souls, knowing neither city nor village nor household nor any human association [thiasos anthrōpōn]."[182]

The individualism that Philo castigates was the specific temptation of people like himself: wealthy, cultured, "Greek in soul as well as speech,"[183] but chafing at the limits imposed by the ambivalent status of the Jewish community. As Tcherikover says, "Anyone who desired to participate in the cultural and public life of this environment, and to play any part whatever in the world at large, had first to be a citizen of a Greek city."[184] That individuals of Philo's class could readily become citizens cannot be doubted. But at what cost to their Jewishness? The answer is not as simple as it is often made to seem. The case of Philo's nephew, Tiberius Julius Alexander, has already been mentioned. His exceptional career entailed, at least according to Josephus, his abandonment of Judaism.[185] But it may have been possible in other cases for individual Jews to find a way to hold Greek citizenship without directly engaging in acts that most Jews would regard as idolatrous. Certainly at a later period, in cities of western Asia Minor, it was possible. In the great Sardis synagogue, for example, inscriptions record with pride the names of members of the synagogue who were Sardianoi and even city magistrates.[186] And the author of the book of Acts, whether his information was true or fictional, at least thought it credible that Paul's father had been both a citizen of Tarsus and a citizen of Rome, but still sent his son to Jerusalem to study with Rabbi Gamaliel.[187]

Nevertheless, the issue that exercised Alexandrian Jews—and Philo, their spokesman—in the early first century was whether the whole community of Jews would possess citizen rights the same as those of the Greeks. That issue lay behind the continual controversies and periodic violence between gentiles and Jews in Alexandria. The legal question for the period we are interested in was settled by the famous letter of Claudius of A.D. 41, a papyrus copy of which was discovered in the first decade of this century. Claudius reconfirmed the Jews' rights to continue their ancestral customs without molestation, but he categorically denied them the right to be considered citizens. They must be satisfied with the many benefits they already held as resident aliens in "a city not their own."[188] The legal situation was probably not different in other cities, where we have much less evidence. In places like Sardis, however, where relations between Jews and gentiles were evidently much more harmonious over several centuries, there may have been less reason to test the legal limits of Jewish participation in civic life.

Although the Jews of Alexandria were disappointed by Claudius's eventual response to their petition—and they had been terrified for a time by the response of his predecessor—nevertheless it is significant that they had turned to Rome for redress of local grievances. Two factors pressed them to do so. One was the composite character of the Greco-Roman city; the other was the Roman policy begun by Caesar and Augustus of rule by balancing strong local interests and winning their allegiance by making them clients. As a consequence, any sizable, coherent community with ambivalent local status, like the Jews, must cultivate imperial patronage. The diaspora Jews did so, generally with success. Popular treatments of early Christianity and early Judaism have focused so one-sidedly on Palestine and especially on the failed revolts of 66–70 and 132–135 that we tend to think of Rome as the implacable enemy of the Jews. The documents collected by Josephus, the two political tracts of Philo, and other evidence suggest rather that Jews of the cities more often regarded Rome as their protector. During the two Palestinian revolts, the Jews of the diaspora cities seem to have offered almost no direct support to the revolutionaries, and they suffered no visible consequences of the latter's defeat. Even during the wars there were incidents in which Roman officials intervened to protect Jews from attacks from local opponents, who had taken advantage of the anti-Jewish sentiment evoked by the revolutions. The best known took place in Antioch, when in the year 67 an apostate Jew incited a pogrom against his own people (his father was *archōn* of the Antiochene Jews) by alleging a plot to burn the city. After an interval,[189] the outbreak of a real fire in 70/71 provoked new hostilities, but the temporary governor, Gnaeus Collega, succeeded in restraining the Antiochenes and in proving by investigation that the Jews were innocent. Unsatisfied, the Antiochenes petitioned Titus, when he appeared in Syria in the spring, to expel the Jews or, when he would not, at least to take away their privileges. He refused, "leaving the status of the Jews of Antioch exactly as it was before."[190] To be sure, Roman rule was not always benign. The Jewish uprisings in Egypt and Cyrenaica between 112 and 115 were put down so ruthlessly that in large regions of North Africa whole Jewish communities simply ceased to exist.[191] Yet even that war and the Palestinian debacle of Bar Kochba two decades later did not much affect the situation of Jews living in cities of the other provinces. By and large the diaspora Jews found it prudent to view Roman power in just the way that one of them, though a convert to the sect of the Christians, advised his fellows at Rome: "Rulers are not a terror to good conduct, but to bad. Would you have no fear of him who is in authority? Then do what is good, and you will receive his approval, for he is God's servant for your good" (Rom. 13:3–4, RSV).[192]

Evidence for the economic status of Jews in the cities is scattered and much of it is late, but what there is indicates that Jews in most places were distributed through the whole range of statuses and occupations.[193] For example, Applebaum finds in the Jewish population of Cyrenaica a few Jews who were wealthy and landowners, for their sons were admitted to the ephebate of Cyrene, Teucheira, and Ptolemais, but also impoverished tenant farmers, slaves, a stonecutter, makers of clay lamps, painters, and perhaps seamen and mint workers.[194] The number of artisans who appear in inscriptions, papyri, and literary and legal texts is especially notable. The newly discovered synagogue list from Aphrodisias includes a goldsmith, a coppersmith, two confectioners, a fowler(?), possibly a greengrocer, and, among those listed separately as *theosebeis,* coppersmiths, fullers, a stonecutter, a purple-dealer or -dyer, two carpenters, a moneychanger(?), a sausagemaker, and a braceletmaker.[195] There is a tradition preserved in the Tosefta that the Great Synagogue of Alexandria had special places set apart for guilds of silversmiths, blacksmiths, weavers, carpetmakers, and such.[196] And there is evidence for connection of guilds with synagogues also in Hierapolis (Phrygia) and Corcyros (Cilicia) and perhaps elsewhere.[197] References to Jewish merchants are rarer but not altogether lacking, and Applebaum develops an ingenious and not implausible argument that the impressive wealth of Alexander the Alabarch, Philo's brother and the father of Tiberius Julius Alexander, must have come in part from commerce, for he had money on deposit at Puteoli.[198] Naturally there were many tradesmen of more modest standing among the Jews, like the shipowners and merchants (*nauklēroi, emporoi*) who, along with farmers and artisans (*geōrgoi, technitai*), were deprived of livelihood by the riots in Alexandria during the reign of Caligula.[199] A visitor to the cities with which we are concerned would thus have found Jews in virtually every stratum of society. The ambivalences which affected their lives as simultaneously members of the Jewish community and residents of the Greek city would have varied somewhat from place to place[200] and considerably with their means and rank.

THE CITIES OF PAULINE CHRISTIANITY

Paul's own summary of his mission speaks of a crescent "from Jerusalem around as far as Illyricum" (Rom. 15:19). The termini of this arc are problematical, for although Acts has Paul preaching in Jerusalem immediately after his conversion (9:26–30), Paul vigorously denies any connection with Jerusalem at this point (Gal. 1:17–24), and neither Acts nor the letters mention any activity in Illyricum.[201] It is easy to understand why Paul would take Jerusalem as the rhetorical starting point, however, and if he or his fellow workers did not in fact press into Dalmatia or Moesia, their extended work in Macedonia brought them near the borders of those Illyrian areas.[202] Still, the difficulties remind us that our sources do not fully inform us about the movements of the Pauline missionaries. The dates of the authentic letters span scarcely more than a decade of Paul's life, roughly the last third of his Christian career, and their reports of travel plans are fragmentary. The Acts account is more systematic, but much of its plausible order probably results from the author's deductions and his theological intent (such as the centrality of Jerusalem) rather than from accurate sources. Nevertheless, by using both the authentic and the deutero-Pauline letters and supplementing them cautiously with information from Acts, it is possible to gain a picture of the main locations where Paul and his associates were active. Arguments from silence will be very precarious, for we do not know how many letters from Paul may have been lost.

Missionary activity is reported or may be inferred from the sources in a number of places on the Jerusalem-Illyricum crescent for which we have little or no evidence of later activities by Paul and his co-workers to maintain Christian congregations. Consequently, it remains uncertain whether Christianity in those places, if successfully established at all in the first century, was in any way distinctively Pauline. Immediately after his conversion, according to Galatians 1:17, Paul went from Damascus to "Arabia," that is, the area south or east of Damascus under the control of the Nabatean native kings. Acts reports nothing of this activity or of the hostility it aroused from the ethnarch of King Aretas (2 Cor. 11:32f.; contrast Acts 9:19–25). Yet most of the "three years" (perhaps not much more than two by modern reckoning) before his first visit to Jerusalem (Gal. 1:18) was presumably spent in the Nabatean realm, for the pursuit by royal forces and Paul's escape from them at Damascus are most readily understood as occurring very soon after his return. We hear of no further contact between Paul and the Christians in Damascus, nor anything about congregations in "Arabia."

The locale of the next fourteen years (or thirteen or, if both periods are counted from the conversion, only eleven; Gal. 2:1) is more problematic. Paul speaks of work only in Syria and Cilicia (Gal. 1:21; the latter, according to Acts, his native province). The conventional way of harmonizing Acts and Galatians, by identifying Paul's second visit to Jerusalem with the "apostolic council" of Acts 15, requires, however, the inclusion in that period of the preaching in Cyprus (Acts 13:4–12), in Antioch by Pisidia (13:14–52), and in the Lycaonian cities of Iconium, Lystra, and Derbe (14:1–20). Some scholars, following a suggestion of John Knox, would place the major part of Paul's activity in Galatia, Macedonia, Greece, and Asia also in the time prior to the council.[203] Whatever the chronology, it was in these latter areas that Pauline Christianity put down its enduring roots. There is little evidence of lasting results from the so-called first missionary journey in the Acts scheme, even though the author's summary of the return trip presupposes that converts were made and congregations organized in Lystra, Iconium, and Pisidian Antioch[204]—unless these last three, which were in fact in the Roman province Galatia, are the places addressed in Paul's letter "to the Galatians."[205]

In Macedonia, Greece, and western and central Asia Minor the story is quite different. The preaching in Macedonia began in Philippi, and although Paul, Silvanus, and Timothy experienced hostility there (1 Thess. 2:2; Acts 16:12–40), the congregation they founded had a very special role of "partnership" (koinōnia) in the Pauline circle's further mission, including financial help for the mission to Thessalonica and Achaia and for Paul in his later (final?) imprisonment (2 Cor. 11:8f.; Phil. passim, especially 4:15–18). They were also early and strong participants in the collection undertaken by Paul for the Jerusalem Christians (2 Cor. 8:1–6; 9:2–4; Rom. 15:26). From Philippi the missionary route lay southward. Groups were formed in Thessalonica (1 Thess. 2:2; Acts 17:1–9)—these would receive the earliest letter from Paul and his colleagues that has been preserved—then, according to Acts alone, in Beroea (17:10–14) and Athens (17:15–34). The sole mention of Athens in the letters is 1 Thess. 3:1, which merely confirms that Paul spent some time there waiting until Timothy could return from inspecting the situation in Thessalonica.

The southernmost point of Paul's expedition to Greece was Corinth (Acts 18:1–17), where he founded the church known to us in greatest detail, because of his extended correspondence with it, attested and partially embodied in 1 and 2 Corinthians. The recommendation of Phoebe, "diakonos of the church in Cenchreae," in Rom. 16:1 shows that a congregation was also established in Corinth's eastern port, and 2 Corinthians 1:1 suggests that there were yet others "in the whole of Achaia." Acts does not credit Paul with the introduction of Christianity in Ephesus, but it does speak of an extended work there by Paul and his associates, especially Prisca and Aquila (Acts 18:19–21, 24–28; 19:1–40). It was from there that Paul wrote the first of the extant letters to Corinth (1 Cor. 16:8), and there that he experienced grave difficulties of some kind (2 Cor. 1:8–11; cf. 1 Cor. 15:32), leading some to suppose that he was imprisoned for a time and perhaps from there wrote the letters to Philemon and to the Philippians. With some plausibility, Ephesus has been seen as the center of the Pauline circle's subsequent activity.[206]

Unmentioned in Acts are the churches of the Lycus valley in western Asia Minor, Colossae, Laodicea, and Hierapolis. But we know from the authentic letter to Philemon and the letter of a Pauline disciple to Colossae that these lay in the Pauline orbit (Col. 4:12–17; Philem. 1–2, 23–24). It is less certain how much reliance should be placed on the geography of the Pastorals. For whatever it is worth, the second-century author connects the Pauline retinue with churches in Ephesus (1 Tim. 1:3; 2 Tim. 4:12), Galatia or, in a variant reading, Gaul (2 Tim. 4:10), Dalmatia (2 Tim. 4:10), Troas (2 Tim. 4:13), Corinth (2 Tim. 4:20), Miletus (2 Tim. 4:20), Crete (Titus 1:5), and Nicopolis (Titus 3:12).

If we limit ourselves to the evidence from the letters of Paul and his immediate associates, then, we find that the Pauline movement took root in at least four provinces of the Roman Empire: Galatia, Asia, Macedonia, and Achaia. A few remarks about the most obvious characteristics of the cities in each will help to set the stage for the next part of our investigation.

The location of "the churches of Galatia," to which Paul wrote a letter and which he mentioned to the Corinthian Christians (Gal. 1:2; 1 Cor. 16:1), cannot be determined with any certainty. In other cases, although Paul speaks of "believers in Macedonia and in Achaia" (1 Thess. 1:7; cf. Rom. 16:26; 1 Cor. 16:15; 2 Cor. 9:2; 11:9f.) or in the province Asia (Rom. 16:5; 1 Cor. 16:19), his letters are addressed to Christians in specific cities. Yet nowhere in Paul's letters is a city mentioned that lay within the Galatian province. The account in Acts only complicates the puzzle further. Acts does describe evangelization by Paul and his companions in Pisidian Antioch, Iconium, Lystra, and Derbe—four of the Roman colonies established as part of the romanization program undertaken by the province's first governor, Marcus Lollius, under Augustus.[207] The author of Acts, however, does not use the name Galatia to refer to these places, but the ethnic regional terms Pisidia and Lycaonia.[208] Further, Acts reports a journey through "the Phrygian and Galatian country" (16:6) and, although it records no missionary activity and names no specific locations, later tells of a return trip "strengthening all the disciples" in the same areas (18:23).

One widely held solution simply identifies the "Galatians" of Paul's letters with Christians in those Roman colonies in the central part of the province that are mentioned in Acts. This identification has been particularly popular with scholars who have seen the central problem to be the harmonization of Acts and the letters.[209] As we have just seen, however, this hypothesis does not really do justice to the evidence of Acts, for Acts does not call these cities "Galatian," and the sequence of Acts 16 implies a distinction between them and "the Galatian country." As for Paul, one might well argue that he could have referred to Christians in, say, Lystra as "the churches in Galatia" in the third person. But it is hardly imaginable that he would address them as "O *Galatai!* [O Celts, or Gauls]" (Gal. 3:1). Even Augustus, reporting in his *Res gestae* his founding of the colonies in question, did not call them "Galatian" but "Pisidian."[210]

We are left, then, with two rather awkward facts: in the extant letters of Paul there is no reference to the Pisidian and Lycaonian cities of Antioch,

Iconium, Lystra, and Derbe, all lying in the Roman province Galatia, which are mentioned in Acts; and neither Paul nor Acts tells us in what city or cities of Galatia, in the narrow, ethnic sense, Paul established communities. If we must guess, however, evidence points to one or more of the capitals of the three tribal "republics" organized by Mark Antony: Tavium (capital of the old Celtic tribe of the Trocmi), Pessinus (of the Tolistobogii), and Ancyra (of the Tectosages). Marcus Lollius made Ancyra (modern Ankara) capital of the province. These three small cities lay in the central highlands of Anatolia, where the marauding tribes of the Celts, after their migration down through Thrace, had been settled in Hellenistic times, probably by Nicomedes I of Bithynia, Mithridates of Pontus, and Antiochus I of Syria.[211] Their remoteness does not count too heavily against this identification of Paul's Galatians, for Roman roads gave fairly ready access. A road ran through Tavium and Ancyra to Sardis on the west, on the east connecting with Megalopolis and branching south to Melitene, north to Satala and Nicopolis; another ran to Nicomedia from Ancyra; one route from Sinope to Tarsus ran through Tavium.[212] Evidently Augustus and his successors did not think these Galatian cities too remote to be important; for different reasons, Paul agreed.[213]

West of Galatia was the province Asia, quite different in history and culture. The coast had been colonized by Greeks in the Bronze Age; in the interior were such ancient civilizations as the Lydian and the Phrygian. A large part of the territory had been consolidated by the Attalid kings who ruled from Pergamum. The last of them, Attalus III, on his death in 133 B.C. willed the kingdom to the Roman people. Perhaps his intention was that only his own property should go to Rome, while the cities of his realm were to be free, but the subsequent wars against the pretender Aristonicus and, in the following century, against Mithridates VI of Pontus, drew the Romans more deeply into the governance of the area than perhaps either they or Attalus had foreseen.[214] It was organized as a senatorial province, with a governor of consular rank, resident in Ephesus. Phrygia and Cibyratis had been annexed to the original bequest, resulting in a territory a little larger than England.[215] At the time Rome acquired it, the towns of the interior, as distinct from the old Greek cities on the western coast, were of several types:

ancient Asianic cities which at the end of the third century had the municipal institutions of a *polis;* Seleucid foundations which in some cases replaced an older town; Pergamene settlements built for the purpose of controlling a region of strategic importance; and communities which were originally temple-villages but grew into cities. Alongside of these were the rural village-centres, sometimes on "royal" sometimes on "sacred" domain-land, which, obtaining more and more organization, developed with the increasing urbanization of the country from villages into communities that resembled, more or less closely, the Hellenic *polis.*[216]

The end of the Roman Republic brought also the end of the depredations by the equestrian tax-farmers.[217] In the century and a quarter of relative peace and of imperial support for urbanization that followed Octavian's victory at

Actium, the cities of Asia enjoyed greater prosperity than they had ever known before.[218]

The cities where we know of Pauline communities in Asia all participated in that general prosperity; all were centers of trade. That is particularly evident in the case of the cluster of cities in the Lycus valley, whose Christian communities we learn about almost incidentally through the letter written in Paul's name to one of them: Colossae, Laodicea, and Hierapolis.[219] All owed their importance to the wool industry, of which Laodicea was the center. It was the most important of the three and was also the capital of the judicial circuit (*dioikēsis/conventus*) to which all three belonged; the least of the three in the Roman period was Colossae,[220] although it had been a Phrygian city of great importance in earlier times.[221] The inscriptions from Laodicea and Hierapolis (Colossae has not been excavated) show that associations of traders and craftsmen were numerous and important in the life of the towns. These included not only those directly connected with the wool trade, like "the most august guild of the wool washers," the fullers, dyers, and so on, but also smiths, nailmakers, gardeners, and others.[222]

Of course Ephesus, the governmental center of the province, possessing a harbor and situated on the Cayster River and close to the broad Maeander valley, profited from the burgeoning trade of the province most of all. A free city (that is, having home rule, with a Greek constitution) probably even under the Attalids,[223] it also owned a very large territory extending inland from the coast. The fame of its huge temple to Artemis, regarded in antiquity as one of the seven wonders of the world, was not diminished by the fact that the movement of peoples had brought many other cults to the city as well. The imposing temple of Sarapis near the commercial (lower) agora, for example, testifies to the importance of Egyptian cults here. However, like most of the monuments that immediately impress the visitor to the excavated site today, it was built at a period later than the one that interests us.

Jewish communities were especially vigorous in Ephesus and in most of the other cities of the province.[224] Josephus preserves a series of edicts by Roman officials guaranteeing the rights of the Jews of Ephesus and exempting from military service those of them who were Roman citizens.[225] As we have seen, those documents represent the generally favorable policy of Rome toward the Jewish diaspora communities from Caesar until well after Constantine. In the province of Asia, moreover, the Jews seem to have been more successful than elsewhere in maintaining cordial relations with the local powers in their host cities. Whether one thinks of the section of seats in the Miletus theater reserved for "the Jews who are also *theosebeis*," or the inscriptions of Jews who were municipal senators and held various magistracies in Sardis, Aphrodisias, Acmonia, and elsewhere, or the high status of some of the patrons and patronesses of synagogues, like Julia Severa of Acmonia[226] or Capitolina of Tralles,[227] or the location of the magnificent synagogue in Sardis at the heart of the city's civic, educational, and commercial center, the evidence points toward active participation by Jews in the

urban life of the province. Although most of the inscriptional and archaeological evidence is from the second and third centuries, what evidence survives from earlier times suggests continuity in the Jews' situation rather than
major changes in the second century. It is interesting to note that in the two
cities where available evidence attests the strongest Jewish communities in the
area, and those best integrated into the larger society, namely Sardis and
Apameia, we know of no Pauline mission, although both lay close to places
where Paul or his associates and disciples preached.[228]

Macedonia, dismembered by Rome in 167 B.C., was organized as a
Roman province twenty years later, with the proconsul residing in Thessalonica. Like the later provinces in Asia Minor, it suffered greatly in the first
Mithridatic war and even more in the Roman civil wars but blossomed under
Augustus.[229] The region was a crossroads of land routes from the Adriatic,
the Danube, and Thrace, and its ports offered access by sea to the East. The
two Macedonian cities, Philippi and Thessalonica, that were so important to
the Pauline mission were also important in the Roman scheme of control.

Philippi had been founded as Krenides ("Springs") by the Athenian exile
Callistratus, and then, after less than five years, seized and refounded by
Philip II, who gave it his name.[230] That was only the beginning of its transfor-
mations. After Octavian and Antony defeated Brutus and Cassius there, in
the battle that marked the end of the Roman Republic (42/41 B.C.) Antony
refounded the city as Antoni Iussu Colonia Victrix Philippensium[231] and
settled a group of his veterans (of the twenty-eighth legion) there. About
eleven years later Octavian, having destroyed Antony's forces at Actium,
reorganized the colony yet again, planting there some of his own veterans,
including a cohort of praetorians, and also a number of Italians who had
supported Antony and therefore had now to give up their Italian lands to
other veterans of Octavian. The new name was Colonia Iulia Philippensis, to
which the epithet "Augusta" was added to fit the new honor voted Octavian
by the Senate in January of 27 B.C.[232]

The double colonization and the constant passage of troops through
Philippi thereafter, because of its strategic location, assured to this city a
much more Latin character than any of the others we have considered so far.
For example, Barbara Levick counts 421 inscriptions from Philippi, only 60
of which are in Greek—and some of those may be precolonial. In contrast,
only about 41 percent of the inscriptions from Antioch-in-Pisidia are in Latin.
The coins show the same persistence of the Italian element: military motifs
predominate and the city's full Latin title persists until the reign of Gallienus,
while Latin legends on Pisidian coinage quickly decline into barbarous mis-
spellings.[233] The plan of the city is also distinctively Roman, with the Via
Egnatia itself forming the main axis (*decumanus*). At the center of this axis,
on the southern edge, is located the forum, a "self-contained architectonic
ensemble," with its open side oriented to the magnificent view of the acropolis.[234]

Other evidence, however, points to the persistence of a large native population, including a strong Thracian element, and to a steady influx of immigrants from Egypt, Anatolia, and elsewhere.[235] The language of all these groups was Greek.[236] Among the foreign groups were undoubtedly the Jews, but so far no archaeological evidence has been found to confirm or enlarge the New Testament reports.[237]

Philippi is also different from the other Pauline towns in having been primarily a center of agriculture rather than of commerce. The Italian colonists were dispersed in villages throughout the plain and in the valleys opening from it,[238] and the farming around their villages was the base for the economic development of the area. The city itself always remained very small—not more than six hundred to eight hundred meters from wall to wall along its east-west axis.[239] On the other hand, the Egyptian, Anatolian, and other immigrants must have been engaged primarily in commerce and crafts, although there is little direct evidence. A Latin inscription marks a dedication "to Fortune and the Genius of the Market."[240]

Paradoxically Thessalonica, which was larger and more important in the Roman period, is less well known than Philippi. Human disaster is the archaeologist's good fortune, but Thessalonica, although it has suffered more than its share of disasters, has survived continuously on its original site since its founding in 316 B.C. Much of what the archaeologists would like to see therefore remains buried under modern buildings and streets, many of which follow the ancient plan.[241] There have been important chance discoveries, including the Roman forum found in 1962, whose buildings span the second and third centuries, and the Serapeion, found in the southwestern part of the city after the great fire of 1917 and excavated but never published.[242] The corpus of Greek inscriptions has been published by Charles Edson.[243]

Thessalonica had an excellent harbor on the Thermaic Gulf and was near the midpoint of the Via Egnatia, besides being the terminus of an important road that ran up the valley of the Axius to that of the Morava and eventually to the Danube.[244] It thus became one of the two most important trading centers in Roman Greece, the other being Corinth.[245] Among the crafts that flourished there was the purple-dyeing industry, supplied with dye-bearing mollusks by the fisheries of the district.[246] Commerce brought a cosmopolitan population, and these as always brought with them their foreign cults. The Egyptians were among the earliest arrivals; probably the Jews were not far behind, although so far little archaeological evidence for the Jewish community in the Hellenistic and Roman periods has been reported.[247] There is no reason to doubt the report in Acts of a strong Jewish community there. Only recently evidence has been found confirming the early existence of a synagogue in Stobi, which lay directly on the northern road, some one hundred fifty kilometers from Thessalonica.[248] A composite inscription partly in Samaritan Hebrew and Aramaic, partly in Greek indicates that there was also a Samaritan community in Thessalonica.[249]

Unlike Philippi, Thessalonica remained a visibly Greek city under Roman rule. It was made the capital of the second of the four regions into which

Macedonia was divided in 167, then the capital of the whole province when that was organized in 146. However, it remained a free city, with a Greek republican form of government for its internal affairs—that is, it had a *boulē*, a citizens' assembly, the right to strike coins, and no Roman garrison within its walls.[250] Greek far outweighs Latin in the known inscriptions.[251] Of the two Thessalonian delegates who accompanied Paul on his journey to deliver the Jerusalem collection, according to the list preserved in Acts 20:4, one bore a Greek name, Aristarchus, the other a Latin, Secundus. Nearby Beroea sent Sopater son of Pyrrhus, another Greek. The only other name we have is the unfortunate Jason, according to Acts 17:5–9 the first host of the Christians.

The senatorial province Achaia had its capital at Corinth. Like Thessalonica, Corinth owed its great commercial importance to its location, as Strabo observed: "Corinth is called 'wealthy'[252] because of its commerce, since it lies at the Isthmus and controls two harbors, one of which is near Asia, the other near Italy, and it makes reciprocal exchange of cargoes easy. . . ."[253] The two ports were Lechaeon, on the Gulf of Corinth, and Cenchreae, on the Saronian Gulf. The isthmus was narrow enough at Schoenus, just to the north of both these ports, that some ships were actually hauled across.[254] Corinth was not so fortunate in survival as Thessalonica, however. In 146, during Rome's campaign against the Achaean League, Lucius Mummius destroyed the city, and it lay desolate until Julius Caesar refounded it as a Roman colony, Colonia Laus Julia Corinthiensis, in 44.[255] Rebuilding began at once, and by the time of Nero the public center of the city was one of the largest and handsomest of Greece. Augustus favored his own colony at Patrae over Corinth,[256] but nevertheless his reign saw the building of the theater, the northwest stoa and its shops on the agora, the shops along the west side of the Lechaeon Road and the basilica on a terrace above them, and the monumental limestone arch over the entrance from the Lechaeon Road to the agora.[257] In the reigns of Tiberius, Gaius, and Claudius there was a great burst of building activity, which gave Corinth more and more the appearance of a Roman city. This was most visible in the agora, one of the largest known. It was divided into two parts by the buildings of a central terrace, running east to west, "the lower [northern] and larger of which became the forum of the people, the upper and smaller section the administrative quarter."[258]

The Italian face of the colony was apparent in other ways as well. In the first century virtually all public inscriptions were in Latin.[259] The proportion of Italian pottery to eastern wares was much higher than, for example, in nearby Athens.[260] The government was typical of a Roman colony, with annually elected *duoviri* and aediles.[261] The depth of this "romanization," however, should not be exaggerated. The fact that the relation between Latin and Greek inscriptions suddenly reverses itself in the reign of Hadrian, with Greek increasingly dominant thereafter,[262] suggests that the fashion approved for public display may not have represented quite accurately the ordinary languages of the population. Furthermore, even some of the earlier Latin inscriptions were ordered by former freedmen who have telltale Greek-derived names, like Babbius or Erastus or Cleogenes.[263] It is interesting that about half the persons connected in the New Testament with the Corinthian church have Latin names, the others Greek.[264]

As Strabo said, it was commerce that made Corinth wealthy, and it was doubtless commerce that gave its individual colonists and other residents the opportunity for wealth. Agriculture around Corinth seems to have been very poor, but its handicrafts were widely known in antiquity.[265] There is some evidence to support the view that "this new city attracted individualist, entrepreneurial types."[266] Strabo says that Caesar colonized Corinth "with people that belonged for the most part to the freedmen class."[267] With no indigenous aristocracy to snub them or to frustrate their ambitions, the freedmen colonists had the rare opportunity to compete with one another for the marks of status that would enable some of them to *become* the local aristocracy. They did that in the way well known in the Greco-Roman cities: by giving conspicuous presents to the city in return for offices and public honors. For example, the best known of Roman Corinth's private benefactors, active in the reign of Tiberius, was Cn. Babbius Philinus, whose lack of a patronymic indicates that he was probably a freedman, while his cognomen betrays his Greek origin. He served as aedile and then, "in return for his generous gifts, the colony made him *pontifex* and *duumvir*"; his family became one of the first houses of Corinth.[268] Similar though less prominent was Babbius's younger contemporary Erastus, who paved the square east of the theater's stage building "in return for his aedileship, at his own expense," and who was perhaps the same Erastus who was "city treasurer" and a member of the Christian community in Corinth (Rom. 16:23).[269] There were evidently a number of such success stories in Corinth. A freedman of Augustus was one of the two *primi* ("most outstanding members") of a collegium of the Lares of the Imperial House charged with erecting a monument;[270] a group of *liberti qui Corinthi habitan[t]* erected a small marble building, perhaps a clubhouse or a monument, in the Augustan period.[271] A member of the family who donated a meat and fish market early in the first century was a woman who had married her maternal grandfather's freedman, with the Greek cognomen Cleogenes.[272]

One may be sure that the freedmen from Italy were soon joined in this booming commercial center by many "Greeks and foreigners," as H. N. Fowler says, adding, "among them many orientals and especially Jews. . . ." But for the last he is able to cite only Acts 18.[273] Was there in fact a major Jewish community in Roman Corinth? It seems so, for besides the New Testament evidence, Philo singles out only the cities Corinth and Argos in his list of regions of the Diaspora.[274] Other literary reports are lacking, and archaeological evidence is disappointing: a single fragment of a terracotta lamp from the fifth or sixth century A.D., decorated with what is *probably* a menorah,[275] and a broken piece of what was perhaps the lintel over a doorway, inscribed *[Syna]gōgē Hebr[aiōn]*.[276] Because the stone was found on the Lechaeon Road, at the foot of the steps leading through the Propylaea into the agora, it is tempting to associate the Jewish community with the crafts and trades that flourished in that area of markets and workshops.[277] However, the violence with which stones were smashed and scattered in the Herulian and Gothic attacks on Corinth[278] somewhat undercuts Powell's confident claim that the stone was too large to have been moved far from its site.[279] As elsewhere in Greece, we are left with only tantalizing hints of the Jewish community here.

The other Achaian town in which the Pauline group established a community was Corinth's eastern port, Cenchreae, but we learn nothing about it except the name of Phoebe, its *diakonos* ("minister"? "helper"?) and *prostatis* ("patroness"?) (Rom. 16:1–2). Excavations begun in 1963 by the American School in Athens, the University of Chicago, and Indiana University cleared the harbor installations on the northern and southern extremes of the basin. Among the fascinating discoveries on the south pier was an apsidal structure plausibly identified with the Temple of Isis mentioned by Pausanius (2.2.3) and prominent in book 11 of Apuleius's *Metamorphoses*.[280] Otherwise, there is nothing that sheds any direct light on the origins of Christianity there.

We thus reach the end of our survey of the "cities of St. Paul" and his associates. These places for which we have some evidence from our first line of sources, the letters of Paul and his school, for persistence of Christian communities some time after the initial evangelization, are irregularly distributed along a rough arc from the middle of Asia Minor across Macedonia and down to the Peloponnesus. In size they range from rather small towns, like Philippi, to sprawling cities like Ephesus and Corinth, but they are all cities in terms of government, culture, and the perception of their inhabitants. Two, Philippi and Corinth, are Roman colonies, but of very different types, the one primarily an agricultural center, the other a center of crafts and commerce. If we were to be convinced that the Pisidian cities Antioch, Iconium, and Lystra were the places Paul meant by "Galatia," these would be added to our list of colonies. The dominant language is Greek in all except the two colonies in Greece, Philippi and Corinth, and even in those there was a substantial population for whom Greek was the normal language. All except Philippi are centers of trade, and even in Philippi there are reasons to think that there were alongside the Italian farmers a good many foreigners who made their living by trade. Every one is well located for access by sea or land or both; even the cities of northern Galatia are connected by good Roman roads with the rest of Asia Minor.

The areas not included in the Pauline mission nor mentioned in the Pauline documents are also interesting: Egypt, despite relatively frequent communications between Palestine and Egypt;[281] and, less surprisingly, proconsular Africa and the transalpine provinces. There is no mention of anything beyond the *limes* of the empire except the proverbial Scythians in Col. 3:11; none, for example, of anything in the Persian realm, despite the important Jewish Diaspora in Mesopotamia. We might also wonder why we do not hear of any Pauline mission to certain cities that lay within the arc of the group's travels—like Apameia, mercantile center second only to Ephesus in western Asia Minor, or Sardis, like Apameia the home of a thriving Jewish community. Because the limitations of our sources have forced us to eschew an argument from silence, these omissions can do no more than pique our curiosity.

The Pauline world was one in which, for urban and mobile people, Greek was the lingua franca, but upon which the overwhelming political fact of Rome was superimposed. These somewhat discordant cultural and political grids are both evident in the mental map which Paul reveals in his letter to the Roman Christians. When he chooses a rhetorical phrase to signify the whole human world, he speaks as any Greek orator might, of "Greeks and barbarians, wise and ignorant" (Rom. 1:14). Of course he includes Romans under "Greeks,"[282] but a Latin writer would hardly have divided the world in this way. Moreover, when Paul shifts to the theme of his letter in the following verses, the significant division becomes the one between Jew and Greek. Paul's mental world is that of the Greek-speaking eastern provinces, specifically that of the Greek-speaking Jew. Still it is a *Roman* world—the existence of this letter and the travel plans outlined in its chapter 15 indicate how central Rome is, even to one who at this moment is worried about Jerusalem—even though it is Rome as seen from the cities of the East.[283]

2

THE SOCIAL LEVEL OF
PAULINE CHRISTIANS

"PROLETARIANS" OR "MIDDLE CLASS"?

Celsus, the first pagan author we know of who took Christianity seriously enough to write a book against it, alleged that the church deliberately excluded educated people because the religion was attractive only to "the foolish, dishonourable and stupid, and only slaves, women, and little children."[1] The Christian evangelists, he said, were "wool-workers, cobblers, laundry-workers, and the most illiterate and bucolic yokels," who enticed "children . . . and stupid women" to come along "to the wooldresser's shop, or to the cobbler's or the washerwoman's shop, that they may learn perfection."[2] Celsus lived in the second century, but he was sure that Christianity had always been a movement of the lowest classes, for Jesus himself had only been able to win disciples among "tax-collectors and sailors," people "who had not even a primary education."[3] This was the sort of jeer to which the second-century apologists for Christianity had frequently to respond,[4] and modern authors have more often than not assumed that the early critics were right. Did not Luke's Jesus pronounce a woe against the rich (Luke 6:24), James warn against kowtowing to "the rich who oppress you" (James 2:1–7), and Paul himself write that God had chosen "what is foolish in the world . . . what is weak . . . what is low and despised" (1 Cor. 1:27)? The notion of early Christianity as a proletarian movement was equally congenial, though for quite different reasons, to Marxist historians and to those bourgeois writers who tended to romanticize poverty.[5]

Of particular importance in shaping this century's common view of Paul and his congregations was the opinion of Adolf Deissmann, professor of the New Testament at Heidelberg, then at Berlin. Deissmann saw that the hundreds of newly discovered documents written on papyrus or ostraca—letters, contracts, school lessons, bills of sale, magical spells—had revolutionary implications for understanding not only the vocabulary and grammar but also the social setting of the New Testament. He had a genius for popularizing the results of his own and others' research, and two extended trips through the Middle East enabled him to reconstruct "the world of St. Paul" in terms of a vivid, thoroughly romantic travelogue.[6] In general his identification of the language of the New Testament with the vulgar *koinē* of the nonliterary papyri supported the view that the writers had belonged to the lower classes, but Deissmann had some difficulty in situating Paul himself. His occupation would have placed him among the lowest of the free poor, like the weaver whom Deissmann had watched in Tarsus in 1909, "making a coarse cloth on his poverty-stricken primitive loom," yet "the very fact that he was born a Roman citizen shows that his family cannot have lived in absolutely humble circumstances."[7] Paul wrote unliterary Greek, yet "not vulgar to the degree that finds expression in many contemporary papyri. On the ground of his language rather Paul should be assigned to a higher class."[8] Still, Deissmann was confident that Paul's closest ties were to the "middle and lower classes. . . . As a missionary chiefly working amongst the unliterary masses of the great cities Paul did not patronizingly descend into a world strange to him: he remained in his own social world."[9] Until recently most scholars who troubled to ask Deissmann's question at all ignored the ambiguities of the evidence that Deissmann had at least mentioned. The prevailing viewpoint has been that the constituency of early Christianity, the Pauline congregations included, came from the poor and dispossessed of the Roman provinces.

Within the past two decades, however, a number of scholars have looked at the evidence afresh and come to conclusions very different from Deissmann's about the social level of the first-century Christians. The convergence of these inquiries, which have been undertaken from diverse viewpoints, has led Abraham Malherbe to suggest that "a new consensus may be emerging" which would approve Floyd Filson's dictum of more than forty years ago, "The apostolic church was more nearly a cross section of society than we have sometimes thought."[10] The role of the upper classes is particularly emphasized by E. A. Judge, who points to the pervasive but seldom-mentioned importance of *amicitia* and *clientela* in Roman society to support his conviction that "Christianity was a movement sponsored by local patrons to their social dependents."[11] Robert M. Grant, looking primarily at evidence from the second through the fourth centuries, concurs: "The triumph of Christianity in a hierarchically organized society necessarily took place from the top down." He infers that, also in the earlier period, Christianity should be viewed "not as a proletarian mass movement but as a relatively small cluster of more or less intense groups, largely middle class in origin."[12] Malherbe has drawn significant clues for the social level of the New Testament writers and their audiences from recent studies of language, style, and genre, which have the effect of refuting Deissmann in the area of the latter's central contributions. Malherbe emphasizes the ambiguities of the linguistic data that Deissmann noted but chose to set aside in his general conclusions.[13] These studies, too, suggest that the educational and therefore probably the social level of Paul and at least some members of his congregations was a good bit higher than has commonly been assumed. The most careful, consciously sociological analysis of social stratification in the Pauline communities, however, is found in the series of articles published by Gerd Theissen, which discuss the situation in Corinth. He, too, finds leading figures in the Christian groups of that city who belong to a relatively high economic and social level, but Theissen emphasizes the evidence that the church, like the larger society, is stratified. The conflicts in the congregation are in large part conflicts between people of different strata and, within individuals, between the expectations of a hierarchical society and those of an egalitarian community.[14]

If these studies and others like them are indeed moving toward a consensus, it it still not clear just what this consensus will tell us about the social characteristics of the Pauline groups. Some of the scholars just mentioned emphasize the status of the leading figures; others, the social distance between those figures and the majority of the members. To one observer the mixture of classes in the church simply shows that the Christian movement inevitably conforms to the social structure of the society as a whole; to another, it reveals a fundamental conflict between the values of the Christian group and those of the larger society.[15]

MEASURING SOCIAL STRATIFICATION

Something more is at stake here than merely deciding whether we shall count only the highest, only the lowest, or the average members of the Christian congregation. There is also a more fundamental question, what we mean by "high" or "low." We will do well to follow the lead of M. I. Finley (who in turn was adapting the views of Max Weber) in distinguishing in ancient society three different kinds of ranking: class, *ordo*, and status.[16] Of these, class is not very helpful. In the everyday speech of popular sociology (such as "lower middle class"), it refers almost exclusively to income level, with perhaps the added qualification of the way in which income is obtained. ("Middle class," for example, usually implies not only an intermediate level of income, but also earned income rather than inherited wealth.) For Marx, class was determined by relation to the means of production, yielding only three: landlords, capitalists, and workers. For Weber, too, class was determined by economic factors, but defined by the market rather than by production. It represented "life chances in the market" for a specifiable group of people.[17] None of these definitions is very helpful in describing ancient society, for they lump together groups who clearly were regarded in antiquity as different.[18]

The "orders" (*ordines*) or "estates" of imperial Roman society, on the other hand, were clear-cut, legally established categories. The two most important and enduring ones were the senators and the knights: the *ordo senatorius* and the *ordo equester*. In addition, the families whose members had served or were eligible to serve in the councils or senates of the provincial cities constituted a local order in those places. These orders, and the steps that led to them, the cursus honorum, were of tremendous importance to the ambitious elite of the Roman empire. Yet, given that these three top *ordines* comprised considerably less than 1 percent of the population,[19] the category does not have much discriminating power for the sorts of groups we are investigating. To include as formal *ordines* also the *plebs* (in Rome) and the *ordo libertinorum* would be only slightly more useful than adding "and everybody else."[20]

That leaves us with the category of status as the most generally useful one for forming a picture of stratification in the Greco-Roman cities. Here some of the discussion of social stratification by modern sociologists may help us toward greater conceptual clarity. All the writers reviewed in the first part of this chapter seem to regard an individual's status as a single thing. One is high or low or middle or perhaps somewhere in between, but still measured along a single scale. In recent years, however, most sociologists have come to see social stratification as a multidimensional phenomenon; to describe the social level of an individual or a group, one must attempt to measure their rank along *each* of the relevant dimensions. For example, one might discover that, in a given society, the following variables affect how an individual is ranked: power (defined as "the capacity for achieving goals in social systems"), occupational prestige, income or wealth, education and knowledge, religious and ritual purity, family and ethnic-group position, and local-community status (evaluation within some subgroup, independent of the larger society but perhaps interacting with it).[21] It would be a rare individual who occupied exactly the same rank, in either his own view or that of others, in terms of all these factors. The generalized status of a person is a composite of his or her ranks in all the relevant dimensions.

Moreover, the resultant status is not just the average of one's ranks in the several dimensions. Several other considerations are involved. First, not all the dimensions have the same weight. Wealth, especially if displayed in conspicuously stylish ways, might count more heavily than religious purity, but being the scion of an old and famous family might bring even more prestige than wealth would. Second, the weight of each dimension depends upon who is doing the weighing. For example, Seymour Martin Lipset distinguishes three perspectives: "objective" status, that is, "aspects of stratification that structure environments differently enough to evoke differences in behavior"; accorded status, or "prestige accorded to individuals and groups by others"; and subjective status, or "personal sense of location within the social hierarchy felt by various individuals."[22] Most individuals tend to measure themselves by the standards of some group that is very important to them—their reference group, whether or not they belong to it—rather than by the standards of the whole society.[23] Third, the degree of correlation among one's various rankings constitutes another kind of variable that affects how one is evaluated by others and how one evaluates oneself. This is the dimension of status consistency, status congruence, or status crystallization, mentioned briefly in the previous chapter.

If prestige was distributed in some analogous ways in antiquity, then to describe the early Christians' social status by some single, general category—say, "of the middle class"—is not only vague but misleading. It is vague because it ignores the multidimensionality of stratification. It is misleading because it tacitly assumes that there was something in the ancient Greek city corresponding to the middle class of modern industrial society.

There is a further reason for being alert to the multiple dimensions of status. A series of studies has demonstrated that, in present-day American society, persons of low status crystallization, that is, those who are ranked high in some important dimensions but low in others, tend to behave in certain predictable ways. Some may take political action favoring change in the society. Some may withdraw from groups and tend to become unsocial. Others may develop psychophysiological symptoms of stress. All these kinds of behavior, some sociologists believe, show that a high degree of status inconsistency produces unpleasant experiences that lead people to try to remove the inconsistency by changing the society, themselves, or perceptions of themselves.[24]

We must, of course, be cautious in applying to ancient society a theory that has been empirically generated from observations about a modern society. The hierarchies among voters of Detroit are not the same as those among citizens of ancient Corinth. The explanations and predictions incorporated in the theories of status consistency may include latent assumptions about motivation and perception—such as an exaggerated individualism and post-Freudian or at least post-Augustinian introspection—that are culturally determined. Nevertheless, these theories can have great heuristic power. They can help to keep us from oversimplifying the indexes of status, and they can suggest the sorts of connections to look for in our sources. We have already seen how Tony Reekmans could employ the concept of status inconsistency in analyzing Juvenal's attitudes toward social change, or P. R. C. Weaver in describing the upward mobility of imperial slaves and freedmen. The "criss-crossing categories" described by Finley are another term for the same phenomenon. The "dictionary of snobbery" compiled by Ramsay MacMullen[25] provides valuable material for defining the dimensions of hierarchy, as seen from above.

When we consider individuals and groups who joined the Pauline congregations, then, we should not too quickly assign them to some general level. Rather, we should ask what clues we have that would indicate ranking in the several hierarchies which were relevant in that time and place. For example, in adapting to the provincial situation Reekmans's categories, which apply only to Rome, we should look for rankings in such categories as ethnic origins, *ordo,* citizenship, personal liberty, wealth, occupation, age, sex, and public offices or honors. We must ask, too, about the context within which each of these rankings is valid; for example, to be a freedman in the early years in Roman Corinth, a colony whose first settlers were mostly freedmen, would surely have been less of a social disability than it would have been in Rome or in Antioch.

PROSOPOGRAPHIC EVIDENCE

In the letters of Paul and his disciples written in the first century (that is, leaving aside the Pastorals) sixty-five individuals besides Paul are named or otherwise identified as persons active in local congregations, as traveling companions or agents of Paul, or as both. Some of these are also mentioned in Acts, which adds thirteen other names and an anonymous household. Thus it is possible to draw up a prosopography of Pauline Christianity containing nearly eighty names. About most of them little information is to be found besides the name, and of some not even that. A close look at the whole list, however, does yield some clues about the social texture of the Pauline circle.

The long list of persons to whom Paul sends greetings in Romans 16 poses a problem. Paul may know some of these individuals or groups only by reputation; others he may have met only as individuals traveling in the East. Hence we should count only those whom the text specifically calls Paul's "fellow workers" or the equivalent, or who had earlier belonged to one of the Pauline congregations.[26] That eliminates Apelles (vs. 10); the members of the household of Aristobulus, probably including Herodion (vss. 10–11); the members of the household represented by Asyncritus, Phlegon, Hermes, Patrobas, and Hermas (vs. 14); Mary (vs. 6); the members of the household of Narcissus (vs. 11); Persis, Tryphaena, and Tryphosa (vs. 12); the members of the household represented by Philologus and Julia, Nereus and his sister, and Olympas (vs. 15); and Stachys (vs. 9).

Of the remaining persons mentioned in the letters, sixteen probably or certainly belong to the Pauline groups but lack any clear indicator of their social standing. These are Archippus of Colossae (Philem. 1; Col. 4:17); Aristarchus (Philem. 24; Col. 4:10f.; Acts 19:29; 20:4; 27:2); Demas (Philem. 24; Col. 4:14); Epaphras (Philem. 23; Col. 1:7; 4:12); Epaphroditus of Philippi (Phil. 2:25; 4:18); Jason (Rom. 16:21; not the Jason of Thessalonica in Acts 17:5, 9); Jesus Justus (Col. 4:11); Sosipater (Rom. 16:21; Acts 20:4?); Sosthenes (1 Cor. 1:1);[27] Timothy (1 Thess. 1:1; 3:2, 6; 1 Cor. 4:17; 16:10; 2 Cor. 1:1, 19; Phil. 1:1; 2:19; 2 Thess. 1:1; Col. 1:1; Rom. 16:21; Philem. 1; Acts 16:1–17:14; 18:5; 19:22; 20:4);[28] Titus (2 Cor. 2:13; 7:6–16; 8:6, 16–24; 12:18; Gal. 2:1–3); Tychicus (Col. 4:7f.; Eph. 6:21f.; Acts 20:4); Urbanus (Rom. 16:9); the anonymous "true yokefellow" (Phil. 4:3); and the two anonymous (in the extant text) "brothers" and "delegates of the churches" connected with the collection (2 Cor. 8:18f., 22f.)

We are left with thirty individuals about whose status we have at least a clue. For several the clue is nothing more than the name itself, which in the particular context may be significant. Thus Achaicus (1 Cor. 16:17), Fortunatus (ibid.), Quartus (Rom. 16:23), and Lucius (Rom. 16:21) in Corinth and Clement in Philippi (Phil. 4:3) have Latin names in the two Roman colonies where Latin was the dominant official language. This *may* indicate that their families belonged to the original stock of colonists, who tended to get ahead. One of these, Lucius, is a Jew besides.[29] The case of Achaicus is interesting, for a resident of Corinth would hardly receive *there* the geographical nickname (it was not on Crete but in Toledo that Domenikos Theotokopoulos was named "El Greco"). The man or his father must have lived for a time in Italy, received the name there, and then returned to Corinth, probably as one of the freedmen colonists. If so, we would have an example of the phenomenon suggested by Bowersock, Italians of Greek ancestry re-turning as Roman colonists to Greece.[30] On the other hand, the Greek names of Euodia and Syntyche (Phil. 4:2f.) may hint that they were among the merchant groups who were metics in Philippi. It is to be noted besides that they were women who had sufficient independence to be recognized in their own right as activists in the Pauline mission. Tertius is another Latin name among the Corinthian Christians (Rom. 16:22); in his case we have the further hint of a profession, or at least training, as a scribe.[31] Another profes-sional with a Latin name is Luke (Philem. 24), a physician (Col. 4:14) with Paul, probably in Ephesus. Doctors were often slaves; we might speculate that Luke had been a *medicus* in some Roman *familia,* receiving the name of his master (Lucius, of which Lukas is a hypocorism) on his manumission.

The ability to travel bespeaks some financial means,[32] but not neces-sarily the traveler's own. Many slaves and freedmen traveled as agents of their masters or mistresses, like the members of Chloe's household who told Paul in Ephesus about Corinthian troubles (1 Cor. 1:11). Ampliatus (Rom. 16:8), who is in Rome after Paul knew him in the East, may be a similar case, for his is a common Latin slave name.[33] Andronicus and Junia(s) (Rom. 16:7) have also moved from the East, where they were imprisoned with Paul some-where, sometime,[34] to Rome. Eck assumes that Andronicus's name marks him as a freedman and that therefore Junia, too, must be a freedwoman of the *gens Iunia,*[35] but not every Jew with a Greek name in Rome was a former slave. If, with John Chrysostom, we are to take *Iounian* as the accusative of the feminine *Iounia* rather than the masculine *Iounias,* then very likely An-dronicus and Junia are husband and wife, like Prisca and Aquila (vs. 3) and Philologus and Julia (vs. 15).[36] Epaenetus (Rom. 16:5), honored as the first Christian convert in Asia, has also traveled to Rome. His name, like that of Ampliatus, suggests but does not prove servile origins. Silvanus (1 Thess. 1:1; 2 Cor. 1:19; 2 Thess. 1:1; cf. 1 Pet. 5:12 and often in Acts), who bears the name of a Latin deity,[37] traveled widely with Paul but perhaps not at his own expense. Acts reports that he had been one of the leaders of the Jerusalem church (15:22) as well as a prophet (15:32), but neither necessarily implies anything about status in the larger society.

We can be slightly more definite about the status of the remaining individuals. Gaius (1 Cor. 1:14; Rom. 16:23) has a good Roman praenomen, thus resembling several Corinthian Christians already mentioned, but in addi-tion he has a house ample enough not only to put up Paul, but also to accommodate all the Christian groups in Corinth meeting together (Rom. 16:23). He is evidently a man of some wealth.[38] The same is true of Crispus, whose office as *archisynagōgos* shows that he not only has high prestige in the Jewish community but is also probably well to do.[39] It is noteworthy that these two are singled out by Paul as people whom he personally baptized at the beginning of Christianity in Corinth (1 Cor. 1:14). It is tempting to assume that the third person mentioned in the same context, Stephanas, the members of whose household were the very first converts (*aparchē*) in Achaia (1 Cor.

16:15), was also a person of wealth. That would be too hasty an inference, however.[40] His Greek name might indicate that his family was not part of the original colony, but either indigenous Greek or immigrant, in either case not of the highest social stratum. His having traveled with Achaicus and Fortunatus to see Paul in Ephesus suggests some independence, but they seem to be a more or less official delegation, so their expenses may have been paid by the Corinthian congregations. On the other hand, he heads a household important enough for Paul to mention twice. And the services he has rendered to the Corinthian Christians (16:15b) seem from the context to be of the sort rendered by patrons rather than by charismatic gifts (*charismata*). It is precisely in contrast to the sometimes disruptive roles of the *pneumatikoi* that Paul urges recognition due to "people like those" (*toioutoi*), namely Stephanas, Achaicus, and Fortunatus. We are probably safe, then, in placing Stephanas fairly high on the scale of wealth, though probably not so high as Gaius and Crispus. In prestige within the Christian group he was their equal, but probably not in Corinth at large, and not so high in civic recognition as our next figure, Erastus.

Alone among the persons mentioned by Paul, Erastus is named with an official title that refers not to his role in the Christian group but to his role in the city: *oikonomos tēs poleōs*. There has been a long debate, however, over the precise meaning of that title or its equivalent in the official Latin titulature of Corinth. The Greek title is rather widely attested by inscriptions, especially in Asia Minor, in both the Hellenistic and Roman periods.[41] However, although many of these inscriptions refer to high officials charged with administering public funds or property, the title is also applied in some cases (in Chalcedon and Cos, for example) to persons who apparently were public slaves.[42] One might argue that Paul would not have mentioned the title if it were not a public office of some consequence, but that would fail to take account of the *philotimia* which was so constant a factor in the life of the Greco-Roman world. We may be sure that if Erastus had been a city slave charged with keeping the municipal accounts, that would have been quite ample occasion for pride and congratulation within his own circle, and his children would have been glad to record *oikonomos tēs poleōs* on his tombstone.

The debate took a new turn with the discovery of a Latin inscription naming an Erastus as donor of the paving of the courtyard east of the theater in Corinth.[43] This Erastus announced his gift "in return for his aedileship."[44] Two aediles were elected annually in a colony; together with the two duoviri they constituted the four highest offices in the city's administration. Against the identification of aedile with *oikonomos tēs poleōs* stood the objection that the normal Greek translation is *agoranomos*. However, the editor of the Corinthian inscriptions was persuaded that, because one of the main tasks of aediles in most colonies, management of public games, was taken over in Corinth by a special officer in charge of the famous Isthmian Games, *oikonomos* would be appropriate to the actual functions of a Corinthian aedile.[45] Theissen, however, challenges that argument on the grounds that because separate officials for games are widely attested, Corinth's situation was not unique.[46] Instead, Theissen proposes a new solution, in which *oikonomos tēs poleōs* is not the same office as aedile but a lesser one, perhaps equivalent to quaestor, but still part of the municipal cursus honorum. The Erastus mentioned in Romans, in that case, would have been an important official and the same person who soon thereafter was elected aedile.[47] This conclusion, though far from certain, is persuasive. If it is correct, the Christian Erastus was a person of both wealth and high civic status, and we can add one further deduction made by Kent from the fact that there was no room in the broken part of the inscription for a patronymic before Erastus's (Greek) name: "Like his contemporary, Cn. Babbius Philinus,[48] Erastus was probably a Corinthian freedman who had acquired considerable wealth in commercial activities."[49]

It was also in Corinth, according to Acts 18:2f, that Paul met Prisca and Aquila. Two letters mention a Christian community in their house: 1 Corinthians, when Paul sends greetings from Ephesus (16:19); and Romans, when he sends greetings from Corinth (16:3–5). Moreover, we hear that they have "risked their necks" for Paul (Rom. 16:4). The author of Acts has other information about them: that Aquila's family came from Pontus, that he was a Jew, that they lived in Rome until forced to leave by Claudius's expulsion of the Jews, and that they were tentmakers (18:2–3). Both have good Roman names, but in Rome that was quite common for Jews, Greek- as well as Latin-speaking, especially for women.[50] We may summarize their known indicators of status as follows: wealth: relatively high. They have been able to move from place to place, and in three cities to establish a sizable household; they have acted as patrons for Paul and for Christian congregations. Occupation: low, but not at the bottom.[51] They are artisans, but independent, and by ancient standards they operate on a fairly large scale. Extraction: middling to low. They are eastern provincials and Jews besides, but assimilated to Greco-Roman culture. One thing more: the fact that Prisca's name is mentioned before her husband's once by Paul and two out of three times in Acts suggests that she has higher status than her husband.[52]

"Chloe's people" (*hoi Chloēs,* 1 Cor. 1:11) are slaves or freedmen or both[53] who have brought news from Corinth to Ephesus. Whether the *familia* was situated in Corinth, with business in Ephesus, or vice versa, is not certain, but the fact that Paul expects the name to be recognized by the Corinthian Christians suggests that Chloe lived there. Whether she herself was a Christian is not stated and cannot be inferred with any confidence.[54] The case of Onesimus and his owners is clearer. Onesimus of Colossae (Philem. 10 and passim; Col. 4:9) was not only a slave but a runaway. There is no indication what his particular task had been in Philemon's service, but Paul's eagerness to have him help in the mission suggests, despite the pun on his former uselessness (Philem. 11), that he may have had some education or special skills.[55] Philemon himself ranks high at least on the dimension of wealth and on evaluation within the sect: he has a house large enough to accommodate a meeting of Christians (Philem. 2) and guests (22) and has been a patron of Christians in other ways as well (5–7). He owns at least one slave, probably a number of them, for Paul's strongly implied request to send the slave Onesimus back to work with him (8–14) evidently is not expected to be a great hardship for Philemon or the household. Apphia is usually taken to be Philemon's wife, but she is mentioned in her own right as "the sister," as Philemon is "beloved" and Timothy "the brother." Otherwise there is no separate indicator of her status.

Another "sister" is particularly interesting: Phoebe, who is recommended to the Roman Christians as *diakonos* of the church in Cenchreae and "*prostatis* of many [others][56] and myself as well" (Rom. 16:1–2). The two titles (if that is what they are) have evoked endless discussion. Whether *diakonos* represents an office, as perhaps in Phil. 1:1, or whether it means "missionary"[57] or more generally "helper"[58] is of considerable interest for questions of the internal governance of the early Christian groups and for questions about the role of women. It cannot, however, tell us anything directly about Phoebe's status in the macrosociety. Nor could *prostatis* if, as some commentators have recently urged, it is to be translated as "president" or the like.[59] The term was used in that official sense in some Hellenistic cities, in the place of the more usual *prytaneis* ("executive officers"),[60] and as a title, or in the general sense of "leader," of officers of clubs or guilds.[61] If it were a title in Rom. 16:2, it would be in this latter sense, which is the way Paul uses the cognate participle in 1 Thess. 5:12: "those who labor among you and preside [*proistamenoi*] over you in the Lord and admonish you." That meaning, however, is rendered impossible by the context, for it is difficult to imagine what Paul could have meant by describing Phoebe as "also presiding over me." The sensible solution is to follow E. A. Judge in taking *prostatis* in the sense that it often has where Roman influence is strong, as an equivalent of *euergetēs* and the Latin *patrona*.[62] Paul says that Phoebe has been the protector or patroness of many Christians, including himself, and "for that reason" (*gar*) he asks that the Roman Christians provide her with whatever she needs during her stay in Rome. We may then infer that Phoebe is an independent woman (she is probably traveling to Rome on business of her own, not solely to carry Paul's letter) who has some wealth and is also one of the leaders of the Christian group in the harbor town of Cenchreae.

Another woman, then living in Rome, may have served as a patroness of Paul in the same loose sense. This is the mother of Rufus (Rom. 16:13). If what Paul means by calling her "my mother, too," is that she was his benefactress, then she, too, had traveled or resided for a time in the East and had some wealth. We obviously cannot put much weight on this possibility, however. We are in only a slightly more secure position to assess the status of Mark, sometime fellow worker of Paul and of Mark's cousin, Barnabas (Philem. 24; Col. 4:10). Mark's mother, according to Acts 12:12, had a house in Jerusalem that accommodated a meeting of the Christians. If that report is trustworthy, the family had some means, and the Latin surname, in a Jerusalem Jew, may imply some social ambition.

The last two persons to be considered from the letters can be reckoned as part of the Pauline circle only with some injustice to them, for they were missionaries in their own right before they met Paul. Barnabas was a leader of the Antioch group before Paul's conversion; there is good reason to call Paul his fellow worker, in the early years, rather than the reverse.[63] There is not much in the letters to indicate Barnabas's social standing, but 1 Cor. 9:6 says that he and Paul were alone among the apostles in their policy of working with their own hands rather than receiving regular support. Hock has argued that Paul's manner of talking about his own work resembles that found in rhetoricians and philosophers who come from higher social levels and thus think their decision to do menial work something worthy of comment.[64] The parallel between Paul and Barnabas suggests that they might have determined this policy jointly in the earliest stage of their mission, in Antioch and its environs. The picture of Barnabas as a reasonably well-to-do man who deliberately chose the life of an itinerant artisan to support his mission is reinforced by the report in Acts that he was the owner of a farm that he sold, the proceeds going to the Jerusalem Christians (4:36f.). He is also described there as a Levite, of a family that had settled in Cyprus.

Apollos seems to have been more or less a free agent who was drawn into the Pauline orbit—according to Acts, through the good offices of Prisca. Despite a certain competitiveness among their partisans in Corinth (1 Cor. 1:12; 3:1–4:6), there seem to have been good relations between Paul and Apollos (16:12). Again we are dependent on the account in Acts for any clues about status. Acts describes him as an Alexandrian Jew, *logios* and "powerful in the scriptures" (18:24). *Logios* here implies at least rhetorical ability, perhaps also rhetorical training. There is some support for that claim in 1 Corinthians 1–4, where Paul contrasts the "wisdom of God" with, among other things, a human wisdom exhibited in rhetoric.[65] Apollos's apparent ability to travel independently may further indicate some wealth.

The reports of the Pauline associates and converts in Acts must be treated with somewhat more caution, for the account is written a generation later than Paul's letters and depends on traditions that may have been distorted by time and the accidents of transmission. In addition, we must remember that the author of Luke-Acts evidently was interested in portraying the Christian sect as one that obtained favor from well-placed, substantial citizens. A number of women, including Joanna, the wife of Herod's *epitropos* Chuza, support Jesus and his companions from their own possessions (Luke 8:2f.). The proconsul of Cyprus, Sergius Paulus, summons Barnabas and Paul, is impressed by their miracle as well as by their teaching, and "believes" (Acts 13:7–12). "Not a few Greek women of high standing as well as men" become believers in Thessalonica (17:12, RSV); an Areopagite is converted in Athens (17:34); the procurator Felix converses with Paul often, if not for the highest of motives (24:26); King Agrippa is impressed by Paul's arguments

(26:2–31); the "first man" of Malta entertains him, and he heals the official's father (28:7–10). Some or even all of these episodes may be true, but it is well to remember that the author of Luke-Acts is a sophisticated writer who is also capable of inventing typical occasions to make his points.

The list of early leaders of the Antioch congregation (Acts 13:1) is probably a reliable piece of tradition, but because Symeon Niger, Lucius of Cyrene, and Manaen, the *syntrophos* of Herod Agrippa, were most likely active there before Paul's arrival, I include only Barnabas among the Pauline associates. The asiarchs of Ephesus who were "friends" of Paul (Acts 19:31) had best be left out of account as sounding a bit too much like a Lucan invention; besides, the story does not hint that they became Christians.[66] It would be precarious, too, to draw inferences from the story of the Philippian jailer and his household, converted in response to a familiar sort of miracle (Acts 16:23–34).[67] It is true that this legend might still preserve some local tradition about early converts, but in that case we would expect a name to be remembered. A name we have, and a very prominent one, in Acts 13:7–12, which reports the impression made by yet another miracle on Sergius Paulus, proconsul of Cyprus. Still, we do not hear of his being baptized, nor anything else about him or Christianity in Cyprus—although Barnabas goes there later, 15:39—and again we should err on the side of caution by omitting him.[68] The same is true of Dionysius of Athens, whose position as a member of the court of the Areopagus would otherwise have supplied good material for speculation,[69] and with him Damaris, about whom we know nothing anyway (Acts 17:34).

Erastus, associated with Timothy as an assistant of Paul (19:22) and surely not the *oikonomos* of Corinth; Sopater of Beroea (20:4); and Trophimus of Ephesus (20:4; 21:29; 2 Tim. 4:20) all certainly belonged to the Pauline circle, but we know too little about them to make judgments about their social level. Eutychus of Troas, famous forever as the first recorded Christian to fall asleep during a long-winded sermon (20:9–12), does not seriously warrant inclusion. Of Gaius of Macedonia (19:29) we have only the Latin name and the fact that he was free to travel with Paul. The same is true of Secundus of Thessalonica and Gaius of Derbe (20:4).[70]

The three remaining persons named in Acts are all reported to have served as hosts or patrons of Paul and his associates. The most interesting is Lydia, the Thyatiran dealer in purple fabrics, who, as a gentile worshipper of the Jewish God, encounters Paul in Philippi and converts forthwith, with her *oikos* (Acts 16:14f.).[71] She persuades Paul, Silas, and their other companions to move into her house (vss. 15, 40). We have several indicators of her status. First, as a *porphyropōlis* she must have had some wealth, for purple was a luxury item;[72] she also has a household in which several guests can be accommodated. Second, her name, occupation, and place of origin show that she belongs to the Greek-speaking merchants who have settled in Philippi alongside the Italian, agrarian colonists. Third, she is a pagan adherent of the Jewish synagogue.[73] Finally, she is the female head of a household.

A certain Jason (not to be identified with the Jason of Rom. 16:21) is the host of the missionaries in Thessalonica, and consequently is held responsible for their conduct and forced to post bond for them (Acts 17:5–9).[74] He is evidently a gentile, with a good Greek name. He has a house and some wealth. Titius Justus, like Lydia a "worshipper of God," has a house adjacent to the synagogue in Corinth which becomes the temporary domicile of Paul, Silas, and Timothy after their rebuff by the Jews. His name indicates that he may be a Roman citizen;[75] he belongs to the dominant Latin group of the colony. Unfortunately, Acts does not say explicitly whether either Jason or Titius Justus became a Christian.

Our survey of the names mentioned in the Pauline letters and in Acts has yielded few data about the social level of typical Pauline Christians. A statistical analysis of the sort so important in modern, empirical sociology would be entirely unjustified. Yet some patterns have emerged that are not insignificant. Even though many inferences must remain tentative, we can form a cumulative impression of certain types of people who were prominent in the Pauline groups and mission. Before summarizing the results, however, it will be well to look at other, less direct evidence that can be gleaned from the letters. The prosopography may tend to give skewed evidence, for it is after all the leaders, the prominent, and the unusual who would be mentioned by name, and they may very well have stood out in part because their social rankings were different from those of the majority. The letters must be searched for evidence about the social level of anonymous groups within the congregations.

INDIRECT EVIDENCE

Of the anonymous Christians mentioned in the Pauline letters, there is one group for which the text supplies a rather specific social location: the "saints" who belong to "the household of Caesar" and who join Paul in sending greetings from the place of his imprisonment to the Philippians (Phil. 4:22). Paul does not name any of them, nor does he say how many they are. We do not even know with certainty what city they were in, for some commentators have urged Ephesus or Caesarea as the place of writing, although Rome still seems the most likely.[76] We also do not know whether the Christians in the *familia* were slaves, freedmen, or both, nor where they stood in the internal hierarchy of the *familia*, which ranged from menial domestics to heads of important state bureaus. Nevertheless, the imperial slaves and freedmen as a group had greater real opportunities for upward social mobility than did any other nonelite segment of Roman society,[77] and it is a precious bit of information that some members of this group had found reason to be initiated into Christianity at so early a date.

Apart from the imperial household, we have already seen that there were both slaves and slaveowners among the Pauline Christians. Philemon and Apphia represent the latter category, as does probably Chloe; "Chloe's people" are slaves or former slaves, and Onesimus a slave who, though not a

Christian in his master's house, became one as a runaway. How many or what proportion of each category may have been found in each congregation, we have no way of knowing.[78] In 1 Cor. 7:20–24 Paul addresses a slave rhetorically. Although the slave, like the circumcised Jew of verse 18, is introduced *exempli gratia,* since the topic has to do with marriage, divorce, and celibacy, it would be a strange example if there were in fact no slaves among the addressees. On the other hand, it would be a mistake to infer from this passage that the majority of Corinthian Christians were slaves. There are no other admonitions in the authentic letters of Paul addressed explicitly to slaves, but in the later letters written in Paul's name (as in the similar one written in the name of Peter) the common Hellenistic moral topic on the duties of household members appears, the so-called *Haustafel.*[79] In Colossians 3:22–25 the admonition to the slaves is much longer than the sentence addressed to masters (4:1), but this does not necessarily imply, as has sometimes been suggested, that the slaves were a majority of the congregation. The content of the admonitions would certainly be more readily approved by owners than by slaves.[80] The parallel in the letter that later came to be known as Ephesians is more significant; the fact that that letter seems to have been designed as an encyclical addressed to several congregations of the Pauline mission area in western Asia Minor[81] confirms the impression that the admonitions represent general expectations about Christian behavior rather than the situation in one particular congregation. In Ephesians 6:5–9 again the directives to the slaves are more extensive than those to the masters, but there is somewhat greater balance than in Colossians. Clearly the expectation is that a typical Pauline congregation would include both slave owners and slaves, and the ethos of the leaders is rather more that of the owners than of the slaves. It is also important to notice that these admonitions are within the context of advice for maintaining the proper—hierarchical—structure of a household.

Among the collections of moral advice, or *paraenesis,* in the letters there are a number of passages addressed to free handworkers or craftsmen. Since our prosopography includes several leaders of the Pauline mission—not least Paul himself—who belong to that category, these passages may repay a closer look. In what is usually taken to be the oldest of the extant letters, to the Christians in Thessalonica, Paul appeals to them "to strive to lead a quiet life, to mind your own business, and to work with your own hands, according to the instructions we gave you, that your behavior may be decent in the view of the outsiders and that you may not be in need" (4:11f.). This instruction probably implies, as Ernest Best says, "that the great majority of the Thessalonian Christians were manual workers, whether skilled or unskilled."[82] It is also important to notice that this is a paraenetic reminder of instruction given the Thessalonian converts when the church was first organized there. It is not a unique admonition fitted to special needs of the Thessalonians, then, but represents the kind of instruction that Paul and his associates generally gave to new converts.[83] That is confirmed by the appearance of a similar sentence in the paraenesis of the later deutero-Pauline encyclical, Eph. 4:28: "Let the thief no longer steal, but rather let him labor, working the good with his (own) hands, that he may have (the means) to share with anyone in need." On the other hand, 2 Thess. 3:6–13 (assuming that 2 Thessalonians is a real letter, whether or not Paul wrote it) presupposes the general teaching but applies it to a particular situation in which some Christians are behaving in a disorderly fashion (*ataktōs*) by refusing to work. This behavior, the author says explicitly, violates the "tradition" which they received from Paul (vs. 6). Further, the example of Paul's own manual labor, which was implicitly a model to be imitated in 1 Thess. 2:9 (*mnēmoneuete*), here becomes that explicitly (vss. 7–9).[84] The admonition is pointedly renewed: "That by working in quietness[85] they should eat their own bread" (vs. 12). It is taken for granted that people work in order to eat, even though the prohibition of verse 10 may refer to the Eucharist or other communal meals.

There are a few passages in which the letters directly mention money. Several have to do with the collection for Jerusalem Christians. In 1 Cor. 16:1–4, Paul gives instructions which he says he also gave to the Galatians. Each person, on the first day of the week, is to "set aside and keep whatever he has succeeded in, so there need be no collections when I come" (vs. 2). I have translated as literally as possible, for the phrase *ho ti ean euodōtai* is rather awkward, but it perhaps provides a clue to the economic situation of the Corinthian Christians. The translation suggested by Bauer's *Lexicon*, "as much as he gains,"[86] is a bit overspecific. The verb *euodoun* has taken on a very general metaphoric sense from its original "have a good trip"; it can hardly refer to each individual's whole profit for the previous week, for which Paul's verb would be *kerdainein*. On the other hand, Conzelmann's "whatever he can spare" ("was er wohl erübrigen kann")[87] is too loose. Most translators assume, rather reasonably, that the meaning is the same as in Acts 11:29, "each, as he had prospered," hence the Revised Standard Version here, "as he may prosper."[88] The phrase is in fact quite general, and we should avoid reading very much into it. What we do see clearly is that the collection is to be assembled little by little, week by week. This bespeaks the economy of small people, not destitute, but not commanding capital either. This, too, would fit the picture of fairly well-off artisans and tradespeople as the typical Christians.

The gift for the Jerusalem poor was intended to be quite substantial, as the term *hadrotēs* ("plenty, lavish gift"; 2 Cor. 8:20) suggests, and as the elaborate plans for collecting it confirm. The extant second letter to the Corinthians contains two appeals for participation in the collection, which may have stood originally in separate letters. In chapter 8, Paul uses the Macedonian Christians' generosity in the project to chide and encourage the Corinthians to do better. The size of the collection in Macedonia is the more remarkable, he says, because of their "abysmal poverty" (*hē kata bathous ptōcheia autōn*, vss. 2–3). He implicitly contrasts the economic situation of the addressees. The phrase *ek tou echein*, "from what one has," in verses 11–12, implies that the

Corinthians have the means to "complete" that which was begun the year before. Verse 14 speaks of their abundance (*perisseuma*) in contrast with the Jerusalem Christians' lack (*hysterēma*). The cognate verb in verse 7, which speaks of the Corinthians' abounding in spiritual things, may be a double-entendre, and so may be even the christological formula in verse 9: "For our sakes he, though rich, became poor, that you through his poverty might grow rich." The same word, *charis*, is used for the "grace" of Christ's sacrifice in this verse and for the gift to Jerusalem in verse 7.[89]

On the other hand, we should not take the "abysmal poverty" of the Macedonian Christians too literally, for 2 Cor. 9:2–4 suggests that Paul used the same sort of argument with the Macedonians, in reverse. He has bragged to them of the eagerness of the Corinthians. Moreover, we must remember that whereas Paul had been careful not to accept monetary support from the Corinthians, he had done so more than once from the Macedonians (2 Cor. 11:9; Phil. 4:14–19). Their "poverty" may be partly hyperbole occasioned by the structure of Paul's rhetoric in 2 Cor. 8, which depends upon the antithesis of "poverty" and "wealth," "abundance" and "lack," leading on to the goal, beloved also by Hellenistic moralists, of "equity" (*isotēs*, vs. 14).[90]

Incidentally, Paul's refusal of support from the Corinthians is not absolute, for there are indications that he expected them routinely to help with travel expenses. In 1 Cor. 16:6 he tells of his plans to stay a time with them, perhaps over the winter, "that you may send me on my way [*propempsēte*] wherever I may go." The same expectation is voiced in 2 Cor. 1:16 for his journey to Judea, and he requests the same service in the meantime for Timothy (1 Cor. 16:11). Malherbe has argued that in such a context *propempein* generally "means to equip him with all things necessary for the journey,"[91] which would involve some financial outlay.

The fact that some members of the Corinthian groups conduct lawsuits against other members also implies some financial or mercantile transactions (1 Cor. 6:1–11). Paul's discussion gives no information about the kind of disputes involved, except that they involve *biōtika*, matters of everyday life. Nor can we infer the level of affluence of the parties, for, as the papyri show, it was a litigious age, when even small traders or village farmers could and did appear before magistrates to complain about the encroachments of their neighbors.

It may or may not be significant that the Pauline letters occasionally use commercial language both directly, to describe aspects of the relationship between the apostle and local congregations, and also metaphorically, to make theological statements. Paul makes a very direct promise to reimburse Philemon for any damages incurred by the defection of his slave Onesimus (Philem. 18), but he also uses the formal language of partnership to reinforce the epistolary form of recommendation: "If you hold me as your partner, receive him as myself" (vs. 17). The language associated with commercial partnerships is especially evident in the letter to Philippi, both in the elaborate and carefully nuanced "receipt" that Paul gives for the gift the Philippian Christians have sent to help him in prison (4:15–19), and also, doubtless with that gift and the relationship it represented in view, in the general statements of the opening thanksgiving (1:5, 7).[92] In the same letter[93] Paul can speak of his conversion in terms of gain and loss (3:7f.), and his disciple writing to Colossae could speak of Christ's sacrifice as "canceling the note that was against us" (Col. 2:14). By themselves, these passages would prove nothing about the occupations or wealth of Christians, but they may add one small increment to the cumulative impression that many were artisans and merchants with a modest income. The same is true of the proverb Paul quotes in 2 Cor. 12:14b, "Children ought not save up for their parents, but the parents for their children." That does not sound like the ethos of people at the lowest end of the economic scale, who generally regarded their children, at least their sons, as economic assets, added hands in the workshop, and sometimes direct means for escape from financial straits by sale into slavery. It is wealthy misers whom Plutarch castigates for keeping and storing up their wealth for children and heirs.[94]

It is also possible to infer something about social stratification from several of the conflicts that occurred in the Pauline communities.[95] That is clearest in the case of the divisions which appeared when the Corinthian Christians gathered for the Lord's Supper, which Paul rebukes in 1 Cor. 11:17–34. These divisions, about which Paul "hears" (vs. 18), may be connected in some way with the incipient factions reported by Chloe's people (1:10f.), but nothing that is said here hints that either the jealousy between followers of Apollos and partisans of Paul or the "realized eschatology" of the *pneumatikoi* is involved. It is true that Paul introduces an eschatological element, for he combines here, as often elsewhere, the notion of testing by difficult circumstances, so popular with pagan moralists as well, with the eschatological notion that the Day of the Lord alone reveals one's true worth.[96] Thus the divisions "must" come—this sounds like apocalyptic determinism—"in order to show who are the ones who meet the test" (*hoi dokimoi,* vs. 19). The notion of testing is resumed in verses 28–32. Each person must test himself before eating and drinking, lest by failing to "distinguish [*diakrinein*] the body" his behavior may be liable to God's judgment (*krima*), which already manifests itself in magical punishments (vs. 30). Even these, however, are "discipline" (*paideia*) intended to save the erring from the far worse fate of being "condemned along with the world" (vs. 32). But just what is the unacceptable behavior that Paul attacks with these heavy warnings and taboos? Instead of the Lord's Supper (*kyriakon deipnon*), "each proceeds with his private supper [*to idion deipnon*], and one goes hungry and another gets drunk" (vs. 21). These private suppers ought to be eaten "at home" (22a, 34). But what specific behavior is it that in Paul's view breaks up the communal Lord's meal? The nub of the problem seems to be stated in verse 22, a series of rhetorical questions. This form, of course, is used when the speaker wants to force his audience to draw conclusions for themselves, here, to acknowledge certain unacceptable inferences from their own behavior. Their actions imply that they "despise the congregation of God," because[97] they "humiliate those who do not have." The last phrase, *hoi mē echontes,* could be read quite concretely as continuing the *oikias ouk echete* of the preceding question; that is, those who have houses are blamed for humiliating those who do not. More likely, the phrase is to be taken absolutely, "the have-nots," that is, the poor. Either way, this verse makes it clear that the basic division is between the (relatively) rich and the (relatively) poor.

We can go a bit further, thanks to a very illuminating study of this passage by Gerd Theissen.[98] Theissen compares the divisions in the Corinthian Eucharist with two situations familiar in Roman society and therefore, he surmises, also in a Roman colony like Corinth. One was in collegia, where officers were sometimes assigned larger quantities of food than ordinary members. Theissen points out that most clubs and guilds were more socially homogeneous than the Corinthian congregation seems to have been, and therefore conflicting expectations might arise in the latter that would have no occasion in the former.[99] The other situation was a banquet held by a patron, to which his freedmen clients as well as friends of his own social rank were invited. In the society of the principate it was apparently not uncommon for these to become occasions for conspicuous display of social distance and even for humiliation of the clients of the rich, by means of the quality and quantity of food provided to different tables. Theissen cites both Martial and Juvenal, who presented the viewpoint of the inferiors, and Pliny's letter of advice to a young friend, advocating a less offensive policy for the patronal class. The latter is worth quoting at length:

. . . I happened to be dining with a man—though no particular friend of his—whose elegant economy, as he called it, seemed to me a sort of stingy extravagance. The best dishes were set in front of himself and a select few, and cheap scraps of food before the rest of the company. He had even put the wine into tiny little flasks, divided into three categories, not with the idea of giving his guests the opportunity of choosing, but to make it impossible for them to refuse what they were given. One lot was intended for himself and for us, another for his lesser friends (all his friends are graded) and the third for his and our freedmen. My neighbor at table noticed this and asked me if I approved. I said I did not. "So what do you do?" he asked. "I serve the same to everyone, for when I invite guests it is for a meal, not to make class distinctions; I have brought them as equals to the same table, so I give them the same treatment in everything." "Even the freedmen?" "Of course, for then they are my fellow-diners, not freedmen." "That must cost you a lot." "On the contrary." "How is that?" "Because my freedmen do not drink the sort of wine I do, but I drink theirs."[100]

If a person like Gaius, who opened his house for gatherings of the whole *ekklēsia* of Corinthian Christians, regarded himself very much in the way that the wealthy patron of a private association or a pagan cultic society might do, that would not be surprising. If at the common meals of the Christian community, held in his dining room, he moreover made distinctions in the food he provided for those of his own social level and those who were of lower rank, that would not have been at all out of the ordinary, even though there were some voices even in pagan society who protested the practice. It was precisely the humiliation of the have-nots to which Pliny and the satirists objected. Paul objects on quite different grounds, but Theissen has given good reason for seeking the roots of the denounced behavior in the "status-specific expectations" of a sharply stratified society.

Theissen has argued that differing perspectives of people of different social levels were involved also in another of the conflicts that perturbed Christians at Corinth, the issue of "meat offered to idols," addressed in 1 Corinthians 8–10.[101] Several aspects of this issue will be discussed in chapter 3, Purity and Boundaries, and chapter 6, The Lord's Supper: Ritual of Solidarity. At the moment what is relevant is the identity of the two factions. On one side are "the strong,"[102] who have "knowledge" (*gnōsis*) that "there is [really] no idol in the world" (8:1,4) and who therefore insist upon their "right" (*exousia:* 8:9; 9:4, 5, 6, 12, 18; 10:23, 24) and "freedom" (*eleutheria:* 10:29; cf. 9:1, 19) to eat what they please. They are the ones to whom Paul directs his reply to the inquiry the Corinthians have sent, and with whom to some extent he identifies.[103] On the other side are "the weak" (8:10f.; cf. 9:22), further specified as having "weak consciences" (8:7, 12), who lack this *gnōsis* and, because of their previous customs in paganism, regard the eating of sacrificed meat as a real and dangerous matter (8:7). Many attempts have been made to define these positions in terms of their theological beliefs or ideologies. Theissen does not dismiss all these efforts, but undertakes to show that there is also a social dimension of the conflict, to which the ideological factors would have to be related. In his reading, the "strong" are the socially powerful also referred to in 1 Cor. 1:26f. It is indeed plausible that those who, after conversion to Christianity, may still have had reason to accept invitations to dinner where meat would be served (10:27), perhaps in the shrine of a pagan deity (8:10), are likely to have been the more affluent members of the group, who would still have had some social or business obligations that were more important to their roles in the larger society than were comparable connections among people of lower status. The difference is not absolute, however, for Christian clients of non-Christian patrons would surely also sometimes have found themselves in this position. Theissen also argues, though, that the whole perception of what it meant to eat meat would have been different for people of different economic levels. The poor in fact rarely ate meat; the occasions when they did tended to be cultic, whether public or private. For wealthy people, who could have meat as a more or less regular item in their diet, it would have had far fewer numinous associations. For the poor, moreover, the Christian community provided a more than adequate substitute for the sort of friendly association, including common meals, that one might otherwise have sought in clubs, guilds, or cultic associations. For an Erastus, if indeed he was the rising public servant who in a few years would be aedile in charge of all the Corinthian meat-markets, a restriction of his social intercourse to fellow Christians would mean a drastic reduction of his horizons and a disruption of his career.

On the whole Theissen's case, which is more elaborate than can be conveniently summarized here, is convincing, and makes the conflict between the "weak" and the "strong" further evidence for the presence within the Corinthian congregation of persons of significantly different strata.[104] There is one problem with his construction, however, that may warrant a refinement in the concept of social stratification that he has employed. Theissen moves directly from his demonstration that the "strong" are relatively higher in economic status than the "weak" to the assumption that they are consequently better integrated socially into the larger society. John Schütz has pointed out difficulties with this inference.[105] First, Theissen compares the "strong" with later Christian gnostics. "It is plainly difficult," as Schütz says, "to think of gnostics, with their dour cosmologies and clannish sense of separate identity, as paradigms of social integration." Second, in Theissen's view, the high-status Christians in Corinth include former "god-fearers." This, too, is surprising, if high status entails high social integration, for why would well-integrated gentiles "forsake common civic and religious traditions in favor of Judaism"?[106] There are two orders of problems at issue here. One has to do with adequacy of evidence and argument: Are there adequate grounds for extrapolating from second-century Gnostics to the "gnostics" of Corinth? Because some god-fearers are known to have been of higher status than most proselytes, is it valid to assume that all god-fearers had high general status? What is relevant to our immediate concern, however, is another sort of question, which we have raised before: Is social status best understood as a single dimension or as the resultant of several different dimensions? Because Theissen has assumed a single dimension, or an average of several dimensions, he concludes that high status entails a high degee of integration, an assumption which other evidence seems to contradict. We would avoid these contradictions if we recognized that the "strong" of the Corinthian congregation are inconsistent in status. They may enjoy a high rank in some dimensions, such as wealth, identification with the Latin element in the colony, support by dependents and clients, and in one or two cases perhaps also civic office, but they may be ranked lower in others, such as origin, occupation, or sex. Such people would share many of the attitudes, values, and sentiments of unambiguously higher social levels yet still lack status crystallization. Other persons in the Corinthian congregation who were much lower on all these scales than the "strong" might suffer a much lower degree of inconsistency among their dimensions of status, and thus, within their own social circles, might be better integrated than those who were more mobile and more exposed.

Also in Corinth the status of women became a matter of controversy, as we see in 1 Cor. 11:2–16 and 14:33b–36. These are not the most lucid passages in the Pauline letters, and a small mountain of literature about them has by no means relieved their obscurity. Fortunately we do not have to solve all their problems in order to make the few observations that are germane to our present question. We have already seen that there were a number of women prominently involved in the Pauline circle who exhibited the sorts of status inconsistency that would inspire a Juvenal to eloquent indignation.

There were women who headed households, who ran businesses and had independent wealth, who traveled with their own slaves and helpers. Some who are married have become converts to this exclusive religious cult without the consent of their husbands (1 Cor. 7:13), and they may, though Paul advises against it, initiate divorce (ibid.). Moreover, women have taken on some of the same roles as men's within the sect itself. Some exercise charismatic functions like prayer and prophecy in the congregation (1 Cor. 11:2–16); others, as we have seen in our prosopography, are Paul's fellow workers as evangelists and teachers. Both in terms of their position in the larger society and in terms of their participation in the Christian communities, then, a number of women broke through the normal expectations of female roles.

It is not surprising that this produced tensions within the groups, and that the tortuous theological compromise stated by Paul in 1 Cor. 11:2–16[107] would not settle the issue. Later in the received form of the same letter, a discussion of ecstatic speech and prophecy in the assemblies is interrupted by an absolute prohibition of women from speaking in the meetings, requiring them to be "subordinate" and to "ask their own husbands at home if they want to learn something" (14:33b–36).[108] The subordination of women within the household order was taught in the paraenesis of the Pauline congregations, and reinforced in the letters to Asian churches written by disciples of Paul (Col. 3:18; Eph. 5:22–24).[109] In the second century the roles of women were still controversial among people who wrote fictional accounts claiming the authority of Paul. In the Acts of Paul and Thecla a virgin of Iconium on the eve of her marriage is won to celibate Christianity by Paul's preaching. After miraculously confounding the (male) authorities who try to silence her, but supported by the women of the city and saved on one occasion by a lioness, she baptizes herself. Then she cuts her hair short, dresses like a man, and goes off to follow Paul as an itinerant apostle.[110] On the other hand, the author of the Pastoral Epistles rejects the sort of asceticism represented by Thecla and all teaching by women (1 Tim. 2:9–15; 4:3), except that older women should become "good teachers" by instructing younger women to be good wives and mothers, always subordinate to their husbands (Titus 2:3–5).[111] These second-century documents furnish no direct evidence that can help to describe the social constituency of Pauline Christianity as I have defined it, but they do illustrate the variety and the strength of reactions to status inconsistency (and violation of conventions) of one kind.

The other conflicts which are addressed in the letters of Paul and his immediate disciples did not, so far as the evidence permits us to judge, have anything directly to do with different social levels in the groups. There is one possible exception: the rivalry in Corinth between Paul and the people whom he called sarcastically the "superapostles" (*hyperlian apostoloi*: 2 Cor. 11:5; 12:11). In the invidious comparisons which were made in Corinth between them, certain signs of status seem to have figured. That is, there were members of the Corinthian church sufficiently numerous or persuasive that Paul could address his complaints to the whole congregation, who accorded greater prestige to the recent arrivals than to Paul. Since we have only Paul's description of the situation, and that heavily laden with sarcasm and hostile interpretation, we cannot hope to reconstruct an accurate picture of the superapostles or of their reception by the Corinthians,[112] but it may be useful to note quickly those status factors to which the text alludes. First, rhetorical ability and imposing physical presence are valued. Some Corinthians have complained that, while Paul's letters are "weighty and strong," his "bodily presence is weak and [his] speech despicable" (2 Cor. 10:10). The claims which Paul makes just before this (10:1–6) are themselves claims about rhetorical ability, the ability "to take every thought captive." In 11:6 he admits to nonprofessional status (*idiōtēs*) as an orator, but claims to possess *gnōsis*. That is an argument of the same order: Paul rhetorically boasts that he is no mere sophist.[113] Second, wealth and income appear only in a curiously inverted way: not the amount of wealth or income possessed by Paul and the rivals, but the manner of self-support. The superapostles receive support from the Corinthians, which Paul interprets in a negative way (11:20); the Corinthians now are unhappy with Paul because he did *not* take money from them (11:7–12; 12:13–15). The situation is further complicated by the fact that someone has apparently suggested that the Jerusalem collection is really a fraudulent scheme by which in fact Paul is going to enrich himself while piously declining support (12:16–18). But that is a secondary calumny; the primary issue is the qualification of an apostle by the way he is supported. We may take it, to simplify a complex situation, that expecting to be paid for one's eloquence is seen by the Corinthians as a mark of professional eminence; in contrast Paul is depicted as an amateur or worse.[114] Third and finally, peculiar religious qualifications play a major role: visions and revelations (12:1–10), miracles (12:12), specific divine commissioning (10:13–18), pure Jewish background (11:22f.). Paul argues, first, that if these things really counted, he could claim them, too, and, second, that they are devalued by the surpassing and novel criterion of a life in conformity with the crucifixion/resurrection pattern, which he but not his opponents exemplifies. All this tells us little about the status dimensions of typical Corinthian Christians, except that they share certain measures of status that are generally recognized in the larger society, especially those having to do with rhetorical ability, and that they have superimposed on these some specifically religious qualifications. Whether this implies that a number of Corinthian Christians themselves possessed the signs of prestige that they held in esteem is far from obvious.

MIXED STRATA, AMBIGUOUS STATUS

The evidence we have surveyed is fragmentary, random, and often unclear. We cannot draw up a statistical profile of the constituency of the Pauline communities nor fully describe the social level of a single Pauline Christian. We have found a number of converging clues, however, that permit an impressionistic sketch of these groups. It is a picture in which people of several social levels are brought together. The extreme top and bottom of the Greco-Roman social scale are missing from the picture. It is hardly surprising that we meet no landed aristocrats, no senators, *equites,* nor (unless Erastus might qualify) decurions. But there is also no specific evidence of people who are destitute—such as the hired menials and dependent handworkers; the poorest of the poor, peasants, agricultural slaves, and hired agricultural day laborers, are absent because of the urban setting of the Pauline groups.[115] There may well have been members of the Pauline communities who lived at the subsistence level, but we hear nothing of them.

The levels in between, however, are well represented. There are slaves, although we cannot tell how many. The "typical" Christian, however, the one who most often signals his presence in the letters by one or another small clue, is a free artisan or small trader. Some even in those occupational categories had houses, slaves, the ability to travel, and other signs of wealth. Some of the wealthy provided housing, meeting places, and other services for individual Christians and for whole groups. In effect, they filled the roles of patrons.

Not only was there a mixture of social levels in each congregation; but also, in each individual or category that we are able to identify there is evidence of divergent rankings in the different dimensions of status. Thus we find Christians in the *familia caesaris,* whose members were so often among the few upwardly mobile people in the Roman Empire. We find, too, other probable freedmen or descendents of freedmen who have advanced in wealth and position, especially in the Roman colonies of Corinth and Philippi. We find wealthy artisans and traders: high in income, low in occupational prestige. We find wealthy, independent women. We find wealthy Jews. And, if we are to believe Acts, we find gentiles whose adherence to the synagogue testifies to some kind of dissonance in their relation to their society.

The "emerging consensus" that Malherbe reports seems to be valid: a Pauline congregation generally reflected a fair cross-section of urban society. Moreover, those persons prominent enough in the mission or in the local community for their names to be mentioned or to be identifiable in some other way usually—when we have evidence to make any judgment at all about them—exhibit signs of a high ranking in one or more dimensions of status. But that is typically accompanied by low rankings in other dimensions. Although the evidence is not abundant, we may venture the generalization that the most active and prominent members of Paul's circle (including Paul himself) are people of high status inconsistency (low status crystallization). They are upwardly mobile; their achieved status is higher than their attributed status. Is that more than accidental? Are there some specific characteristics of early Christianity that would be attractive to status-inconsistents? Or is it only that people with the sorts of drive, abilities, and opportunities that produced such mixed status would tend to stand out in any group they joined, and thus to be noticed for the record? It may not be possible to answer these questions, but they suggest some possible correlations to be explored in subsequent chapters.

3

THE FORMATION OF THE *EKKLĒSIA*

One cannot read far in the letters of Paul and his disciples without discovering that it was concern about the internal life of the Christian groups in each city that prompted most of the correspondence. The letters also reveal that those groups enjoyed an unusual degree of intimacy, high levels of interaction among members, and a very strong sense of internal cohesion and of distinction both from outsiders and from "the world."

The aim of this chapter and the next is to describe the social structure of those groups. The Pauline congregations belong to the category studied extensively by modern sociologists, especially American sociologists, and called "small groups" or simply "groups." George C. Homans's definition is representative and has the virtue of simplicity: "a number of persons, or members, each of whom, while the group is meeting, interacts with every other, or is able to do so, or can at least take personal cognizance of every other."[1] Although my purpose is not sociological but historical, the sorts of questions these sociologists ask, even though they deal almost exclusively with groups in modern industrial democracies, are helpful in suggesting the order of our inquiry. In this chapter we shall deal with matters that are more basic, I believe, but also more elusive than the process of organization of the group. What makes a group a group? How does it come together and how does it hold together? These questions have to do with sentiments and attitudes, with perceptions and expectations, as much as with overt structure. It is especially in these realms that the historian needs to be most wary about making anachronistic assumptions about behavior.

Accordingly, we shall begin by comparing the Pauline *ekklēsiai* with groups and organizations in the Greco-Roman city to which they bear at least a family resemblance. Even though it will turn out that none of these categories quite fits, this procedure has the advantage of approximating the way in which a curious contemporary observer might have tried to identify and understand the Christians.

Second, we shall canvass the letters for evidence of how the early Christians regarded their own groups. In particular, we shall seek the factors that contributed to their sense of belonging to a distinct group and the ways in which they distinguished that group from its social environment. Indeed, the

74

question just how far they *did* distinguish and separate it is as important as the question how they did so.

As we focus attention on the local congregations, we shall recurrently glimpse another dimension of the life of these aggregations, one not captured by the net "small group." One peculiar thing about early Christianity was the way in which the intimate, close-knit life of the local groups was seen to be simultaneously part of a much larger, indeed ultimately worldwide, movement or entity. Hence we must also investigate the ways in which that trans-local sensibility was generated and reinforced.

MODELS FROM THE ENVIRONMENT

The Household

The meeting places of the Pauline groups, and probably of most other early Christian groups, were private houses. In four places in the Pauline letters specific congregations are designated by the phrase *hē kat' oikon* (+ posses-sive pronoun) *ekklēsia*, which we may tentatively translate "the assembly at N.'s household."[2] An intimate connection with existing households is also suggested by 1 Cor. 1:16, where Paul says he baptized the "house [*oikos*] of Stephanas," and later in the same letter (16:15f.), where he commends the Stephanas household (*oikia*) as the "firstfruits of Achaia," who have "de-voted themselves to service for the saints." The conversion of a person "with (all) his/her house" is mentioned several times in Acts as well.[3] The letters also mention other groups, not necessarily founded by members of the Pauline circle, that are identified by the households to which their members belong. These include members of the households of Aristobulus and of Narcissus (Rom. 16:10f.). The lists in Rom. 16:14f. of Asyncritus, Phlegon, Hermes, Patrobas, and Hermas; Philologus, Julia, Nereus and his sister; and Olympas probably represent members of three other households whose heads are not mentioned. We hear, too, of Christians in the household of Chloe (1 Cor. 1:11), and even in the household of Caesar (Phil. 4:22). The local structure of the early Christian groups was thus linked with what was com-monly regarded as the basic unit of the society.[4]

The phrase *kat' oikon* does not designate merely the place where the *ekklēsia* met, although the commonest English translation is "the church in N.'s house." For that, *en oikō* would be the more natural expression (see 1 Cor. 11:34; 14:35). Rather, Paul probably uses *kat' oikon* to distinguish these individual household-based groups from "the whole church" (*holē hē ekklēsia*), which could also assemble on occasion (1 Cor. 14:23; Rom. 16:23; cf. 1 Cor. 11:20), or from the still larger manifestations of the Christian movement, for which he could use the same term, *ekklēsia*.[5] The *kat' oikon ekklēsia* is thus the "basic cell"[6] of the Christian movement, and its nucleus was often an existing household. As we saw earlier, the household was much broader than the family in modern Western societies, including not only immediate relatives but also slaves, freedmen, hired workers, and sometimes tenants and partners in trade or craft. However, the *kat' oikon ekklēsia* was not simply the household gathered for prayer; it was not coterminous with the household. Other preexisting relations, such as common trades, are also suggested in the sources, and new converts would certainly have been added to existing household communities. Furthermore, there were groups formed in households headed by non-Christians, like the four mentioned in Romans 16:10, 11, 14, 15, not to mention the *familia caesaris.* Conversely, not every member of a household always became a Christian when its head did, as the case of Onesimus shows.

The number of such household assemblies in each city will have varied from place to place and from time to time, but we may assume that there were ordinarily several in each place. In Corinth, for example, Paul gives special prominence to the household of Stephanas, as we have seen (1 Cor. 1:16; 16:15f.). Acts mentions, besides Aquila and Prisca, who soon moved on, Titius Justus as a host (Acts 18:7), and the conversion of the "whole household" of Crispus (18:8; cf. 1 Cor. 1:14). Gaius, before he became "host . . . of the whole church" (Rom. 16:23), was probably host of one of the household groups. The household assembly in Philemon's house was apparently not the whole of the Colossian church, nor that in Nympha's household the only one in Laodicea (Col. 4:15).[7]

The adaptation of the Christian groups to the household had certain implications both for the internal structure of the groups and for their relationship to the larger society. The new group was thus inserted into or superimposed upon an existing network of relationships, both internal—kinship, *clientela,* and subordination—and external—ties of friendship and perhaps of occupation. The house as meeting place afforded some privacy, a degree of intimacy, and stability of place.[8] However, it also created the potential for the emergence of factions within the Christian body of a city. It may well be the case that the incipient factions addressed by Paul in 1 Cor. 1–4 were based in different households.[9] The household context also set the stage for some conflicts in the allocation of power and in the understanding of roles in the community. The head of the household, by normal expectations of the society, would exercise some authority over the group and would have some legal responsibility for it.[10] The structure of the *oikos* was hierarchical, and contemporary political and moral thought regarded the structure of superior and inferior roles as basic to the well-being of the whole society. Yet, as we shall see, there were certain countervailing modes and centers of authority in the Christian movement that ran contrary to the power of the paterfamilias, and certain egalitarian beliefs and attitudes that conflicted with the hierarchical structure. It is significant that in the later letters of the Pauline circle, Ephesians and Colossians, the pattern of the common rhetorical topic, *peri oikonomias,* "on the ordering of the household," is adapted for moral instruction among Christians, in the form of the so-called *Haustafel* (Col. 3:18–4:1; Eph. 5:21–6:9; cf. 1 Pet. 2:13–3:7).[11] In time, in circles that appealed to the memory of Paul as an authority, whether or not they stood in any concrete social continuity with the Pauline mission, the whole church would be construed as "the household of God," with great stress upon the hierarchical order of the various roles peculiar to the ecclesiastical organization.[12]

The centrality of the household has a further implication for the way we conceive of the Pauline mission: it shows our modern, individualistic conceptions of evangelism and conversion to be quite inappropriate. If the existing household was the basic cell of the mission, then it follows that motivational bases for becoming part of the *ekklēsia* would likely vary from one member to another. If a household became Christian more or less en bloc, not everyone who went along with the new practices would do so with the same understanding or inner participation. Social solidarity might be more important in persuading some members to be baptized than would understanding or convictions about specific beliefs. Differential qualities and degrees of engagement with the group from the beginning would not be surprising.

Important as the household was for Pauline Christianity, it leaves a number of aspects of the groups' life unexplained. It is not merely that the peculiar ritual processes, the central symbols and beliefs, of the Christians have scarcely any point of contact with the domestic cult of a Roman or Greek house;[13] that is hardly surprising. Also, in purely social terms there are elements that are strange to the household structure. That hierarchy offers no clue to the source of the kinds of power and leadership that rival and prevail over the position of the householder, either in the persons of the itinerant apostle and his fellow workers or in the charismatic figures in the local group. It leaves unexplained not only the occasional expression of antihierarchical sentiments but also the sense of unity among Christians in the whole city, the region or province, and even beyond. Apparently there were other models and social ideas at work.

The Voluntary Association

As we saw in the previous chapter, the early Roman Empire witnessed a luxuriant growth of clubs, guilds, and associations of all sorts. In the second century, Roman officials and literary opponents of Christianity often identified the Christian groups with such clubs, especially the sort of secret and uncontrolled gatherings that were regarded as seedbeds of immorality and sedition and often, but not very effectively, banned.[14] Some modern scholars, especially those in the nineteenth century, have speculated that the first Christian groups may in fact have imitated the pattern of voluntary associations, especially the common *collegia tenuiorum,* or burial societies.[15] Although those proposals did not win much support at the time, recently there have been new calls for a fresh examination of analogies between the associations and the early churches.[16] This model would not be an exclusive alternative to the household, for we know of instances in which associations were formed in close conjunction with specific households.[17]

There are indeed some important similarities between the Pauline groups and the private associations known to us from innumerable inscriptions. Both were small groups in which intensive face-to-face interactions were possible and encouraged. Membership was established by the free decision to associate rather than by birth, although factors of ethnic connection, rank, office, and profession were often important as the context for the associations. Both the Christian groups and the associations often incorporated persons who shared a common trade or craft. Both had a more or less important place for rituals and cultic activities, and also engaged in common meals and other "fraternal" activities. The provision of proper burial and the commemoration of the departed on later anniversaries was an important function in many of the associations. We have no evidence about the funeral practices of Pauline Christians—a silence that in itself would be grounds for doubting a direct identification of the Christian groups with *collegia tenuiorum*—but we can hardly doubt, in the face of the sort of sentiment expressed in, say, 1 Thess. 4:13–5:11 or the enigmatic reference to "baptism for the dead" in 1 Cor. 15:29, that these groups made appropriate provision for the burial of deceased Christians.

Both the private associations and the Christian groups also depended to some extent on the beneficence of wealthier persons who acted as patrons, as we have had occasion to observe in several contexts. The client collegium would reward its patron with encomiastic inscriptions, honorary titles, wreaths, perhaps even a statue—and with effective control of the club's life, for there were no strong countervailing powers in the association. In this respect, as we have seen, the Christian congregation was quite different, and the patrons may have had reason to feel somewhat slighted.[18] Paul even admonishes the Corinthians to show a little more respect for such people, such as Stephanas (1 Cor. 16:15–18). On the other hand, the collegia preserved at least the semblance of democratic internal governance, imitating the classical polis in organization and procedures for elections and decisionmaking. It is arguable that such democratic procedures were also at work in the Pauline congregations, but the question is much complicated by charismatic functions and spirit possession, which receive full discussion in the next chapter.

There were also important differences between the Christian groups and typical voluntary associations. First of all, the Christian groups were exclusive and totalistic in a way that no club nor even any pagan cultic association was. Although we shall see later that the boundaries of the Pauline groups were somewhat more open than those of some other early Christian circles, to be "baptized into Christ Jesus" nevertheless signaled for Pauline converts an extraordinarily thoroughgoing resocialization, in which the sect was intended to become virtually the primary group for its members, supplanting all other loyalties. The only convincing parallel in antiquity was conversion to Judaism, although adherence to the sects of the Pythagoreans or the Epicureans may in some cases have come close.[19] Corresponding to this more exclusive and organic conception of membership was a deeper motivational basis for association. Students of private associations generally agree that their primary goals were fellowship and conviviality. Cultic associations had in addition certain specific functions in connection with the festivals, processions, and shrines of the gods. The goals of the Christians were less segmented; they had to do with "salvation" in a comprehensive sense.

On the other hand, the Christian groups were much more inclusive in terms of social stratification and other social categories than were the voluntary associations. There was some crossing of social boundaries in the associations, especially under Roman influence in the period we are interested in, so that lists of members and of officers not infrequently include both men and women, or freeborn, freedpersons, and slaves. Rarely, however, is there evidence of equality of role among these categories, and for the most part the clubs tended to draw together people who were socially homogeneous.[20] As we saw in the preceding chapter, it was precisely the heterogeneity of status that characterized the Pauline Christian groups.

That the Christian groups did not consciously model themselves on the associations is apparent from the almost complete absence of common terminology for the groups themselves or for their leaders. Although in later literature the Christian group is occasionally called a *thiasos, factio, curia, corpus,* and so on,[21] nowhere in the Pauline letters are any of the terms used that are characteristic of Greek and Roman associations.[22] Paul uses the verb *synagein* only once, to refer not to the foundation of a group but to a meeting for a specific purpose (1 Cor. 5:4), and the corresponding noun, *synagōgē,* never.[23] On the other hand, I can find no example of *ekklēsia,* nor of the epithets used by Paul in letter openings—"the holy ones," "called" (or "elect"), or "beloved of God"—in the titulature of clubs.[24] The choice of *ekklēsia* might appear to have a structural parallel in the language of the associations, for they commonly imitated the technical terms for the structure of the republican city, and the best-known use of the term *ekklēsia* was for the voting assembly of free citizens in Athens and other free cities of Greek constitution. In fact, however, the Christian usage seems to have been mediated by the Septuagint translation of the biblical phrase *qᵉhal yhwh* and by the extension of that use by Greek Jewish writers.[25] The names of municipal offices that were so often adopted by the clubs, *prytanis,* treasurer, secretary, *decuriones, quinquennales,* and so on,[26] are absent from the Pauline letters. The only candidates for titles common to the Pauline groups and associations are *episkopos* (Phil. 1:1) and *diakonos* (Phil. 1:1; Rom. 16:1), which in these passages *may* have a technical sense designating a local "office," and *prostatis* (Rom. 16:2), which almost certainly does not. *Prostatēs* is often used in inscriptions of associations, either as a functional designation (presiding officer; cf. 1 Thess. 5:12) or as a title, but where Roman influence is strong, as it certainly was in Corinth and Cenchreae, it often translates *patronus.*[27] That is the sense in which the feminine form is applied to the *diakonos* Phoebe.[28] When *diakonos* appears in association inscriptions, it seems always to refer to persons whose function more or less directly involved waiting on tables; the

Christian technical usage is quite different.[29] Only *episkopos,* then, is likely to have been taken over from the usage of associations,[30] and it has scarcely begun to make its appearance in Christian terminology in Paul's time.

Finally, the associations offer as little help as does the household in explaining the extralocal linkages of the Christian movement. Each association, even those that served the internationally popular deities, was a self-contained local phenomenon.

The Synagogue

Because Christianity was an offshoot of Judaism, the urban Christian groups obviously had the diaspora synagogue as the nearest and most natural model. Further, the synagogue incorporated features of both the two types of groups we have already looked at, the association and the household. The Jewish communities were construed legally as collegia and adopted many aspects of collegial structure.[31] And the characteristics of Jewish ritual required that the household become, in a pagan environment, a closed cultic community of its own.[32] In addition, Jews possessed what is most visibly lacking in these two models compared with Pauline Christianity, the sense of belonging to a larger entity: Israel, the People of God, concretely represented by the land of Israel and the Temple in Jerusalem.[33]

There are in fact a number of similarities between the Jewish communities in the Greco-Roman cities and the Pauline groups that grew up alongside them. As we have noted, the term *ekklēsia* as used by Paul seems to presuppose the special usage of Greek-speaking Jews, even though we have no evidence that it was ever applied to the Jewish community in a given place.[34] The practice of meeting in private houses was probably an expedient used by Jews in many places as it was for the Pauline Christians, to judge from the remains of synagogue buildings at Dura-Europos, Stobi, Delos, and elsewhere that were adapted from private dwellings.[35] In the cities where Paul founded congregations, however, the Jews had probably already advanced to the stage of possessing buildings used exclusively for the community's functions. The sorts of activities in the meetings were also probably similar, including scripture reading and interpretation, prayers, common meals, but in neither case the sacrifices that were characteristic in pagan cults. The Pauline meetings were also marked by prophecy, admonitions, the reading of apostolic letters, and by glossolalia and other phenomena of spirit possession. Whether these things, too, had analogies in the synagogues is impossible to say; in the light of Philo's description of the vigils of the Therapeutae, it would be foolish to deny the possibility.[36] Of course there were rituals peculiar to Christianity, although these, too, had at least some analogies in Judaism, in ritual washings, the initiation of proselytes, and communal meals.[37] In addition, the Jewish community took responsibility for the adjudication of internal disputes, and Paul at least expected the same to be done in the *ekklēsia.*[38] Most important, the Pauline Christians took over the scripture, large and basic parts of the belief system, and a great many norms and traditions, either whole or with some modification, from the Greek-speaking synagogues.

In view of these similarities and palpable connections, it is surprising how little evidence there is in the Pauline letters of any imitation of the specific organization of the synagogue. To be sure, we have too little information about the internal structure of the synagogues in the early empire to be quite certain what to look for; most of our evidence comes from a later time.[39] But again, as in the case of the collegia, the terminology of functions and honors is different. We do not meet an *archisynagōgos* or any *archontes*—except mythical and Roman imperial ones—in Paul's letters, nor is the term *synagōgē* used for the assembly. Accordingly, although there are persons who function as patrons, they receive no honorifics like *patēr* or *matēr synagōgēs*. The role of women in the Pauline movement is much greater and much more nearly equal to that of men than in contemporary Judaism.[40] And, of course, membership requirements are drastically different. The ethnic community is no longer the base; Paul describes his own mission as primarily to "the gentiles" (Gal. 2:1–10; Rom. 1:5, 13f.; 11:13; 15:14–21), even though the unity of Jew and gentile within the *ekklēsia* was a matter of central concern to him. Paul explicitly and emphatically rejected the ritual of circumcision and the other observances that distinguished Jew from gentile, although the controversy in Galatia shows that this was by no means a self-evident step. In that conflict, in the earlier one in Antioch recalled by Paul in that context, Gal. 2:11–14, possibly in the rivalry between Paul and other apostles addressed in 2 Cor. 10–13, and probably in the later conflict in Colossae addressed by a disciple of Paul in his name, some Christian leaders evidently wanted to ensure that the tested, traditionally and biblically sanctioned means by which the Jews had maintained their identity in a pagan culture would continue to serve the community of Messiah Jesus.[41] The vehemence with which Paul and the other leaders of his circle closest to him combat that position suggests that for them some other conception of the community was operative, one not directly derivable from the experience of the synagogues.

Philosophic or Rhetorical School
There is a fourth model from antiquity with which early Christian groups, and particularly the Pauline ones, have been compared: the school. The comparison was made already in the second century, when Justin Martyr presented Christianity as "the true philosophy," and later by other apologists of the second and third centuries. Robert Wilken has argued that this analogy was put forward quite deliberately and shrewdly to deflect the suspicion that had fallen on the movement as a newfangled cultic association of the sort that was always regarded with distaste by the aristocracy and by imperial officers on the watch for groups that might turn subversive.[42] Recently, however, it

has been proposed that the communities of disciples around noted teachers, both philosophers and rhetors, that became so important in the high and late Roman Empire are a close parallel to the organization of the Pauline mission.

To be sure, it is not usually the local congregation as such that is most often described as the "school of Paul," but more often the circle of fellow workers and leaders. Often the phrase has been used quite loosely, referring merely to some continuity of thought and traditions that persisted for a time and could be distinguished from other trends in early Christianity. In 1966, however, Hans Conzelmann proposed that there was a "school of Paul" in a more concrete sense, "a school operation consciously organized by Paul . . . where one methodically pursued 'Wisdom' or carried on theology as wisdom-instruction."[43] The school was located, Conzelmann thought, in Ephesus, although the only evidence he cited was the presence there of Apollos, Aquila, and Prisca, and the "dialogues" in the *scholē* of Tyrannus mentioned in Acts 19:9.[44] Conzelmann is content to discuss the reworking of traditions as evidence for school-like activity; he offers no suggestions about the structure of the supposed school, nor does he relate it to any contemporary social forms except the very vague category "Jewish wisdom."[45]

Six years earlier, E. A. Judge had gone even further, suggesting that Paul and his "retinue" had followed principally rhetorical models, founding local groups that were not organized as cultic communities, as the ancients understood cult, but as "scholastic communities," pursuing an "intellectual mission" in ways that often resembled a "debating society."[46] Contemporaries would have understood Paul and his followers as "sophists," a category which by the Roman period included philosophers as well as rhetoricians.[47] Judge's sketch is bold and impressionistic, based more on the account in Acts than on evidence from the letters, and ignores critical questions about both kinds of sources. Nevertheless, it has evoked considerable discussion, for it raises specific questions about how new groups in the Greco-Roman cities supported themselves, found places to meet, and gained a hearing, and it proposes answers on the basis of specific, known analogies in that environment. Judge himself grants that his model is not adequate alone, for Paul's mode of operation differed in important ways from that of a typical sophist: "What other touring preacher established a set of corporate societies independent of himself and yet linked to him by a constant traffic of delegations?"[48]

It certainly is true that Paul and the other leaders of his circle did carry on teaching activities. Converts were instructed in the beliefs and norms of the new movement, which were to some extent formulated and handed on as specific traditions (*paradoseis*),[49] and those traditions were discussed and argued about. Furthermore, these beliefs and norms were applied in a continual process of admonition and exhortation which is abundantly represented in the letters and was the responsibility of leaders in each congregation.[50] All this corresponded to some degree to the tradition of the "guidance of souls" that in the Hellenistic and Roman periods was considered more and more to be the province of philosophers and of the popular philosophic preachers. Moreover, the leaders of the Pauline circle were apparently acquainted with major topics current in Hellenistic moral discourse and with some aspects of the style of that discourse.[51]

It is true that the philosophic schools offered not only ideas and patterns of language that may fruitfully be compared with early Christian modes of discourse, but also a social model. Students of ancient philosophy have given relatively little attention to the form and organization of the schools themselves, but a few have observed that, even in the classical period of Greek philosophy, the school was sometimes organized as "a religious fellowship, *thiasos,* dedicated to the goddesses of culture."[52] In offering this description, Marrou may have exaggerated the influence of the Pythagoreans on other schools; there is hardly anything in Arrian's report of Epictetus's lectures or in the extant writings of Musonius Rufus and Seneca, for example, that suggests such a closed organization of initiated disciples. Such is the prevailing picture, however, not only of the Pythagoreans but also of the Epicureans—the two schools about which we unfortunately know least, especially in the Roman period.

Most of our information about the Pythagoreans comes from the five-part collection made by the enthusiastic neoplatonist Iamblichus around the end of the third century A.D.[53] and from the *Life of Apollonius* by Philostratus, a first-century Pythagorean teacher and miracle-worker, written under the patronage of Julia Domna (but perhaps after her death, ca. 217).[54] The account by Iamblichus contains a description of the school founded by Pythagoras himself at Croton, in southern Italy, into which young men personally selected by Pythagoras were inducted after a three-year period of testing, followed by a five-year novitiate of silence (*Vit. Pyth.* 17.71–74). They entered a fellowship characterized by community of goods, a carefully ordered daily regimen, and strict taboos on diet and clothing (21.95–100). It is impossible to be sure how much of this picture is the result of later idealizing or, unfortunately, whether any communities of (neo-)Pythagoreans existed at the time of the early Roman principate.[55]

Although much remains mysterious about the Epicureans also, at least we know that there were thriving Epicurean communities in Roman times and that some of them actively propagandized to win proselytes.[56] There is much in the life of these communities that reminds us of the Pauline congregations. Based on "that highly adaptable institution, the Hellenic household,"[57] they strove to produce the intimacy of a family among the members, who included male and female, slave and free, bound together by love (*philia*), "the immortal good."[58] There was no rigid hierarchy of office, but some functional differentiation, based on one's stage of advancement in the school's thought. The training of recruits and especially the regular practice of admonition, "a manifold art," were worked out in great detail.[59] The unity and perseverance of the school attracted jealous admiration in antiquity. Numenius, for example, said, "The school of Epicurus resembles a true commonwealth [*politeia*], altogether free of factionalism, sharing one mind and one disposition [*hena noun, mian gnōmēn*], of which they were and are and, it appears, will be willing followers."[60] Moreover, it is recorded that Epicurus undertook to maintain that unity among groups of his followers settled in different places, by writing letters "to the friends" in those places.[61] In a number of ways, then, the groups founded by Paul and his circle and the groups that traced their basis to Epicurus seem to have arrived at similar solutions for a number of parallel goals and practical requirements. The analogies would repay a more careful investigation than the present context permits.[62]

What becomes most obvious from this quick survey of the Pythagorean and Epicurean schools, however, is that they resemble the Pauline communities just to the extent that they take the form of modified households or voluntary associations—that is, the two other models from antiquity that, along with the special case of the Jews, we examined earlier. This fact should introduce a certain caution into any discussion of a Pauline school. It is useful to know that there was a strong scholarly, academic, and rhetorical element in the activities of the Pauline groups, but it will not do to make those elements constitutive of the movement. They are ancillary. Judge, for example, rejects far too quickly the cultic association as an analogy to the Pauline groups. It is true that Christianity did not yet have a *cultus* of the sort that most established cultic associations practiced, by public or private sacrifices, public processions, and festivals. It also differed in significant ways from the initiatory mysteries. Nevertheless, it did have an initiatory ritual, one that figures very importantly in the Pauline and deutero-Pauline letters, a ritual meal central to its common life, and rapidly growing traditions of other sorts of ritualized behavior. (See chapter 5, below.)

The fact is that none of the four models we have now surveyed captures the whole of the Pauline *ekklēsia,* although all offer significant analogies. At the least, the household remains the basic context within which most if not all the local Pauline groups established themselves, and the manifold life of voluntary associations, the special adaptation of the synagogue to urban life, and the organization of instruction and exhortation in philosophical schools all provide examples of groups solving certain problems that the Christians, too, had to face. For the structures worked out by the Pauline movement itself, however, which may after all have been unique, we must turn to the primary sources it has left us.

THE FELLOWSHIP AND ITS BOUNDARIES

In order to persist, a social organization must have boundaries, must maintain structural stability as well as flexibility, and must create a unique culture.[63] The second factor, the social structure of the organization, is concerned largely with leadership, the allocation of power, the differentiation of roles, and the management of conflict. All these topics are deferred until the following chapter. How the Pauline Christians developed "a unique culture" is an extremely complicated matter, and one that recurs in various guises throughout the rest of this book. For now, I wish only to inquire about the ways in which these groups identified themselves as groups or as a movement, and that entails investigating mainly the first factor, the boundaries drawn between the groups and their social environment, and one part of what made their culture unique, that is, the aspects of language, practice, and expressed sentiments and attitudes that gave the group cohesion. For our purposes "social cohesion" can conveniently be defined the way Leon Festinger does, as "the resultant of all the forces acting on the members to remain in the group."[64] Internal cohesion and the creation of boundaries against outsiders are complementary factors and can best be considered together. The question of boundaries can be extended somewhat to bear on the larger issue of the group's "response to the world," the issue by which Brian R. Wilson has undertaken to classify the various sorts of "sects."[65]

The categories that follow have not been systematically derived from any sociological theory, but are adopted merely as convenient pigeonholes for keeping track of certain kinds of evidence that appear in and between the lines of the Pauline letters.

The Language of Belonging

The letters of the Pauline circle are rich in words and phrases that speak of the Christians as a very special group and of the relations between them in terms charged with emotion. Very often the addressees of the letters are called "saints" or "holy ones" (*hagioi;* once *hēgiasmenoi;* 1 Cor. 1:2; 2 Cor. 1:1; Phil. 1:1; Rom. 1:7; Eph. 1:1; Col. 1:2). The term is the functional equivalent of *ekklēsia* in the letter openings, as it is elsewhere when used in the third person (Philem. 5 and 7; 1 Cor. 6:1f. in contrast to the "unjust" outsiders; Col. 1:4; many manuscripts of 1 Thess. 5:27). It is also used of Christians in other places, especially in conveying greetings from one place to the other (2 Cor. 13:12; Phil. 4:21f.; Rom. 16:15) and in statements about the collection for "the saints" in Jerusalem (Rom. 15:25f.; 1 Cor. 16:1, 15; 2 Cor. 8:4; 9:1, 12). Notice also the practical consequences drawn in Romans 16:2: Phoebe is to be received "as befits *hagioi.*" The term *elect* and its cognates are important, too (1 Thess. 1:4; Rom. 8:33; Col. 3:12; 1 Cor. 1:27; Eph. 1:4; of an individual in Rom. 16:13), as is the related set, *calling* (1 Cor. 1:9; 7:15, 17–24; Gal. 1:6, 15; 5:8, 13; 1 Thess. 2:12; 4:7; 5:24; 2 Thess. 2:14; Col. 3:15; Eph. 4:4; cf. Rom. 8:30; 9:24–26; and 2 Thess. 1:11). The notions that the members are peculiarly "loved" by God (Rom. 1:7; Col. 3:12; 1 Thess. 1:4; 2 Thess. 2:13; cf. Rom. 5:5, 8; 8:35, 39; 15:30; 2 Cor. 5:14; 13:11, 13; Eph. 2:4; 3:19; 5:2, 25; 2 Thess. 2:16) and that they are "known" by him (1 Cor. 8:3; Gal. 4:9) are also striking. All these terms are drawn from biblical language referring to Israel; Paul himself still uses several of them of the Jewish people in Romans 9–11.

Repetitive use of such special terms for the group and its members plays a role in the process of resocialization by which an individual's identity is revised and knit together with the identity of the group, especially when it is accompanied by special terms also for "the outsiders," "the world." By this kind of talk members are taught to conceive of only two classes of humanity: the sect and the outsiders. To the extent that this process is effective, each should think of himself in every activity in terms of the new typification: "I am a believer" or "I am in Christ." Stigmatization by outsiders in the same or equivalent terms—"He is a Christian"—but with hostile connotations reinforces the self-stigmatization. This is a point to which we shall return.

Especially striking is the language that speaks of the members of the Pauline groups as if they were a family. They are children of God and also of the apostle. They are brothers and sisters; they refer to one another as "beloved." The Pauline letters are unusually rich in emotional language—joy and rejoicing, anxiety, longing.[66] For example, the earliest of them in its opening thanksgiving addresses the Thessalonian Christians as "brothers beloved by God" and mentions the "joy of the Holy Spirit" associated with their conversion (1 Thess. 1:4, 6). To be sure, it was (and is) common for letters to include near the beginning some philophronetic phrases, language intended to convey the writer's esteem for the recipient and to encourage the latter's positive sentiments toward the writer,[67] but both the number and intensity of the affective phrases in the Pauline letters are extremely unusual. The apostles have been "gentle among you, as a nurse would care for her own children" (2:7).[68] They report that they felt "so affectionate toward you that we were willing to give you not only the gospel of God but also our own souls, because you had become so beloved to us" (2:8). In 2:17 an epistolographic cliché ("absent in person but present in heart/mind") is intensified by use of emotionally charged words: "Bereft [*aporphanisthentes*] of you for a time, in person but not in heart, we were the more determined, with eager longing, to see your face." The section 2:17–3:11 is especially dense with such language, emphasizing the high regard of the author[69] for the recipients, the pain of separation, his longing to see them, and narrating the suspense he felt while waiting for Timothy to confirm that the regard was mutual and that they were still sound, which in turn only heightened Paul's desire to see them in person. The topos "concerning brotherly affection" (*peri philadelphia*) is formally introduced in 4:9 with the statement that the recipients already fulfill the God-taught commandment to "love one another" toward "all the brothers in the whole of Macedonia" (4:10). The eschatological section 4:13–5:11 focuses on the anguish of separation between the living and those members of the community who have died, as we shall see in more detail later in this chapter and in chapter 6.

The concluding series of brief admonitions speaks, again with many affective terms, of attitudes and sentiments and of interactions in the group, beginning with the admonition to regard local leaders "in love" (5:13) and concluding with the directive to "greet all the brothers with a holy kiss" (vs. 26).

One of the latest of the authentic letters, Philippians, contains if possible even more such language expressing close personal ties between the addressees and the writers. Further, in this instance the Christians in Philippi have reinforced these ties by sending a gift to Paul (4:10–20), an act that according to 4:15 represents a unique relationship (cf. 2 Cor. 11:7–9). The connection is also emphasized by the warm language used of both the Philippians' and Paul's messengers: Paul's description of Epaphroditus (and of the latter's concern for his home congregation and theirs for him: 2:25–30), who has come from Philippi to him, and of Timothy, whom he will soon send to Philippi (2:19–24). These intermediaries thus become mediators not only of information but also of the personal relations which the leaders are careful to emphasize.

Early Christians of all sorts seem to have called one another "brothers" and "sisters," but these terms occur far more frequently in the Pauline letters than anywhere else in the earliest Christian literature.[70] The commonest use by Paul himself—about half the occurrences—is in the diatribal form of address, "My brothers, . . . " This appears sixty-five times in the undoubtedly authentic letters and seven times in 2 Thessalonians but not at all in Colossians, Ephesians, or the Pastorals, so it may be peculiar to Paul. The same is true of the general usage, "a brother, a sister" (twenty times in the homologoumena, twice in 2 Thessalonians), but that occurs only in certain contexts, such as rules formulated as cases. References to individuals as "N., a brother," or "N., a sister," are found both in the undoubted letters (twelve times) and in Colossians and Ephesians (four), and the plural in the third person is used to refer to Christians in general in both (eighteen and three times, respectively), as well as in the Pastorals. Paul can also speak of the members of a church founded by him as his "children" (*tekna:* Gal. 4:19; 1 Cor. 4:14f.; 2 Cor. 6:13; 12:14), although this expression, too, can serve as a common rhetorical metaphor for the relation between teacher and pupil (as in 1 Thess. 2:7, 11; 1 Cor. 4:14; 2 Cor. 6:13).[71] On three occasions he refers to an individual as his child: once to Philemon (Philem. 10) and twice to Timothy (1 Cor. 4:17; Phil. 2:22). In each case Paul is commending to the addressees a person coming to them from him.[72] Like other early Christian circles, the Pauline groups could also speak of members as "children of God" (*tekna:* Rom. 8:16, 21; 9:8; Phil. 2:15; Eph. 5:1; *hyioi:* Gal. 3:26).

The use of family terms to refer to members was not unknown in pagan clubs and cult associations, particularly in Rome and in areas where Roman customs influenced the Greek associations.[73] Most likely, however, the early Christians took their usage from the Jews.[74] Not only was there biblical precedent for referring to all Israel as brothers, a usage that continued in the Greek-speaking Diaspora,[75] but that usage could be restricted to members of a purist sect, as we know from the documents of Qumran.[76] The notion of "adoptive brothers," which occurs in several inscriptions of a Jewish-syncretistic cult of "the Highest God" in the Bosporan kingdom in Roman imperial times,[77] is especially interesting, because the metaphor of adoption plays a role also in Paul's allusions to baptismal ritual.

When Paul in Galatians 3:26–4:6 (cf. Rom. 8:15–17) uses the metaphor of adoption to describe initiation into the Christian fellowship, he is evidently drawing on common baptismal language. The ritual symbolizes "putting on Christ," who is the "new human" and "the Son of God." The ecstatic response of the baptized person, "Abba! Father!" is at the same time a sign of the gift of the Spirit and of the "sonship" (*hyiothesia*) that the Spirit conveys by incorporating the person into the one Son of God. The facts that this cry is retained in Aramaic in the Greek-speaking Pauline congregations and that it is also familiar to the non-Pauline Roman groups show that this is a quite early tradition.[78] Whatever else is involved, the image of the initiate being adopted as God's child and thus receiving a new family of human brothers and sisters is a vivid way of portraying what a modern sociologist might call the resocialization of conversion. The natural kinship structure into which the person has been born and which previously defined his place and connections with the society is here supplanted by a new set of relationships.

A second way of dramatizing the break with the past and integration into the new community is found also in the language of the baptismal ritual, to which allusions are made in Galatians 3:28, 1 Corinthians 12:13, and Colossians 3:11. Here we learn that those who have been "baptized into Christ" or "into one body" have "put on Christ" or the "new human," in whom such divisions as those between Jew and Gentile, Greek and barbarian, slave and free, even male and female, are done away with and "all are one." This baptismal reunification formula, which is almost certainly pre-Pauline, has its roots in certain aspects of the Adam legends. These legends spoke of the image of God (Gen. 1:26) as a "garment of light" with which the first human was clothed, lost when he sinned, and replaced by the "garments of skin" (Gen. 3:21), or the physical body. Moreover, the legends construed that image as both male and female (Gen. 1:27), so that the separation of Eve from Adam (Gen. 2:21f.) represented the loss of the original unity. At the same time the clothing imagery interprets the ritual actions naturally associated with nude baptism. The removal of clothing for baptism represents a "stripping away of the body of flesh" (Col. 2:11). Reclothing afterward represents "putting on Christ," who is the "new human," and begins the process of being "renewed . . . according to the image of the Creator" (Col. 3:10). The structural antinomies that establish one's social place, one's identity, are dissolved and replaced by a paradisiacal unity: "All are one."[79]

Both the fictive use of kinship terms with strong language of affection and the reunification pattern correspond with phenomena found in many initiatory rituals. Victor Turner, expanding on Arnold van Gennep's classic analysis of "The Rites of Passage," has proposed the term *liminality* to refer to the antistructural quality of the initiatory phase between separation and reintegration, and *communitas* to refer to the close, undifferentiated mode of social relationship that initiates experience with one another.[80] Liminality, as the word suggests, is ordinarily temporary, a transitional stage between two modes of integration into a society that is structured by roles and statuses. However, if the initiatory rituals are exercised not for the dominant society but within a sect or "marginal" group that distinguishes itself sharply from the society, that group may continue for some time to exhibit features of *communitas*.[81] The regular use of terms like *brother* and *sister*, the emphasis on mutual love; the prominent role accorded to the Spirit and its "gifts" (*charismata*), which result in spontaneous actions by members of the community; and epistolary reminders of the initiatory experience—all reinforce the *communitas* of the Christian groups. Implicitly they contrast the group's life with that of "the world": the closely structured, hierarchical society of the Greco-Roman city. On the other hand, these groups, like every social movement, clearly are in the process of developing their own structures, and in fact they can scarcely ever have evaded altogether the structures that surrounded them—even in the very households in which they met. Thus the dialectic between "structure and anti-structure" that Turner describes appears again and again in the tensions addressed by the Pauline letters. For example, Paul insists that male and female prophets, even though they are filled with the "one Spirit," and even though (as they would doubtless remind him, though he perhaps pointedly does *not* mention it in 1 Cor. 12:13) in Christ there was "no more male and female," must keep the different hair styles and different dress that are customary for men and women (1 Cor. 11:2–16). In this instance he is speaking in support of "structure," and he sets limits to the anticipation of eschatological *communitas*.[82] Similarly, in a later chapter of the same letter, he lays down rules for controlling the exuberance of spirit-possessed behavior, "because God is not God of disorder but of peace" (14:33) and because outsiders who witness the uncontrolled spontaneity of speaking in tongues may think the Christians insane (vs. 23). Initiation into the new family of God's children produces strong forces of cohesion, but apparently it also releases some fissiparous forces that must be curbed, if the groups are to continue, by imposing patterns of order, including subordination.

Something of the same dialectic may be observed in the use by Paul and his disciples of the metaphor "the body of Christ."[83] The use of the human body as a metaphor for society was a commonplace in ancient rhetoric, a favorite of the late Stoics, and was readily adapted by Jewish writers to speak of Israel.[84] What makes the Pauline usage extraordinary, and what has attracted so much theological comment, is the fact that so often the phrase "the body of Christ" or its equivalent is used with a concrete allusion to the human body of Jesus, crucified and raised from the dead.[85] That special significance was reinforced by the language of the two major rituals, which spoke of dying and rising with Christ in baptism as well as of baptism into his "one body," and of the giving of his body and blood, represented in the supper. It is not easy, however, to decide whether readers would have recognized overtones of that particular reference in passages in the letters that sound like the ordinary figurative usage.[86] In 1 Cor. 12:12–30 the use of the metaphor is not very different from that in the pagan moralists. The Corinthian congregations have experienced a process that is normal in groups or social movements: the differentiation of roles, with some accorded higher prestige than others, and consequently the rise of competitiveness, jealousy, and the other shocks that threaten group life. The picture is complicated by the fact that different roles are regarded as gifts of the Spirit and therefore are evaluated not pragmatically, but in terms of the degree to which they are thought to demonstrate an individual's unusual quality of possession of or by the Spirit. Paul uses the image of the body as pagan moralists do, to suggest that differentiation does not compromise but promotes the unity of the group, so long as the interdependence of the members is recognized. That attitude is certainly not incompatible with steep stratification, as the common usage amply shows, in which the king is head, peasants the feet, and so forth. And the way in which Paul lists certain roles, even numbering the first three (vs. 28), implies acceptance of a hierarchy of roles in the congregation, though perhaps not the same as that prized by the glossolalists of Corinth. On the other hand, Paul's emphasis on the "one Spirit," his stress on the inversion of prestige ("honor") in the divine economy of the body (vss. 23f.), and especially the insertion of the poem of love (ch. 13) into the middle of the discussion of exhibitions by the *pneumatikoi*[87] indicate that he is concerned to limit if possible the developing stratification and above all to reinforce the cohesion of the group. The irony of the situation thus becomes fully manifest: the Spirit is the principle par excellence of *communitas,* of spontaneous, direct interaction apart from the roles and antinomies of "the world," but some members quickly claim to have more Spirit than others. Paul does not want to allow that claim.[88]

The Letter to Colossians and the encyclical "to Ephesians" show how the Pauline school has later (how much later, we cannot really tell) extended and elaborated the body metaphor. The image itself has been articulated, so that Christ is now the "head," while the ordinary members make up the "body" (Col. 1:18; 2:19; cf. 2:10; Eph. 1:22; 4:15; cf. 5:23). Even more striking is the connection of the body metaphor here with a myth of cosmic restoration. In the traditional material which the two authors have worked into these compositions, much of it evidently connected with the ritual of baptism in the Pauline communities, Christ is portrayed as the head not only of the church but also "of every rule and authority" (Col. 2:10); as the firstborn of the whole creation, "everything in the heavens and on earth" (Col. 1:15f.); as the one whose exaltation brings about reconciliation of heaven and earth (Col. 1:20).[89] However, both authors have used this picture of cosmic reconciliation in order to glorify the unity of the Christian community and to appeal to their audiences to maintain that unity.[90] Internal cohesion and harmony is the central paraenetic aim of both letters.

Even these superficial observations about the development of the "body of Christ" figure in Pauline groups illustrate another powerful factor that operated to draw the early Christians together. A group of people who strongly hold a set of beliefs about what is real and valuable, different in some salient aspects from beliefs commonly held in the general society, and who also share evocative symbols for those beliefs, naturally find communication with one another easier and more satisfying than communication with those who do not share their way of seeing. Furthermore, unless some countervailing factors work to divide the group, the more frequently and intensively the members interact, the more strongly these common, distinctive patterns of belief will be reinforced.[91] To be sure, "distinctive" never means "absolutely unique." A century of study by historians of religions has demonstrated that there is hardly a belief attested in the New Testament for which some parallel cannot be found somewhere in its environment or antecedents. But on balance these studies have also shown that these parallels, though often immensely illuminating, rarely explain the meaning and function of the given beliefs in their Christian contexts. The first few decades after the death of Jesus were apparently a time of extraordinarily rapid emergence of new combinations of symbols and beliefs among Jesus' followers and early posthumous converts; these quickly gave to the Christian movement a character different from that of any other Jewish sect of the time.[92] The social function of some of those distinctive belief constellations is the subject of chapter 6. We can anticipate that discussion here by mentioning three examples of the ways in which distinctive beliefs could have encouraged group coherence.

Paul, Silvanus, and Timothy remind the Thessalonian believers of their conversion by recalling "how you turned to God from the idols, to serve a living and genuine God" (1 Thess. 1:9). They back their code of strict sexual morality by urging the Christians not to be "like the gentiles who do not know God" (4:5). In both cases the source of the language in the traditions of the Jewish synagogue is palpable. To the Corinthians Paul writes, " . . . although there may be so-called gods in heaven or on earth—as indeed there are many 'gods' and many 'lords'—yet for us there is one God, the Father, from whom are all things and for whom we exist, and one Lord, Jesus Christ, through whom are all things and through whom we exist" (1 Cor. 8:5f., RSV). As a matter of fact, there was an old and expanding tradition of intellectual monotheism in Hellenistic culture, and the series of prepositional phrases appended to "one God, the Father," and "one Lord, Jesus Christ" in Paul's formulalike statement can be found in almost identical form in writings of the Roman Stoics and others.[93] Jews in the Greek cities capitalized on that trend in presenting their beliefs to cultured pagans, often with great success.[94] At the same time, the exclusivity of Jewish monotheism was quite different from the tolerant attitude of the philosophic monotheists, who regarded the various deities worshiped by different people as either many names for the one divine principle or as the lesser agents, powers, or manifestations of the highest but ineffable God. It was precisely their single devotion to the One God, their abhorrence of sharing his worship with that of any other, that gave to the Jews their sense of being a unique people. That exclusive monotheism was part of the very fabric of the life within which the earliest followers of Jesus grew up, and it was no less a part of the premises with which the Pauline wing began.[95] For them as for the Jews in a Greek city, it served as the focus of their difference from others and signified also the basis for unity among the believers.

There was, however, an important difference. Whereas the Jewish communities in the diaspora cities welcomed both proselytes and "god-fearers" who were not yet ready to make the full commitment signified by circumcision, Paul and the other urban missionaries of the new sect took a much more radical approach toward the non-Jews. They proclaimed in the death and resurrection of Messiah Jesus the beginning of a new age, in which Jew and gentile were to be joined together without distinction in the people of God. The ritual markers that protected the identity of the Jews in pagan cities— particularly circumcision, *kashrut,* sabbath observance—were now abandoned (though not without dissent). Paul argued that this eschatological unity of Jews and gentiles in the new household of Christ was the logical implication of monotheism itself: "Or is God [the God] of Jews alone? Is he not also [God] of gentiles? Yes, certainly of the gentiles, since God is one, who will justify circumcision from faith and uncircumcision through faith" (Rom. 3:29f.).[96] And others in the Pauline school employed the lesson, for the author of Ephesians makes the unity of Jew and gentile in the one household the paradigm instance and starting point of a cosmic reconciliation, the "summing up of all things in Christ."[97]

A second example of special beliefs that promoted a sense of distinctive identity is more formal: the belief in revelation made uniquely to believers. That belief also was part of the Jewish heritage, and the form in which it appears in early Christianity is rooted especially in the forms of Jewish apocalyptic. In an apocalypse, things which have been hidden from people on earth are revealed from heaven to a specially chosen figure (usually a hero of the ancient past) and through him made known to the faithful community. This pattern was important in the speech of the first Christians, and it echoes several times in the Pauline and deutero-Pauline letters. In 1 Corinthians 2:6–9, for example:

Yet among the mature we do impart wisdom, although it is not a wisdom of this age or of the rulers of this age, who are doomed to pass away. But we impart a secret and hidden wisdom of God, which God decreed before the ages for our glorification. None of the rulers of this age understood this; for if they had, they would not have crucified the Lord of glory. But, as it is written, "What no eye has seen, nor ear heard, nor the heart of man conceived, what God has prepared for those who love him," God has revealed to us through the Spirit.[98]

Certainly a group that possesses information to which no one else has access is a group strongly conscious of the boundaries between itself and nonmembers. The content of the secret held by the Christians was malleable; it could be expanded to include the whole constellation of their special combinations of beliefs. For the Pauline Christians, the heart of the secret was the significance of Jesus' death as God's messiah and his resurrection.

That announcement, the fulcrum of Pauline christology, serves as our third example of beliefs that reinforced group solidarity. The messiah of God—but crucified by men. Dead and buried—but raised the third day. Rejected by Jew and killed by Roman—but revealed as son of God. Here were assertions fraught with paradox, freighted with allusions to traditional longings for all who knew the Jewish traditions, and resonant with archetypal human fears and hopes. The assertions take the form of claims of fact, yet the claim is not open to verification or falsification by outsiders. It belongs to the secret hidden for ages but now revealed only to the believers. It is a claim of fact, but at the same time it is patient of elaboration into complex metaphors and analogies. The fundamental claim, "the gospel," can be stated in extremely compact formulas: "Christ Jesus, who died; indeed, who was raised" (Rom. 8:34a); "Jesus our Lord . . . , who was handed over for our transgressions and raised for our justification" (Rom. 4:25).[99] It gives rise to a pattern of parallel antithetical statements that occur again and again in Paul's letters and those of his followers. The pattern is dramatized in the ritual of baptism, in which believers are "buried with him through baptism into [his] death, in order that as Christ was raised from the dead through the Father's glory, so we may walk in newness of life" (Rom. 6:4), and regularly recalled in the Supper, in which, as Paul summarizes, "you proclaim the Lord's death until he comes" (1 Cor. 11:26). Paul and the other leaders deliberately unfold the metaphoric potential of this core belief in monitory, paraenetic, and argumentative contexts, constantly suggesting in numerous small and large matters that the behavior of members in the community ought somehow to exhibit the pattern of dying and rising. Apostolic authority is manifested in troubles and weakness, not in overt power, "always carrying about the death of Jesus in the body, in order that the life of Jesus may be displayed in our body" (2 Cor. 4:10). Sexual connections are not a matter of indifference, as if the body were only transitory and unimportant to the spirit, for "God raised the Lord and will raise us through his power" (1 Cor. 6:14). Christians in Corinth ought to share their money with Christians in Jerusalem when they remember "the grace of our Lord Jesus Christ: he was rich but for your sakes he became poor, that you might become rich through his poverty" (2 Cor. 8:9). Later we shall look in more detail at the particular uses of such statements in the life of the congregations. For now the point to be made is only how prolific and pervasive in the discourse of the Pauline Christians were statements about the dying and rising of Christ Jesus. Those who shared this belief, which could be stated with such dramatic simplicity, shared a religious symbol of enormous generative power.

As the foregoing discussion shows, not just the shared content of beliefs but also shared forms by which the beliefs are expressed are important in promoting cohesiveness. Every close-knit group develops its own argot, and the use of that argot in speech among members knits them more closely still.[100] In-group jargon employs a variety of linguistic strategies. Ordinary words may be used with special nuances; the term *ekklēsia* itself, applied to the company of Christians whether gathered in a house, or comprising many such gatherings in a city or province or all Christians everywhere, is an example. In ordinary Greek it referred to the voting assembly of citizens of the free Greek city. On the other hand, the words themselves may be unusual or foreign; for example, the Pauline groups retain in liturgical contexts the Aramaic terms *Abba* (Gal. 4:6; Rom. 8:15) and *marana tha* (1 Cor. 16:22). And of course the title "Christ" (*christos*), the literal translation of the Hebrew "messiah" (*mešiaḥ*), would be unintelligible to an ordinary Greek speaker, for whom the everyday meaning of the word was "ointment."[101] The special texture of a group's idiom is not confined to individual words, however, nor to vocabulary in general. Certain phrases tend to become fused by repetition in a small-group situation, so that they function as single units of speech, and not so much any more to convey information as to serve as tags or signals.[102] We have seen, too, that certain syntactical patterns could become habitual, like the antithetical formulas about Jesus' death and resurrection. Perhaps the extraordinary chain of synonyms and prepositional phrases in the opening doxology of Ephesians is an extended example. Fused language appears especially often in ritual contexts; the blessings, doxologies, and confessional formulas that punctuate Pauline and even more the deutero-Pauline letters all exhibit to some degree the influence of ritual language on epistolary language. The language of letters tends to be highly conventional in any case, especially at the beginning and ending. Modern study of the Pauline letters has compared them with ancient rhetorical handbooks for letter writers and with actual letters, both literary and private, that have survived. As a result, we have learned that Paul and his imitators were thoroughly familiar with the standard patterns, but also that they used them flexibly and imposed on them their own special character.[103]

To a significant extent the Christians inherited their jargon from Judaism. A great many of the unusual words and phrases in the early Christian documents are translation Greek, either taken directly from the Septuagint or influenced by its idiom.[104] The liturgy of the Greek-speaking synagogues also contributed patterns and style.[105] Very quickly, though, the Pauline Christians developed their own slogans and patterns of speech that distinguished them from other Jewish groups as well as from the general environment.

The Language of Separation

The Pauline groups have special terms not only to refer to themselves but also to distinguish those who do not belong. The latter are simply "the outsiders" (*hoi exō:* 1 Cor. 5:12, 13; 1 Thess. 4:12; Col. 4:5).[106] Sometimes they are lumped together as "the world" or "this world," although *ho kosmos* is often used with a quite neutral connotation in the Pauline letters and never with quite so negative a cast as it receives in the Johannine circle and in later gnostic texts.[107] However, the outsiders may be further stigmatized not only matter-of-factly as "nonbelievers" (*apistoi*)[108] but also as "unrighteous" (*adikoi;* 1 Cor. 6:1, 9), "those despised in the church" (1 Cor. 6:4), "those who do not know God" (1 Thess. 4:5; Gal. 4:8; 2 Thess. 1:8). They are characterized, as pagan society had been in Jewish apologetic traditions, by catalogs of vices (as in 1 Cor. 5:10; 6:9–11), which stem from the primary sin of idolatry (Rom. 1:18–32; compare Wisd. of Sol. 13–15).

The insider/outsider language invariably implies a negative perception of the outside society, even when the immediate function of the dualistic expressions is to reinforce the internal ordering of the group. When Paul refers to the beginning of the Christian group at Thessalonica, he distinguishes the believers from the remainder of society as those who "turned to God from idols" (1 Thess. 1:9). This is language inherited from the Diaspora, but it is immediately reinforced by an eschatological clause with distinctive Christian content: "And to await from the heavens his Son, whom he raised from the dead, Jesus who rescues us from the wrath to come" (vs. 10). In Philippians the same note is sounded, and the social consequences are candidly expressed. In contrast to those who are "enemies of the cross of Christ" (Phil. 3:18f.), whether these are pagans or, more likely, deviant Christians, Paul describes himself and his readers as those whose *politeuma* is in heaven. This is an interesting twist in the use of a term that usually described the corporate organization of a group of resident aliens, especially the Jewish communities in Greek cities.[109] Here, too, there is an eschatological sanction added in the immediate context. The heavenly *politeuma* and heavenly Savior correspond to a future transformation both of the bodily existence of the individual Christians and of their social life, when "all things" will be subjected to Christ and God. This typical apocalyptic belief is advanced here to reinforce attitudes of loyalty and confidence within the Christian groups (3:17, 4:1). In other passages, despite Paul's insistence that there is "no more distinction" between Jew and gentile, *gentiles* is nevertheless used as a pejorative term for outsiders (1 Cor. 5:1; 12:2, Eph. 4:17).

Several recurrent patterns that evidently characterized early Christian preaching reinforce this consciousness of a qualitative difference between outsiders and insiders. For example, the "soteriological contrast pattern" reminds the Christians that "once" their life was characterized by vices and hopelessness, "but now" by eschatological security and a life of virtue.[110] Gal. 4:1–11 is a vivid instance of the use of this schema to sanction a pattern of belief and practice within the group. Formerly the Galatian Christians were "enslaved to things which were nongods by nature," namely the "elements of the world" (*stoicheia tou kosmou*). Their life then was characterized by "not knowing God" (vs. 8), their new life by "knowing—rather being known by—God" (vs. 9). This again is language appropriated from Judaism,[111] but Paul has placed the Jews too among the outsiders, because of the special issue involved here: before the coming of Christ and faith the Jews are "enslaved" under the Law, as are pagans under the *stoicheia* ("elements"). For the Galatian Christians to accept the Judeo-Christian practices urged by Paul's opponents would be to fall again into the power sphere of the *stoicheia*. Thus Paul is attacking a rival interpretation of Christianity by associating it with the "outside," evil, and dangerous world from which the Christians were "rescued" by conversion (1:4).[112] There are a few places in the Pauline letters, all in paraenetic contexts, where the Christians are urged sharply to separate themselves as "children of light" from the "children of darkness" in the rest of society—language that is best known from the Essene writings found at Qumran.[113] As we shall see, however, the Pauline Christians did not emulate the Qumran group's withdrawal from society.

If a sect expects the larger society to be hostile toward it, and if society obliges by attacking the sect, the experience is a very strong reinforcement of the group's boundaries.[114] Sufferings and persecution form a complex set of notions in the Pauline and deutero-Pauline letters, and these notions are bound up with Paul's most fundamental theological and christological beliefs. Some aspects of this complex are discussed in the final chapter of this book. It is clear, however, that one function of the talk about suffering is to strengthen group solidarity by emphasizing the dangers from without. The paraenetic reminder in 1 Thess. 3:3f. shows that the instruction of new converts early on included warnings that sufferings must be expected. In a time of actual stress, Timothy has been sent to remind the congregation that "when we were with you, we told you beforehand that we were to suffer affliction" (3:4, RSV).[115] Furthermore, the convert is given powerful models for the endurance of suffering. The apostle himself and his fellow workers have experienced great hostility and danger, which Paul often recites, as in the so-called peristasis catalogs of the Corinthian correspondence.[116] Other Christian congregations can also be cited as examples, as in 1 Thess. 2:14.[117] All these are related finally to the comprehensive image of Christ's sufferings and death. What other fate could believers expect so long as they live in the world that crucified the Son of God? The common paraenetic motif of imitation permits Paul to link the various models: "You became imitators both of us and of the Lord, by receiving the word in great affliction with joy [inspired by] the Holy Spirit, so that you [in turn] became a model [*typon*] for all the believers in Macedonia and in Achaia" (1 Thess. 1:6; cf. 2:14). The result is a series of structurally analogous examples which combine to present a compelling picture of a world hostile to God's intentions and to his chosen agents. The convert who does eventually experience hostility, even in such mild forms as perhaps the jibes of friends and relatives, readily understands it as confirming the sect's picture of the way the world is.

The picture may be further reinforced by two mythic elements. The antidivine opposition may be said to be instigated by the devil or by demonic forces (as in 1 Cor. 2:6–8; 2 Cor. 4:4; Eph. 6:11–18). Indeed, "the god of this world" may be pictured as one who opposes the true God (2 Cor. 4:4). And this opposition can be integrated into a two-age dualism, characteristic of Jewish and Christian apocalyptic literature. Present sufferings will yield to future "glory" (2 Cor. 4:17; Rom. 8:18). There will be an eschatological recompense, when a judgment theophany will render punishment to the opponents and comfort to the afflicted faithful (2 Thess. 1:3–12).[118]

Purity and Boundaries

"The human body," writes Mary Douglas, "is always treated as an image of society."[119] Where social boundaries are carefully guarded, we may expect to find concern about the boundaries of the body. This principle finds ready illustration in the functions of purity rules in other sects of Judaism contemporary with early Christianity. The Pharisees distinguished themselves from the ordinary population, the *'amme ha-'areṣ*, by scrupulously observing the rules of purity that had in biblical times applied to the priesthood and to others only when they entered the sacred precincts of the Temple.[120] The monastic, hierocratic community at Qumran used yet more rigorous practices to assure their purity and to reinforce their separation, already accomplished spatially by withdrawal into the wilderness, from the world of the Prince and the children of Darkness.

Bodily controls and purity meant tight social boundaries not only for Jews of special sectarian allegiances, who were thus isolated from other, latitudinarian Jews, but also to some extent for all Jews who wished to maintain their identity in diaspora cities. Philo puts their situation succinctly in his interpretation (quoted above in chapter 1) of Balaam's prophecy: Israel cannot be harmed by its opponents so long as it is "a people dwelling alone" (Num. 23:9), "because in virtue of the distinction of their peculiar customs they do not mix with others to depart from the ways of their fathers."[121] The most important of the "peculiar customs" were circumcision, *kashrut*, sabbath observance, and avoidance of civic rituals that implied recognition of pagan gods.

The Pauline school abolished circumcision of proselytes and other rules that distinguished Jew from gentile within the new community. In the new era inaugurated by the death and resurrection of Jesus the Messiah "there is no distinction" (Rom. 3:22; 10:12) between Jew and gentile. Yet by abandoning these rules, the Pauline Christians gave up one of the most effective ways by which the Jewish community had maintained its separate identity in the pagan society. That was the practical issue at dispute between Paul and his opponents in Galatia, although the complexity of Paul's theological and midrashic arguments has often led later interpreters to forget this simple question. Would the abolition of the symbolic boundaries between Jew and gentile *within* the Christian groups mean also lowering the boundaries between the Christian sect and the world? The Pauline Christians answered this question with a significant ambivalence, illustrated by two cases discussed in Pauline letters; the issue of idolatry and rules for marriage and sex.

Interaction between sect members and non-Christians is directly at issue in the question posed by the Corinthian Christians, whether one is allowed to eat "meat offered to idols" (1 Cor. 8:1). The delicacy of the problem and its importance are apparent from the complex and far from univocal reply, which comprises three chapters of the present form of 1 Corinthians,[122] and from the fact that Paul repeats his admonitions in a more general form in

Romans 14:1–23. The letter from Corinth has put this issue to Paul because there is a division of opinion among the Corinthians themselves. Paul labels the two sides "the strong" and "the weak." "The strong" adopt a weak-boundary position: they need no taboos against idolatry in order to protect their Christian faith, because they know that the idols are not real; they are proud both of their knowledge (*gnōsis*) and of the power (*exousia*) and freedom (*eleutheria*) which this knowledge, the grace they have received as believers in Christ, gives them. "The weak," on the other hand, are accustomed to associate the eating of meat with participation in the cults of pagan gods; for them, "idolatry" is real and dangerous.

Thus, members of the group perceive its boundaries quite differently. Many commentators have held that the division must have been one between Jewish Christians and gentile Christians, but the passage defies interpretation on that assumption.[123] The truth behind that attempted interpretation is that the symbolization of identity and religious loyalty by absolute exclusivity of cult was peculiarly Jewish, so that the terms by which idolatry is defined in the Corinth Christian controversy are inherited from Judaism. In fact there is nothing in the text that requires us to assume that the line was drawn between two self-conscious factions. It is more likely, as Gerd Theissen has argued, that the issue of eating meat tended to divide people according to their social status. It was the more affluent members, "the strong," whose business and social relationships would be sharply curtailed if the ban on "meat offered to idols" were to be enforced; the poorer classes would be little affected. Moreover, poorer people ate meat so rarely that they would tend to associate it with cultic occasions and situations. The issue is complicated by the fact that the affluent few were patrons of the church in Corinth.[124]

Paul's response is addressed to "the strong," to "the weak" only obliquely, and affirms the intellectual position of the former. The idols are nonexistent (8:4)—although this statement is qualified in 8:5f. and 10:19f. Eating and not eating are ultimately matters of indifference; as a Stoic moralist might say, they are *adiaphora* (8:8). Therefore, a Christian may eat anything sold in the *macellum* without any scruples of conscience, "for the earth is the Lord's and its fullness" (10:25). And one may accept invitations by pagans and eat anything served by them, so long as the eating is not explicitly designated a cultic act by someone else (10:27f.). However, the enlightened believer must be prepared to sacrifice this freedom to avoid harming the "weak" brother, for whom the association of meat with pagan sacrifices is still a serious matter (8:7–13; 10:24, 28f.)

The chief difficulty in understanding the passage is that this rather pragmatic rule, oriented toward responsibility between persons, stands alongside an absolute prohibition of "idolatry" in 10:1–22, backed by a biblical example (vss. 1–13) and by a deduction from the Christian ritual of the Lord's Supper (vss. 16–22). Some commentators have supposed that Paul vacillated, now taking the position of the "strong," then that of the "weak." Others have maintained that the situation addressed in 10:1–22 is different from that of chapters 8 and 10:23–11:1; a few have even proposed that these were parts of originally separate letters. The transitions are abrupt, but there is nevertheless a logic to the sequence of arguments in the present form of chapters 8–10. Chapter 8 sketches out the problem and Paul's dialectical answer in lively, diatribal style, using slogans and phrases from the Corinthians' internal debate. Chapters 9 and 10:1–22 support Paul's answer with examples drawn from his own missionary practice (ch. 9), from the biblical account of Israel in the wilderness (10:1–13), and, in the light of that same account, from an implication of the Eucharist (10:16–22). Finally, Paul sums up with a series of rules, formulated in imperatives and introduced by his modification of a Corinthian slogan (10:23–11:1).

The first of the two main examples accords admirably with Paul's general rule. The apostle's rights (*exousia*)—to be accompanied by a wife or to accept financial support—are by no means abolished by his decision not to assert them. He has not ceased to be free (*eleutheros*) by freely "enslaving" himself to others. So also "the strong" will not deny their freedom of conscience if on occasion they relinquish their rights for the sake of "the weak"; on the contrary, they will "become imitators of me as I am of Christ" (11:1). The second major example, however, does not fit the context so well. Indeed, 10:1–13 gives every appearance of having been composed independently of its present context.[125] It is a midrashic homily, based on the scripture verse cited in verse 7, from Exod. 32:6; "The people sat down to eat and drink and rose up to play." Each element of the verse is expounded. "To eat and drink" is explained as the eating and drinking of "spiritual food" (manna) and "spiritual drink" (the water from the rock). "To play" is interpreted according to various nuances the verb translated "to play" could have and illustrated by other passages from the biblical account of the wilderness period: "to commit idolatry," "to fornicate," "to test the Lord [or Christ]," "to grumble." After explicit warnings not to commit these sins there is a word of reassurance, that God always provides for the faithful the means to escape temptation. The homily, which otherwise would have been appropriate in any synagogue, has been Christianized by identifying Christ with the legendary rock that followed the Israelites and gave water (vs. 4b) and by finding in the crossing of the Red Sea an equivalent to baptism (vs. 2). The point of the homily remains rather general: even the wilderness generation, for whom God performed great miracles, did not escape temptation; one must therefore be vigilant.

Paul has extracted from the homily the central warning against idolatry, which of course follows naturally from the quoted verse, for Exodus 32:6 refers to the episode of the Golden Calf, the classic instance in Jewish tradition of Israel's idolatry.[126] He has stated it first in a general rule, which was evidently widely used in early Christianity.[127] Then he backs this rule by connecting an interpretation of the Lord's Supper (known to the Corinthians) with a further deduction from the Golden Calf episode. The cup of blessing and the broken bread represent "partnership" with Christ. In Israel, too, those who ate the sacrifices were "partners of the altar," but by the same principle those who participated in the sacrifices to the Golden Calf committed the self-contradiction of becoming "partners of demons" (vss. 18–20). Notice that the diatribal question that Paul inserts in verse 19 reveals that he is aware that he seems to be contradicting his agreement with "the strong" in 8:4, namely, that the idols are not real. (This is rather clear evidence of the integrity of the three chapters, despite the looseness of connectives.) Evidently he wants to say that the pagan gods are not what their worshipers think they are; they are "by nature not gods" (Gal. 4:8). Nevertheless, they have some reality, as "demons," and any participation in their cults is absolutely excluded for those who belong to the One God and One Lord.

The effect of the argument is to leave the issue of the Christian group's boundaries somewhat ambiguous. On the one hand, social intercourse with outsiders is not discouraged. The mere act of eating meat is desacralized in order to remove a taboo that would prevent such intercourse.[128] It is thus not idolatry. On the other hand, any activity that would imply actual participation in another cult is strictly prohibited. Thus the exclusivity of cult, which had been a unique mark of Judaism difficult for pagans in the Hellenistic cities to understand, would remain characteristic also of the Pauline congregations.[129] The emphasis in Paul's paraenesis, however, is not upon the maintenance of boundaries, but upon internal cohesion: the mutual responsibility of members, especially that of strong for weak, and the undiluted loyalty of all to the One God and One Lord.

There are similar ambiguities in the rules about sex. The key passages are 1 Thess. 4:1–8 and 1 Cor. 7:1–16. The former is especially important because it is specified as tradition: it belongs to the catechetical instruction which new Christians received either before or after their baptism (4:1–2). In 1 Cor. 7:2–5 Paul takes up the same rule cited in 1 Thess. 4:4–6, but elaborates and reinterprets it.[130] In 1 Thess. 4 the controlling category is "holiness."[131] Its opposite is "impurity" (4:7), understood here as a metaphor for forbidden sexual connections. "Holiness" implies separation; it is contrasted with passions attributed to "the gentiles who do not know God" (1 Thess. 4:5). The admonitions of 1 Corinthians 5 and 6 also presuppose a conception of the community as a pure and holy space, and of the outside world as impure and profane. As we have seen before, the life of the outsiders is characterized not only by abhorred sexual practices but also by a variety of other vices. In baptismal initiation the believer has been purified—"washed" and "made holy"—from these corruptions (1 Cor. 6:11).

The marriage rule in 1 Thess. 4:3–8 and 1 Cor. 7:2 stands under the general rubric "avoid *porneia*," a term used of all sorts of illicit sexual connections. This general warning appears in several traditional formulations that belonged to early Christian instructions or paraenesis.[132] The Jewish abhorrence of homosexuality and the equation of irregular sex with idolatry were retained by the Pauline Christians.[133] Indeed, the way in which the general marriage rule was formulated, with the phrase "not as the gentiles who do not know God," suggests strongly that this whole tradition had its origins in the diaspora synagogue. The rule shows that monogamy was understood by the Pauline Christians, as it had come to be for Jews in the Hellenistic and Roman periods, as normative and the normal means for avoiding *porneia*. The rules for ordering households (*Haustafeln*) incorporated into the deutero-Pauline letters to Colossians and Ephesians (as well as in other contemporary and later Christian documents, including 1 Peter, the Pastorals, and the Letter of Polycarp) show that monogamy continued to be the normal expectation in the mainstream of Pauline thought.[134] Monogamy as such, however, can hardly be what distinguished them from "the gentiles that do not know God," for it had long been the norm approved in Greek and Roman as well as Jewish law and sentiment.[135] The assertion that the "gentiles" indulge in "the passion of lust" is not an objective description of pagan society, but another example of the labeling of outsiders as vicious, a practice that we have already encountered. There are abundant parallels not only in Jewish apologists but also in pagan satirists and moralists. In fact, pagan moralists habitually denounce "passion" (*epithymia*) and "pleasure" (*hēdonē*); the wise man indulges in sex for neither, but solely in order to beget children. Greek-speaking Jewish authors agree.[136] The surprising thing, in view of the wide attestation of this attitude, is that neither the rule Paul quotes nor his own discussion of sexual norms mentions procreation. Very likely his eschatological expectations made the question of procreation seem moot, but in that event the fact that he still allows normal sexual relations would be the more remarkable. On the whole, though, the sexual purity for which the Pauline Christians strive in an impure world is defined mostly in terms of values that are widely affirmed by the larger society.

There are two possible exceptions. First, we learn from 1 Cor. 7:10 that the saying of Jesus rejecting divorce, forms of which are also known in the synoptic Gospels, was used in the Pauline circle as a rule.[137] In comparison with both Jewish and pagan practice at the time, this norm would have appeared quite unusual. It could be regarded as a radicalization of the norm of monogamy and thus a distinguishing feature of the Christian groups. However, we see that Paul applied the norm rather freely (1 Cor. 7:11–16), especially in cases of marriage between Christians and non-Christians. The discussion of these cases calls attention to a second way in which the Pauline rules about marriage deviated from norms of the larger society. It is clear that Paul's preference is that believers marry "in the Lord," that they marry other believers. Very likely this expectation was generally known among the churches of his circle, for this would help to explain why the issue of continuing or severing marriages between Christian and non-Christian spouses was raised in Corinth. The phrase "a sister as wife" in 1 Cor. 9:5 presupposes the norm. Notice that Paul does *not* advocate separation; the divorce rule takes precedence over the preference for group endogamy. So long as the unbeliever is willing to live "in peace" with the believer, the sphere of "holiness" is actually extended to include the pagan spouse as well as the children (7:14).

The limit of the divorce rule appears when the unbeliever wishes to separate; in that case the believing brother or sister is not "enslaved" (vs. 15). Most commentators take verse 16 as a reference to the practical and reasonable hope that, if the marriage continues, the pagan partner may be won over to the faith.

Second, the Corinthian correspondence also shows that the notion of sexual purity could be radicalized in another way: by asceticism. Thus some of the Corinthian Christians reason that "it is good for man not to touch a woman," even if they are married. Celibacy could be a powerful symbol as well as a practical means of separation from the connections and responsibilities of ordinary society. That this was one of the principal functions of celibacy in later encratite Christianity may be seen in some of the sayings attributed to Jesus in the Gospel of Thomas, in the narratives and speeches of several apocryphal Acts of apostles—notably the Acts of Thomas—and in much of the literature and ritual of early Syriac Christianity.[138] In the second-century Acts of Paul and Thecla, we see that such an ideology could be attributed to Paul. And well it might, since he and Barnabas and probably several of the other prominent itinerants of his school were celibate, and he agrees with his Corinthian questioners that celibacy is preferable. However, the reasons he gives in support of celibacy, for those who like himself have the *charisma* for it, are pragmatic: it enables them to give undivided attention to the work of the Lord, in view of the impending end of all things (1 Cor. 7:25–40). Paul's argument, together with his citation of the monogamy rule "on account of *porneia*" and his careful restatement of it in terms of the reciprocal sexual obligations of man and woman (7:2–5), tends rather to undercut the use of asceticism as a means for establishing social boundaries.

Purity is very often associated with ritual, and that is true also in the Pauline communities. I shall reserve a full discussion of the social functions of the Christian rituals for chapter 5 below, but a few observations are warranted here. We have already seen that some of the actions and language of the baptismal initiation emphasize the internal cohesion of the community. The reverse of that is emphasis on separation from the outside world. The fact that a water bath serves not just as a preparatory rite, as in most contemporary initiations, but as the central act of the whole ceremony vividly portrays life prior to the event—and outside the sect—as unclean. All who enter the pure community must do so by being "washed" and "sanctified" and "justified" (1 Cor. 6:11). Furthermore, the whole ritual represents a dying and rising with Christ. It entails dying with respect to the structures and powers of the world (see Col. 2:20), "taking off" the "old human" with his vices and his divisions and entanglements, and putting on a new life in Christ, the "new human," distinguished by the unity of a new family of brothers and sisters, children of God. Clearly, then, baptism is a boundary-establishing ritual.

The other major ritual of the Christian groups, the Lord's Supper, also provided symbolic expression of the group's solidarity and of its boundaries.

Two examples show how important common meals were for defining fellow-ship. In Antioch it was the decision of some Jewish Christians to stop eating with uncircumcised fellow Christians that led to the confrontation between Paul and Peter and, apparently, to the break between Paul and Barnabas and even between Paul and the Antioch church (Gal. 2:11–14). Second, one mode of discipline for serious violators of the community's moral norms is their exclusion from the gatherings and the warning that other members are "not even to eat with such a one" (1 Cor. 5:11; see also 2 Thess. 3:14). Other meals besides the Eucharist may well be included in this sanction, but cer-tainly the Eucharist would be the occasion par excellence for shunning the person under discipline. Some such bounding of the ritual meal is probably reflected in the curse pronounced at the conclusion of First Corinthians: "If anyone does not love the Lord, let him be banned. *Marana tha*" (16:22). The marked similarity between this anathema and a line in the eucharistic ritual prescribed by the Didache (the earliest extant "manual of church order," dating perhaps from the beginning of the second century) has persuaded a number of modern commentators that such a solemn pronouncement was already in use in the meetings of the Pauline groups.[139] We have already seen that Paul interpreted the "communion" with Christ represented in the eating of bread and drinking of wine in a way that precluded Christian participation in any recognizably cultic meal in a pagan setting (1 Cor. 10:15–22).

These examples indicate that the Pauline groups were having to discover workable means for drawing boundaries around themselves. The Pauline school had self-consciously abandoned the rules of purity that helped to maintain the social boundaries of the Jewish communities, for in a communi-ty composed largely of former gentiles these rules were dysfunctional—and, for Paul, they appeared to deny the newness of the gospel of the crucified and risen Messiah. A whole second-order or symbolic system for mapping the sacred and the profane was thus discarded. It was no longer particular foods or closely defined events or actions that rendered a person "unclean," and there were new rituals and occasions that established "holiness" or "purity." It was necessary, therefore, to define the purity of the community more directly in social terms. For example, Paul declares that the Supper has certain magical effects, including physical illness or even death, on people who vio-late the norms appropriate to the sacred occasion (1 Cor. 11:29f.). Yet these violations are not ritual errors in the narrow sense, but offenses against the social cohesion of the group caused by tensions between people of higher and lower social and economic positions. So, too, the one excluded from fellow-ship by the curse in 1 Cor. 16:22 is not one stigmatized by a ritual flaw, but whoever "does not love the Lord."[140]

Autonomous Institutions
One means of promoting the isolation of the group was the creation of institutions to perform services for which its members would otherwise have relied upon municipal or other outside organizations. The term *institution* is

used here in a broad sense and does not imply a high level of formality or complexity in the organized activities in question. The communal meals would be one example. For many members, especially those of the humbler social strata, the Christian assemblies and meals provided a more than adequate substitute for benefits, both physical and social, that they might otherwise have obtained from membership in collegia of various sorts or from the various municipal festivals.[141] A still clearer example appears in the admonitions of 1 Cor. 6:1–11. Verses 2–5 imply that Paul expects the church to establish internal procedures to judge civil disputes between Christians, with selected "sages" among them acting as arbiters. The fact that the second half of the passage (vss. 6–11) chides them for having suits at all and urges an other-regarding ethic that would eliminate such competition[142] does not cancel the practical directive. The Christians, as those destined to share in the eschatological judgment of the whole world, of men as well as of angels, are surely competent to set up a panel to arbitrate matters of everyday life (*biō-tika pragmata*) among themselves. They must not perpetrate the absurdity of letting outsiders ("unjust," "unbelievers," "those despised in the assembly") decide internal conflicts.[143]

There are other, less specific, more pervasive ways in which the life of these close-knit groups tends to displace a member's dependence on other groups and on the culture of the larger society. One of the fundamental services that groups perform for their members in our modern, highly complex and differentiated society is provision of a limited social space within which a consensus may be attained about a perceived reality and its requirements.[144] That function is of course greatly enhanced in a religious or ideological group, in which the adherence of recruits has been focused on a peculiar set of images or explanations of things to be believed, felt, and responded to. Urban society in the early Roman Empire was scarcely less complicated than our own, in proportion to the scale of knowledge available to an individual and of demands made upon him. Its complexity—its untidiness to the mind—may well have been felt with special acuteness by people who were marginal or transient, either physically or socially or both, as so many of the identifiable members of the Pauline churches seem to have been. In any case, Paul and the other founders and leaders of those groups engaged aggressively in the business of creating a new social reality. They held and elaborated a distinctive set of beliefs, some of them expressed in dramatic claims that proved pregnant with metaphor: "Jesus the Messiah, and him crucified." They developed norms and patterns of moral admonition and social control that, however many commonplaces from the moral discourse of the larger culture they might contain, still in ensemble constituted a distinctive ethos. They received, practiced, and explicated distinctive ritual actions. None of these was made *ex nihilo*. All drew upon the common language and culture of the Greek-speaking, Roman provincial cities as well as upon the special subculture of Judaism, which had already over generations adapted to those cities. The resultant, nevertheless, was an evolving definition of a new, visibly different subculture. Each of these three major components of the new subculture will be the subject of a later chapter.

Gates in the Boundaries

The Pauline groups' strong and intimate sense of belonging, their special beliefs and norms, their perception of their own discreteness from "the world," did not lead them to withdraw into the desert, like the Essenes of Qumran. They remained in the cities, and their members continued to go about their ordinary lives in the streets and neighborhoods, the shops and agora. Paul and the other leaders did not merely permit this continued interaction as something inevitable; in several instances they positively encouraged it.

The most direct statement to this point is in 1 Cor. 5:9–13, in which Paul corrects a misunderstanding of a previous admonition:

I wrote to you in the [previous] letter not to mix with *pornoi* [violators of the various norms of sexual behavior]—not at all [or, perhaps, "not in the absolute sense"][145] [meaning] the *pornoi* of this world or the greedy people and robbers or idolaters, since in that case you would be obliged to get out of the world. On the contrary, I wrote "not to mix" if someone called a brother were a *pornos* or a greedy person or idolater or slanderer or drunkard or robber—not even to eat with someone like that. For what business is it of mine to judge the outsiders? Is it not rather the insiders that you judge? As for the outsiders, God will judge them.

In this context, in which he directs the expulsion of a member who has violated the incest taboo, the purity of the community is Paul's central concern. However, he is at pains to make clear that this purity is contaminated only from within, not by contact with the outsiders, even though the latter are considered typically immoral. In some later ascetic forms of Christianity, including some that appealed to Paul as an example, "going out of the world" was the chief preoccupation of a Christian. Here it is treated as an impossibility within an argument of *reductio ad absurdum*.

We have already seen that similar sentiments were at work in the discussion of eating "meat offered to idols" in 1 Cor. 8–10. Although Paul strongly defends the conscience of the "weak" Christian for whom sacrificial meat seemed a real threat to purity, and although he forbids any action that could be construed as real participation in a pagan cult, yet he is careful to preserve the freedom of Christians to use the pagan meatmarkets and to accept invitations for meals in pagan homes. We have also seen that, despite the stated preference for marriages only between Christians, Paul encouraged the preservation of existing marriages with pagan spouses whenever possible (1 Cor. 7:12–16). Both the mission and the self-defense of the church are reasons to encourage openness toward the world in these instances. Paul states the missionary motivation candidly in the case of marriages with pagans: "What do you know, woman, may you not save your husband? What do you know, man, may you not save your wife?"[146]

Further, the ordering of the internal life of the sect takes place not in complete isolation, but with an eye toward how outsiders will perceive the Christians. The artisan ethic of "a quiet life" (*hēsychia*), supported by hard work and minding one's own business, has as its purpose "that your behavior may be decent in the view of the outsiders" (1 Thess. 4:11f.). Ecstatic demonstrations in assemblies of the church are to be curbed lest unbelievers coming in (they are thus assumed to have free access to these meetings) should think the Christians possessed or insane (1 Cor. 14:23). The Corinthian Christians are urged to put no stumbling block before "Jews and Greeks and God's assembly" (1 Cor. 10:32), and Paul cites here again his own missionary adaptability (vs. 33; cf. 9:19–23). The same pattern persists in the later letters of the Pauline school and in other groups of later Christians.[147] Colossians 4:5 lays down a general rule, parallel to that already attested in 1 Thess. 4:12: "Behave wisely toward the outsiders, and cash in your opportunity." To behave wisely means here to behave in a manner that is in accord not only with the moral norms of the community, which are "the will of God" (compare the parallel in Eph. 5:15f.), but also with standards that the outsiders recognize as good.[148] More and more, the deutero-Pauline paraenesis depicts the basic structure of the Christian groups in terms of the hierarchically ordered household that was regarded as fundamental to all Greco-Roman society. Emphasis upon that order, by means of so-called *Haustafeln* (such as Col. 3:18–4:1; Eph. 5:21–6:9), serves as a defense against the typical objection which Greco-Roman writers urged against novel cults: that they corrupt households and hence threaten the basis of the whole social fabric.[149]

In only one passage in the authentic Pauline letters is attention explicitly directed to the political authorities. The Christian groups' interactions and difficulties with the larger society seem to have come about, at this early stage, through the less formal social structures. It is commonly acknowledged that in Rom. 13:1–7 Paul is using a form of paraenesis that had been formulated by the diaspora Jewish communities. The "authorities" to which Christians are urged here to be submissive are the functionaries of the imperial government rather than the municipal magistrates. Jews in the provincial cities habitually depended upon good relations with the imperial court and its delegates, especially when local opposition arose.[150] The picture of the state is idealized in this context, but the experience of urban Jews on numerous occasions vindicated the advocacy of this ideal as their best policy, and the Pauline Christians followed their example. It is significant that the dualistic language that the Pauline groups sometimes used in their paraenesis (even later in the same chapter, Rom. 13:11–14) is not applied to the Roman power. The demonic "rulers" (*archontes*) are not identified as the real power behind the human ones, as they were, for example, in the Qumran Jewish sect's ideology or in Revelation.[151]

In addition to these practical concerns that led the Pauline Christians to continue their participation in the broader life of their cities, their special language contained a number of metaphorical and symbolic complexes that could be construed to imply some ultimate unity among all people. The initiatory ritual of baptism, although it was evidently a boundary-setting ceremony, stressing the liminal unity of the initiates as distinct from the divisive structures of the "old human," nevertheless also portrayed that sectarian unity with images of universal import. The Christ who was "put on" with clothing after baptism was the "new human," the "last Adam," the "image of the Creator." At least some of the Pauline Christians spoke in their reminders of baptism of a cosmic reconciliation between superhuman as well as human powers. That sort of imagery is particularly evident in the deutero-Pauline Ephesians and Colossians.[152] For Paul himself and for his disciple who wrote Ephesians the unity of humankind is dramatically realized in the equality of Jew and gentile within the church. The joining together in one household of those who were formerly at enmity and estranged is in Ephesians the chief instance of God's secret plan of "the fullness of times, to sum up the universe in Christ, the things in heaven and the things on earth" (1:9f.; 2:11–22). In the peroration of his long discourse to the Roman Christians on the problem of the Jews' having mostly rejected Jesus as Messiah, Paul enunciates an extraordinary vision of the time "when the fullness of the gentiles comes in, and thus all Israel will be saved" (Rom. 11:25f.).

The import of this universal imagery is ambiguous. A sect that claims to be the unique possessor of what it construes to be a universally desirable value—a monopoly on salvation—does not necessarily welcome free interchange with outsiders; more often the contrary. The cosmic imagery of the Pauline school's baptismal language was used in the admonitions of Colossians and Ephesians specifically to strengthen the internal cohesion of the Christian groups.[153] Yet one of the most obvious facts about the movement associated with Paul and his fellows was the vigor of its missionary drive, which saw in the outsider a potential insider and did not want to cut off communication with him or her. In this respect the ethos of Pauline Christianity is significantly more open than that, say, of the introverted Johannine groups.[154] There is a tension in the literature of the Pauline groups between measures needed to promote a strong internal cohesion, including rather clear boundaries separating it from the larger society, and the intention to continue normal and generally acceptable interactions with outsiders.

A WORLDWIDE PEOPLE

The local groups of Christians not only enjoyed a high level of cohesion and group identity, they also were made aware that they belonged to a larger movement, "with all who invoke the name of our Lord Jesus Christ in every place" (1 Cor. 1:2).[155] In time they would invent a unique network of institutions to embody and protect this connection, and the resultant combination of intimate, disciplined local communities with a supralocal organization was a major factor in the social and political success of Christianity in the age of Constantine. Our earliest sources show both aspects of that double identity already at work. According to Adolf von Harnack, "It was this, and not any evangelist, which proved to be the most effective missionary."[156]

The unusual nature of the claim being made about the identity of the believers in Messiah Jesus becomes apparent from the way in which Paul and his associates used the term *ekklēsia*—a word that we habitually translate "church." We employ this anachronism, which cannot fail to mislead, because the urban Christians seem early on to have begun using the term in a peculiar way that must have been puzzling to any ordinary Greek. The commonest use of *ekklēsia* was to refer to the town meeting of free male citizens of a city of Greek constitution, and it continued to be so employed even though the Hellenistic and then the Roman monarchies had robbed the voting assemblies of much of their power.[157] There are passages in the Pauline letters which seem almost to mimic or parody that usage, as when those addressed are "the *ekklēsia* of the Thessalonians" or of the Laodiceans (1 Thess. 1:1; 2 Thess. 1:1; Col. 4:16),[158] or when all in a given town "come together in *ekklēsia*" (1 Cor. 11:18; cf. 14:19, 23, 28, 35).[159] The term is also used, though, for the smallest cell of the Christian movement, the household assembly (*hē kat' oikon ekklēsia*).[160] This usage superficially resembles the designation by some Greek clubs of their business meetings,[161] but the epistolary context shows that "meeting" would not be an adequate translation—unless, perhaps, we think of "The Friends' Meeting of Newtown." *Ekklēsia* names not just the occasional gathering, but the group itself.

Moreover, it names all Christian groups everywhere, considered either severally or as a whole. Paul can speak of the *ekklēsiai* (plural) of a province—Galatia, Asia, Macedonia, Judea (1 Cor. 16:1; 16:19; Gal. 1:2; 2 Cor. 8:1; 1 Thess. 2:14)—but also of "all the *ekklēsiai* of the gentiles" (Rom. 16:4) and "all the *ekklēsiai* of Christ" (Rom. 16:16) or "of God" (1 Cor. 11:16, 22; 2 Thess. 1:4).[162] But he, and even more often his disciples who wrote Ephesians and Colossians, can use the singular not only in general rules that apply to any local assembly, but also in phrases that embrace the entire Christian movement.[163] Most striking among these passages is the phrase "the *ekklēsia* of God," which stands alongside "Jews and Greeks" (1 Cor. 10:32), but which was also used of a local community, as in the case of "the *ekklēsia* of God that is in Corinth" (1 Cor. 1:2).[164] The roots of this usage are certainly in the biblical phrase "assembly of the Lord" (*ekklēsia tou kyriou*, translating *qᵉhal yhwh*), which referred to a formal gathering of all the tribes of ancient Israel or their representatives.[165] Jewish writers near the time of Paul repeat this biblical usage with minor modifications, and the Qumran community used the phrase "assembly of God" to refer to a cultic assembly of the faithful at the end of days, for the final war or for a solemn meal with the anointed priest and prince.[166] The precise connection between such usage and that of Paul is elusive, but there can be little doubt that the concept of belonging to a single, universal people of God, which so distinguished the Pauline Christians from other clubs and cults, came directly from Judaism.

It is evident, too, that Paul and the other leaders of the mission worked actively to inculcate the notion of a universal brotherhood of the believers in Messiah Jesus. The letters themselves, the messengers who brought them, and the repeated visits to the local assemblies by Paul and his associates all emphasized this interrelatedness. It is noteworthy that the places where the household assemblies are mentioned are all in the context of greetings in letter closings or (in Philemon) openings. The smallest unit of the movement is addressed precisely in the epistolary context that reminds the readers of the larger fellowship by mentioning names and groups in other places. The salutations and greetings sometimes link the addressees with all Christians in their province or elsewhere, say, not only Corinth but also "all the saints who are in the whole of Achaia" (2 Cor. 1:1), "all who invoke the name of our Lord Jesus Christ in every place" (1 Cor. 1:2). In Colossians 4:13 the churches of the Lycus valley are associated, and Laodicea and Colossae are especially connected by the directive in 4:16 that the letter to each should be read to the other.[167] The close of First Corinthians is also suggestive: "The *ekklēsiai* of Asia greet you; Aquila and Prisca and their household *ekklēsia* greet you much in the Lord. All the brothers greet you. Greet one another with a holy kiss. I, Paul, greet you in my own hand" (16:19–21). The ritual kiss—a most intimate expression of the *communitas* experienced in the local meeting—is thus placed within the context of reminders of a much wider fellowship. The language is at once formal and personal.

If the letters were reminders of connections beyond the local scene, the apostolic visits, for which the letters were interim substitutes,[168] were even more direct ones. The amount of travel by the leaders of the Pauline mission has often surprised ancient and modern readers. Embedded in the letters are a number of passages that serve as letters of recommendation, requesting hospitality for travelers.[169] Later, such letters of recommendation would benefit all traveling Christians, not just the leaders.[170] There are hints in the Pauline letters and elsewhere in the New Testament that ordinary Christians traveling to another city could already expect to find accommodation with "brothers," very likely following a custom established among diaspora Jews.[171] Thus hospitality is already among the virtues of the Christian common life stressed in the traditional admonitions Paul includes in his letter to the Romans (12:13). Later the Epistle to the Hebrews and the letter of the Roman church to Corinth would, like contemporary Jews, adduce the example of Abraham (Heb. 13:2; 1 Clem. 10:7), and hospitality becomes a virtue especially required of bishops.[172] E. A. Judge's comments about the later practice can with scant exaggeration be applied already to the first century:

Security and hospitality when traveling had traditionally been the privilege of the powerful, who had relied upon a network of patronage and friendship, created by wealth. The letters of recommendation disclose the fact that these domestic advantages were now extended to the whole household of faith, who are accepted on trust, though complete strangers.[173]

Here was a most concrete reminder of what it meant to belong to the *ekklēsia* of God that could welcome one as "brother" or "sister" in Laodicea, Ephesus, Corinth, or Rome.

Quite a different sort of reminder of Christians' obligations to one another across geographic boundaries is the collection of money for "the poor among the saints in Jerusalem," to which Paul seems to have devoted a great deal of his energy during the final years of his career. At the meeting in Jerusalem between the Antioch representatives and the Jerusalem "pillars," Paul and Barnabas had undertaken a formal obligation to "remember the poor" (Gal. 2:10), and Paul evidently regarded that obligation as incumbent not only on the Antiochene Christians but also on the later converts of Asia Minor and Greece. Despite some resistance and suspicions among the latter, he mobilized a large effort, with the aid of Titus and certain unnamed delegates appointed by the churches, to collect the money and send it, accompanied by a whole retinue of representatives from the local groups, to Jerusalem.[174] Paul's motivation and theological grounds for this undertaking have been the object of several inquiries in recent years,[175] but as Klaus Berger and Bengt Holmberg have complained, not enough attention has been paid to the way the collection was understood by the local Pauline congregations and by the Jewish Christians and Jews in Jerusalem.[176] Each may have had a quite different view, as Berger suggests: for the Jerusalem group, it provided a means of legitimating the Pauline mission on terms familiar in Judaism; as far as the Jews were concerned, the Pauline groups were gentiles, but their alms could show sympathy and unity with Israel. For the Pauline communities themselves, "the alms for the poor Jewish-Christians means nothing less than their oneness with the congregation in Jerusalem; it has demonstrative character, and its acceptance by the Jerusalem congregation confirms their own groups' status. . . ."[177] The collection effort proved disastrous. If it was accepted at all by the Jerusalem group, it must have been in such a way as to imply the second-class status of the gentile Christians.[178] Even so, the presence of Paul with the representatives of the gentile churches was a provocation to some faction in the Jewish community, leading to Paul's arrest and the end of his career. Nevertheless, these results should not obscure the fact that the Pauline communities did join together in an extraordinary labor to demonstrate their sense that they, "like branches of wild olive, contrary to nature," had been grafted into the one people of God. Long after the Jerusalem community ceased to exist, that concept would continue, in divers ways, to affect the self-understanding of the Christian movement.

4

GOVERNANCE

In the previous chapter we considered some of the elements that gave the Pauline Christians a sense of belonging, a cohesiveness both in the intimate household groups in particular cities and in their knowledge of being part of a larger movement, the "*ekklēsia* of God." We now need to examine the organizational dimension of their solidarity. No group can persist for any appreciable time without developing some patterns of leadership, some differentiation of roles among its members, some means of managing conflict, some ways of articulating shared values and norms, and some sanctions to assure acceptable levels of conformity to those norms. We would like to know what sorts of persons were able to issue commands or make recommendations that would ordinarily be accepted by members of the churches Paul and his associates had founded. And we want to know why the followers obeyed. These questions bring us into the obscure territory of the structure of authority, which fortunately has been explored in some detail in two recent monographs by Schütz (1975) and Holmberg (1978). The following discussion owes much to both.

DEALING WITH CONFLICT

A good way to begin our inquiry is to consider several specific instances of conflict reflected in the letters, to see who asserts or exercises authority, what kinds of norms are stated or implied, what sanctions used, and with what results. Here we are interested not so much in the substantive issues under dispute, about which much has been written in recent years, as in their forms and in the procedures by which they were handled.

Jerusalem and Antioch

The question on what terms gentiles would be admitted to the Christian movement was a divisive one, as we have already seen. The issue first erupted at Antioch, and Barnabas and Paul, as representatives of the Christian community there, went up to Jerusalem to consult with leaders of the original congregation. According to Paul, the decision to go to Jerusalem was made "by revelation" (Gal. 2:2). That statement does not necessarily contradict the

111

report in Acts 15:2 that the Antioch assembly "ordered" them to go, for the revelation may well have occurred through a congregational prophet, the casting of lots, or some other means of inspired decision. We cannot so easily resolve some of the other differences between the two accounts, but there is no need to rehearse here the long debate about them.[1] The author of Acts was using a source or sources that in some respects contradicted what Paul reports to the Galatians, and the didactic purposes of Acts may have still further obscured the events. Paul, even more obviously, has an apologetic purpose in the Letter to Galatians, but as a participant writing within at most a decade of the events he has first claim on our credence. Fortunately the facts most important for our inquiry are reasonably clear.

The dispute was about circumcision,[2] that is, whether the gentiles who had joined the followers of Jesus at Antioch must now undergo the normal rite of incorporation into the Jewish community. Nevertheless, the dispute was internal to the Christian movement. It was not members of the larger Jewish community who raised the issue, but "brothers"—though to be sure Paul brands them "false brothers." Accordingly, in the attempt to settle the issue, the congregation resorts not to the *archontes* or *gerousia* of the Antiochene Jews, but to the eminent people (*hoi dokountes*) or "pillars" of the church in Jerusalem. The author of Acts supposes a more complex organization in Jerusalem: like other religious associations, the whole community, led by a council of elders (*gerousia*), assembles for important decisions with the twelve apostles, who are perhaps construed as a sort of executive committee (*prytania* or *decania*). Such an organization, unmentioned by Paul, may in fact have existed, but it is also possible that the Acts picture is of a later style of organization, which it projects onto the past. Both accounts report full agreement between the principals: the gentile converts are not required to be circumcised. Beyond that the sources diverge on the style and scope of the decision. In Acts a solemn decree is issued by authority of "the apostles and the elders with the whole assembly" (15:22),[3] laying down ritual as well as moral rules for the gentile Christians. The author of Acts was not the first to believe that Jerusalem had issued such a formal regulation, for Paul finds it necessary to insist that the leaders "added nothing to me," except "only that we should remember the poor" (Gal. 2:6, 10).[4] And Paul reports not an edict but an agreement between equal parties, with the "eminent" Cephas, James, and John on the one side, Paul and Barnabas on the other, sealed by "the right hand of partnership."[5]

The agreement was short-lived. For a time the solidarity of Jew and gentile in the Antioch groups was celebrated by common meals, in which even Peter, who had arrived from Jerusalem, participated.[6] Yet when "certain persons from James" appeared, Peter and all the other Jewish Christians except Paul—even Barnabas, his closest associate—withdrew from such meals, and Paul was left isolated (Gal. 2:11–13). Did the Jerusalem agreement not deal with the question of commensality between those who did and did not observe *kashrut*? Or had the situation in Jerusalem changed abruptly when Peter's departure broke up the triumvirate and left James, as "the Lord's brother," in effective control? We do not know. We see only that this time the dispute was settled at the cost of a division among the Christians at Antioch—a clear defeat for Paul, however effectively, in his defense to the Galatians, he contrasts his consistency with the inconsistency of the others. After the showdown with Peter, Paul's activities shifted to Asia Minor and mainland Greece.[7]

What does this episode, or what we can know of it, teach us about the development of organization among the early Christians? First, we see that within two decades of Jesus' death the community of those who believed in his messiahship and resurrection had become a distinct sect among the Jews, not only in Jerusalem but in several places outside Palestine, including the metropolis of Antioch. Their own leaders had emerged, though their relationships were still fluid, and they settled their disputes within their own movement. Moreover, the sect had already reached beyond the Jewish community to convert, on its own, gentiles—although exactly what that meant was precisely the point in dispute. Second, we see a concern for unity and conformity. What happened among Christians in Antioch mattered to those in Jerusalem, and vice versa. The free movement of figures from one "church" to another, some as delegates (apostoloi ekklēsiōn), others with no other authorization or legitimation than their conviction that the Spirit had called them, was a constant fact of early Christian life, and these figures often intervened to "correct" the beliefs or practices of the communities they visited. Third, the primary means for resolving conflict seems to have been meeting and talking. Later, as we shall see, the apostolic letter becomes a substitute for face-to-face discussion when travel is inconvenient. No formal means for settling disputes had been established, but some leaders had emerged both in Jerusalem and in Antioch, and the very process of dealing with dissent was leading to the consolidation of authority and the discovery or invention of more formal means of making decisions.

None of this tells us much about the specific organization of Pauline Christianity. Indeed, there is reason to take Paul's defeat in Antioch as the starting point for his formation of a more clearly distinct and self-conscious missionary organization of his own.[8] That did not mean, of course, that he ceased to be interested in continuity with the traditions of Israel or in unity with the Jewish Christians of Jerusalem. But he and the associates whom he now gathered around him would develop their own techniques for maintaining contact among the new congregations they were founding.

Letters and Visits

Foremost among the techniques that the Pauline mission invented were return visits by the missionaries to the groups they had planted and, when a visit was not possible, letters. We noted already in chapter 3 the importance of these contacts for the development of perceptions and attitudes, a sense of solidarity transcending the local groups. But these communications also afforded the means of more direct and specific attempts at social control. There were instructions to be given, often in response to reports of specific local problems; there were general reminders of the mode of life deemed appropriate for the new faith; there were arguments against viewpoints that Paul regarded as unacceptable; there were even directives for quite specific actions such as the discipline of deviants and procedures for the Jerusalem collection.

A REMINDER TO THESSALONICA. The importance of emissaries and the potential of the letter as a means of social control are already evident in the earliest Christian letter that has survived, that from Paul, Silvanus, and Timothy to the Thessalonian Christians. After establishing Christian cells in the Macedonian cities, Paul and his companions had moved southward into Greece (the Roman province of Achaia). In Athens Paul became anxious about the recent converts in Thessalonica, apparently having heard that they were experiencing some hostile pressure from their neighbors,[9] and dispatched Timothy to "strengthen and exhort" them and to find out how they were faring (1 Thess. 3:1–5). When Timothy returned with good news, Paul sent off the letter we have, the purpose of which was also "to strengthen and exhort."[10]

Very little in 1 Thessalonians is presented as new instruction. Apart from the words of consolation in 4:13–18, with the apocalyptic scene of Jesus' imminent return, the admonitions of the letter consist of reminders of things that "you yourselves know." Such reminders are typical, as Malherbe has shown,[11] of the Hellenistic moral rhetoric called paraenesis, and the kind of morality advocated in 1 Thessalonians is not much different, in terms of the behavior advocated, from what one might hear from an Epictetus or a Dio Chrysostom. Nevertheless, the writers cite some specific examples of rules that were taught the converts earlier, in which we see the beginnings of a special Christian language of moral obligation. Like the exhortations themselves, the warrants for obeying also take the form of reminders.

Formally the most striking feature of the letter is the disproportionately long opening thanksgiving. As we saw in the previous chapter, it dwells in rich, affective language on the personal connections between the authors and the recipients. As such, it goes far beyond the standard expressions of friendly feeling in ordinary private letters,[12] first by extending the lines of friendship to other groups of Christians elsewhere in Macedonia, in Achaia, and in Judea,[13] and second by placing the whole in a christological and theological context. And this complex reminder of the previously established relationships becomes the basis for and context of the exhortations.

The warrants for behavior are thus not so candidly stated here as they would be in situations of conflict, but are implicit in the design of the letter. Authoritative models are cited for imitation—the apostles, Christ himself, and other groups of Christians. And the Thessalonian Christians themselves are congratulated for having served as models (typoi: 1:7) for others, with the implication that the eyes of those others are still upon them. Their good beginning is repeatedly stressed; they must continue in the same road, only "abundantly." These human obligations, however, are set within the context of the eschatological action of God.[14] The Thessalonians are admonished to "behave in a way worthy of the God who calls you into his kingdom and glory" (2:12). The pleasure of the affection between apostle and congregation is itself connected with the joy to be experienced at the coming (*parousia*) of Jesus and the final judgment and reward (2:19f.), and the stresses they have experienced are defined as belonging to those that were "destined" in the eschatological plan (3:2–4).

First Thessalonians thus shows how Paul fashioned the letter into an instrument for extending through time and space his instruction of converts. In this instance, in which no conflict demands specific attention, the paraenetic letter serves to reinforce previous instruction and, by emphasis on the personal network to which the addressees belong and on the theological basis and context of that network, to shape the community's ways of thinking and talking about itself that go to make a distinctive group ethos. When conflict did break out in Pauline groups, Paul and his fellow missionaries were ready to adapt the letter quite boldly to deal with new issues.

REFORMERS IN GALATIA. The letter that is most clearly a response to a particular conflict is that to the Galatians. In Paul's absence other Christian missionaries had appeared in the Anatolian cities, seeking to persuade Paul's converts that their faith was imperfect and their salvation in question unless they were circumcised and observed at least Sabbath and Jewish festivals (*kashrut* is not specifically mentioned). Paul sees this as a direct attack on his own authority as apostle and founder of the Galatian churches and as a perversion of the one gospel. Accordingly he mounts a counterattack through this carefully composed letter. He undertakes to persuade the Galatian Christians that he is a true and reliable apostle. To abandon the form of the gospel that he proclaimed to them would not mean an advance toward perfection, but a falling away from Christ, back into a slavery no better than paganism. The freedom from the Jewish law that he had announced to gentile converts was no mere strategy, but the will of God for the messianic age, taught consistently by Paul everywhere, solemnly acknowledged by the Jerusalem Christian leaders, and defended with great pain by Paul when others proved inconstant.[15]

The argument is too intricate to unfold here, but it is important for our purposes to see the kinds of appeals it contains.[16] First, there is an appeal to revelation. Paul insists that the gospel the Galatians heard from him was not based on human tradition and teaching, but was "a revelation of Jesus Christ" (1:12). He does not mean, presumably, that he did not receive and hand on certain traditional forms of preaching, creedal statements, ritual patterns, and the like, for elsewhere he states flatly that he did (1 Cor. 15:1–8; 11:2, 23–26), and some of those traditions, especially from the baptismal ritual, are important to the argument of Galatians. Rather, it is Paul's manner of preaching the gospel that he here defends as "revealed." His special revelation was a commission, like that to the classic scriptural prophets, "to preach [God's Son] among the gentiles" (1:16); it was his apostolate that was "not from humans nor through human agency" (1:1).

The appeal to revelation occurs within the autobiographical apology that occupies the first part of Paul's argument. The personal experience of the apostle is thus the second basis of appeal. He insists that his radicalness in releasing gentile proselytes from the Law was not *his* idea. On the contrary, he had been a "zealot" for the "traditions of the fathers" before God intervened and set him on a different road (1:13–16). Further, his actions after that revelation showed his indifference henceforth to human authorities (1:16–2:14). The "pillars" in Jerusalem could add nothing to his authority, and although he was happy to report their approval of his mission and to join them in partnership so long as they did, he had been ready to stand alone against even Peter and all the Jewish Christians at Antioch when he saw them "not walking straight toward the truth of the gospel" (2:14). Thus Paul's narrative of his own experiences serves to refute the rumors circulating in Galatia that he preaches circumcision elsewhere (5:11) but omitted the requirement in Galatia "to please human beings" (1:10). At the same time it shows that his consistency, to the point of obstinacy, is rooted in a unique revelation. The first two appeals are thus so presented that they reinforce one another.

The third appeal is also to experience—the experience of the Galatian Christians themselves. This appeal, too, is partly interwoven with his own apologia, for the addressees are part of that narrative, and the extraordinary trust and affection which they showed Paul when he first appeared in their cities (4:12–14) are now cited as a reminder of the sort of relationship that is threatened (4:15–20). In part, the reminder refers to benefits that the converts received, without assistance from the Law: the Spirit, miracles (3:1–5), freedom from the demonic powers of paganism (4:8f.). A wealth of rhetorical devices clothes this appeal: curses and threats on the one hand, reminders of blessings on the other, ironic rebukes, shaming and sarcasm. All are ways of suggesting to the addressees that they are in danger of committing irreparable folly and of recalling them to their earlier sound judgment. Very likely the admonitions at the end of the letter, for which commentators have devised such improbable hypotheses as "a second front" and "gnostic libertinism in Galatia," are also an extension of the reminder; the string of imperatives begins already in 4:12: "Become like me, as I (have become) like you, brothers," introducing the reminder of Paul's first arrival. The paraenesis that follows, introduced by the allegory of Sarah and Hagar, summons the addressees to a life of freedom, led by the Spirit not by law; this life produces mutual care and responsibility, precludes vices, and produces virtues as "the Spirit's fruit." As usual in paraenesis, these are not novelties, but reminders of the life the Christians already enjoyed after their initiation by Paul, for they had been "running well" (5:7).

A fourth major appeal, central to the construction of the letter, is to scripture. Paul does not merely quote proof-texts here, but in 3:1–4:11 constructs an extremely subtle argument in which an ingenious interplay among several texts serves as the fundamental warrant. The techniques are similar to those found commonly in the later collections of rabbinic midrash. Moreover, an understanding of the argument requires not only knowledge of the texts cited and alluded to, but also of certain traditions of interpretation, some of which have become recognizable to us only since the recovery of the Dead Sea Scrolls.[17] In a quite different style, in 4:21–31, Paul introduces the story of Sarah and Hagar as a homiletic model supporting the admonitions that follow.[18]

CONFUSION IN CORINTH. The extended correspondence between Paul and the Corinthian Christians has left us a picture of conflict on several levels, about several issues. We have already examined some aspects of this situation in chapters 2 and 3. The words *power* and *authority* and derivatives occur frequently in these letters,[19] often in a context of irony, that is, in a context that requires reversal of their ordinary meaning. The use of irony suggests both that power was important to the addressees and that the writers wanted to alter the way power was conceived. The conflicts are in large measure directly *about* authority; they are questions about who makes decisions and who has to obey, and why. Furthermore, the letters themselves are instruments used intentionally to exert authority; they therefore exhibit the strategies of influence that Paul and his co-workers thought would be effective.

One way of experiencing power in a group is to identify oneself with a figure regarded by the group as powerful. That tendency was at least one of the latent motives among the factions that Paul had heard about, whatever else may have been implied by the enigmatic slogans he attributes to the Corinthians in 1 Cor. 1:10–13: "I am Paul's, I am Apollos's, I am Cephas's, I am Christ's." Notwithstanding the title of F. C. Baur's famous article published a century ago,[20] it is doubtful that there was a "Christ-party" in Corinth, or even a "Cephas-party." The argument in 1 Cor. 1–4 really deals only with Paul and Apollos, who are mentioned in its rather cryptic peroration: "These things, brothers, I have modified to speak of myself and Apollos, for your sake, that you may learn 'nothing beyond what is written,' and may not be inflated, each for the one and against the other" (4:6). The jealousy between the partisans of the two great teachers that this rebuke implies evidently stemmed in part from invidious comparisons between the rhetorical abilities of Apollos (called an *anēr logios,* "a man of rhetoric," in Acts 18:24) and of Paul, for Paul's apology in these four chapters contains quite a few disparaging comments about rhetoric. There was more to the division than that, however; it also had to do with being baptized by or in the name of one or another personage, so that Paul is reluctant to admit that he baptized anyone in Corinth (1:14–17). For at least some of the Corinthian Christians, baptism meant initiation into a spiritual realm, to enjoy already the benefits of the world to come: possession of the Spirit, heavenly knowledge, and wisdom. Evidently some felt that they had received from *their* apostle a richer endowment than others had, while perhaps others felt independent of both, being themselves "Christ's persons." In any case certain leaders, of whom Stephanas was probably the principal, persuaded the church to send a formal letter to Paul, by an official delegation, to ask his advice about a whole series of problems (7:1, 25; 8:1; 12:1; 16:1, 15–18). Nils Dahl has ingeniously suggested that the decision to send that delegation may itself have precipitated the factions, with some wanting to inquire of Apollos instead, others of the famous Cephas (although there is no evidence that he had ever visited Corinth), while others, claiming to embody Christ's spirit themselves, saw no need for any outside help.[21] Certainly there were some at Corinth who doubted the wisdom of asking Paul's advice, for they expected never to see him again (4:18). And it was not from the official letter that Paul heard about the factions, but from members of Chloe's household who happened to come to Ephesus (1:11).

Paul's letter must have accomplished some of its objectives, for we hear nothing in 2 Corinthians about the factions named in 1 Cor. 1:12, nor about comparisons of Paul with Apollos, nor about the specific problems dealt with in 1 Cor. 7–15.[22] The letter had not, however, put to rest the discontent with Paul's authority, nor the longing of some Corinthian Christians to attach themselves to leaders more self-evidently grand. At some time later, some new traveling apostles not of Paul's circle arrived in Corinth. Disparaging Paul as "weak" and his rhetorical ability as "contemptible," they quickly found an enthusiastic following. We can see how deeply Paul was stung, and how seriously he viewed the danger, from the fierceness of his sarcasm in 2 Cor. 10–13. We also get glimpses of some of the features of "the superapostles" (as Paul contemptuously labels them) that won the admiration of their Corinthian partisans: a Jewish pedigree (11:22); impressive physical presence (10:7, 10); perhaps letters of recommendation (3:1–3); and, above all, rhetorical skill (10:10; 11:6), including mastery of rhetorical boasting to show by means of *synkrisis* (rhetorical comparison) their superiority to other practitioners of the art (10:12–18)[23] and a "professional" attitude toward financial support by their admirers (11:7–11; 12:14–18);[24] probably also reports of mystical or apocalyptic revelations (12:1–10); possibly performance of miracles (12:12). Paul manages through his sarcasm to remind the Corinthian Christians that he, too, could claim many of these same legitimacy norms if that were a game worth playing. By bracketing such statements with the disclaimer that it is all "foolishness," he contrives simultaneously to demonstrate his own rhetorical skill and to denigrate rhetorical efforts generally, but he appears also to be trying to set forth a different vision of authority altogether.[25] We shall examine that vision later.

Apart from alliances with significant outsiders, there were people in the Corinthian groups who could be called strong in their own right. In chapter 2 we found reason to conclude that a number of these owed their power to wealth and position in the city. It was not that they belonged to the Corinthian aristocracy—only Erastus may have had that distinction—but that their relative affluence gave them the means to do things for the Christian groups that most members could not and gave them, too, connections in the city at large that affected their perceptions of social obligation and rights. Not surprisingly, tensions arose between them and poorer members of the church, who doubtless were the majority. In connection with at least two issues the tensions produced overt conflict: the question whether to accept invitations to eat with pagans (1 Cor. 8–10) and the humiliation of the poor in the meetings for the Lord's Supper (1 Cor. 11:17–34).[26] In both cases Paul deplores the exhibition of social and financial advantage in a way that offended the poor or those with "weak" consciences. Nevertheless, he addresses his admonitions primarily to the "strong" and speaks as if he were one of them. The three whom Paul personally baptized in Corinth, Crispus, Gaius, and "the house of Stephanas" (1 Cor. 1:14–16), all belong to this category. Crispus had been head of the synagogue (Acts 18:8); Gaius was "host of the whole assembly" and of Paul himself (Rom. 16:23); Stephanas was probably the leader of the delegation that brought the Corinthians' letter to Paul. Paul singles out Stephanas's household for particular praise because they were the first converts in Achaia and because they have been patrons of the Christian groups in Corinth (1 Cor. 16:15). He admonishes the congregation to "obey such people and all the fellow workers and laborers," and to "acknowledge" them along with the other messengers, Fortunatus and Achaicus (16:16–18).

There was a third means of gaining and using prestige and influence in the Corinthian church: by behavior that the Pauline Christians recognized as directly manifesting the Spirit of God. The sign of the Spirit most highly prized in the Corinthian congregations was "speaking in tongues." If the phenomenon was like that often exhibited in modern groups and which, adopting Paul's Greek term, we call glossolalia—and there is good reason to think that it was[27]—then we can well understand why it would have seemed the premier instance of possession of or by the Spirit. Glossolalia occurs in a trance that exhibits most fully the loss of conscious control and at the same time extraordinary levels of energy, poured out in involuntary utterances and in rapid or sudden bodily movements, profuse sweating, salivation, and so on. The organs of speech seem to be activated, with enormous power, by something beyond the subject's will. That is why the linguist and ethnographer Felicitas Goodman calls the condition "a state of dissociation," in which "the glossolalist switches off cortical control" and then "establishes a connection between his speech center and some subcortical structure."[28] Or, as Paul puts it, "If I pray in a tongue, my spirit is praying, but my mind is barren" (1 Cor. 14:14). The groups that practice glossolalia do not speak of the power that gets control of the speech center as "some subcortical structure," but as a nonhuman power or spirit. For the Christians in Corinth, including Paul, it was the Holy Spirit of God.

Now a person who could so visibly demonstrate, in the assembly of Christians, that the Spirit of God was speaking through him or her certainly held some currency of social power. The difficult question is how that currency was related to the other, more ordinary media of social exchange—linkage with authoritative others and access to money and status. There are some reasons to believe that the different modes of power had come into direct conflict. That glossolalia was a source of some kind of conflict is apparent from the amount of space Paul gives it in his letter—three chapters in our modern versions. Not everyone in the church spoke in tongues (12:30), and those who did—or their followers—looked down on those who did not. But did those who did not speak in tongues include some who exercised other kinds of power? It is plausible. The Spirit is no respecter of persons. Glossolalia is, to pun on Peter Brown's phrase, a kind of "inarticulate power";[29] such power does not usually flow only in the normal channels of authority created by society, with its roles and statuses. A characteristic experience in the onset of the trance is the lifting of inhibitions; conflict between possessed behavior and more structured forms of power would not be surprising. Paul's argument for the control of glossolalia and other *charismata* goes some way toward confirming our suspicion, for he insists that everything in the assemblies should be done "decently and in order" (14:40), he warns that outsiders may think the tongue-speaking Christians are crazy (14:23), he insists that male and female prophets should observe customary codes of sex-specific dress and hair style (11:2–16), and he supports the authority of householders and patrons like Stephanas (16:15–18).

On the other hand, there are reasons to be wary of forming too simple a notion of the structural and antistructural modes of power in Corinth. An extensive body of studies of possession phenomena by modern anthropologists has shown that such behavior is not without structure and is far from independent of its social and cultural settings.[30] Goodman has shown the same for the specific case of glossolalia. Glossolalia is a learned skill, however unconscious its mechanism. The occasions on which it is manifest are to a high degree dependent upon expectations of a specific group, expressed in part through ritualized procedures. Even the characteristic bodily motions accompanying dissociation and some aspects of modulations in the utterances are specific to a particular group and even to the leader who has "taught" the glossolalist. And the interpretation given to glossolalia depends upon the belief system of the group.[31] It is significant that Paul does not reject out of hand the positive evaluation that the Corinthians gave to speaking in tongues, as he might easily have done, say, by deeming it the result of possession by Satan rather than the Holy Spirit. It seems instead that all concerned share the general framework of interpretation, within which it is God's spirit that is at work in glossolalia. It is within that framework that Paul tries to reduce glossolalia's importance in comparison with other gifts. Further, while the social distance between the poorer and wealthier members of the community leads us to expect the more articulated forms of power to be exercised by the latter and the less articulate by the former, it will be recalled from chapter 2 that the prominent members of the Pauline congregations did not enjoy unambiguously high status, but showed instead many signs of status inconsistency. Such people might well be candidates for the more dissociative experiences of the Spirit. Then, too, leaders of a community in which the enthusiasm for glossolalia ran as high as it evidently did at Corinth would find it difficult to remain leaders, no matter what their original platform, unless they were able to exhibit equivalent signs of the Spirit. No wonder Paul is careful to say, "I thank God that I speak in tongues more than all of you" (14:18).

This statement raises the question whether it may not have been Paul himself who taught the Corinthian Christians to value so highly the experience of speaking "in the Spirit," however unhappy he may have become about the direction in which they have taken it. "Receiving the Spirit" is closely connected with baptism in the teachings of the Pauline circle (and probably in most circles of early Christianity), and Paul often harks back to that experience—in his rebuke of the Galatians, as we have seen, and here in 1 Cor. 12.[32] Not only was the moment of baptism surrounded with symbols of a radical change of life—death and rebirth, change of body, destruction of antinomies and restoration of unity[33]—but there is at least some evidence that the baptizand commonly experienced mild dissociation. "God sent the spirit of his Son into our hearts, crying out 'Abba! Father!'" (Gal. 4:6).[34] Crying out on cue the Aramaic word *Abba* presumably bespeaks a lower level of arousal than glossolalia,[35] but it is still a sign of a dissociative state—of control by the Spirit. Paul taught his converts to expect other kinds of experience of the Spirit, too, such as miracles (Gal. 3:5; 1 Cor. 12:10; 2:4; 2 Cor. 12:12). It would be a short step to the discovery, with or without Paul's example, of the deeper and emotionally more powerful trance of glossolalia. We cannot be sure, though, whether there was such a progression.

Tantalizing, too, is the question whether the factions addressed in the first four chapters of 1 Corinthians had anything to do with the problem of "spiritual gifts" discussed in chapters 12–14. As we saw, the factions, too, were connected with some special understanding of baptism, and with the "wisdom" and "knowledge" available to "spiritual" people but not to others. The *communis opinio* among New Testament scholars is that all the problems addressed in 1 Corinthians are somehow connected with the beliefs about the resurrection addressed in chapter 15. It was not, according to this view, that the Corinthians who did "not believe in the resurrection of the dead" were simply skeptical of a future life or that they rejected the "Jewish" notion of bodily resurrection in favor of a "Greek" conception of the soul's escape from the body at death. Rather, they considered that spiritually they were *already* raised up with Christ and "enthroned with him in the heavenly places," as the baptismal liturgy probably stated (Eph. 2:6; cf. 1 Cor. 4:8). Now if we ask how people could imagine and continue to believe over some time that their physical life was unreal or of no consequence and their real life spiritual and transcendent, we might well guess that trance experiences of the sort that produce glossolalia *could* have served as strong reinforcement of that belief. Still, this is only a conjecture. The letter does not refer explicitly to any connection between the Corinthian Christians' realized eschatology and their glossolalia.

We are left then with more suspicions than positive evidence for the interactions among the authority of apostles and their loyal adherents, the authority of wealth and position, and the authority of the spirit-possessed in Corinth. Probably there were conflicts not only between persons but also between different kinds of authority. Undoubtedly the real alignments were more complex than any picture we might construct.

The response by Paul was complex, too. The media he used were those that had already proven themselves: visits by himself and by emissaries, and letters. None was unequivocally successful. Conflicts continued for some time, and although some issues were resolved, others emerged with the arrival of the superapostles, a visit by Paul during which he was insulted, and a painful reaction to a letter (now lost) that he wrote thereafter. A reconstruction of the precise sequence of those events and their ultimate resolution, if any, depends on one's solution to literary problems in 2 Corinthians, which we cannot pursue here. As before, we must be satisfied to catalog the major kinds of appeal that Paul makes.

John Schütz, in his important monograph on Paul's authority, shows that authority is "the interpretation of power."[36] The person in authority focuses and directs the power of those who recognize his authority, not under force, but by their acknowledgment that his directives are "right." Authority is thus "a quality of communication," which entails the belief that the "rightness" of the communication could be demonstrated if need be.[37]

The letters to the Corinthians amply demonstrate the attempt to exert authority as an interpretative enterprise. Paul (with Sosthenes and Timothy) undertakes to reform the Corinthian Christians' perception of power and thereby to persuade them to modify their behavior. The language Paul uses seems chosen to persuade the recipients that the beliefs, attitudes, and behavior that he advocates are in accord with what the Corinthians themselves know or can know. He alludes to things they have learned from him earlier, what is now reported to them, and the experiences they have had. Accordingly, there is very extensive use in these letters of indirect modes of speech, especially irony, sarcasm, and metaphor. The diatribal style, used by teachers to engage their audiences and draw them into the first steps of philosophic reasoning, is used by Paul more in these letters than anywhere else except Romans, where it serves to introduce Paul's gospel to strangers.[38] Much of the discourse here is also corrective, second-order speech; that is, it takes up specific language or specific experiences known to the readers and reinterprets them. Part of the language quoted comes from early Christian traditions, including traditional formulas that Paul himself taught the Corinthian Christians, some of which they have interpreted in ways he finds unsatisfactory.[39] In addition, he parodies, modifies, or refutes slogans that some people are using:

"Everything is permitted me"—but not everything is helpful.
"Everything is permitted me"—but I will not be dominated by anything.

"Food is for the belly and the belly for food, and God will destroy both the one and the other." But the body is not for prostitution, but for the Lord, and the Lord for the body, and God both raised the Lord and will raise us through his power. [1 Cor. 6:12–14]

"We all have *gnōsis.*" *Gnōsis* puffs up; love builds up. If someone thinks he knows something, he does not yet know as he ought to know, but if anyone loves God, he is known by him. [8:1–3]

For the reinterpretation of experiences, Paul's comments on glossolalia are a particularly vivid example. He insists on the equality of all spiritual *charismata,* but he puts the Corinthians' favorite, "tongues," at the bottom of his lists (1 Cor. 12:8–10, 28, 29f.). He includes in his list of gifts functions that involve no extraordinary mental state, such as "assistance" and "leadership," probably with patrons like Stephanas and Gaius in mind. Among those that do involve mental dissociation, he elevates those that function at lower levels of arousal, especially prophecy, for "He who speaks in a tongue builds up himself, but he who prophesies builds up the church" (1 Cor. 14:4). The experience of dissociation itself he robs of its awe by declaring, "In the assembly I would rather speak five words with my mind, in order to instruct others, than ten thousand words in a tongue" (14:19). He belittles the exotic nature of the "speech" itself by comparing it with a badly played flute or lyre or an indistinct bugle call in battle (14:6–10). The value of the spiritual gifts is thus strictly derived from their usefulness in solidifying and "building" the group. "Building" is understood as occurring through rational means. The highest of all gifts is accordingly other-regarding love (ch. 13).

By the very fact of writing as he does, Paul asserts his authority as an apostle and, to a lesser degree, the authority of the co-workers who join him in the formal letter openings. Apart from this implicit exercise of authority, he also makes explicit claims to personal authority in a variety of ways. First, he claims a unique personal relationship with the Corinthian groups, as their founder: "For though you may have tens of thousands of pedagogues in Christ, yet you have not many fathers—for in Christ Jesus, through the gospel, I begot you" (1 Cor. 4:15). It is this right of the founder that he defends against the "superapostles," whom he depicts as interlopers (2 Cor. 10:12–18). Narrative recollection of the beginnings does not figure as prominently here as in 1 Thessalonians and Galatians, but it does play some role, as in 1 Cor. 1:26–3:17. There is also extensive reporting of the apostle's experiences, travels, and plans in the first chapters of 2 Corinthians. The theme of receiving divine comfort in the midst of affliction, introduced in the opening doxology (2 Cor. 1:3–7), continues through the first seven chapters. Paul draws parallels between his experiences of affliction and those of the congregation. This reference is especially pointed, since their affliction was in part caused by one of his letters (7:8–11). He connects this theme with repeated assertions of confidence, which dominate this part of the correspondence.[40]

These parallels between the Corinthians' experiences and the apostle's touch on another, more fundamental way in which Paul's reports of his own experiences serve his interpretation of power. They are narrated frequently in the Corinthian correspondence as terse catalogs of difficulties (1 Cor. 4:11–13; 2 Cor. 6:4–10; 11:23–29) and as ironic boasting against the superapostles. What they have in common is the dialectical structure of weakness and power. Paul emphasizes his visible weakness; that he nevertheless not only survives but flourishes in his accomplishments "for the gospel" he declares to be testimony to the hidden power of God. Further, this dialectic is homologous with his central affirmation about Christ: that he was crucified but raised by God from the dead. Through Paul's scheme of double imitation the apostolic career becomes a mimesis of Christ and thus a fit paradigm by which to test what is an authentic mode of authority in the church.[41]

Yet these letters also contain some rather undialectical assertions of power. If there are some "inflated" people at Corinth who think Paul will not return, he will come quickly and will "learn not the talk of these inflated people but their power" (1 Cor. 4:18f.). He threatens to come "with a rod" (vs. 21) but does not elaborate what practical form this threat might take, since it is only the rhetorical foil for the desirable "love and a spirit of humility" (ibid.). More seriously meant is the threat in 2 Cor. 13:1–4. To those seeking "proof of the Christ who speaks in me," Paul will be "unsparing"; out of his weakness he will show the "power of God." How? Apparently through some judicial process, for he has just quoted Deut. 19:15; "By the word of two witnesses or three everything will be established" (vs. 1). Yet the threat could then be carried out only if the issue is resolved in Paul's favor, that is, if the Corinthians assent to his authority, so that his judgment wins the consensus of the assembly. In the earlier judicial proceeding against the individual deviant in 1 Cor. 5, he could so take that consensus for granted that he could announce the decision in advance. Because he knew, as it were, the Spirit's will in the case, he could be sure that the Spirit-guided assembly would confirm it. The same inner certainty may be implied in 2 Cor. 13, but the situation is very different, for it is precisely his own charismatic authority that his rivals have challenged.

Elsewhere, too, Paul can claim to speak directly the will of God, giving his "opinion, as one given mercy by the Lord to be faithful" (1 Cor. 7:25), for "I think that I also have the Spirit of God" (7:40). He is careful, though, to distinguish such statements from "commands of the Lord" that he knows by tradition (7:10, 12, 25).

Paul appeals to the authority of tradition in several ways. The long chapter on the resurrection (1 Cor. 15) is in effect an elaborate exposition of the formula quoted at the beginning, which he introduces by the reminder that it is tradition which he has received and which the Corinthians accepted from him. It is a very subtle exposition that aims at overthrowing the interpretation that the "spirituals" in the congregation have made of the same beliefs. Thus there is a dialectic between the tradition's authorizing his own position as an apostle who, though "last of all, like an *abortus*," nevertheless is at one with all the other apostles as witness of the resurrection (vss. 8–11), and on the other hand his giving an authoritative interpretation of that tradition.[42] The same sort of dialectic may be seen, though in not so extended a form, in his use of other bits of tradition: the Lord's command about divorce (1 Cor. 7:10), the rule for avoiding *porneia* through monogamous marriage (7:2–5; cf. 1 Thess. 4:3–8), the "words of institution" of the Lord's Supper (1 Cor. 11:23–25).

More broadly, he can appeal to "custom." Thus, if a contentious person is not persuaded by his arguments about the dress of male and female prophets, the last word is "We have no such custom, nor do the assemblies of God" (1 Cor. 11:16). Later he, or more likely a later interpolator, claimed that it was customary, "as in all the assemblies of the saints," for women to "be silent in the assemblies" (14:33f.). Timothy had been sent to Corinth to "remind you of my ways in Christ Jesus, as I teach everywhere in every assembly" (4:17). The rule that each should remain in the status he had when "called" to Christianity is backed by the remark, "And thus I enjoin in all the assemblies" (7:17). Not surprisingly, since no sect can isolate itself completely from the larger culture, customs of the macrosociety also have some weight with Paul, though it is seldom explicit. The way in which outsiders would view glossolalia is a strike against it (14:23); the violation of the incest rule is a kind of *porneia* not to be found "even among the gentiles" (5:1); and the appeal to "nature" in 11:14 is of course really an appeal to custom—Paul was not the first or the last moralist to conflate the two.

A DISCIPLE USES PAUL'S NAME. The letter to Colossians provides a valuable instance of the extension of Paul's apostolic authority by pseudonymous use of his favorite instrument, the letter. Walter Bujard's thorough stylistic analysis[43] ought to put to rest the long debate whether Paul himself could have written the letter: he did not. That does not completely settle the question of Paul's authority for the letter, however, for it must have been written by some fairly close associate. Wolf-Henning Ollrog, for example, makes a particularly lucid but not absolutely convincing argument that it was written by Timothy, who after all appears as a coauthor in the opening.[44] If that were true, then the appended greeting (4:18), which claims to be in Paul's own handwriting (cf. Gal. 6:11; 1 Cor. 16:21; but also the disputed 2 Thess. 3:17), might well be authentic, and the letter written at Paul's suggestion. On the other hand, although the close similiarities between the greetings at the end of Philemon and in Col. 4:7–14 could suggest that the two letters were dispatched at about the same time (Ollrog), what is said about Onesimus (4:9) is more easily understood on the assumption that the author both uses and consciously imitates the letter to Philemon and also knows that the slave's case had a happy outcome. To be sure, that affair could have been resolved quickly and the information brought back to Ephesus (assuming that that was where Paul was imprisoned) in time for Timothy to compose the letter to Colossians and Paul to approve its dispatch. But it could also have been written later, depending on local knowledge or even traditions about Onesimus, by Timothy, or Epaphras, or Tychicus, or some disciple of Paul completely unknown to us.[45]

Whoever the author, the situation is real. There is no reason to doubt the address to Colossae, with attention to other congregations in the Lycus valley cities (4:13, 15f.), nor the actuality of the specific conflict that occasioned the letter. Although it is even more difficult than in the case of Galatians and 1 Corinthians to guess the precise contours of the *philosophia* (2:8) here opposed, it is certain that there was, again, a conflict over authority. There were people in the Colossian congregation who had arrogated to themselves the right to disqualify people who did not share their perceptions and practices (2:14–19) and to lay down dogmas requiring ritual practices related to Judaism (2:16; cf. 2:11?) and ascetic taboos (2:20–23). They based their authority upon "traditions" somehow related to "the elements of the world" (2:8) and upon visions connected somehow with "the religion of angels" and "humility" (2:18). "Humility" probably meant for them fasting and other ascetic exercises (2:23).[46]

Against these ascetic and mystical innovations, the author sets the authority of Paul. It is particularly interesting to see how he has idealized and generalized the apostolic autobiography (1:24–2:5). We have seen that Paul's mention of his sufferings often served as a means both of identifying his experience with the troubles of his followers and of connecting his authority, dialectically construed, with the fundamental paradigm of Christ's crucifixion. Here, though, his disciple adopts a bold new interpretation. The apostle's sufferings "make up, in my flesh, what is lacking of the afflictions of the Christ, for the sake of his body, which is the church" (1:24). The labors of the apostle become universal in scope: "admonishing every human being [*panta anthrōpon*] and teaching every human being in all wisdom, that I may present every human being perfect in Christ" (1:28). The epistolary cliché, "absent in the flesh but with you in the spirit," (2:5) takes on perhaps a special nuance in this context, for the letter is intended not only for the Colossian and Laodicean Christians, but perhaps also for others "who have not seen my [Paul's] face in flesh" (2:1). The pseudonymous writer wants to make the apostolic authority and personal example available to a wider audience. He thus sets in motion a way of employing Paul's memory for institutional purposes that would be vastly important in future generations, beginning with the pseudonymous letter that directly imitates his own, the encyclical that most biblical manuscripts wrongly address "to the saints who are in Ephesus."[47]

Even more striking is the way Colossians uses tradition. Paul had set the example for that, too, as we have seen. Yet none of the authentic letters is so filled with quotations of and allusions to traditional material—most of it connected directly or indirectly with baptism—as Colossians. However, the author of Colossians does not argue against the human traditions of the "angelic cult" in Colossae by systematically expounding the older traditions. Indeed, there is little progressive argument of any kind in Colossians, nor does tight logical sequence characterize its grammatical style.[48] Instead, the letter as a whole is paraenetic; the readers are recalled to the truths and practices that they already know. The admonitions to "watch out" for the false "philosophers" and not to submit to them are of the same sort as the admonitions about how to behave.[49] The whole is a "reminder of baptism,"[50] or rather of the whole process of receiving instruction and entering the Christian community that culminated in baptism. The theme of the letter is stated in 2:6f.: "So as you received Christ Jesus the Lord, walk in him, rooted and built up in him and confirmed in faith as you were taught, abounding in thanksgiving."

Emphasis on elements that promote the cohesion of the group and its internal harmony is even greater in Colossians than in the authentic letters of Paul. The author adapts the rich imagery of cosmic reconciliation, which is probably drawn from the language of the baptismal ritual, to speak of the unity of the congregation. He does the same with traditional language about the Christian mission. The Colossians are not admonished to engage in active mission to the world so much as to cultivate the internal peace and loyalty of their community, which is part of one growing and thriving "body" throughout the world.[51] It is in the same context and to the same end that the author employs the topos "On Household Governance" (*peri oikonomias,* or what Luther called *Die Haustafel,* 3:18–4:1). This hierarchical outline of the duties incumbent upon each person according to his role, either ruling or ruled, in the household, microcosm of society, was well loved by Hellenistic moralists and readily adapted by Jewish apologetic self-descriptions in the Hellenistic environment.[52] Here it is used to underline the stability and harmony of the Christian household, in contrast to the mystical preoccupations and sexual asceticism of the opponents. The "things above," the life "hidden with Christ in God," are to be realized, it seems, in rather mundane ways. There is a curious irony here. The author uses the baptismal imagery in 2:20–3:4 in a way almost exactly opposite from Paul's polemic in 1 Corinthians 4 and 15; indeed, this author's description of the postbaptismal exaltation of the Christian sounds much like the position that Paul opposes. Nevertheless, he manages to advocate a communal behavior that is not much different practically from that which Paul urged by his emphasis on the unfinished state of the Christian's salvation.

Controlling Individual Deviance

One actually hears of sexual misconduct [*porneia*] among you—and such misconduct that is not [to be found] even among the gentiles—so that someone possesses his father's wife. And you are inflated! Have you not rather gone into mourning, [praying] that the person who did this deed be removed from your midst? Well, for my part, absent in body but present in spirit, I have already decided the case of the one who has thus done this, as in fact present when in the name of our Lord Jesus you and my spirit assemble, with the power of our Lord Jesus to hand over such a person to Satan, for destruction of [his] flesh, that [his] spirit may be saved on the Day of the Lord. Your boasting is not fine! [1 Cor. 5:1–6a]

This is a very important passage for the glimpses it affords both of procedures for discipline in at least one Pauline congregation and of some aspects of the sensibilities of these groups. I have translated rather woodenly to bring out

some of the difficulties in the text as well as some of the connectives ordinarily severed by smoother English renderings. Even so, I have had to make
a number of exegetical decisions that will not be argued here; for the options
the reader may consult the standard commentaries.[53]

Despite modern paragraphing and the older chapter divisions, the passage quoted is not to be separated completely from the issues Paul dealt with
in chapters 1–4. The ironic exclamation, "And you are inflated!" (vs. 2a),
recalls 4:6, 18, 19. The verb occurs twice more later, in 1 Cor. 8:1 and 13:4,
and nowhere else in the authentic letters.[54] Apparently Paul finds the image
of the *pneumatikoi* being "puffed up" wryly appropriate. The matter but not
the image is picked up again in the litotes of vs. 6a, "Your boasting is not
fine!" The direct discussion of the case is thus placed within brackets that
connect it with Paul's concern about members of the Corinthian group who
are "inflated" with their sense of spiritual power, knowledge, and wisdom,
and who believe that they are free from Paul's interference because he will not
return to Corinth (4:18f.).

Within that context we may be able to make more sense of the peculiar
way in which Paul describes the judicial procedure. On the one hand, he
presents a *fait accompli:* "I have already decided." On the other, he gives
unmistakable directions for a solemn assembly of the whole congregation to
expel the wrongdoer and "hand him over to Satan." Paul takes for granted
that such a plenary meeting is the way such a solemn action is to be taken.
Matthew records a similar procedure (18:15–18); its antecedents were probably in the Jewish community's self-governance. Yet Paul's directive about
the assembly is hardly a limitation of his apostolic authority in deference to a
more democratic polity.[55] It is more nearly the opposite. In the decision of the
assembly, about which he allows no doubt, it will become apparent to the
Corinthian doubters that the apostle's physical absence makes no difference.
The phrase *hōs parōn* (vs. 3b) is not to be translated "as *if* present." It is the
effectiveness of his real presence ("in spirit") that Paul insists on in the
striking phrase "you and my spirit" (vs. 4). What is at issue is not just an
egregious case of moral laxity, but also a tension between local, charismatic
authority and supralocal, unitive governance through the apostle and his
itinerant associates. Paul does not relax that tension. The local leaders ought
to have solved this problem already; but because they did not he is fully
prepared to call them to account.

Once we see that 1 Corinthians 5 is concerned not only with the particular case but also with shaping the congregation's understanding of its responsibility for self-discipline and the relation between self-discipline and wider
forms of authority, we may also make more sense of what follows. The order
of topics in chapters 5 and 6 has seemed disjointed to most commentators.
Paul jumps from the case just described to a complaint about lawsuits between Christians, then back to the topic of *porneia* in 6:12–20. How are they
connected? After using the metaphor of cleansing out old leaven before Passover (5:6b–8) to support his decision to expel the deviate, Paul reveals that he

has written a previous letter about keeping separate from sinful people, and asserts that the Corinthians have misunderstood it. They took it to be an admonition about group boundaries, about keeping themselves separate from the wickedness of "the world." Nonsense, says Paul now; one could do that only by leaving the world altogether (vs. 10).[56] If they had understood the former letter, they would presumably have already taken the action here called for, since they are required to "judge the insiders yourselves" but to leave the outsiders to God (vss. 12f.). Then he turns to the question of lawsuits, not just because the topic of judgment has come up[57] but because again it illustrates their confusion about the lines dividing "inside" from "outside." Not only have they left a shocking misdeed in their midst un-judged; for trivial disputes over finance between members of the community they have turned to outside judges, presumably colonial magistrates (6:1–11). Although Paul finds it deplorable that such disputes should even arise (vss. 7–11), it is still clear that he expects the Christians to find a mechanism within the community to settle them when they do arise, just as the assembly must deal with the even more deplorable sin of *porneia*.

But then the quotation in verse 12 of the pneumatics' slogan, "Everything is permitted me," seems another abrupt shift. Paul is reverting to the subject of chapter 5, *porneia*, but the transition begins in vss. 9–11, where he quotes the catechetical rule, "Those who do [*x, y,* . . . and *n;* a variable list of vices] will not inherit the Kingdom of God." He has alluded to this rule in 5:9–11; evidently it loomed large in the previous letter. Because *porneia* figures prom-inently in the rule, he thus reintroduces the topic, now understood not in the general sense common in the New Testament, "sexual immorality," but in its older, specific one, "prostitution." He also sets the stage for his answer in chapter 7 to the first question of the Corinthians' letter, where he will in-terpret the other traditional rule, "Avoid *porneia*" (7:2; also in 6:18). More-over, the quotation in 6:12f. of the pneumatics' slogans gives more content to the "boasting" and "inflation" mentioned at 4:6, 18, 19; and at 5:2, 6. The charismatics' self-confidence is unfazed by the most flagrant deviations from the community's—and the macrosociety's—sexual norms. It is tempting to say that they "boast" just *because* these violations demonstrate their spiritual transcendence of the rules having to do with the body, but Paul does not explicitly accuse them of that. Were some of the *pneumatikoi* actually fre-quenting the city's brothels? Perhaps. But perhaps that is only Paul's *reductio ad absurdum* of their vaunted freedom. It is striking that there is no threat here of juridical action, but only a careful and rhetorically powerful theologi-cal and christological argument, backed by a traditional rule, scriptural ex-egesis, and the metaphor of the community as temple (6:14–20). The discus-sion has thus led from a flat assertion of apostolic decision, through insistence on finding internal organs of discipline, to a rational appeal for submission to divine norms. The thread that runs through all is concern for the purity of the community.

Let us return briefly to the man living with his father's wife, to see what sanctions are imposed. Centrally, he is to be "removed" from the community (5:2). Paul concludes discussion of the matter by quoting the sentence that recurs often in the Deuteronomic code (but changing the verb to the plural): "Remove the evil [one] from yourselves" (vs. 13). He does not construe the action primarily as a sanction against the offender, but as a way of purging the community. That it nevertheless would certainly function as a sanction is more evident when Paul quotes the formula of his misunderstood earlier letter, which commanded "not to mix with anyone called a brother if he be a fornicator or a greedy person or an idolater or an abusive person or a drunkard or a robber, not even to eat with such a one" (5:11). To shun the offender, especially at common meals—the Lord's Supper and others—would be an effective way of letting him know that he no longer had access to that special fellowship indicated by use of the term *brother* (cf. 2 Thess. 3:14f. and Gal. 6:1). But there is more. He is to be delivered formally into the sphere of Satan, perhaps by means of a curse, "for the destruction of the flesh" (vs. 5). Some commentators, in antiquity and more recently, have wanted to take "flesh" here in Paul's special, metaphorical sense, of life in rebellion against God, but the plain sense is to be preferred. The notion that misdeeds could be punished by sickness or death is one that Paul expresses elsewhere as well (11:29f.). All was not lost for the offender, however, for the shunning and the diabolic punishment were "in order that [his] spirit may be saved in the Day of the Lord" (5:5–7; cf. 2 Thess. 3:15).

The obverse of the disciplinary procedure appears in 2 Cor. 2:5–11, where Paul urges the restoration of an offender who has been chastised and now repents. The details of this case are obscure. Although many commentators have identified the offender with the man of 1 Cor. 5,[58] the offenses are described rather differently. The episode alluded to in 2 Cor. 2 involves a personal insult to Paul (vss. 5, 10; cf. 7:8–12). A plausible conjecture is that the unnamed individual was a leader in the local faction who rejected Paul's authority in favor of the superapostles (chs. 10–13)—if those chapters are from a letter earlier than all or part of chapters 1–8. Only two points are sufficiently firm to give us some insight into the disciplinary process, and both suggest the same kind of proceeding as in the earlier case of incest. The individual has been censured by "the majority" or "the main body" (*hoi pleiones*).[59] The term variously rendered "punishment," "penalty," or "reproof" (*epitimia*, vs. 6) cannot tell us how severe the sanction was; a verbal rebuke is perhaps more likely than a stronger penalty,[60] but the latter cannot be excluded. We must assume that the action was taken formally by "the whole assembly" of Corinthian Christians, not just one of the house assemblies, since it is to the whole that Paul's words are addressed. Furthermore, this action, like that demanded in 1 Cor. 5, was taken in response to a letter from the apostle that "grieved" the whole community as well as the person rebuked (7:8–12). Accordingly, Paul is now careful to identify their act of restoration with his own forgiveness (2:10). Just as the verdict was given in 1

Cor. 5:4 by an assembly "in the name of the Lord Jesus," here forgiveness is "in the presence (*en prosōpō*) of Christ" (vs. 10).

INFERENCES

From the examples of conflict and from the letters sent to deal with them, what patterns emerge? Who exercises authority? That is, what sorts of persons are in a position to issue effective imperatives? And what explicit and implicit answers are given to the question, "Why should I obey?"

Leaders

APOSTLES. It may seem too obvious to mention that the chief figure in the records we have of these little groups, scattered from Anatolia to Corinth, is Paul. Of course, one may say: that is because our firsthand records are his letters and those by people very close to him. That statement has a converse, however: it is because of the extraordinary personal authority exerted by this man that we have his letters as the earliest extant Christian writings. The form of the letters reinforces that observation. Like any good Hellenistic moralist, Paul puts forth his own life as a model to be imitated, but by his "biography of reversal"[61] and his application of the Cross as a metaphor to his own mishaps and sufferings, he transforms that commonplace into something new. Moreover, in his letters there recur not only examples but also direct commands: "I have already decided"; "I command—not I, but the Lord—" when he has a saying of Jesus that applies; "I tell you—not the Lord—" when he does not. He sees himself as the "father" of the community he founded. "What do you want? Shall I come to you with a rod or in love and a spirit of gentleness?"

The title "apostle" was important to Paul. Not everyone in the Christian movement of his time was willing to acknowledge his right to it. To the Corinthians he writes, "If to others I am not an apostle, at least I am to you" (1 Cor. 9:2). His first words in the letter to the troubled Galatian congregations are "Paul, apostle not from human beings nor through a human being, but through Jesus Christ and God the Father" (Gal. 1:1). Yet his first biographer, years later, avoids using the term for him or for anyone else besides the Jerusalem Twelve, except for one passage (Acts 14:4, 14).

It is now commonly recognized that the term represented no office in Paul's own time, but it did point to functions that carried authority in the missionary activities of the Christians. We need not enter into the long discussion by modern scholars about the origins of the notion and its historical development. The Greek word we transliterate *apostle* meant at its simplest level "agent" or "envoy," and Paul could use the word *ambassador* or its verb as a synonym: "For Christ, then, we are acting as ambassadors, as God is making his appeal through us" (2 Cor. 5:20).[62] That analogy approaches the claim of being messengers of God that was characteristic of the classical prophets of Israel. Indeed, Paul could allude to words of Jeremiah in reference to his own revelation (Gal. 1:15f.) and tacitly compare himself with Moses (2 Cor. 3; Rom. 9:3; 10:1).[63]

For Paul, apostleship involved a commission, somehow directly received in a revelation of the risen Christ, to "preach among the gentiles" and, moreover, to gather the converts into communities—"lay foundations," "build," and "plant" are favorite metaphors. Moreover, in his conception of the apostolate these were *new* foundations, where no other apostle had worked. Not everyone shared that view, however.

There were in fact a good many apostles in the early Christian movement, and some of them crossed paths with Paul and had some effect on the way that patterns of authority were taking shape in his mission area. First of all, there were the ones in Jerusalem, "the apostles before me" (Gal. 1:17), but they appear in the Pauline literature only negatively and indirectly. Paul vows, under oath, that he had nothing to do with them (Gal. 1:17, 19). The reformers who followed him into Galatia must have been independent of Jerusalem, too, or Paul's counterargument in Galatians 1–2 would make little sense. Jerusalem leaders were very much involved, on the other hand, in the earlier crisis at Antioch, but in Paul's account of that series of events nothing is said about either apostles or the Twelve, only about the three "pillars" subsequently supplanted by James. What the Corinthians meant who called themselves "Cephas's" (1 Cor. 1:12; 3:21f.) we cannot know, but there is no evidence of any attempt by Peter or agents of his to claim authority over Pauline congregations. The original apostles of Jerusalem thus seem to have had little or no direct authority so far as the Pauline churches were concerned.

The earlier apostles, in Paul's terms, were in fact a large and, so far as we can see, not well-defined group. His list of witnesses of the resurrection names, in order, Cephas, the Twelve, "more than five hundred brothers," James, "all the apostles," and then himself, "last of all . . . least of the apostles" (1 Cor. 15:5–9). There are also Andronicus and (his wife?) Junia (if that is the correct text), who were probably fellow Tarsians or fellow Cilicians,[64] became Christians before Paul did, and were "notable among the apostles." The last phrase, however, does not absolutely have to mean that they themselves were apostles (Rom. 16:7).

The rivals who appeared in Corinth in Paul's absence and won some considerable following there with their claims to superior authority were also "apostles," as Paul's attack on them makes clear (2 Cor. 11:5, 13). Where they came from we do not know, for there is nothing in the text to connect them with Jerusalem. The would-be reformers of Galatian Christianity were similar and probably to be identified as apostles in the same sense, although the Letter to Galatians gives no definite indication that they were called that.

Besides these itinerant charismatics, who like Paul represented no one but Christ, we hear once of *apostoloi ekklēsiōn,* "delegates of churches" (2

Cor. 8:23). These are people designated to accompany the collection to Jeru-
salem. We hear a number of times in the letters about messengers from one
church to another or between the churches and Paul, with various functions.
One of these, Epaphroditus, who has brought money from the Philippian
Christians to Paul in prison, is also called "your apostle" (Phil. 2:25). It
would not be out of line to use the term in the same sense for such people as
Stephanas, Fortunatus, and Achaicus, who brought the letter from Corinth to
Paul.[65] Their authority seems to be derivative and limited. In later centuries
both rabbinic and non-Jewish sources would speak of "apostles" (šlîḥîm) of
the rabbinic court, who collected money and conveyed rulings about festivals
and the like. Functionally, the Christian "apostles of churches" resemble
them much more than they do Paul and the other itinerant, charismatic
apostles.[66]

FELLOW WORKERS. Apart from apostles, who are distinguished by their
conviction of a direct, divine commission (except perhaps in the case of
"apostles of churches"), we repeatedly encounter in the letters and Acts other
leaders more or less closely associated with Paul and more or less dependent
on him. E. A. Judge once called these Paul's "retinue."[67] From the beginning
the Pauline mission was a collective enterprise, with something that can
loosely be called a staff. Its corporate nature was one of the most effective
elements in the mission's successful adaptation to what Gerd Theissen calls
"socio-ecological factors" of its urban territory.[68] This arrangement for
planting, nurturing, and connecting the Christian household cells was probably not Paul's invention but something he learned at Antioch. Indeed, Ollrog
argues shrewdly that Paul's missionary career began as a "fellow worker" of
Barnabas.[69] When Barnabas and Paul split, after the confrontation described
in Gal. 2:11–14, each took one or more partners. In the New Testament
reports, none of the other apostles, such as Peter, Apollos, or Philip, seems to
have done that.[70]

The Pauline associates assumed a wide range of functions. Silvanus,
Timothy, and Sosthenes all appear one or more times as coauthors of letters.
Timothy could be sent from Athens to Thessalonica to check on the group
recently founded there and to reinforce them in various ways (1 Thess. 3:2,
6). With Paul and Silvanus he took part in establishing Christianity at Corinth (2 Cor. 1:19) and was later sent from Ephesus with an apostolic reminder for the Corinthians (1 Cor. 4:17; 16:10). When Paul wrote to the
Philippians (Phil. 2:19), Timothy was with him (in Rome? Ephesus?) but
apparently not imprisoned. Titus, mentioned less often, had a major role in
the tangled relations between Paul and the Corinthian groups (2 Cor. 2:13;
7:6–16) and in arrangements for their participation in the Jerusalem collection (8:6, 16–24).[71] The roles of Prisca and Aquila are different; they served
as patrons and protectors of Paul himself and of local house-assemblies, but
they moved several times and were evidently evangelists and, according to
Acts 18:26, theological instructors of considerable power. There are many
other "fellow workers," "fellow athletes," "laborers," and so on of whom

we know little more than place and name, from the greetings and occasional admonitions included in the letters.[72] From the contexts in which they are mentioned, some of these seem to have been local leaders; others were itinerants. There seems to have been no hard-and-fast distinction.[73] Local leaders could become missionary "founders," too, like Epaphras of Colossae (Col. 1:7f.; 4:12). The "apostles of churches" could conceivably include or become "fellow workers"—like the Epaphroditus from Philippi (Phil. 2:25–29; 4:18).

There is also a range of relationships between these workers and Paul. At one end there is the independence, but with some communication maintained, of a Barnabas (after the Antioch debacle) and an Apollos—hence I have listed them among the apostles. At the other there is Timothy's very close dependence upon Paul's direction and authority—although that does not mean that he or Titus could not be given considerable discretion in carrying out delicate assignments. Further, the relationship could extend over a very long period—Timothy and Titus again, and Prisca and Aquila—or it could be limited to a particular time and place, as with some of those whose work was mostly in one town, or some of those whom Paul calls "fellow prisoners" or "fellow captives." Indeed, what is perhaps most impressive is the complexity and fluidity of the network of leaders that tied the Pauline *ekklēsiai* together.

LOCAL LEADERS. Acts and the Pauline letters make no mention of formal offices in the early Pauline congregations. This fact is striking when we compare these groups with the typical Greek or Roman private association. The clubs' inscriptions show a positive exuberance in the awarding and holding of offices, which, as we saw earlier, commonly imitated those of the city government.[74] We find nothing comparable when leading roles in the Pauline congregations are mentioned. The New Testament writers do not use the word *archē* in the sense of "office," nor its synonyms. We do find, however, that roles have begun to be differentiated and that their relative importance is being discussed at the time of our earliest information. The first letter admonishes the Thessalonian Christians to acknowledge "those who labor among you and are over you in the Lord and admonish you" (1 Thess. 5:12, RSV). The three parallel participles do not name three roles, but three functions of one role. "Laboring" (*kopiōntes*) is quite general, Paul's usual verb for all sorts of work in the missionary enterprise and the "building up" of the communities. "Admonishing" (*nouthetountes*) implies (verbal) discipline in moral questions. *Proistamenoi* ("are over you") is more problematic, for the verb may mean to "preside over" or to "act as patron or protector."[75] The latter is more appropriate here, but if the patron can also "admonish," then he or she certainly is being accorded some governing authority.[76] The Corinthian correspondence offers clues to the same relationship: a position of authority grows out of the benefits that persons of relatively higher wealth and status could confer on the community. The three participles, then, name functions rather than offices. The passage provides no evidence for a formal process for the selection of leaders.

The same is true in the longer lists of leaders and functions in 1 Cor. 12:8–10, 28–30; Rom. 12:6–8; Eph. 4:11:

1 Cor. 12:28–30	1 Cor. 12:8–10	Rom. 12:6–8	Eph. 4:11
apostles (first)	wisdom	prophecy	apostles
prophets (second)	*gnōsis*	*diakonia*	prophets
teachers (third)	faith	the teacher	evangelists
miracles	healing gifts	the exhorter	shepherds
healing gifts	working miracles	the donor[77]	teachers
assistances	prophecy	the patron	
guidances	distinguishing	the one who	
kinds of tongues	spirits	shows mercy	
(interpret: 30)	kinds of tongues		
	interpretation		
	of tongues		

These passages have in common the conception of the principal roles in the local communities as gifts (*charismata*)—by God, Christ, the Spirit. The variety among the lists shows that there is local variation and considerable freedom for charismatic leadership. In the Corinthian lists the curious mixture of nouns or participles designating persons and abstract nouns denoting activities draws attention to the functions themselves rather than the status of those who exercise them. However, we must remember that it is Paul who is trying to play down differences of status and to stress cohesion of the group, even while allowing room for diversity of individual powers. For the Corinthian Christians, status was already important.

Further, the few roles common to all the lists are signs that some degree of formalization had already taken place. So is Paul's ranking of apostles, prophets, and teachers in 1 Cor. 12:28. And, although some leaders were financial benefactors of the congregations, other types of leaders were supported by the congregations from a very early time. That is most likely the meaning of Galatians 6:6: "Let him who is being instructed in the Word share in all good things with the instructor."[78] The principle is the same as that generally applied to the itinerant ministries (backed by a saying of Jesus and other arguments in 1 Cor. 9:4–14), here applied to local teachers. In the Ephesians list and in the opening of Philippians, there is possible evidence for some advance in the process of formalizing offices. Roles do not become fully institutionalized, though, until the turn of the century and afterward, as we see in the letter of Clement from Rome, the letters of Ignatius, and the Pastorals. None of these unambiguously represents the continuation of the Pauline organization as such. By then, qualifications for office are being defined, rules for selection are laid down, and the offices become constitutive of good order.[79]

Adolf von Harnack undertook to distinguish various local functions and, later, offices from the three great charismatic and universal callings, apostles, prophets, and teachers.[80] That schema has not held up under subsequent inquiry,[81] and we, too, have seen that the lines are often hard to draw between local and wider functions, between charismatic and other kinds of authority. Instead, I have proposed a simpler and more flexible, tripartite classification of the modes of authority exercised by various people in the local communities: visible manifestations of Spirit-possession, position, and association with apostles and other supralocal persons of authority. These were not mutually exclusive, but tensions and conflicts could arise among them.

Warrants for Authority

On the basis of our analysis of a number of exemplary cases of conflict and control and our attempt to expose the structure of the claims and counterclaims, we can now list the more general and more specific warrants we found supporting assertions of power.

A COMMON ETHOS. Informal modes of control predominate. Face-to-face meetings, emissaries, and letters are the means for responding to difficulties. Advice, persuasion, and argument fill the letters; they can be effective only if writers and addressees share a set of common assumptions, beliefs, goals, and relations. The philophronetic sections of the letters are elaborate and often very long: the relationship between writer and readers is fundamental to the attempt to persuade. This relationship is described in a way that stresses the common experience, the shared biography, so to speak, of apostle and congregation. Reminders of the beginning—the first preaching, the early instruction, the conversion, the baptism—become the basis for appeals for appropriate behavior. Moreover, these reminders are set into a theological context. They are described in such a way that the experiences of the Christians in the place addressed are seen to be not only parallel to those of Christians in other places and especially of the apostle, but also homologous to actions by God. The kinds of behavior recommended are thus joined with a set of sacred symbols and a historical ethos unique to the Christians. Yet we have seen that Paul and his co-workers also take for granted many norms that are shared by the sect with society at large. That is hardly surprising. When such norms are expressed, they are often in forms that were especially common in the Greek-speaking Jewish communities of the Mediterranean cities, but often they have parallels also in works of the contemporary pagan philosophers and sophists. The Christians might be resident aliens in the world, their *politeuma* in heaven (Phil. 3:20), but they were neither withdrawing from the world (1 Cor. 5:10) nor completely denying its realities and values.

SPECIFIC WARRANTS. The fluid but recognizable set of beliefs, attitudes, and dispositions that constituted the common ethos of the Pauline groups would tend to produce a certain level of consensus about most behavior expected in these communities. When things are running smoothly, there need be little talk about authority, and outside observers may be hard put to discern the hidden means of control. That is why we have looked especially at situations of conflict, in which the question "Why should I obey?" is more likely to come into the open. Authority distinguishes itself from naked power by its ability to produce acceptable answers to that question.[82] To be sure, we can know only some of the answers that Paul and other leaders proposed; we are rarely in a position to say whether the followers accepted them. We do see some hints that problems at Corinth and in Galatia diminished over time (the fact that the letters were preserved and Paul was still honored seems to justify such an inference); and the fact that some of the warrants are repeated in different situations, not only by Paul but by some who imitated him, indicates that they knew what they were doing.

We have seen that the position of some individuals provided warrant for heeding their advice. Paul expects to be obeyed because he is an apostle. Stephanas should be recognized because he is the first convert of the province and because he is a benefactor of the church. The teacher should be supported because he is a teacher. This kind of assertion, however, proves to be quite diffuse. Either it resolves itself into one or more of the other warrants—the apostle is to be obeyed because he has received a revelation, because he has the Spirit of God, because the readers know him and have found him trustworthy, and so on—or it turns into a question of legitimacy. Apostleship becomes an institutionalized role, and the question becomes whether the claimant to apostolic authority shows the marks required of one who properly occupies that role—legitimacy norms. Schütz has shown that Paul's own concept of authority prevented his appealing to legitimacy norms, but he suggests that the rival apostles in Corinth did introduce that sort of issue.[83] As institutionalization progressed, legitimation would become more and more a central issue.

Among the other warrants upholding imperatives between leaders and the Pauline Christians, the claim of revelation is one often made. The central beliefs about Jesus are a "mystery," hidden for ages but which "God has revealed to us"—a common pattern in early Christian preaching.[84] A revelation also authorized Paul's peculiar mission to the gentiles (Gal. 1:15f.). Revelations from prophets in the congregational assemblies provided instruction and guidance; a "word of the Lord" obtained by that means or from the tradition of Jesus' sayings could count as a warrant for behavior.

Statements and directives could also be authorized by scripture, in quite a variety of ways. Paul quotes scripture frequently, though by no means with the same frequency or in the same fashion in all letters. He also engages at times in detailed exegesis of texts. Furthermore, for a full understanding, his interpretations sometimes require knowledge of certain Judaic exegetical traditions. This leaves us with the nice question whether the predominantly gentile congregations he had gathered received special instruction in the scriptures and traditions of Judaism. If so, it interpreted them from the special perspective of believers in the crucified Messiah Jesus. Like the followers of

the Teacher of Righteousness at Qumran, Paul believed that the things recorded in the Bible "happened as models [*typikōs*], but they were written
down for the admonition of ourselves, to whom the end of the ages has
come" (1 Cor. 10:11; see also Rom. 15:4).

We have also seen Paul appeal to Christian tradition. By citing explicit
traditions that he had received and handed on, he could reinforce his arguments by emphasizing the solidarity between him and the other apostles, as in
1 Cor. 15:3–11, call the Corinthians to account for behavior not fitting the
tradition of the Lord's Supper, and so on. Yet he interprets tradition with
considerable freedom, and treats with ambivalence both tradition and agreement among the apostles (especially in Gal. 1–2). Related to this is the appeal
to custom of "all the churches of God." Paul's imitators, in the letters they
wrote in his name, used tradition even more extensively, but somewhat less
dialectically.

The Spirit counted as authority par excellence in the Pauline communities. Paul's advice is to be taken, when any specific directive is lacking from
the tradition of Jesus' sayings, because "I think I have the Spirit of God" (1
Cor. 7:40). Not law but the Spirit is the guide for proper behavior. But what
was the evidence that the Spirit was present? We found the Corinthian *pneumatikoi* prizing dramatic, visible manifestations, especially glossolalia. Paul
tried to dampen their enthusiasm and to interpret all important functions of
the community's life as gifts of the Spirit. Yet he did not deny the visible signs;
he claimed not only to speak in tongues but also to work miracles, as did
others in the congregations he founded. He could even speak of miracles as
"signs of an apostle" (2 Cor. 12:12; cf. Rom. 15:19), however inconsistent
with his profounder theology that claim might appear to us.

The most characteristic form of expression of authority for Paul, however, is the dialectical, even at times paradoxical pattern by which he tries to
employ the fundamental proclamation of Christ's death and resurrection as a
paradigm of authentic power. It is the center, for example, of his heavily
ironic argument against the "superapostles" in 2 Cor. 10–13. This frequently
recurring paradigm is one we must consider again in the final chapter, which
examines the pattern of beliefs involved. Whether the paradox impressed his
original readers as much as it has modern theologians, we cannot be sure. The
"biography of reversal" (as Schütz calls it) did find an echo, though rather
flat and lacking nuance, in the writers who used Paul's name later. The "least
of the apostles" (1 Cor. 15:8f.) becomes for the writer of Ephesians "least of
all the saints" (Eph. 3:8), for the author of the Pastorals the "foremost of
sinners," who received mercy nevertheless as a paradigm of Christ's patience
(1 Tim. 1:12–16).

RULES. In the letters the norms of the Pauline communities are only
rarely stated as rules. We may be tempted to connect that fact with Paul's
polemic against people who wanted to make adherence to aspects of Jewish
halakah a requirement for gentiles who joined the community of salvation,
but we must be careful of distortions created by anachronistic perspectives.[85]

In fact there were rules, and we occasionally find Paul quoting some of them, as traditions that he has received and handed on to the congregations he founded. Instruction in appropriate behavior was assuredly part of the process of resocialization that accompanied baptism (before, after, or both—we do not know). Yet most of the fragments that we can glean from the paraenetic sections of the letters are rather general in scope, more suggestive than prescriptive. "Avoid fornication." "Neither fornicators nor idolaters nor adulterers nor catamites nor sodomites nor thieves nor greedy persons nor drunkards nor abusive persons nor robbers [the list can vary] will inherit the Kingdom of God." Some are more specific: "Let each acquire his own spouse in holiness and honor . . . ," or the "command of the Lord" that there should be no divorce. Even so, the two most striking features of Paul's application of these rules are the remarkable freedom of his interpretation and the flexibility of decision apparently required of his readers.[86] A great many of the norms are taken for granted: Paul does not define *porneia*, for anyone in his right mind is expected to know that to live with one's father's wife is unacceptable. Or the community is expected to grasp intuitively or by reflection what kinds of behavior are "worthy" of the way in which its members "received Christ." Or prophets and apostles in their midst receive "in the spirit" revelations that will guide decisions. The impression is one of great fluidity, of a complex, multipolar, open-ended process of mutual discipline. Perhaps this fluid structure of authority in some measure expressed the perception, at least for Paul himself, that the crucifixion of the Messiah marked the end of the time when "the Law" shaped the limits of God's people and the beginning of the new age that would yield soon to his Kingdom.

5

RITUAL

Was early Christianity a religion? Not at all, declares E. A. Judge. To first-century observers,

the talkative, passionate and sometimes quarrelsome circles that met to read Paul's letters over their evening meal in private houses, or the pre-dawn conclaves of ethical rigorists that alarmed Pliny, were a disconcerting novelty. Without temple, cult statue or ritual, they lacked the time-honoured and reassuring routine of sacrifice that would have been necessary to link them with religion.[1]

To use religion as a model for describing early Christian groups would amount, in Judge's view, to "mislocating them under . . . an unhistorical rubric."[2] This is a useful warning, especially given the array of visible forms by which cults in the Roman Empire publicly displayed themselves. Ramsay MacMullen has assembled examples of these forms in the first chapter of his recent book on paganism. Not only did the first-century Christians lack shrines, temples, cult statues, and sacrifices; they staged no public festivals, dances, musical performances, pilgrimages, and as far as we know they set up no inscriptions.[3]

Christianity's difference from other cults should not be exaggerated, however. Judge's assertion that the early Christian communities were "without . . . ritual" is manifestly false. Not only does Pliny describe some of their rituals to Trajan, but it is surely ingenuous to describe the Christians of sixty years earlier as meeting merely "to read Paul's letters over their evening meal," as if their meeting and that meal had not been set about with ritual from the beginning. In fact Pliny did not think of Christianity as "conclaves of ethical rigorists," but as "a perverse, uncontrolled superstition."[4] It is hard to see why not only Pliny, but also Tacitus and Suetonius[5] would apply the term *superstitio* to an ethical debating society that had no ritual.[6] One uses such a term to characterize someone else's rituals that one does not like. If they had not been "perverse and uncontrolled" or, as Judge puts it, "a disconcerting novelty," they could have been called *religio*.

The early Christian movement also fits reasonably well under the rubric of religion as described by some modern social scientists. The anthropologist Melford E. Spiro, for example, defines religion as "an institution consisting of culturally patterned interaction with culturally postulated superhuman beings."[7] That the Pauline Christians believed in superhuman beings can hardly be doubted; we shall examine some of those beliefs more closely in the next chapter. For Spiro, interactions with those beings include both ritual behavior and moral behavior, behavior believed to be in accord with the "will or desire of supernatural beings or powers."[8] Pauline groups exhibited both. In the previous chapter we discussed some of the ways in which the groups shaped and regulated behavior to accord with what they took to be "the will or desire of" God and Christ. Here we shall examine what we can see of their ritual system.

A large and growing number of social scientists construe ritual as a form of communication. It does not just include certain patterns of language; it is itself a kind of speech. To interpret ritual is, "in effect, trying to discover the rules of grammar and syntax of an unknown language."[9]

Many of the scholars who adopt this perspective would say that ritual communicates the fundamental beliefs and values of a society or a group. Ritual is often said to be symbolic action, representing what the society holds to be of primary importance, or indeed the very structure of the society. There are a number of problems with this view, however, not least of which is the difficulty of clearly distinguishing between representation in the mind of the actor and in the mind of the external observer.[10] If it is the latter case, this definition does not distinguish ritual from other social behavior. Moreover, the observer's deductions are likely to be circular, as Jack Goody has pointed out:

For it can be said, in an important sense, that all social action [and not just mag-icoreligious behavior] is "expressive" or "symbolic" of the social structure, because the more general concept is simply an abstraction from the more specific. It is not, however, "expressive" in the way many sociologists implicitly assume, that is, it does not express major principles of social behaviour. Indeed such an approach simply involves the reification of an organizing abstraction into a causal factor.[11]

For Emile Durkheim, who with Robertson Smith initiated the modern discussion of ritual, the relation of ritual to language was more intrinsic. Ritual did not merely encode ideas that could be expressed otherwise; rather, it *created* the essential categories of human thought. For Durkheim, ritual solved the Kantian problem of the origin of the necessary concepts. "Ritual and religion did publicly," says Ernest Gellner, "what the Kantian transcendental ego did only behind the impassable iron curtain of the noumenal."[12] Thus Mary Douglas, one of the most imaginative of Durkheimian anthropologists, treats "ritual forms, like speech forms, as transmitters of culture," but insists that they create as well as reflect social reality. She adds: "Ritual is more to society than words are to thought. For it is very possible to know something and then find words for it. But it is impossible to have social relations without symbolic acts."[13] Other communications-oriented students of ritual take a similar position with more or less important variations. Berger and Luckmann, for example, describe "the social construction of reality," and Clifford Geertz proposes that "sacred symbols" serve to synthesize "world view" and "ethos" of a community.[14]

There are a number of problems with the Durkheimian perspective. For Durkheim, ritual was able to do its work only by perpetrating a benign fraud. The actor in a rite spoke of "God" or "the gods," but Durkheim knew that he really meant "society." Nevertheless, Durkheim's followers preserve an insight often forgotten in modern interpretations of myth and ritual: ritual does not only or primarily convey information. It does something. If we are to think of ritual as a kind of speech, then perhaps we ought to think preeminently of the kind that J. L. Austin called "performative."[15] The appropriate question, as we undertake to describe the rituals mentioned in the Pauline letters, is "What do they *do*?"

MINOR RITUALS

The obvious starting point for our search might seem to be the two great ritual complexes, baptism and the Lord's Supper, which were of self-evident importance in the earliest Christian communities. However, the very fact that these ceremonies continued to be central to Christian worship in subsequent centuries caused them to accrete increasingly complex actions and meanings. That accretion makes it difficult to divest these rituals of the accumulated "theology of the sacraments" and to avoid an anachronism in performing the needed act of historical imagination. When the Christians of the Pauline mission baptized converts and gathered for common meals in memory of Jesus, they framed these special occasions with a very fluid and rapidly developing system of small ritualized actions. By these gestures, formulas, and patterns of speaking they discovered and expressed their identity as "brothers and sisters in Christ," "the assembly of God," "the holy and elect," "the body of Christ," and so on. Unfortunately no written description of these little rites survives, but we do find clues about a number of them in the letters. These clues may help to correct our perspective on the larger, more familiar sacraments.

Coming Together

The regular meeting of a group at a familiar time and place itself becomes a ritual, in the broad sense of the word we have adopted. And the meeting begets rituals to define and accent its activities, to signal its beginning and end, to separate friendly milling around and gossip from more serious business, to call attention to the leaders' authoritative utterances.

"When you come together" is a clause that Paul uses several times in his correspondence with the Corinthian saints. The verb *synerchesthai*, quite simply "to come together," occurs in 1 Cor. 11:17, 18, 20, 33, 34—all referring to meetings "to eat the Lord's Supper" (for Paul's chiding negative in vs. 20 shows that that was supposed to be the purpose of the meetings)—

and in 14:23, 26. Two phrases underline the commonality of the meeting: *en ekklēsia* (in *synerchomenōn hymōn en ekklēsia*) in 11:18 and *epi to auto* (in *synerchomenōn . . . epi to auto*) in 11:20. Given that these phrases are combined in 14:23, the regulations set forth there for spirit-possessed communication when "the whole *ekklēsia*" gathers probably also refer to occasions at which the common meal is the central ritual. Paul uses the alternative verb, *synagein*, "to gather," which is fairly frequent in Acts, only at 1 Cor. 5:4, where a solemn assembly is ordered for the purpose of expelling a member who has violated the sexual taboos (discussed above, chapter 4).

The earliest extant letter specifies that the letter is to be read "to all the brothers" (1 Thess. 5:27). In the Letter to Colossae, Paul's surrogate takes for granted the reading of this letter in the assembly, and gives instructions that it also be read in Laodicea, and the Laodicean letter in Colossae (Col. 4:16). The form of all the Pauline letters assumes that they will be read at a regular gathering of the *ekklēsia*,[16] but not necessarily to all the groups of a given city at once. Galatians affords the special instance of addressees belonging to a wider area than one city, and the plural in the address makes it plain that several assemblies are expected to receive the letter, either in multiple copies or in successive meetings as Paul's messenger takes it from one place to the next. It may also be that in some cities the letters were read successively in individual household assemblies rather than to "the whole assembly" gathered in a place like Gaius's house in Corinth. The *ekklēsia* that meets in Nympha's house in Laodicea (Col. 4:15) is probably not the entirety of the *Laodikeōn ekklēsia* (vs. 16), nor is the meeting in the house of Philemon and Apphia the only such in Colossae (Philem. 2). So also in Rome there are several household assemblies (Rom. 16), and we cannot be sure whether there was one common meeting place for all of them.[17] The practice doubtless depended on the practical problem of finding adequate room for a citywide assembly in a given place.[18] Gaius's contribution was important enough to be singled out in the remark identifying him (Rom. 16:23); it was probably unusual at this early date.

How often did the groups meet? We do not know. By Pliny's time the Christians in Bithynia were meeting weekly, on a "set day" (*stato die*).[19] Around 150, Justin confirms that that day was Sunday.[20] Acts 20:7 and Ignatius, Magnesians 9:1 provide earlier evidence. We might guess that the gatherings for common meals would have been weekly from the beginning, the Christian "family" following the example of Jewish sabbath observance, but no text confirms this surmise. A weekly rhythm to the life of the congregation and the ascription of some importance to Sunday are suggested by Paul's directive to the Corinthians and the Galatians about the collection for the Jerusalem poor: "The first day of every week, let each of you set aside privately and save up whatever his prosperity permits, so there need be no collections when I come" (1 Cor. 16:2). However, since the directive is for "each one" to set aside money at home (*par' heautō*), it offers no proof that the assembly was also on "the first day of every week."[21]

In the Ekklēsia

What happened in the assemblies? The closest thing we have in the letters to outright description is the series of admonitions in 1 Corinthians 11 and 14. Some of the actions mentioned there are confirmed for other places by mention in other letters. "When you assemble," writes Paul, "each has a psalm, a teaching, a revelation, a tongue, an interpretation" (14:26). As Barrett remarks, "Church meetings in Corinth can scarcely have suffered from dullness."[22] Let us begin with the psalm. There are a number of clues that chanting and singing were normal parts of the Christian meetings. Both Col. 3:16f. and the parallel text, Eph. 5:18–20—both probably adapting traditional language—speak of "psalms, hymns, and spiritual odes." There is not much use trying to distinguish among the three synonyms, although some ancient and modern commentators have tried. Gregory of Nyssa, for example, thought of psalms as accompanied by instruments.[23] The psalms may have included some from the biblical psalter,[24] which was very important in early Christian interpretation and apologetic;[25] but the fact that all three are seen as manifesting in the singers the presence of the Spirit or the *logos* of Christ (Col. 3:16) indicates that most were probably original Christian compositions or adaptations. The likelihood that many of them followed Jewish models is confirmed by some fragments sifted from the letters. As Lightfoot observed, "Psalmody and hymnody were highly developed in the religious services of the Jews at this time."[26] To his references to Philo we may now add the important evidence from Qumran, including the "Hymns" or "Thanksgivings" scroll from Cave 1.[27] This does not exclude general Hellenistic influence as well, for hymns to and about the deities were prominent in cults of all sorts, and sometimes the forms were not altogether different from the Jewish ones.[28]

Perhaps we even have some examples of those psalms, hymns, and spiritual odes. It is widely agreed that Paul quoted one in Phil. 2:6–11, which originally would have sounded something like this:

> [Give thanks to Christ,]
> who being in the form of God
> did not count it his good luck
>   to be equal to God,
> but emptied himself,
> taking the form of a slave,
> taking human likeness
>   and found in shape a man,
> he humbled himself
>   and was obedient to the point of death.
> That is the reason God has raised him on high
> and given him the name
>   higher than any name,
>   that in the name of Jesus
>   "every knee should bend,"
>   of earthly and heavenly and chthonic beings,

> "and every tongue confess":
> "The Lord is Jesus Christ"
> —to the glory of God the Father.

Analysts of the Pauline letter style have identifed a great many other "hymns" or "confessional poems" or fragments thereof, including Col. 1:15–20, Eph. 1:3–14, and 1 Tim. 3:16. Not all are equally convincing. In its present form Eph. 1:3–14, for example, like 2 Cor. 1:3–7, is a literary "blessing" that belongs to formal epistolary style, but it probably also incorporates elements of liturgical blessings used at baptism. That is not the same as a hymn, however.[29] It is also disappointing that the enormous diligence and ingenuity displayed by many exegetes to restore the "original" strophes, stichoi, and meter of these liturgical fragments have almost never resulted in agreement between any two scholars. It is fair to infer that a large subjective factor is involved. We may also wonder whether the chants of the early Christians were necessarily any more regular than the present form of these putative fragments. If they had been as precisely balanced and metrically true as some of the reconstructions, then we would have to suppose that the letter writers who edited them into their present misshape were tone deaf indeed.[30] More likely, the "spiritual" chants were composed freely according to sense-lines, rhythmic but not precisely scannable. They probably followed a few common patterns and used stereotyped turns of phrase (including scriptural lines, as in Phil. 2:11, as well as Christian formulas). In that case they would not have been exactly the same on any two occasions.

There is one surprising detail in the verses just quoted from Colossians and Ephesians. Although the singing is addressed to "the Lord" (Eph. 5:19) or to "God" (Col. 3:16), it is also the means for "speaking to one another" (Ephesians) or, more specifically, for "teaching and admonishing one another" (Colossians).[31] That community-oriented function is consistent with the reason for Paul's preference for prophecy in clear speech to glossolalia: the glossolalist speaks only to God; the prophet, to human beings (1 Cor. 14:2f.). The test is whether speech in the assembly "builds up" the *ekklēsia* (vss. 3–5); that is the summary rule Paul applies in the verse we started with, 1 Cor. 14:26: "Let all [psalm, teaching, revelation, tongue, interpretation] be for upbuilding [*oikodomē*]." Here is a candid statement of the social function that Paul and his associates see for the distinctive sorts of singing and speaking that take place in the spirit-filled meetings. By chanting psalms, hymns, and odes to God (or to the Lord), among other things the congregation also "taught" and "admonished" themselves and "built up" the community. One large role of ritual speech and music is thus to promote group cohesion, as we emphasized in chapter 2. *Oikodomē* is more than social cohesion, however.[32] It involves, by "teaching and admonition," the formation of the community's ethos. By the images of the group's special language, the poetic reiteration of statements and metaphors of fundamental beliefs, reinforced by musical rhythms and charged with the high emotional level induced by cumulative interaction in the meetings, the group's peculiar "knowledge" grows. With it, attitudes and dispositions take form; the kinds of behavior "worthy of the way you received Christ" are learned.

"Instruction" and "admonition" in Col. 3:16 are functions of the whole congregation—by means of their singing or chanting. Elsewhere, too, the letters appeal to the addressees to "admonish" or "exhort" one another (as in 1 Thess. 4:18; 5:11, 14; 1 Cor. 14:31; Rom. 15:14). That does not mean that these functions were not led by individuals or performed by individuals on behalf of the congregation. "Each one" could offer "a psalm, a teaching," and so on. Instruction, exhortation, and consolation were especially to be expected from prophets (1 Cor. 14:3, 19), but admonition is also a function of the local leaders who "labor" and "protect/preside"[33] (1 Thess. 5:12). These are individual *charismata* (1 Cor. 12:8–10, 28–30; Rom. 12:8), but given to the "one body"; so Paul wants them understood, and so his disciples who wrote Colossians and Ephesians construed them.

Historians of liturgy commonly assume that the Christian meetings included, from the beginning, the reading and exposition of scripture—that is, of what the second-century church would begin to call the Old Testament. The primary reason for that assumption is the supposed example of the Jewish synagogue. We must be careful, however, not to explain one unknown quantity in terms of another, equally unknown. The fact is that extant descriptions of synagogue worship and orders for it are from the New Testament itself or from much later sources. Only by means of small allusions in the writings of Philo and Josephus and a few other writers, and by more or less plausible deductions from the style of these and of other Jewish literature is it possible to guess what synagogue liturgies in the first century may have included.[34] That scripture texts were read and homilies were based on them seems very credible indeed, but details are quite uncertain. Is there anything in the Pauline letters themselves that suggests that reading and exposition of scripture took place in the Christian assemblies—perhaps as part of the activity indicated by "instruction," "teaching," "admonition," "consolation," "words of wisdom," "words of knowledge"? There is nothing explicit. However, the rich allusions to and arguments from scripture that Paul sometimes includes in his letters, a practice also visible in the work of his disciple in, say, Eph. 2:11–22; 4:8–12; 5:21–33, presuppose *some* means for learning both text and traditions of interpretation. Regular readings and homilies in the assemblies are the most plausible.

Besides exposition of scripture, preaching in the assemblies must have included other things, preeminently statements about Jesus Christ, and inferences, appeals, warnings, and the like, connected logically or rhetorically with those statements. Examining some of the recurrent patterns of language in the Pauline corpus and in other early Christian letters, Rudolf Bultmann and, more systematically, Nils Dahl have suggested that several reproduce typical rhetoric of preachers. Dahl describes five such patterns. The "revelation pattern" says that what the Christians now know (about Christ) is "a secret, hidden for ages," "but now revealed" to the elect. The "soteriological contrast pattern" sets the preconversion life of the Christians ("Once you were . . .") against their new status, which they must live up to ("but now you are . . ."). The "conformity pattern" is hortatory: "Just as the Lord forgave you, so also you [ought to forgive one another]." The "teleological pattern" permits a broad range of implications to be drawn from christological statements, as in 2 Cor. 8:9: "You know the grace of our Lord Jesus Christ, that, rich as he was, he became poor for your sakes, that you might be enriched by his poverty [and therefore ought to be ready to send money to the poor in Jerusalem]." Finally, there is the simple introduction of exhortations or advice by "I appeal to you by the name of the Lord Jesus," or ". . . in the Lord," or the like.[35] Some of these had wider application than preaching. They could also shape formulas that are liturgical in a narrower sense, like the doxology added in most manuscripts to one of the last chapters of Romans.[36]

Moreover, we may assume that the paraenetic sections of the Pauline letters are fairly close to the sort of exhortations that would have been made orally in the regular meetings. Given that the letters include not only specifically Christian forms but also many of the topics, forms of argument, and figures common to popular rhetoric, oral exhortation doubtless used them, too. Joining the meeting in Gaius's overcrowded dining room, we might have heard, along with reminders of our life before baptism and our new life now, revelations of "words of the Lord," prophecies about things to come, admonitions to love each other as Christ loved us, as well as discourses on the topos "on marriage," or "on brotherly love." We would have been urged to exercise body and mind for the great contest of life, pressing on to the goal, not fearing the pain or the difficulties, which would prove our character.[37] The Christian prophets and exhorters did not speak only novelties, a "Holy Ghost language." The uninstructed outsider (*idiōtēs*) who came in off the street to hear this kind of preaching would not think he was hearing the gibberish of some frenzy, but nevertheless he would find something strange, perhaps numinous about it (1 Cor. 14:23–25). What was odd was just the blend of the familiar and the novel.

Of course the assemblies included prayer. How formal was it? The fact that one could pray either "by tongue" or "rationally" ("with the mind," 1 Cor. 14:13–15) suggests some mixture of the spontaneous and the customary—though further reflection may show that the line between rational and spiritual prayer is not identical to the dichotomy between formal and formless (see further below). The best-known form of Jewish prayer is of the style, "Blessed art thou, Lord our God, King of the Universe [or other suitable epithets], who doest . . . [or, "because thou has done . . ."]. This is the style of the standard daily prayer that is among the oldest parts of the synagogue liturgy, the Tefillah (*"the* Prayer"). That the early Pauline groups adapted this pattern of prayer is suggested by numerous echoes in epistolary forms, some of which we have already noticed, such as "Blessed be the God and Father of our Lord Jesus Christ, the Father of mercies and God of all consolation, who consoles us in our every affliction. . ." (2 Cor. 1:3f.). The third-person formulation in lieu of the second-person in fact accords with an older prayer style, but its appearance in the letters is dictated by the epistolary situation. In worship the Christians may well have said, "Blessed are you, God and Father of our Lord Jesus, . . ."[38]

A great many other small forms, "acclamations," "doxologies," and the like that are embedded in the letters also probably reflect the common language of prayer: "Thanks be to God who gives us the victory through our Lord Jesus Christ" (1 Cor. 15:57; cf. Rom. 7:25; 2 Cor. 2:14; further adapted, Rom. 6:17; 2 Cor. 8:16; 9:15); "God . . . to whom be glory for ever and ever. Amen" (Gal. 1:5; Rom. 11:36; 16:27; more elaborate, Eph. 3:21; still in use, 2 Tim. 4:18; elaborated 1 Tim. 1:17).[39] The "amen" that follows the doxology in many instances was also liturgical, following a Jewish pattern (1 Cor. 14:16) of congregational response to a prayer.[40]

The formula "in the Name of Jesus" or similar phrases must also have punctuated Christian worship very frequently, because the admonition about congregational singing in Col. 3:17 concludes, "And everything you do, in word or in deed, (do it) all in the name of the Lord Jesus, giving thanks to God the Father through him" (see also Eph. 5:20). Indeed, early Christians including Paul adapted from Joel 3:5 the phrase "every one who calls on the name of the Lord," understanding "Lord" to mean "our Lord Jesus Christ" (1 Cor. 1:2 and often). Moreover, the "hymn" that Paul quotes in Phil. 2:6–11 pictures a heavenly enthronement of Christ in which, at the signal "in the Name of Jesus," everyone kneels. Those doing obeisance in the mythic picture are superhuman powers; we would probably not go far wrong to imagine that the Philippian Christians were accustomed, on hearing the same formula at some point in their worship, probably in connection with baptism,[41] to bend *their* knees and confess, "The Lord is Jesus Christ." What is done on earth is confirmed in heaven—or, rather, the reverse.

We have been talking about "forms," "rites," "customs or practices of a formal kind."[42] Yet one of the most vivid (and noisiest) activities in the Pauline assemblies was glossolalia—at least that was the case in Corinth, and the source used by the author of Acts for his Pentecost story probably presupposes a widespread phenomenon in the early churches. Surely glossolalia and ritual are polar opposites? Paul certainly saw a dangerous tension between the extravagance of speaking in tongues at Corinth and the rational behavior he preferred—between uncontrolled enthusiasm and "decency and order." We would form a seriously distorted picture of these meetings, however, if we were to assume that glossolalia and other manifestations of spirit possession were formless, while ritual behavior was pure form. Neither is true. The formal procedure, the known pattern, was the framework within which the individual Christian more or less spontaneously sang "his" psalm or prayed "his" prayer. Anyone who has attended modern-day services of the free church traditions will know how large a proportion of supposedly spontaneous prayer consists of endlessly repeated linguistic patterns.

Moreover, even the extreme form of antistructural behavior, glossolalia, has also its forms and occasions, some of them very specific and rigid, as is evident from the discoveries of Felicitas Goodman, mentioned in the previous chapter. Not only does glossolalia in modern groups occur at predictable times in the service, framed by rather clearly defined ritual procedures; there are also quite specific verbal formulas and physical actions that to some extent channel and limit the ecstatic behavior. In adepts, there are even "trigger words" that can induce or terminate the trance.[43] Paul, at least, thought the same was true at Corinth, for he gives explicit directions about the number of glossolalists who are to be permitted to speak and clearly expects that the *charisma* can be controlled within the framework of the other ritual procedures we have been describing. Thus we are led to a conclusion that at first might have seemed paradoxical: that such exotic and presumably spontaneous behavior as speaking in tongues was also ritual. It occurred within the framework of the assembly, performed by persons who were expected to do it. It happened at predictable times, accompanied by distinctive bodily movements, perhaps introduced and followed by characteristic phrases in natural language. It did what rituals do: it stimulated feelings of group solidarity (except, as at Corinth, for those nonspeakers made to feel excluded); it increased the prestige of individuals, thus creating or underlining roles, and marked the occasion as one of solemnity (in the older sense, not the now common one of being dull and humorless).

A number of other hints of ritual are to be found in the letters, but it is impossible to be sure what their contexts may have been. Were there formulas for beginning and ending a meeting? In 1 Cor. 5:4 the Corinthians are told what to do when they "gather in the name of the Lord Jesus," a formula we have met in other contexts. Does that mean that this formula is pronounced in some suitable sentence to call the assembly to order? Again, we know that the use of the Shema ("Hear O Israel, the Lord our God is one Lord . . . ," Deut. 6:4f.) had a prominent place early in the synagogue liturgy. Is familiarity with it through a similar use in the Christian gatherings presupposed by Paul's pointed allusions in 1 Thess. 1:9 and Rom. 3:30? A "holy kiss," is mentioned in the conclusions of four of Paul's letters and also in 1 Peter (1 Thess. 5:26; Rom. 16:16; 1 Cor. 16:20; 2 Cor. 13:12; 1 Pet. 5:14). Was it a ritual marking the end of a meeting? Or did it, as in some later liturgies, mark the transition to the Supper? The same sort of question often arises about the *anathema* against anyone who "does not love the Lord" and the Aramaic prayer, *marana tha*, of 1 Cor. 16:22. To these questions we find no definitive answers.

We have found a wide range of little actions and verbal formulas and references to larger, more general activities that occurred, it seems, with fair regularity in the Pauline communities. Although most of our evidence comes from a few passing references, particularly in the Corinthian correspondence, we are safe in assuming that many if not all of these were common. The earliest of the letters reassures us that this was so, for it speaks already of instruction, admonition, prayer, thanksgiving, prophesying and perhaps other "ecstatic" demonstrations (the *pneuma* is not to be "quenched"), the holy kiss, and the reading of the apostolic letter (1 Thess. 5:12–27); and it ends, as a meeting might, with a benediction (vs. 28). We discover a very free, charismatic order, but an order nonetheless: there are customary forms. These assemblies, marked by these forms, were also the setting for the two major ritual complexes, baptism and the Lord's Supper.

BAPTISM: RITUAL OF INITIATION

Exactly what did Paul do and say when he baptized the household of Stephanas? To what symbolic action do he and the author of Colossians refer when they speak of "being buried with [Christ] in baptism"? Nowhere in the letters do we find a straightforward description of the ritual. The people to whom Paul and his disciples were writing knew what the procedure was; it was the implications of the event that the leaders had to interpret and reinterpret. Consequently, we are fairly well supplied with interpretations of baptism, with examples of what it meant in at least one sense, or what Paul and his co-workers wanted it to mean. Yet we have to rely on inference to answer the simplest questions about what happened, and we will remain ignorant, however clever our detection, of many details that might, if we knew them, alter our total picture of the ritual. Nevertheless it is neither impossible nor useless to sort out what we *do* know and can with fair probability infer about Pauline baptism, along the lines that an ethnographer might use to describe initiation into some modern sect.

Our task is made easier by the efforts of a number of scholars in this century to detect, by stylistic analysis, formulas quoted or paraphrased by the letter writers.[44] We have already noticed a number of these forms and observed in passing that several of them probably were at home in the baptismal ritual. We shall now examine them more systematically.

The center of the ritual, as the terms *baptizein* and *baptisma* indicate, was simply a water bath. In one of Paul's reminders, the conversion of Corinthian Christians from their former life of vice is summarized thus: "But you were washed, you were made holy, you were justified in [or, by] the name of our Lord Jesus Christ and in [or, by] the Spirit of our God" (1 Cor. 6:11). The fact that baptism could be construed as a symbolic burial with Christ (Rom. 6:4; Col. 2:12) suggests a complete immersion in water. That was the case with the normal Jewish rite of purification, the *ṭebilah,* which was probably, at whatever distance, the primary antecedent of Christian baptism. The first full description of the Christian rite, in Hippolytus's *Apostolic Tradition,* which probably represents Roman practice at the end of the second century, attests a threefold immersion.[45] However, the little manual of church order called the Didache ("Teaching of the Twelve Apostles"), which may represent traditions as much as a century older than Hippolytus, probably in Syria, provides for pouring water thrice over the head, in case sufficient water for immersion is not at hand (7:3). Most of the artistic depictions of baptism, in Roman catacombs and sarcophagi of the third and succeeding centuries, show the candidate (usually depicted as a child) standing in water, with the officiant pouring water over his head. The earliest identifiable Christian meetinghouse discovered by archaeologists, at Dura-Europos on the Euphrates, contained a basin that would hardly suffice for immersion.[46] Perhaps the Pauline groups, too, had to adjust symbolism to physical necessity.

Where *did* they baptize? In the "living water" of a stream? That was what the Didache preferred, no doubt on the model of some of the biblical prescriptions for purification.[47] Most often, however, the Levitical rules mention only "water," without specifying "living water," and by the time of Christianity's beginnings Pharisaic sages seem already to have invented the *mikveh*, an immersion pool deemed pure if it had adequate dimensions and the prescribed construction even though its water was still.[48] Yet we cannot very well imagine the synagogue officers in an eastern city admitting to their mikveh one of Paul's groups of uncircumcised gentiles, chanting about a messiah equal to God, crucified, resurrected, and reigning in heaven. It is only slightly less fantastic to picture them taking over a room in a public bath.[49] And even a Gaius or an Erastus is not likely to have had a private bath. The river seems our best guess, or else a tub and a bowl.

The Christian converts were baptized naked. Analogy with the Jewish rites might suggest that; it is explicit in the Roman practice described by Hippolytus and indicated in all the early portrayals of baptism in Christian art. What confirms the fact for the Pauline groups is the variety of metaphorical allusions to taking off and putting on clothing that we find in those parts of the letters that refer to baptism. Those allusions are of two sorts, as we shall see: the mythical notion of taking off the body, the "old human," and putting on instead Christ, the "new human"; and the rather common ethical figure of taking off bad habits and putting on virtuous ones. The convergence of both types in the baptismal reminders of Pauline paraenesis is most easily accounted for on the assumption that the candidates from the beginning took off their clothes to be baptized and put them back on afterward, and that these natural actions were given metaphorical significance.[50]

Anointing, which would play a significant role in later baptismal liturgies,[51] is mentioned in the Pauline corpus only once, 2 Cor. 1:21. The context, which hearkens back to the conversion of the Corinthian Christians, suggests that it was connected already with baptism.[52] The gift of the Holy Spirit, mentioned in the same passage and frequently elsewhere, was also associated with baptism, but there is nothing in the letters to indicate how this gift was symbolized. We have seen that some of the *pneumatikoi* at Corinth took glossolalia to be the sign par excellence of possession of (or by) the Spirit, and that belief was still known when Acts was written (10:44–46). We can scarcely believe that every convert on emerging from the water of baptism fell into a trance and spoke in tongues, however, if for no other reason than that it would then be hard to understand either the divisions over the practice at Corinth or Paul's arguments in trying to bring it under control. The Acts passage just cited suggests an alternative sign, for the Cornelius household were both "speaking in tongues" and "extolling God" (RSV)— more precisely, "magnifying [*megalynōn*] God." That is, they were shouting out the kind of acclamation found also in pagan contexts, "Great [*megas*] is God!"[53] The response in the Pauline groups may have been simpler: Gal. 4:6 and Rom. 8:15f. suggest that the newly baptized person shouted out the Aramaic word *Abba* ("Father"), and that this was understood as the Spirit speaking through him, at the same time indicating his adoption as "child of God."

Whether in the Pauline communities there was a formal creed, or confession of faith, at baptism is debated.[54] Baptism is the most likely setting for the simple confession mentioned by Paul in Rom. 10:9, "The Lord is Jesus!" (*kyrios Iēsous*). That corresponds, as we saw above, to the acclamation of the exalted Jesus by cosmic powers, depicted in the hymn quoted in Phil. 2:10f. Such a declaration was at least one referent of early Christian interpretation of the Joel passage, "Everyone who calls upon the name of the Lord will be saved" (as, for example, in Rom. 10:13); Paul's biographer still associates this with baptism in his description of Paul's conversion (Acts 22:16). Furthermore, the connection with Phil. 2:10f. suggests that baptism was the *Sitz im Leben* for this and similar poems or canticles that depict Jesus' descent or humiliation followed by cosmic exaltation. "Singing to Christ as to a god," which Pliny discovered the Christians of Bithynia doing at their dawn meetings for (initiatory?) oaths, may thus have been the practice sixty years earlier among Christians of Asia and Macedonia.[55]

So far we have examined clues from the Pauline and deutero-Pauline letters for what the congregations concretely did when they initiated new members. Some of these may become a little clearer when we turn to the ways in which the letters *interpret* baptism. Before taking up those applications of baptismal motifs, however, let us consider what it may have meant to the participants that their initiatory ritual was a rite of cleansing. It was not preceded by a washing; baptism *was* a washing.[56]

The significance of this fact begins to emerge when we compare baptism with activities that both ancient and modern observers have regarded as its closest analogies, the Jewish immersion of proselytes and the initiations into pagan mysteries. In the mysteries, some ceremony of washing or sprinkling often prepared candidates for admission to the mysteries proper. In the Eleusinian mysteries, for example, there was an official in charge of such rites, called a *hydranos*. A marble relief from the fourth century B.C. depicts a goddess, probably Persephone, in this role, pouring water from a phial over a young, nude figure; it cannot fail to remind us of the earliest pictures of Christian baptism, six centuries later.[57] These lustrations, and perhaps also bathing in the river Ilissos, were among the preparatory rites of the Lesser Mysteries held at Agrai, which were as a whole a preparatory purification for the Greater Mysteries held later in the year at Eleusis.[58] On the second day of the latter (16 Boedromion), the cry went up, "To the sea, O Mystai!" where-upon the whole company, each initiate and his pig, bathed, and later the pigs were sacrificed. But all this took place in Athens, three days before the great procession to Eleusis. It was all public and well known, no part of the secret *teletē*.[59] Similarly the initiate of Isis first received a washing, then fasted for ten days before the initiation proper.[60] One had to be pure before entering a sacred space and time.

The same was true of the water rites of Judaism, which in ancient Israel were closely associated with the temple and cult. The extension and democra-tization of the concept of purity and the means for attaining and restoring it were part of the religious revolution of the Pharisees. To a remarkable degree they seem to have transformed the notion of the sacred by associating it, and the cleanness that represented it, with the group that keeps itself pure and loyal to the commandments—not just in temple precincts at festival time, but daily in the home, in the midst of the unclean world. The immersion pool was one of the innovations of that revised conception of purity and its uses.[61] Yet among the Pharisees there is implied, so far as I can see, no permanent transition from the impure world into the pure community. The line between is constantly in flux; purity must be continually reestablished in response to voluntary or involuntary actions of the member of the sect, or to acci-dents that befall him. Thus the boundary between the sect and the world is wavering and porous, and the Pharisee does not, accordingly, represent his sect as the only "real" Israel, nor does the immersion in the mikveh be-come an initiation. Even the immersion required of proselytes is only a special case of the ordinary purifications and not an initiation in itself, despite the attempts of some scholars to make it the direct antecedent of Christian baptism.[62]

By making the cleansing rite alone bear the whole function of initiation, and by making initiation the decisive point of entry into an exclusive commu-nity, the Christian groups created something new. For them the bath becomes a permanent threshold between the "clean" group and the "dirty" world, between those who have been initiated and everyone who has not. It is that obvious sense of the rite separating pure from impure on which Paul trades in his admonitions of 1 Cor. 5–6, which we examined in the previous chapter. There he takes as self-evident that pure/impure can be a metaphor for moral/immoral, and thus he can shift to the figure "cleanse out the leaven," like a Jewish family before Passover, to command the removal of a sexual deviant from the group. It is plausible that the Corinthian Christians, or some of them, had understood the rules they had learned and that Paul had earlier written to them to mean that they should avoid contamination by the pollut-ing world, but that the group's own purity was impregnable. Paul tries to reverse that understanding (1 Cor. 5:9–13). The world is impure, but this is not their concern; what is polluting is internal misbehavior. They are not to try to withdraw from the world. To be sure, to sue one another in pagan courts is an appalling transgression of the boundaries, but what is really

polluting is that their suits imply a desire to cheat one's "brother," which is
behavior typical of what they were, as outsiders, before "you were washed,
you were made holy, you were justified. . ." (6:1–11). That allusion to baptism, as we saw, led Paul's argument back to concern with sexual matters,
now in terms of the purity of the individual body: united with Christ as if
(spiritually) in marriage, the body (like the community: 3:16) is a "temple of
the Holy Spirit within you" (6:12–20). As we shall see, those motifs also are
closely connected with baptism. Paul's argument depends on common recognition that baptism draws a line between the unwashed world and the washed
Christians, and that "clean" is a metaphor for "behaving properly." In the
second century, the Church would further emphasize the height of the threshold between outside and inside by a dramatic series of exorcisms leading up
to baptism,[63] but there is no evidence for such a procedure in the Pauline
communities.

Allusions to baptism occur principally in passages in which Paul tries to
correct misunderstandings or to argue on the basis of a common starting
point, as in the passage just mentioned and in Rom. 6; 8:12–17; Gal. 3:26–
4:6; 1 Cor. 1–4; 12, and in the paraenetic reminders that make up most of
Colossians and Ephesians. Paraenetic reminders are appeals to recall what
happened when the addressees first became Christians, both the ritual of
baptism and the instruction that accompanied it, and to behave in ways
appropriate to that memory.[64] These passages have often been analyzed for
their ideational content and for their parallels, connections, and possible
antecedents in the history of religions. Our purpose is different; we are trying
to see what baptism did for ordinary Christians, disregarding the question of
where its elements may have come from and even the profounder theological
beliefs that Paul and some of the other leaders associated with it, unless we
can be sure those were integral to the common understanding. I shall begin by
listing the most prominent motifs and then try to determine some of their
interrelationships in the pattern of ritual action.

Foremost among the motifs that Paul takes for granted, known not only
to members of groups he founded but also to the Christians in Rome, is the
image of dying and rising with Christ. This is expressed not only in the
language of analogy ("As Christ was raised from the dead . . . so also
we . . .") but also in the language of participation ("We have been baptized
into his death . . . ," Rom. 6:3f.), as well as by verbs compounded in $syn-$,
"with" (Rom. 6:4, 8; Col. 2:12f.; Eph. 2:5f.). A variation of this theme is
that the state of the convert prior to his baptism is itself death; baptism is a
death of death, the beginning of life (Col. 2:13; Eph. 2:1,5).

Were death and rising mimed somehow in the ritual? In liturgies of the
later church, sometimes the usual posture of prayer, standing with arms
raised and palms forward, was taken to represent crucifixion,[65] but there is
no hint of anything similar in the Pauline literature. Attempts to find in Paul's
reference to the "stigmata of Jesus" he carried (Gal. 6:17) evidence for sign-
ing or even tattooing with the cross at baptism have not been convincing.[66]

Descent into the water obviously did not mime Jesus' death, but it could be construed as "being buried with Christ" (Rom. 6:4; Col. 2:12), and rising from the water could very well signify "being raised with Christ" (Col. 2:12; 3:1; Eph. 2:6). For death itself, some other action would have to be found; the Pauline Christians found it in the removal of clothing before entering the water. That became "taking off the body" or "the old human." Reclothing afterward could then represent the new life of resurrection.

The clothing imagery comprises an elaborate complex of metaphors. What is "taken off" is variously construed as "the old human," "the body of flesh," and the vices associated therewith. This "removal of the body of flesh" is "the circumcision of Christ," that is, the Christian equivalent of Jewish circumcision of proselytes (Col. 2:11). What is "put on" is Christ himself, as "the new human," who is "being renewed . . . according to the image of his creator" (Col. 3:10). Characteristic of the "new human" is unity, the end of the opposed sets of roles that typified the "old human": Jew/Greek, slave/free, male/female (Gal. 3:28; 1 Cor. 12:13; Col. 3:10f.; cf. Ignatius, Eph. 6:8). There are patent in this language numerous allusions to the biblical account of the creation of man and to expansions of that account in Jewish lore. Among the latter was a reading of Gen. 1:27 as the creation of an original androgynous human in the image of God, then divided (Gen. 2:21f.) into male and female halves. Moreover, the "garments of skin" made for the fallen couple by God were nothing else than the physical bodies, necessary to replace the "garments of light" (a pun in Hebrew) which had been the "image of God." In view of these elements, baptism suggests a restoration of paradisiac motifs: the lost unity, the lost image, the lost glory.[67] The paraenetic reminders of baptism in the letters blend these mythical motifs with a more commonplace use of clothing imagery that appears frequently in the rhetoric of Hellenistic moralists, including Hellenistic Jewish writers and later Christian writers, both orthodox and gnostic. They admonish the readers to take off vices and to put on virtues in their place.[68]

There is some evidence, principally in Ephesians, that the baptized and now reclothed person was next "enthroned with Christ in the heavenly places."[69] We can perhaps imagine how that could have been mimed, but the texts tell us nothing more.[70] Perhaps this element was present in the baptismal practice of Pauline communities from an early date, for the polemic of Paul in 1 Cor. 15 and his sarcasm in 1 Cor. 4:8 can be understood as opposing a too-enthusiastic appropriation of just such a notion. If the poems celebrating the exaltation of the Lord who had descended from heaven (Phil. 2:6–11; cf. Col. 1:15–20) were chanted at this point in the service, as I suggested above, a symbolic elevation of the believer at the same time would be fitting.

Like the unseen powers mentioned in the poem, the novice most likely then proclaimed, "The Lord is Jesus!" This confession would appropriately signify the change of dominion he had now undergone, from the world ruled by demonic powers, the "elements of the world," to the realm in which "the living God" and his Christ reign. From his new Lord he received certain gifts: the Spirit, adoption as God's child, power. He responded with the cry, "Abba! Father!"

It is immediately apparent that a great many of these motifs sort themselves out as pairs of opposites:

death, dying	life, rising
descending	ascending
burial	enthronement
old *anthrōpos*, body of flesh	new *anthrōpos*, body of Christ
oppositions	unity
taking off	putting on
vices	virtues
idols, demons, rulers of this world	living God, Christ Jesus as Lord

Furthermore, if we array these opposites according to the temporal stages of the ritual, the result is two nearly symmetrical movements. The first, characterized by descending action, climaxes with the "burial" in the water; it signifies the separation of the baptizand from the outside world. The second, a rising action, marks the integration of the baptized into another world,

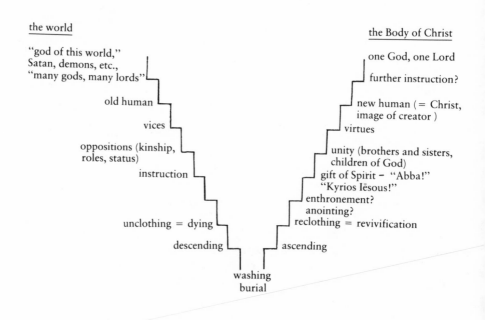

Figure 1

the sect on one plane, the heavenly reality on another. Figure 1 shows the verbal and conceptual progression.

This progression corresponds to the phases of every initiation or rite of passage: separation, transition, and reaggregation.[71] Nudity, symbolic death, rebirth as a child, abolition of distinctions of role and status—all are typical of the transitional or liminal phase in initiations. The most common picture of rites of passage, however, is abstracted from ceremonies that mark transition from one status to another within a small, homogeneous society: from child to man, from elder to chief. Baptism in early Christianity was different from that, different from, say, confirmation or first communion in an Irish Catholic parish, because the group which the initiate enters does not entirely share the same symbolic universe as the society from which he came. It sees itself, as a whole, distinct from "the world" even though, as we have seen at several points, the actual boundary between the two was more ambiguous than that simple statement would suggest. Victor Turner's extension of the concept of liminality to include an "anti-structural" component in more complex social situations, including the condition of marginal groups within complex societies, helps us to relate the early Christian rites to the theory of ritual.

The difference is apparent in the figure 1, in which some liminal elements had to be placed, not at the perigee of the parabola, but high on the "reaggregation" side. It is said of the body of Christ itself that "here there is neither Jew nor Greek, slave nor free, no male and female." The *ekklēsia* itself, not just the initiates during the period of their induction, is supposed to be marked by sacredness, homogeneity, unity, love, equality, humility, and so on—as Turner would say, by *communitas*. However, we have seen abundant evidence (chapters 3 and 4, above) that the Pauline groups suffered some tension between this mode of socialization, which opposes the normal structures of the macrosociety, and the old structures. The latter are not completely escapable, for the Christians continue to live in the city and to interact with its institutions, and besides, they still carry some of its structures in their minds and in the houses where they meet. Thus in the paraenesis of the later letters of the Pauline school, Colossians and Ephesians, reminders of the new "antiworldly" relations introduced in baptism stand alongside admonitions for proper behavior in hierarchically structured roles: husbands/wives, fathers/children, masters/slaves. These tensions also invade the meetings for the Lord's Supper.

THE LORD'S SUPPER: RITUAL OF SOLIDARITY

The Pauline letters yield much less information about the other major ritual of early Christianity, the *kyriakon deipnon* (1 Cor. 11:20). The only explicit references to it are in 1 Cor. 11:17–34 and 10:14–22, and there it is easier to see the social implications that Paul is advocating than it is the ordinary social process of the ritual. He does, however, quote a sacred formula used in the celebration,[72] which differs slightly from the versions found in the later synoptic Gospels, and his polemic against aspects of the Corinthian practice permits some inferences about the usual procedure and understanding. First of all, the basic act is the eating of a common meal, at which it is possible that "one goes hungry, another is drunk" (1 Cor. 11:21). It is "the table of the Lord" (10:21). Festive meals were a common feature of the life of voluntary associations of all sorts, and the Christians' Supper was still understood in this way by Pliny, who early in the second century in Bithynia forbade such meals, in accordance with Trajan's ban against clubs (*Ep.* 10.97.7). A dining room was also "a distinctive and ubiquitous feature of cult centers" in antiquity, and invitations to dine "at the couch of Helios, Great Sarapis," or the like were a familiar part of urban social life.[73] For Christians to meet at intervals for such a meal with their Lord Jesus would not seem out of the ordinary.

In the second place, the ritual action imitates the meal of Jesus with his disciples "on the night in which he was betrayed" (11:23). The rite focuses on two moments: the breaking and distribution of bread at the beginning of the meal, accompanied by thanksgiving and a formulaic saying, "This is my body, which is for you; do this as my memorial"; and the passing of the cup of wine after the meal, with a parallel formula, "This cup is the new covenant in my blood; do this, as often as you drink, as my memorial" (11:24f.).[74]

The repeated injunction, "Do this as my memorial" (not found in the version of Mark and Matthew), shows that in the Pauline and even pre-Pauline tradition the celebration is understood as a cultic commemoration of Jesus. Most pointedly, it is a re-presentation of his death, as Paul's added comment in verse 26 underscores. This concept, too, would have been quite familiar in the environment of the early Christian groups, for, as Bo Reicke says, "The connection of the concept *anamnēsis* ['memorial'] with death is quite typical for people in antiquity."[75] It was also typical that a meal by the family, friends, or fellow burial-club members of the deceased would be the means of commemoration.[76] However, to understand the specific function of the memorial of Jesus it is perhaps most relevant to observe that it repeats under different imagery one of the central motifs of baptism. That is, the repeated sacrament of the Supper re-presents this central content of the initiatory ritual. Both rituals keep in the minds of the believers the fundamental story of the Lord's death. Beginning with this pre-Pauline (Antiochene?) tradition, the motif of commemoration would dominate the way the Eucharist was understood at least into the third century.[77]

Third, the formula contains an allusion to the vicarious meaning of the death in the expression "my body which is for you." This recalls similar expressions in many of the compact, formulaic sentences found in the letters, which are often thought to reproduce early Christian creedal summaries or preaching slogans.[78]

Fourth, there is an eschatological element: "until he comes." To be sure, that phrase belongs to a comment that Paul adds to the tradition, but some connection with Jesus' eschatological coming is found in all versions of the early Eucharistic tradition, though in varied verbal formulations. The Aramaic phrase that Paul quotes in the closing of this letter, *marana tha* (16:22), very likely also belongs to the setting of the Lord's Supper, as it does in the Didache (10:6).

Paul cites the Eucharistic traditions only in order to address certain conflicts which have arisen in the Corinthian congregation. In an illuminating way, Gerd Theissen has undertaken to reconstruct the social conditions underlying the disturbances rebuked by Paul in 1 Cor. 11:17–34 and to analyze Paul's "social intention" in his interpretation of the Supper in that passage.[79] I have already adopted much of Theissen's construction, with a few criticisms, in chapter 2. It may be helpful to recall here the main outline. The divisions in the group (11:18) are primarily between rich and poor. The wealthier members of the church are hosts of the gatherings and probably provide the food for all. Quite in accord with the expectations in many ancient clubs and with the practice often followed at banquets when dependents of a patron were invited, the hosts provide both greater quantity and better quality of food and drink to their social equals than to participants of lower status. The conflict was thus between "different standards of behavior," between "status-specific expectations and the norms of a community of love."[80] Paul's response, Theissen suggests, is a compromise, which asks that the wealthy have their private meal (*idion deipnon*) at home, so that in the Lord's Supper (*kyriakon deipnon*) the norm of equality can prevail. At the same time, Paul sets the social tensions into a larger symbolic universe by making them part of an "eschatological drama." The sacrament is "a zone under taboo, in which violation of norms has as its consequence incalculable disaster."[81] Paul underlines this notion by blaming sickness and deaths which have occurred in the community on such violations (11:30). Paul's social intention in all this is that revealed in 10:16: the transformation of a multiplicity of individuals into a unity.[82] Another way to put this would be to say that the *communitas* experienced in baptism, in which divisions of role and status are replaced by the unity of brothers and sisters in the new human, ought to be visible, in Paul's intention, in the Supper.

For Paul and his co-workers, the corollary of unity in the body of Christ is strict exclusion from all other religious connections. That is, group solidarity entails strong boundaries. Consequently Paul uses traditional language from the Supper ritual,[83] which speaks of the bread as "communion of the body of Christ" and the "cup of blessing" as "communion of the body of Christ," to warn that any participation in pagan cultic meals would be idolatry. The single loaf used in the ritual symbolizes the unity of Christ and of the believer with Christ and, consequently, the unity of the community in its participation in Christ (10:17). Just as in 6:12–20 Paul argues that union with the body of Christ excludes union with a prostitute, so here he insists that the unity presented in the Supper is exclusive. "You cannot drink the cup of the Lord and the cup of demons; you cannot share the table of the Lord and the table of demons" (10:21). It is this exclusivity of cult that was perhaps the strangest characteristic of Christianity, as of Judaism, in the eyes of the ordinary pagan. In this context, the ritual of the Lord's Supper entails for Paul a picture of the world that can be diagrammed as in Figure 2.

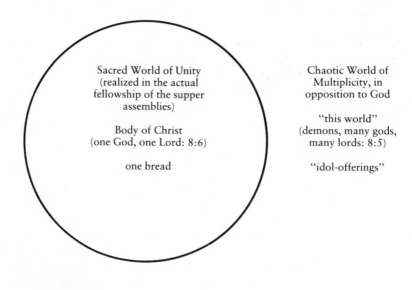

Figure 2

Thus, Paul uses the symbolism of the Supper ritual not only to enhance the internal coherence, unity, and equality of the Christian group, but also to protect its boundaries vis-à-vis other kinds of cultic association.

It must be stressed, however, that this symbolism of exclusivity is only one dimension of the complicated argument in 1 Cor. 8–10 about "meat offered to idols." While the passage just discussed absolutely excludes as idolatrous any participation in a pagan cultic meal, Paul is also at pains to show that nonsymbolic eating of pagan-butchered meat is a matter of indifference (10:25–27). It is only when the meat is deliberately made a symbol— whether through a public location, in an *eidōleion* (8:10), by uninformed belief of the "weak" Christians that idols are real (8:10; cf. vs. 7), or by a statement deliberately calling attention to the religious (sacrifical) character of the meat (10:28)—that it is forbidden for the Christian. To this extent Paul shares and approves the desacralizing *gnōsis* of the "strong" Christians at Corinth, by confirming the right and freedom of Christians to participate in the macrosociety so long as that participation does not upset the internal harmony and development of the Christian community. The complexity of

Paul's interpretation implies that the intrinsic symbolism of the ritual is malleable; it is patient of multiple interpretations.

The unity symbolized by the Lord's Supper, I have suggested, can be seen as a reminder or re-presentation of the liminal transcendence of societal oppositions that was declared in baptism. Now it is commonly asserted that this baptismal unity and egalitarianism is "merely sacramental," that is, as a purely symbolic leveling it signifies an ideal state, perhaps a future eschatological state, but has no effect upon actual social roles.[84] Indeed, that is the way rites of passage ordinarily work in situations in which the boundaries of the religious association are more or less coterminous with the society. The temporary suspension of hierarchical classifications in the liminal period only reinforces their power in the ordinary world into which the initiate is then reintegrated. However, in the case of a group that maintains a strong identity distinct from the larger society, some aspects of liminality may linger in its daily life. The early Pauline communities were understandably not all of one mind about the implications of being, after baptism, all brothers and sisters in the one body.

For Paul, it was a matter of intense concern that at least one of the typical instances of reunification declared in the "baptismal reunification formula"[85] should have concrete social consequences. That there was now no distinction between Jew and gentile was for him (and for his learned disciple who wrote Ephesians) the most dramatic expression of the justification enacted by God through Christ Jesus. When, therefore, Cephas, Barnabas, and the other Jewish Christians at Antioch were persuaded to stop sharing the common meals with uncircumcised Christians, it was not merely a purely spiritual unity in the ritual meal that was at stake, but also the social unity of the church.[86] This unity points to the life of the "new human" now to be manifested in the life of the congregations and, in God's future, in the world. It is expressed in the ritual meal and perhaps also in other meals, for Gal. 2:12 does not restrict its reference to the Lord's Supper.

Yet the result was an ambiguous situation, and the letters reveal some confusion about the implications of the symbols of unity, not only in the practice of the Pauline groups, but even in Paul's own mind. Thus he may say that the slave at conversion has become "the Lord's freedman" and the "free person Christ's slave" (1 Cor. 7:22) and can ask Philemon to receive his runaway back, "no longer as a slave, but more than a slave, a beloved brother" (Philem. 16), but he nowhere urges Philemon or other owners to free their slaves. And the authors of the later letters in his name quote Christianized household rules that require slaves strictly to obey their masters. On the other hand, women do exercise some social roles in the Pauline missionary activity and congregational life that are equivalent to those of men, and Paul himself stresses equivalence of rights and duties in marriage (1 Cor. 7). Still, he objects to *symbolic* disregard for sexual differences in the dress of male and female prophets (1 Cor. 11:2–16). The relation between the symbolic reality presented in the rituals and everyday reality, both in the inner life of the group and in interaction with the larger society, remained an area of controversy and ambiguity. And, of course, this ambiguity remains at the heart of our own hermeneutical perplexity when we try to understand what rituals do for people.

UNKNOWN AND CONTROVERTED RITUALS

We have squeezed about all the information we can from the quotations and allusions in the literature. Yet we surmise that the Pauline Christians used still other ceremonies of which we know virtually nothing. We know, for example, that some of them died during the span of time covered by the letters, and we know that funeral rituals were of enormous importance to people in Greek and Roman society. A great many of the clubs we have mentioned were formed primarily to assure the associates a decent burial and memorial. We can be certain that the congregations Paul founded provided equivalent services for their members, but, apart from one utterly enigmatic remark, the letters say nothing at all about what was done for those who, as they said, "had fallen asleep." Probably the Christians buried their dead in the same places and in the same fashion as their neighbors. Those who could afford it probably erected inscriptions recalling high points of the deceased's life, indicating significant titles of status or profession, and giving the dates—but if they did, either the inscriptions remain lost or there was nothing overtly Christian about them to distinguish them from the others that have been found. The commonest memorial rite was a meal in honor of the departed, often around a table-shaped stone in the cemetery, on several specific anniversaries of the day of death. In later centuries this practice was common among Christians as among pagans—the first clear evidence is in Tertullian.[87] Nothing would seem more natural than for the Christians of Paul's groups, for whom common meals were already so important, to hold funeral meals for deceased brothers as well—either separately, or as part of the Lord's Supper, which was already an *anamnēsis* of the Lord's death. Yet there is not a word about such meals, not even in the consolation that Paul offers the Thessalonian Christians (1 Thess. 4:13–18), where we might have expected it. Perhaps the customs were too well known to mention. Paradoxically, the one practice that is mentioned, in 1 Cor. 15:29, is mystifying to us. Paul is arguing with the *pneumatikoi* at Corinth that resurrection does not mean only spiritual exaltation now, but a real, future resurrection of the dead body. "Otherwise," he asks, "what are they doing who are baptized for the dead? If the dead are not raised at all, why are they baptized on their behalf?" What *are* they doing? The Corinthians presumably knew, but we do not, despite interesting speculations without end.

The Pauline Christians also got married. And if a widow decided to remarry (although Paul preferred that she remain single), she should do so "only in the Lord" (1 Cor. 7:39). Presumably this means that she ought to marry a fellow Christian, and presumably the same rule would apply also to persons not previously married. But did "in the Lord" also imply a Christian ceremony? We do not know.

Besides the regular gatherings of the Christians, which probably but not certainly occurred weekly, did they also observe an annual calendar of seasons or any special festivals? Some Jewish Christians did, and both the missionaries who tried to reform the Pauline churches of Galatia and the syncretistic cult that developed among the Christians in Colossae tried to introduce the celebration of "days and months and seasons and years" (Gal. 4:10; Col. 2:16: "festival or new moon or sabbath"). Paul resisted this innovation vigorously and so did his disciple, the author of Colossians. Yet some commentators have found in 1 Cor. 5:6–8 and 16:8 reason to believe that Paul himself and his churches celebrated both a Christianized Passover and Pentecost (*Shabuoth*).[88] That is a far from necessary conclusion, however.

Acts and the Pauline letters provide only tantalizing glimpses of the rituals practiced by the Pauline groups, but those glimpses are enough for us to see that they had adopted or created a rich variety of ceremonial forms. There is a striking mix of the free and the customary, familiar and novel, simple and complex, in what we can see of their meetings. The *idiōtēs* or unbeliever, entering one of these meetings, might have thought them a bit odd, but he would have recognized them as a cultic community of some kind. Whether he called them a dangerous superstition or a strange religion would depend on personal sympathy or lack of it.

6

PATTERNS OF BELIEF AND PATTERNS OF LIFE

Studies of Pauline theology, which are legion, have all but universally neglected the social context and functions of doctrine. That neglect has led to serious distortions. The force of a belief-statement is determined by the whole matrix of social patterns within which it is uttered. The matrix includes conventions of language but is not limited to them. Abstracted from that setting or placed in a different one, the stated belief is liable to mean something quite different—a happy fact for the religious communities that have had to reinterpret canonical texts in all sorts of new settings and occasions, but a dreaded pitfall for the historian. That is why I have saved until this final chapter a systematic discussion of the beliefs of the Pauline Christians. First it was necessary to describe as fully as possible both the social milieu and the internal social forms of the communities, so that we can hold that context firmly in mind as we now try to supply the lines and shadows of doctrine.

The description that follows avoids strong theoretical assumptions. We will ask whether we can discover correlations between stated beliefs and social forms, but we will not assume that the one *causes* the other; nor shall we assume, when a given belief seems logically to imply a certain kind of behavior, that such behavior really followed, unless we have specific evidence for it.

It will be obvious that yet another attempt to outline Paul's own theology, even if space and wit allowed it, would contribute little to our purpose. Indeed, our aim requires us to neglect some of Paul's most interesting ideas and even, for the most part, his longest and theologically most impressive letter, that to the Christians in Rome. For the present we are interested in the social force of what the typical member of the Pauline churches believed. That information is very difficult to come by, for the typical Christian does not speak in our sources, and it is only by inference that we can guess some lineaments of the common beliefs. On the other hand, I certainly do not want to imply that the stated beliefs of Paul and the other letter writers of his school had no effect on their followers. Sometimes the writers drew from their doctrines direct consequences for the life of the churches. Those deductions are important evidence that we must consider, even though we must be wary of assuming that things really went the way the leaders hoped and argued.

ONE GOD, ONE LORD, ONE BODY

The affirmation that "God is one" is as basic to Pauline Christianity as it was to all Judaism (1 Thess. 1:9; Gal. 3:20; Rom. 3:30; Eph. 4:6; 1 Cor. 8:4, 6; cf. 1 Cor. 11:12; 15:28; 2 Cor. 5:18). To be sure, assertions of God's unity are not infrequent in pagan writers, beginning with the cosmopolitanism of the Stoa. This Hellenistic monotheism seems to have remained the property of certain intellectuals, however, never becoming a widespread or popular belief.[1] Moreover, its social correlates were quite different from the exclusive monotheism of Judaism. The Stoics and the middle Platonists, with their developing conception of one supreme deity synthesizing and incorporating the many gods of popular and traditional belief, provided an ideology for the genial pluralism and tolerance in cultic life that was characteristic of paganism in the imperial age.[2] Because all gods are ultimately aspects of the One, the wise man could acknowledge them all and draw whatever benefit he might from as many of their cults as he chose.

For the Jews of the Greco-Roman city, the pressures to emulate as well as to profit from this general tolerance were considerable. Their usual stance, however, was to match their belief in the one God, in contrast to all the "idols" of "the nations," with the distinctive practices that preserved their communal integrity as a unique people. Philo assimilated much of the middle-Platonic and Stoic programs and wholly shared most aspects of a cultured Hellenist's ethos and ambitions. Yet he illustrates dramatically how exclusive the Jewish monotheism could remain, even when it was explained almost entirely in the terms of the dominant high culture. For example, the Septuagint translators had rendered Exod. 22:27 as "You shall not revile gods," and Philo takes this as a warning that Jews should not speak insultingly of pagan images.[3] The reason he gives, however, has nothing to do with the cultivation of tolerance (which may have motivated the translation and its common application). Rather, the law was intended to keep Jews who might make a habit of reviling "idols" from extending that habit to the one true God. From the context of the Exodus text, he sees this as a special problem for proselytes (the "sojourner" of Exod. 22:20 had become "proselyte" in the Septuagint and in Palestinian Judaism, too). The proselytes must receive "special friendship," he insists, because "they have left . . . their country, their kinsfolk and their friends for the sake of virtue and religion. . . . For the most effectual love-charm, the chain which binds indissolubly the goodwill which makes us one, is to honour the one God."[4]

Christianity took over the Jewish position completely. The world was divided between those who served the "living, true God" and the idol worshipers (1 Thess. 1:9). Pagans have "many gods and many lords," the Christians "one God the Father . . . and one Lord Jesus Christ" (1 Cor. 8:4–6). "The gentiles who do not know God" (1 Thess. 4:5) and are therefore enslaved to nongods (Gal. 4:8) are contrasted with those who "know, rather are known by God" (Gal. 4:9). The language can be even more dualistic, as when "the god of this age" stands in contrast to the God whose image is Christ (2 Cor. 4:4).

For Paul's circle as for Philo, the desired social expression of faith in the one God is the exclusive unity of the worshipers. Paul's admonitions to the Philippian Christians begin, "Only conduct your common life worthily of the gospel of Christ," and continue with a long series of appeals for unity and mutuality: "stand in one spirit, striving with one soul . . . ; think alike; have the same love; joined in soul; have one outlook. . . ."[5] So, too, when Paul was faced with incipient divisions, jealousies, and spiritual elitism among the charismatics of Corinth, it was to the unity of the Lord (Christ) and the Spirit that he appealed (1 Cor. 12). The beginning of this passage has been obscured by the peculiar fascination modern scholars have felt for Paul's hyperbole, "No one speaking in the Spirit of God says 'Jesus is Anathema'" (vs. 3). This does not mean that the Corinthian meetings were full of Gnostics cursing Jesus.[6] Rather, the contrast is between the former life of the Christians ("When you were gentiles . . ."), "led (astray) . . . to speechless idols," and the speech (confessing the one Lord) that is given by the one Spirit of God. The language of verse 2 recalls that of 8:5f., which contrasts the many lords and gods of paganism with the one God and one Lord of Christians, except that here Paul mentions the Spirit as well, because the debate in chapter 12 is about *pneumatika*, "spiritual gifts." The Spirit's gifts are diverse (vs. 4), but there are limits to the diversity. There is an absolute boundary between the confession "the Lord is Jesus" and paganism (vs. 3). Within the community that confesses *kyrios Iēsous* there is diversity of gifts, services, and actions (vss. 4–6), but "the same Spirit . . . the same Lord . . . the same God." That statement sets the theme of the whole chapter and leads to Paul's introduction of the rhetorical commonplace which compares society with the body.

We shall pass over Paul's *tour de force* in Galatians, in which he draws an analogy between the "Judaizing" practices being urged by the latter-day missionaries and pagan polytheism (Gal. 4:8–11).[7] Paul even sets the oneness of God against the multiplicity of mediation by which the Torah itself was given (3:19f.).[8] This contrast, however, tells us more about Paul's argumentative ingenuity than about the effectiveness of these images in Galatia.

We are on slightly firmer ground with the emphasis on unity that pervades the two letters Colossians and Ephesians, written in Paul's name by persons who must have been close associates or disciples. The paraenesis of those letters bears the marks of being largely traditional and is particularly rich in allusions to the common rituals of baptism. As we saw in the previous chapter, the form of baptism used by the Pauline (and probably pre-Pauline) communities included language of what I have called reunification. Moreover, we saw that that language was specifically "sociomorphic."[9] The unity of the "new human," Christ, the Image of the Creator, was set in contrast to just those oppositions that locate a person in society. In short, the unity of the initiates is contrasted with social structure in all its complexity. In the deutero-Pauline letters we see that liminal unity becoming more narrowly circumscribed, for these authors take for granted that the cohesion and normalcy of the community should be preserved in much the same way that it is in ancient society at large: by a hierarchical structure of those who rule (males, parents, owners) and those who are subordinate (women, children, slaves). Nevertheless, the authors appeal to the liminal unity of baptism as the foundation of the church's unity. They can go further in urging that the divine unity should be reflected by a peaceful common life of the congregation. They can even portray cosmic powers as having been reconciled by Christ's exaltation, as a symbolic counterpart of the Christians living in harmony.[10] The admonition of Eph. 4:1–6, for example, begins, "Walk worthily of the calling in which you were called," and goes on to urge mutual forbearance in love, "working hard to keep the oneness of the spirit in the linkage of peace." It climaxes with:

> one body and one spirit,
>   as you were called in one hope of your calling,
> one Lord, one faith, one baptism,
> one God and Father of all,
>   who is over all and through all and in all.

So far, the effective difference from Judaism is slight. The addition of "one Lord" (Christ) and of "God's Son" to the confessional statements might be shocking to Jewish sensibilities, but the social implications of Jewish monotheism remain intact. To the one God (and one Lord and one Spirit) contrasted with the many gods of paganism corresponds the unity of an elect people with strong boundaries separating them from other cults and indeed from "this world."

Yet we know that in one respect Paul and his fellows construed the divine unity in a way that fundamentally departed from Judaism's way of distinguishing itself from the pagan environment. The one God for the Paulinists is precisely the God of Jews and gentiles together in one community. Now this concept, too, was certainly acceptable in some circles of Judaism; what is radical in Paulinism is the transformation of the way in which the community itself is constituted. Philo, for example, welcomed proselytes—as "refugees" from the pagan world to virtue and truth. As we saw earlier, he urged his fellow Jews to incorporate them into the community with bonds of affection that would express precisely the honor of the one God. The reformers that followed Paul into Galatia probably held a view that was not much different: the messianic age could bring more vigorous proselytism of gentiles, but they must then become part of messianic Israel, with the same halakic tests of faithfulness to the covenanting God and thus the same means of social identity and social boundaries as those the Jewish communities had established through long experience. For Paul and his circle, however, the unexpected, almost unthinkable claim that the Messiah had died a death cursed by the Law entailed a sharp break in terms of the way in which the people of God would henceforth be constituted and bounded. When Paul became a Christian, new rituals had already been created to commemorate the dying and rising of Jesus and to incorporate believers into his "body." Among the radicals at Antioch, these rituals and a new set of human relationships were replacing circumcision and other halakic observances as the distinctive boundary markers of the people of the one God.

Socially the most striking thing about the communities revealed in the Pauline letters is that there is no visible connection or even contact between them and the synagogues. The author of Acts, writing a generation later, sought to account for the separation by imagining Paul trying in every place first to win the Jewish community whole and withdrawing to the gentiles only when forced to by Jewish hostility. Perhaps that happened, but Paul says nothing of it. By the time the extant letters were written, the established pattern was instead to found in every city associations of believers in Christ, drawn from gentiles and Jews alike. The groups of believers were linked to one another but were entirely independent of the synagogues. The consequences for the future of Christianity were enormous.

The consequences for Paul's theology were no less great, although we may reasonably doubt whether the nuances of his thought penetrated the common life of his audience. Both in the polemic of Galatians and in the protreptic letter to the Romans, Paul defends his insistence that there is no longer any distinction between Jew and gentile by appealing precisely to the unity of God and his impartiality.[11] Yet this radical change was not a necessary consequence of belief in monotheism; otherwise, the controversy would not have existed. The author of Ephesians still regards the uniting of Jew and gentile in one household as a miracle, as a "mystery" hidden by God for ages and then revealed, as the earthly reflection of a hidden, cosmic drama (Eph. 2:11–22). For Paul himself, the central theological problem is not just to spell out the implications of monotheism, but to explain how the unified purpose of God through history could encompass the *novum* of the crucified Messiah. The theological dialectic of the Letter to Romans, culminating in Paul's essay on Israel's past and future place in God's purpose (chs. 9–11), cannot be separated from this social dimension of Paul's whole missionary career. How could the fact of the separate Christian movement be affirmed theologically as fulfilling God's promises, as representing in itself the "Israel" of God's new covenant, without denying the integrity of God's dealing with historic Israel in the persons of the vast majority of then-living Jews? The later church, for which the separateness of the two communities was a given fact of life, could avoid the problem by ignoring the Jews altogether or by denying their theological right to exist as Israel. For Paul that was impossible. The separation was a present necessity but ultimately a theological anomaly.

An even more difficult question is whether the Pauline Christians conceived of the antithesis between themselves and the larger, pagan society as also anomalous theologically and therefore socially provisional and temporary. The question arises because the assertions of monotheism are not abstract, but exist within the context of a *missionary* theology which has as its object, as Paul's disciple summed it up, "admonishing *everyone* and teaching *everyone* in all wisdom, in order to present *everyone* perfect in Christ" (Col. 1:28, my emphasis). In baptism one spoke of "putting on the new human" as a restoration of the image of God lost in Eden. The logic of these metaphors and of the others we have discussed seems to move in the direction of some kind of universalism, and perhaps this vision provided some of the impetus for the extraordinary zeal of the Pauline missionaries to preach in as many cities of the known world as possible. The thin network of tiny Christian cells represented itself in the audacious images of a restored, universal humanity, the creation of the only true God.

By and large, however, the Pauline Christians used these images when they wanted to insist upon unity and harmony within the sect. The hint in Rom. 11:25–32 that Paul envisaged an ultimate reconciliation of all humankind stands, significantly, within an extended argument in which the fundamental issue is the status of the Jews. Although the Pauline Christians had abandoned the chief Jewish devices for distinguishing the covenanted people from the world of polytheism, that does not mean, as we have seen, that they themselves did not also maintain strong boundaries to define themselves over against that world.

Nevertheless, the "response to the world" by which the sectarian character of the Pauline circle was defined[12] was significantly different from, say, that of the Qumran group of Jews or that of the Johannine Christians.[13] Although they might expect "to judge the world," and so Paul discountenanced some kinds of engagement with "the world's" administration (1 Cor. 6:1–11), they nevertheless did not fear contamination by the world (1 Cor. 5:10). They could continue to enjoy intimate relationships with non-Christians, including existing marriages (1 Cor. 7:12–16) and ordinary social relations (10:27), and their meetings were open to outsiders (14:23f.). This ambiguity about the community's boundaries was one of the important bequests by the Pauline Christians to the literary canon of the later church. Both Tatian's encratite renunciation of the world and a Eusebius's panegyric to a Christian empire could find support in passages from the letters. Within the immediate task of Paul and his associates, however, confession of the one God had as its primary implication the consciousness of unity and singularity of the Christian groups themselves.

There were certain other analogies, too, between the ways in which the Pauline groups talked about God and those in which they talked about themselves. The intimacy of communal life was expressed, as we saw in chapter 3, by language of kinship and affection. Similar language is used of God. He is "the Father," and the Christians are "children of God" (Rom. 8:14, 16, 19, 21; 9:8, 26; Phil. 2:15; Gal. 3:26–4:8; 1 Cor. 8:6; and elsewhere) and his "heirs" (Gal. 4:1–7; Rom. 8:17). They are loved by him (1 Thess. 1:4; Rom. 1:7; Eph. 2:4; cf. Rom.5:5, 8; 8:35; 2 Cor. 13:14) and love him in turn (Rom. 8:28; 1 Cor. 8:3). He has chosen them (Rom. 8:33; 1 Cor. 1:27–29; 2 Thess. 2:13; Col. 3:12), called them (1 Cor. 1:9; 7:17–24; Phil. 3:14), knows them (Gal. 4:9; 1 Cor. 8:3), "makes grace abound" to them (2 Cor. 9:8; cf. Rom. 15:15; 1 Cor. 1:4; 3:10). He may have mercy on an individual and heal his illness (Phil. 2:27) or may humiliate an apostle (2 Cor. 12:21). He puts attitudes into persons' hearts (2 Cor. 8:16), "works" in them (Phil. 2:13; cf. 2 Thess. 3:5), and "measures out faith" to them (Rom. 12:3). Thus the common language of the Pauline leaders, which in these particulars is probably shared generally by the members, represents God as participating personally in the direct, feeling-charged community of the house churches. His Spirit, indeed, was thought to "dwell in" the believers (Rom. 8:9; 1 Cor. 3:16; 2 Cor. 3:3) and to express itself in their ecstatic behavior and in the guidance provided by prophets and leaders (Rom. 8:14; 1 Cor. 7:40; 1 Cor. 12–14; see above, chapter 4, Confusion in Corinth). He reveals secrets to the believers (1 Cor. 2:6–10; Eph. 1:9; cf. 1 Cor. 2:1; 4:1; Col. 1:27; 2:2; Phil. 3:15). A great deal of the Christian language about God, which has its primary source in the scriptures and traditions of Judaism, is language about communication and what Donald Evans has called "the language of self-involvement."[14]

The Pauline Christians speak of God also in more exalted terms. God's power is frequently celebrated, however paradoxically it may be conceived (Rom. 1:16; 1 Cor. 1:18, 24; 2:5; 2 Cor. 4:7; 13:4; Col. 2:12; Eph. 1:19). Both forensic and political metaphors appear. Although the phrase "the kingdom of God," so prominent in the synoptic tradition, is not so frequent in the Pauline letters, it does occur (Rom. 14:17; 1 Cor. 4:20; 15:50; 2 Thess. 1:5; Col. 4:11), especially in the catechetical formulaic warning that the practitioners of vice are excluded (1 Cor. 6:9f.; Gal. 5:21; Eph. 5:5). The image of God as sovereign of the universe, enthroned in heaven, is taken for granted and extended by the depiction of Christ's exaltation to share in his reign (as in Phil. 2:9; Col. 3:3). In that capacity he will pronounce the eschatological judgment on all (Rom. 14:10, 12; 1 Cor. 4:5; 5:13; 2 Thess. 1:5–7), meting out punishment to fit the crime (1 Cor. 3:17). The Pauline Christians, however, seem to have drawn few political implications from these political metaphors, except that "the form of this world is passing away" (1 Cor. 7:31). There is scarcely a hint of the monarchical ideology that appears in so many popular philosophical tracts "on kingship" of the late Hellenistic and early Roman periods, in which the ideal earthly state, with a wise king at its head, imitates the *kosmopolis,* the universal state, whose king is Zeus or Nature.[15] Only in the paraenesis of Rom. 13:1–7 (cf. 1 Pet. 2:13f.) is God's sovereignty used to support an appeal for obedience to the Roman *imperium* and its officers. The apocalyptic element in Pauline thought ran counter to that kind of legitimation.

APOCALYPTIC AND THE MANAGEMENT OF INNOVATION

When Paul reminds the recent converts in Thessalonica of the terms of their initial faith (1 Thess. 1:10), he speaks of their waiting for Jesus to come from heaven as their savior from "the coming wrath." The notions of a swiftly coming day of judgment, pictured as God's anger against human sin, and of salvation brought from heaven to earth are stock images in early Judaism, especially in that hard-to-define genre of literature that modern scholars call "apocalypses." It is remarkable that the former pagans who formed the new Christian congregation in the Macedonian city should have been persuaded that such apocalyptic images were an apt picture of their world and lives. Yet language of this sort is so frequent in Paul's letters that we must suppose that it was intelligible and important to his followers—although we should also note that apocalyptic language has a very small place in the pseudonymous letters to Colossians and Ephesians and therefore probably did not have equal, or equally enduring, significance to all members of the Pauline circle.

Just what was the significance of apocalyptic language in Pauline Christianity has been the subject of intense debate among New Testament scholars since Albert Schweitzer published his provocative book, *The Mysticism of Paul the Apostle,* a half century ago.[16] Schweitzer argued that Paul's thought belonged so thoroughly to Jewish (and early-Christian) eschatology that the Hellenistic Christianity of the generation immediately after him could neither understand nor use it. Few theologians liked Schweitzer's thesis. Rudolf Bultmann took it very seriously but insisted that Paul had already begun the process of "demythologizing" the apocalyptic world view.[17] The earlier Christians really thought, as did Jewish apocalyptists, that the world was soon coming to an end; the coming of the Messiah meant that the end had begun, and his resurrection was the first act of the eschatological scenario. In Bultmann's view, Paul began to understand that these notions were not descriptions of what was to happen in the objective world, but symbols expressing an "existential self-understanding." The end of the world really meant that the Christian in his inner life was now free from everything in the world, to face the future afresh in every moment, naked of every "self-contrived security."

Many writers protested that Bultmann's individualizing and subjective interpretation distorted the meaning of the Pauline texts. None of the critics has provoked as many repercussions as Bultmann's student Ernst Käsemann, who insisted in a 1960 article that "apocalyptic was the mother of all Christian theology."[18] Käsemann argued that it would not do to grant that Paul's theology was eschatological while denying, as Bultmann insisted, that it had any of the central characteristics of apocalyptic. Above all, it would not do to insist that the eschatological myths held only anthropological (that is, symbolic of the individual's human situation) but not cosmological meaning for Paul. On the contrary, it was the individualistic "realized eschatology" of the

"Hellenistic enthusiasts" that Paul opposed in 1 Corinthians, precisely by means of apocalyptic categories. Paul did not demythologize the cosmic and temporal aspects of apocalyptic, for they enabled him to speak of God's purpose for the world, which was just as integral a part of his gospel as was the individual's authentic existence.[19]

The ensuing debate has unfortunately tended to focus on the abstractions represented by the terms *anthropology* versus *cosmology*, both of which the discussants use in peculiar senses.[20] The participants have been unable to agree on a definition of apocalyptic or of eschatology that would settle the question of what counts as evidence for whether Paul's thought was apocalyptic or not.[21]

It is not our purpose to settle the debate about Paul's theological debt to apocalyptic, but to try to see what were the effective uses of apocalyptic language within the part of the Christian movement which he led. To accomplish that, it may be helpful to borrow some observations from anthropologists who have studied modern movements started by prophets who predicted the transformation of the world. The anthropologists have called these variously "nativistic," "renewal," or "revitalization" movements or "cargo cults," and seem to have settled finally on the label "millenarian."[22] The beliefs of such groups are sufficiently like those of apocalyptic that some of the common features in the anthropologists' analyses may help to clarify the functions of apocalyptic beliefs in the Pauline groups.[23]

A millenarian movement looks forward to a series of events in the immediate future that will radically transform the existing relationships of power, prestige, and wealth. The ancestors will send a ship loaded with cargo for the natives which will enable them to live on equal or superior terms with the white colonials. Or miraculous means of warfare will enable the natives finally to obtain their rights by a cathartic battle. This holistic picture of reversal or renewal, which envisions a change of the entire world, presupposes that the participants nurse strongly felt dissatisfactions. They are, of course, almost invariably people who are not competing successfully in the existing scheme of social transactions. Yet it is not enough to say that it is "deprived" groups that develop millennial dreams. First of all, it is not their absolute level of poverty or powerlessness that counts, but the way in which they perceive their status relative to significant other groups.[24] People who have been "big men" in the native society but have been subsequently upstaged by colonial officers may be more likely candidates, for example, than those who have never enjoyed status. So are those who have found opportunities to get ahead in the new situation but now discover that mobility is blocked at a certain point by lack of the dominant culture's skills.

It is therefore not an adequate explanation of apocalyptic beliefs to treat them as compensation in fantasy for real-life deprivation—a widespread scientific version of Nietzsche's notion of "resentment" as the source of religious belief, particularly of early Christianity. Rather, the anthropologists involved in such studies contend that the crucial factor is cognitive or symbolic. What is wrong with the present order is not just that the affected people lack goods or money, but that the rules for getting and using power and prestige, for participating fully in social transactions, have somehow been changed. The traditional ways "of defining the criteria by which the content of manhood is to be measured" no longer work.[25] Their world, their symbolic universe, no longer makes sense; that is, it no longer provides an effective picture of the way things are nor effective recipes for how to cope with that reality.

Accordingly the millennial myth provides not just fantasies of reversal, but also a comprehensive picture of what is wrong and why, and of how life ought to be organized. If the movement is successful, these myths become the basis for lasting rearrangements of social relationships, for building new institutions, even though the myths and the accompanying patterns of leadership will have to undergo more or less drastic modification in the process.

The millennial myth is usually the work of one or more individual prophets. The prophet's formulation is typically based on dreams or hallucinatory visions—on revelations—which the prophet may elaborate into a more or less complex system of beliefs.

The visions and the developed myth or ideology invariably combine the traditional with the radically new. To many anthropologists this has been the most fascinating aspect of millenarian movements, for it affords a means by which a strongly tradition-oriented culture or subculture can radically transform its world view and ethos in the face of a new situation without losing a sense of continuity with the past.

Consequently, these scholars do not regard the Weberian concept of charisma as a very helpful one. The "charismatic" leader is possible only within the tradition from which he springs and which provides the major images of the new myth. On the other hand, his success builds community from the beginning, so that charisma and routinization—or, better, institutionalization—are not antithetical. Indeed, for the millennial group itself the new myth may be very conservative, in the sense that it reinforces the new relationships of power and the new ethos *within the movement* at the same time that it negates for group members the world view held by the dominant society.[26]

This greatly simplified summary of some typical features of the millenarian movement provides a heuristic scheme for sorting out some of the apocalyptic elements in the Pauline groups' language and for relating them to social characteristics that we have noticed. The model will not solve all problems, but it may help explain some elements of Pauline Christianity that have often seemed to contradict one another.

To begin with, the picture of the social level of Pauline Christians we developed in chapter 2 above ill accords with the social and economic deprivation necessary for older concepts of eschatological beliefs and movements as compensatory fantasy. However, the picture does fit a view that apocalyptic movements provide relief from cognitive dissonance,[27] by offering a new or transformed set of fundamental images of the world and of relationships. Cognitive-dissonance theory may suggest further implications of the fact that the typical prominent person in the Pauline groups, insofar as we were able to generate any clues about status, tended to show inconsistency of status indicators, and that the groups included mixtures of people of different levels to a degree unusual in that society. We might guess that people who have advanced or declined socially, who find themselves in an ambiguous relation to hierarchical structures, might be receptive to symbols of the world as itself out of joint and on the brink of radical transformation. They might be attracted to a group that undertook to model its own life on that new picture of reality. Of course it is impossible to prove this, and if such a correlation between social experience and symbolization did exist, it would be hard to tell which was cause and which effect.[28] However, other aspects of the early Christian belief system that we will look at below, especially the paradox of Christ's own "power" and "success," may add to the plausibility of this speculation.

In the letters themselves, we saw in chapter 3 above that apocalyptic language was often used to reinforce attitudes of group solidarity. That is especially clear in 1 Thessalonians.[29] Paul's reminder of the apocalyptic terms of the members' conversion—waiting for Jesus from heaven, salvation from coming wrath—stands in a pivotal place in the opening thanksgiving. It connects the customary philophronetic style of the thanksgiving—which established a mood of friendly relations between writer and recipients—with two major themes: recollection of the beginning of that relationship, at the time of the first preaching in Thessalonica, as a paradigm for the moral reminders and admonitions that make up the chief content of the whole letter; and an interpretation of "affliction" (*thlipsis*) in Christian experience. As we saw above, Paul connects the hostility that the converts have experienced from some of their neighbors with a very broad pattern: the apostle's own sufferings, the sufferings of Christians in other places, and the sufferings of Christ. Furthermore, he reminds them that they had been warned, as part of the first Christian instruction, to expect such affliction (3:2–4). The hostility they have experienced—there is no evidence that it amounted to persecution—now confirms the validity of that teaching and of the comprehensive set of images, including crucifixion-and-resurrection as a root metaphor for seeing the world, to which that teaching belonged. Put in that context, the threat to the community is turned into a reinforcement of the believers' solidarity with one another and with other Christians far away *in the place of* the relations they formerly enjoyed with neighbors and kin (*symphyletai*: 2:14). Whether the initial warning of future sufferings was borrowed from Jewish apocalyptic, as some commentators have plausibly argued, is of little consequence. The important thing is that it functions here as part of a master eschatological picture, which both explains present experience and recommends a specific outlook and set of dispositions.

The passage that is most vividly apocalyptic in style, 1 Thess. 4:13–5:11, has a similar function. Here Paul has assembled three separate bits of tradition, each of an apocalyptic cast: the "saying of the Lord," 4:15–17, which describes the extraordinary events "when the Lord himself, with a cry of command, with the voice of an archangel, with the trumpet of God, shall descend from heaven, and the dead in Christ shall arise first"; the saying about the coming of the Day of the Lord "like a thief in the night" (5:2), which is attested in several places in later Christian literature (Rev. 3:3; 16:15; 2 Pet. 3:10; cf. Matt. 24:43; Luke 12:39); and the dualistic admonition to "watch" addressed to the "sons of light," who are distinguished from "the sons of darkness" (5:4–8). Paul cites all these apocalyptic images in response to worries about members of the congregation who have died. The Thessalonian Christians fear that these people who have died prematurely have somehow lost the hope of sharing the benefits promised those who are waiting for God's son from heaven. Paul's reply does not address the problem of death as a universal phenomenon, only the power of death to shatter the unique bonds of the new community. By using the apocalyptic scenario of the return (*parousia*) of Jesus, Paul declares that the community of Christians crosses even the boundary of death, "that we, the living, who survive until the Parousia of the Lord, will certainly not precede those who have died" (4:15). "Then we the living, the survivors, *together with them* will be caught up in clouds to meet the Lord . . . and thus we shall *always be with the Lord*" (4:17).

In the letter as a whole, apocalyptic language sets the context of paraenesis—reminders and encouragement of the ways in which the Christians are expected to behave. The threat of final judgment, alluded to in 1:10, could of course serve as a sanction for such admonitions, as Paul uses it in Rom. 14:10: "You, why do you judge your brother? You, why do you despise your brother? For we shall all stand before the judgment seat of God." There is a hint of the same sanction at the conclusion of the quoted, traditional rules about sexual norms, "because the Lord is avenger for all these things" (1 Thess. 4:6; cf. vs. 8). The primary function of such doomsday language, however, is less specific. It reinforces the sense of uniqueness and cohesion of the community. And that in turn produces a disposition, if the admonitions are heeded, to act in a way appropriate to the community's well-being. Appropriate behavior includes internal discipline and obedience of leaders (5:13–22), a quiet life that will seem benign to outsiders (4:11f.).

The Letter to Galatians exhibits a rather different use of apocalyptic terms. For the Thessalonian Christians, the apocalyptic imagery was deployed to help them make sense of the sharp changes that had taken place in their lives through the fact of their conversion, and to give stability to the life of those who shared those innovations. Whether such imagery contributed to their motivations for making the decisive step in the first place is beyond our power to discover. In Galatians Paul uses apocalyptic categories as part of an effort to justify the innovative character of his mission as a whole in contrast to the traditional values of Judaism. In Gal. 1:4 is a clause that sounds very much like the one with which we began in 1 Thess. 1:10: "Jesus Christ, who gave himself for our sins, in order to rescue us from the present evil age." But in 1 Thessalonians the emphasis was on *waiting* for Jesus, "who saves us from the *coming* wrath" (my emphasis). Here Jesus is said to have done something already to remove us from "this present evil age." The emphasis throughout Galatians is on present fulfillment of eschatological hopes.

Paul accuses the later missionaries in Galatia of introducing "another gospel," which he insists is false, for there can be no other gospel than the one he preached before.[30] From the point of view of the rival apostles, on the contrary, it is Paul who is the innovator. Paul has radically violated the standards of Judaism by permitting gentiles to join the community without being circumcised and without being required to keep the Sabbath and festivals. These concessions might have been justified to make it easier for gentile proselytes to make the initial step of conversion, but the converts must later complete their induction by observing all the commandments. In contrast, as we have seen, Paul declared that for gentile Christians now to wish to be "under the Law" would be a step not forward but backward, equivalent to a return to paganism (4:8–11). It would not be an act of obedience to God's will, but of disobedience toward the new order established by the Messiah's coming and crucifixion.

To back this extraordinary claim, Paul introduces the language of revelation (*apokalypsis*). He insists that he received the gospel he preaches by no human agency, but "through a revelation of Jesus Christ" (1:12; cf. vs. 1). He then appeals to what is generally known about his career, which the Galatian Christians "have heard" (vs. 13), namely that he was far more of a "zealot" for the laws and customs of Judaism than are those who are now upsetting the Galatians (cf. 4:17). The radical change in the course of his own life is therefore explicable only by this revelation from God (1:13–16). It was because God gave him a special revelation (vs. 16), not because of any instruction or commission from the earlier apostles in Jerusalem (1:16–2:10), that he accepted the nonlegal definition of the gospel and began to preach it himself to gentiles.

The Letter to Galatians illustrates another way as well in which Paul's innovations resemble the model of a millenarian prophet. He defines and defends the radically new order in terms drawn from the old. Not only does his argument presuppose familiarity with the notion of the one God who controls the future in accord with his promises, makes revelations, judges the world, and so on; it also draws its proofs from the scripture and traditions of Israel. This is especially clear in chapters 3 and 4, where he has constructed a dense argument by weaving together a series of specific texts and allusions in a way that depends upon traditional interpretations of certain messianic proof-texts and on rules of exegesis that must have been common in Judaism, for much later they were explicitly formulated in rabbinic literature.[31] For example, the tradition that the term *seed* in 2 Sam. 7:12 and hence also in Gen. 17:7 referred to the Messiah is combined with the promise of Gen. 49:10, understood as "until there shall come the one to whom it belongs." A similar interpretation of Gen. 49:10 occurs in a fragment from the Qumran texts, "Until there comes the legitimate Anointed One, the Shoot of David, for to him and to his seed has been given the covenant of kingship for eternal generations" (4QPB 3f.). The verse is interpreted in the sense of a legal phrase that often occurs in Jewish sources, when a certain rule or institution is valid only "until there shall come" an agent from God. For example, the Rule of the Community from Qumran specifies that the sect is to "walk in these first ordinances until there shall come a Prophet and the Anointed of Aaron and of Israel" (1QS 9:11). Paul is more radical. He not only insists that the Messiah has already come, but the fact that the crucified Jesus falls under a curse in the Torah (Deut. 21:23; Gal. 3:13) leads him to an unprecedented deduction. The temporary ordinances that were valid only until the Messiah came include not just some particular rules, but "the Law" as such, the whole body of commandments that distinguished Jews from gentiles. This insistence that the radically new was already attested in scripture is characteristic of Paul's use of the scripture as authority.[32] It is also characteristic of apocalyptic, as the scriptural commentaries of Qumran abundantly illustrate.

In these two ways, using revelations and eschatological language to legitimate a radically new vision of the divine-human order and incorporating into that vision and that legitimation the old scriptures and traditions, the Pauline movement resembles the modern millenarian model. It also closely resembles a nearly contemporary model, the Jewish sect of Qumran. That group had withdrawn from the main institutions of Judaism in order to establish a "community of the new covenant" in the wilderness by the Dead Sea. They were led by priests who regarded the credentials of the priests in charge of the Jerusalem temple as false and the temple itself as polluted. They undertook to build a new community, composed of "volunteers for the Torah," who would take upon themselves a new, rigorous discipline of separation from all impurity and of radical obedience to the laws of Moses as interpreted by the Teacher of Righteousness and his successors, the priestly leaders of the sect. These radical innovations were justified by the belief that they were living at the End of Days. In a similar way we have seen the even more radical innovations of the Pauline Christians supported by the claim that the Messiah had already come. Obviously the content of the innovations could hardly be more different: instead of rigorous application of the Law and separation from all but the pure remnant of Israel, the Paulinists taught abrogation of the Law's legal use and the unity of Jew and gentile. Yet in both cases eschatological beliefs provided the warrants within a traditional context for sharply modified practice.

The Corinthian correspondence is rich in eschatological language, much of which can be called specifically apocalyptic. Some examples from 1 Corinthians indicate both the range of expression and the epistolary contexts of this language:

. . . so that you are not lacking in any spiritual gift, as you wait for the revealing [*apokalypsis*] of our Lord Jesus Christ; who will sustain you to the end, guiltless in the day of our Lord Jesus Christ. [1:7f., part of the opening thanksgiving]

. . . a secret and hidden wisdom of God, which God decreed before the ages. . . . "What no eye has seen, nor ear heard, nor the heart of man conceived, what God has prepared for those who love him," God has revealed to us through the Spirit. [2:7–10]

. . . each man's work will become manifest; for the Day will disclose it, because it will be revealed with fire. . . . If any one destroys God's temple, God will destroy him. [3:13 (cf. vss. 10–15); 3:17]

Do not pronounce judgment before the time, before the Lord comes, who will bring to light the things now hidden in darkness and will disclose the purposes of the heart. Then every man will receive his commendation from God. [4:5]

You are to deliver this man to Satan for the destruction of the flesh, that his spirit may be saved in the day of the Lord. [5:5]

Do you not know that the saints will judge the world? . . . Do you not know that we are to judge angels? . . . Do you not know that the unrighteous will not inherit the kingdom of God? [6:2,3,9]

The body is not meant for immorality, but for the Lord, and the Lord for the body. And God raised the Lord and will also raise us up by his power. [6:13f.]

I think that in view of the present distress it is well for a person to remain as he is. . . . I mean, brethren, the appointed time has grown very short . . . for the form of this world is passing away. [7:26–31]

For as often as you eat this bread and drink the cup, you proclaim the Lord's death until he comes. . . . But when we are judged by the Lord, we are chastened, so that we may not be condemned along with the world. [11:26,32]

Then comes the end, when he delivers the kingdom to God the Father after destroying every rule and every authority and power. [15:24]

Lo! I tell you a mystery. We shall not all sleep, but we shall all be changed, in a moment, in the twinkling of an eye, at the last trumpet. For the trumpet will sound, and the dead will be raised imperishable, and we shall be changed. [15:51f.]

If any one has no love for the Lord, let him be accursed. Maranatha. [16:22][33]

These examples show that apocalyptic expressions could serve a range of specific functions within the letter's structure, from the initial establishment of friendly relations by praise of the recipients, through warrants for general and specific sorts of behavior, to highly ironic, even sarcastic twists of phrases shared with the addressees. These last must be intended to alter some specific attitudes held by an important group within the Corinthian congregations. The best-known instance of the ironic usage that is characteristic of 1 Corinthians is 4:8, which has become a key for much recent interpretation of this letter: "Already you are filled! Already you have become rich! Without us you have become kings! And would that you did reign, so that we might share the rule with you!" Most exegetes agree that this passage, taken in context with the many statements emphasizing the future and temporal sequence throughout the letter, especially in chapter 15, enables us to discern one major issue behind the varied problems addressed by the letter. As it is commonly put, the issue is between the "realized eschatology" of the group called *pneumatikoi* of Corinth and the "futurist eschatology" or "eschatological reservation" of Paul.[34]

Putting this same issue in functional terms will enable us to compare it with the uses of apocalyptic language we have seen in the other letters. The *pneumatikoi* of Corinth are using eschatological language, especially in forms that had already been adapted in the ritual of baptism. For them it warrants their claim to transcend some norms of ordinary behavior and supports their conviction that their status is superior to that of persons still concerned with the fleshly world, whom they call "weak" and "psychic" Christians.[35] Against them Paul uses eschatological language predominantly in the future tense, in order to emphasize the imperfection of the present status of Christians and the necessity for mutual responsibility.

On the face of it, then, Paul's employment of apocalyptic categories here seems to be the reverse of that in Galatians. There he used the present experience of factors traditionally associated with the messianic age to warrant a radical innovation, abandoning the use of the Mosaic law so as to set boundaries between Jew and gentile. Here he uses eschatological language in the future tense to restrain innovation and to counsel stability and order: "In view of the present [or impending] distress, it is well for a person to remain as he is." However, it is important to recognize that this conservative use of apocalyptic language opposes an innovative use by the *pneumatikoi*, and that the latter is structurally analogous to Paul's own approach in the Letter to Galatians. Members of the Pauline congregation had evidently learned well Paul's use of apocalyptic as a warrant for innovation—but he did not like their application of the lesson.

If we look at the social consequences intended by Paul's diverse use of apocalyptic in these different situations, however, we see more consistency than first appeared. The central focus in all three letters we have examined was the solidarity and stability of the congregations. The mode of life of those congregations was new in the special sense that notions related to the new age of the Messiah were used to warrant the radical changes that former gentiles or former Jews experienced. But any other kind of innovation that threatened the coherence of that communal life was resisted through employing other aspects of the image of the new age. This, too, fits our model of millenarian movements, in which the myth of the coming world-change supports both the shift from traditional social relations to the sect's special relations and also the internal institution-building of the sect. That dialectic, too, is abundantly illustrated by the Qumran community.

We should also remember that when we extract from the letters the elements that we regard as apocalyptic, we are creating an abstraction. No one in the Pauline movement would have used the labels "apocalyptic" or "eschatological" to name aspects of their beliefs. Just as the central accomplishment of a millenarian prophet is to invent (by whatever conscious or unconscious means the revelation occurs) a comprehensive myth that will guide his followers into a transformed way of living, so too the elements that we have singled out as apocalyptic in Paulinism work the way they do only because they are part of a larger, very intricate and flexible complex of beliefs. In that sense, we could as well say that all the other beliefs we are discussing in this chapter are, functionally, apocalyptic.

THE CRUCIFIED MESSIAH

The node around which Pauline beliefs crystallized was the crucifixion and resurrection of God's son, the Messiah. This was destined to prove one of the most powerful symbols that has ever appeared in the history of religions; in the earliest years of the Christian movement, no one seems to have recognized its generative potential so quickly and so comprehensively as Paul and his associates. We have already seen numerous ways in which homologies developed or were declared between "the word of the Cross" and aspects of the communities' life.

For Paul, the paradox of the crucified Messiah became the key to a paradoxical relation between the movement of Jesus' followers and the established structures of Judaism in the Roman world. The Christians identify the "one God" of Jewish worship, the God of the Fathers, as "he who raised Jesus from the dead" (Rom. 4:24; 8:11; 2 Cor. 4:14; Gal. 1:1; Col. 2:12; 1 Thess. 1:10; cf. 2 Cor. 1:9). The result is a structural shift of the whole pattern of beliefs, so that Pauline theology, in the narrow sense, cannot be separated from christology. The belief in the crucified Messiah introduces a new and controlling paradigm of God's mode of action.[36] It is in the affirmation that Christ Jesus was crucified and raised from the dead that the dialectical pattern characteristic of so much Pauline discourse is grounded. The antithetical style so common in Paul's language, which is taken up by his associates and successors and which probably belonged to pre-Pauline traditions, underscores the paradox of this event. Its significance was hidden from the world; it is a secret (*mystērion*) revealed to the Christians alone (1 Cor. 2:1f., 6–10; cf. Rom. 16:25f.).

The novelty of the proclamation, which violates or at least transcends expectations based either on reason or on Jewish traditions (1 Cor. 1:18–25), permits it to serve as a warrant for innovation. In particular, Paul uses the paradox of the Messiah's crucifixion explicitly to support the union of Jew and gentile and the abolition of the distinction between them, by bringing to an end the boundary-setting function of the Torah. That is the centerpiece in the complex argument of Galatians 3–4 and also in Romans, especially 3:21–26. Paul's disciple, writing in the encyclical to the Ephesians, shows the continuing power of this connection in the Pauline school by declaring that the inclusion of the gentiles as members of the "household of God" is itself the content of the *mystērion* (Eph. 3:1–12, 2:11–22).

As metaphor, the crucifixion/resurrection becomes also an interpretative pattern for what we may loosely call theodicy. That is, when one is experiencing suffering or hostility, recalling the action of God in this event becomes the means of comfort. Christians are called to rejoice in being permitted to imitate Christ (as in Rom. 5:1–11; 2 Cor. 1:3–7) and at the same time receive reassurance that it is in weakness that the power of God manifests itself. "He who raised the Lord Jesus will also raise us and present us with him" (2 Cor. 4:14).[37]

The same metaphor functions as a model for evaluating behavior within the church. We have discussed the ways in which Paul asserts that his own apostolic career is homologous with the crucifixion/resurrection pattern, especially against those who deny his authority by appealing to extrinsic indicators of legitimacy.[38] In paraenesis, Christ's voluntary submission to death is taken as a model for other-regarding actions and attitudes. Thus, "We who are strong ought to bear with the failings of the weak, and not to please ourselves; let each of us please his neighbor. . . . For Christ did not please himself. . . ." (Rom. 15:1–3, RSV; cf. Gal. 6:2). Christians should "accept one another, as Christ accepted you" (Rom. 15:7); "forgive one another . . . as the Lord forgave you" (Col. 3:13; Eph. 4:32); "walk in love, as Christ also loved us and gave himself up on our behalf as an offering and sacrifice to God" (Eph. 5:2).[39] They are urged to contribute to the collection for the poor in Jerusalem by the reminder of "the grace of our Lord Jesus Christ, who for our sakes became poor, though he was rich, that you by his poverty might become rich" (2 Cor. 8:9). And the whole mythic pattern of Christ's descent from divine to human form, submission to death, and subsequent exaltation and enthronement can be introduced by quoting a hymn or liturgical poem familiar to the readers, as basis for an appeal for unity and mutual regard (Phil. 2:5–11).

It seems obvious that one effect of the belief in Jesus' death and resurrection would be to provide a powerful warrant for a hope of life after death for the believers. That was certainly true for Paul and his leading associates, and in other circles of early Christianity as well. For good reason many modern historians have suggested that this promise of individuals' resurrection was a major factor in the emotional appeal of Christianity in the pagan world.[40] Yet neither the promise nor the preconceptions that converts brought into the church are quite so clear-cut as they are often made to appear. MacMullen has recently argued that the belief in a personal immortality was not very common in Roman paganism, even in the two centuries following the period we are examining, which has so often been depicted as a time of spiritual hypochondria and flight from the difficult world. He reports that "assurances of immortality prove unexpectedly hard to find in the evidence. Even the longing for it is not much attested."[41] Tombstone epigraphs repeat a joke about death, "I was not, I am not, I care not," so often that it is abbreviated: "n.f.n.s.n.c."[42] MacMullen does not even find much hard evidence that the mysteries promised real immortality, although most previous investigators have thought that the main boon sought by their initiates in the Roman period.[43] In his effort to correct the prevailing consensus MacMullen may put too much weight on the silence of most epitaphs on the hope of another existence. Other evidence, notably the philosophic and rhetorical literature on consolation, seems to assume widely held beliefs in personal immortality.[44] Nevertheless, it is apparent that beliefs and hopes varied considerably. Even in Judaism, beliefs about a future life not only varied from one group to another; they were in flux in the period we are interested in, and even similar beliefs could serve different functions in different contexts and at different times.[45]

In contrast, Paul and his associates are quite clear in their persuasion that God, having raised Jesus, "will also raise us." The consolation passage in 1 Thess. 4:13–18, as we have seen, shows how this confidence could be asserted in a specific situation of anxiety, and how the Christian fellowship could thus be distinguished from "the rest who do not have hope" (vs. 13). Yet the fact that Paul had to write in this way, making use of a special revelation ("a word of the Lord," vs. 15), shows that resurrection of those who had died was by no means self-evident to these recent converts. Furthermore, the concept of resurrection was ambiguous. The dominant image of Jesus' resurrection in pre-Pauline and Pauline Christianity seems to have been not the resuscitation of his corpse, as it is depicted in the passion narratives of the canonical gospels and Acts, but his exaltation and enthronement in heaven.[46] This picture, as a kind of cosmic drama, was especially at home in the celebration of baptism, as we saw in chapter 5. The *pneumatikoi* of Corinth apparently conceived of their own resurrection (in baptism?) analogously, as a spiritual transcendence of the ordinary world, already enjoyed. It was against that conception that Paul presented his much more realistic and apocalyptic picture of the future raising of "spiritual bodies" in 1 Cor. 15. The notion of resurrection could thus be construed quite variously, and different images might have quite different social correlates. For the "spirituals" of Corinth, exaltation with Christ could mean new status for charismatic individuals, release from conventional inhibitions. For Paul, belief in Christ's resurrection as the "firstfruits of those who sleep" meant solidarity of the community, authority manifested in apparent weakness, a dialectical relationship to conventional structures.

From the foregoing discussion it becomes evident that it is not quite accurate to describe the common use or even Paul's own use of the crucifixion/resurrection paradigm as paradoxical. That is, things ordinarily taken as signs of weakness are not simply redefined as powerful because they emulate the weakness of the crucified Jesus, although some of the statements by Paul may plausibly be taken that way.[47] More often the pattern is dialectical or sequential: the Christ was first weak, then powerful; so, too, the Christians are weak and afflicted today, but will be vindicated and glorious. That this is a very common apocalyptic pattern is obvious, and it appears clearly in that most apocalyptic of the Pauline letters, 2 Thessalonians, especially in the consolatory language of the opening thanksgiving (1:3–12).[48] Whether that letter was written by Paul or not, the pattern must have been well known to

Pauline Christians. In fact very similar language appears in the undoubtedly authentic letter to Philippi (Phil. 1:28f.). The fact that very early the declaration of Jesus' death and resurrection was mixed with a different symbolic pattern, that of descent from heaven followed by exaltation and enthronement there,[49] reinforced this compensatory hope.

Even Paul, whose own statements tend toward the paradoxical, can sometimes speak of his own power in nonparadoxical ways. True, he used the crucifixion/resurrection paradigm in his Corinthian letters to argue for a novel way of construing power.[50] However, as Jacob Jervell has pointed out, he does not admit that, even though only weakness is visible in his own career, that very weakness is power in God's eyes. Rather, the paradox is that he is both weak and a charismatic. Paul and others who are weak in terms of the dominant value system nevertheless do powerful things—for example, they survive despite the most extraordinary pressures and afflictions—and therefore this power must be not their own, but God's.[51] So, too, Paul's rhetorical struggle against the "superapostles" in 2 Cor. 10–13, which makes eloquent use of the paradox and irony that could be extracted from the pattern of crucifixion and resurrection, nevertheless culminates in a warning that when he comes to Corinth again "I will not spare (you)": "Since you are looking for proof that the one who speaks in me is Christ—who for you is not weak but powerful in you—for indeed he was crucified out of weakness, but lives from God's power, for we, too, are weak in him, but we live with him from God's power toward you" (2 Cor. 13:2–4).

The deutero-Pauline letters to Colossians and Ephesians show the continuing currency of the symbolism of Christ's exaltation as cosmic victory and reconciliation of cosmic powers. The social implications remained ambiguous. Although some Colossian Christians may have found in this symbolism grounds for their exaggerated ascetic practices, "angel cult," and visionary experiences, the author adapted the same symbolism to polemicize against the deviants. Both he and his imitator, the author of Ephesians, used the cosmic imagery to reinforce the internal cohesion of the churches.[52]

Thus we see once again that the implications of belief were not automatic. The spelling out of the meaning of even so central a belief as the resurrection of Christ was a dialectical process. What we call, crudely, its social consequences were an integral part of that process.

EVIL AND ITS REVERSAL

In the opening formula of a letter, Paul could characterize Jesus Christ as "he who gave himself for our sins in order to rescue us from the present evil age" (Gal. 1:4). Why could he assume that the Christians to whom he was writing would agree that the existing world was evil? What was evil about it? What was the manner of the "rescue" that Christ accomplished?

We have seen that to become a member of the Christian *ekklēsia* meant strong social change. It entailed entry into an association that represented itself as a new family, replacing other relationships and sources of identity. It meant expecting, and experiencing, hostility from the outside society. It meant shunning involvement in any other cult, avoidance of all other rituals. The symbolic counterpart of this exclusive and comprehensive transfer of allegiance, this sectarian commitment, was the representation of "the world" as evil or perverted. This dark picture of the world was not absolute in the Pauline view, just as its boundaries in relation to the larger society were not impenetrable. Nevertheless, the dominant colors are very somber.

The correlation between the social change of conversion and the symbolization of evil and salvation does not imply unidirectional causation. On the one hand, we may reasonably assume that conversion, which intends a radical shift of allegiance, a radical change of ethos and of fundamental symbols, presupposes some kind of strong prior dissatisfaction with the way things are. The sect's symbolism of evil would focus, interpret, and answer that disgruntlement. On the other hand, though, we could argue that once one had made so sharp a change in one's associations and life orientation, it would be necessary to justify and explain that shift, both to oneself and to others, by adopting beliefs that the former life was evil and the present (or future), salvation. Religions both respond to and create needs.

The letters present neither a systematic doctrine nor a comprehensive myth of evil's nature and origin, and attempts to reconstruct a systematic view which could be said to lie behind the express statements remain highly problematical. We shall attempt something more modest: to identify some of the particular ways in which the letters speak of the presence or threat of evil, to note the opposite good with which these evils are usually paired, and to see if there are any hints of the ways in which the beliefs about evil and its cure are related to social motivations, attitudes, and dispositions. We can group the various clusters of metaphors under four headings: bondage and liberation, guilt and justification, estrangement and reconciliation, deformity and transformation.[53]

Bondage and Liberation

The human world is seen as under the control of demonic powers. These include Satan, who can even be called "the god of this eon" (2 Cor. 4:4), and other "rulers and authorities" (Col. 2:15; Eph. 6:12–17), which can be identified with the "elements of the cosmos" (Gal. 4:1–11; Col. 2:20) or with pagan deities (1 Cor. 10:20; Gal. 4:8f.). Death is also treated as a personal power, "the last enemy" that tyrannizes humanity (1 Cor. 15:26), and Paul can describe sin in similar terms (Rom. 5:21–6:23; 7:7–8:2).[54] Once he even describes the Law as a personal, enslaving power (Gal. 4:1–11), but that belongs to the peculiar polemical situation of Galatians and can hardly be part of the regular instruction. By the time Paul wrote Romans 7, he had found a more careful way of stating the relation between the Law and the enslaving power of sin.

The countervailing metaphors speak of freedom. What is required is that the slaves be "liberated" or "ransomed" (Gal. 4:4; 5:1 and passim; Rom. 8:21; 1 Cor. 6:20; 7:23; Rom. 6:12–23; Col. 1:13). This liberation could be depicted as the defeat of the cosmic powers, as in Col. 2:15, a motif that we have found closely connected with the descent/exaltation christology and with the setting of baptism (cf. Eph. 1:21; 2:2; Phil. 2:10), although the reconciliation of those powers is another possible image, as in Col. 1:20.

The subjective side of the plight is weakness, which can be illustrated by the social powerlessness of most of the converts (1 Cor. 1:26–28), but also by physical weakness and vulnerability (2 Cor. 12:9; 4:7–12, 16–18). What is required is to receive God's power, although we have seen that this was understood in the paradoxical or dialectical light of the root metaphor of the Cross. Another way of representing the paradoxical character of the new life was to speak not of liberation but of change of master: the Christian becomes the slave of Christ (1 Cor. 7:22) or of God (Rom. 6:13).[55] But this metaphor is also mixed with that of adoption, coming of age, and inheritance.[56]

The objective side of the picture, however, is the power of opponents to inflict suffering, even on those who believe themselves already in some sense free from the cosmic bondage and enjoying the power of God. There are, of course, human opponents, who persecute the Christians, instigating imprisonments and other punishments. Yet it is interesting that the identity of the opponents of the Pauline communities is never specified. The evidence points to local, sporadic hostility rather than to any organized or official police measures. Pauline paraenesis treats hostility as simply something to be expected and endured. In the cosmic picture, it corresponds to the opposition to God's power by the demons. Satan works mischief in trivial ways, interfering with Paul's travel plans "two or three times" (1 Thess. 2:18);[57] he "tempts" or "tests" by means of sexual desire (1 Cor. 7:5); his designs on an erring member can be thwarted by forgiveness (2 Cor. 2:11). Yet there is little in the language of the letters to connect human opposition with these images of demonic activity. The picture is not so schematic as in, say, the apologists of the second and third centuries, for whom all persecutions were the work of jealous demons.

Guilt and Justification

The traditional language that Paul adapts in the letters speaks not only of rescue from bondage, but also of rescue from "the coming wrath" (1 Thess. 1:10; cf. 5:9; Rom. 5:9; Eph. 2:3). Here, as we have discussed above, we recognize a typical element from Jewish apocalyptic eschatology. God is righteous and demands of human beings righteousness, which will be tested in a final, universal judgment.

The peculiarly Pauline formulation of this eschatological complex is the doctrine that through the faithful death of Christ and God's faithful vindication of him in the resurrection, righteousness is granted as a free gift to all who will receive it by faith. Since Augustine and, more one-sidedly, since Luther and Melanchthon, that doctrine has been deemed, in Western Christianity, the hallmark of Paulinism. In fact, though, Paul speaks this way rarely except in the context of the question of the relation of Jew and gentile in the church, preeminently in the letters to Galatia and Rome. The important text 2 Cor. 5:21 is only a partial exception, for the formulaic statement, "Him who knew no sin he made sin on our behalf, that we should become in him God's righteousness," stands at the climax of Paul's apology for his missionary career. As chapters 3 and 4 show clearly, the question of the relation to Judaism was never far from that apology. To be sure, the doctrine of justification by grace was not so idiosyncratic in Paul that it left no trace in his followers. One of its most compact, if somewhat lapidary, statements is in Ephesians 2:5, 8f.

Nevertheless, the more general usage of the guilt-and-justification complex in the Pauline communities is probably to be discovered in the traditional formulas that the letters occasionally quote, such as Rom. 3:24f., and in the nonpolemical allusions in paraenetic parts of the letters. Rom. 3:24f. speaks of Christ Jesus as a "sin offering," a "means of dealing with sin"[58] that is at the same time a "demonstration of (God's) righteousness in overlooking previously commited sins." The commonest setting for this kind of formulation was probably in the missionary preaching, as indicated by Paul's reminder in 1 Cor. 15:1f. of the tradition "that Christ died for our sins." There is in these passages no more indication that the typical convert was a person who had previously agonized under a subjective sense of guilt than there is that Paul had done so—and in the rare places where he speaks of his former life, he does so with pride (Gal. 1:13f.; Phil. 3:4–6).[59] It does seem, however, that the Christian preachers found some way to persuade their willing hearers that the hearers' lives were, in God's eyes, sinful. That conviction corresponds to the habit of depicting the pagan world as one characterized by vices. The appeals to Christians to avoid the oft-listed vices (1 Cor. 5:11; 6:9f.; Gal. 5:20; Eph. 5:5; Col. 3:5–14) are addressed to those who have been "washed . . . sanctified . . . justified" (1 Cor. 6:11). They have been transferred into a different sphere of power, in which the virtues are "fruit of the Spirit" (Gal. 5:22).

Estrangement and Reconciliation

Alongside the mythic picture of bondage and helplessness under uncanny powers and the forensic and cultic motifs of sin, guilt, and justification, the leaders of the Pauline circle also speak of alienation or enmity vis-à-vis God, which is overcome by his active reconciliation (2 Cor. 5:16–21; Rom. 5:1–11). Paul himself rarely uses this language, and when he does it is closely connected with the language of justification, as in the two passages cited. In 2 Cor. 5:18–20 it epitomizes his missionary career. This appears, significantly, near the climax of the delicate appeal for reconciliation between himself and the church at Corinth. Romans 5:1–11 states themes that are elaborated in chapter 8.[60] The two sections together frame Paul's discussion of a series of problems raised by his argument in chapters 1–3 and form the transition from the first four chapters to the long discourse on the relation between the church and the Jews in chapters 9–11. The latter culminates in an un-paralleled vision of ultimate reconciliation between God and his people Isra-el, who have become "enemies on account of [the gentile Christians]," after "the full number of the gentiles" have "entered" (11:25, 28). The author of Ephesians is thus being especially Pauline when he makes the central instance of cosmic reconciliation the destruction of the barrier between Jew and gen-tile and the induction of the latter into the household of God (Eph. 2:11–22).

In the baptismal allusions that fill Colossians and Ephesians, however, we may come closer to the wider use of this set of metaphors in the ritual and catechetical language of the Pauline groups. Here we find, as we have ob-served before, a cosmic dimension, a mythical picture of spiritual powers at war with one another and with God, but "pacified" and "reconciled" by Christ's ascension through the astral spheres. The notion of the submission of cosmic powers to the exalted Christ was perhaps suggested by the verse that played such a large role in the earliest Christian formation of the exaltation christology:

> The Lord said to my Lord:
> Sit at my right hand,
> until I set your enemies as a footstool
> beneath your feet.[61]

Although Paul himself could use this same familiar text to argue for the incompleteness of Christ's present reign, since "the last enemy, Death," had yet to be "destroyed" (1 Cor. 15:25–28), the common notion suggested by the baptismal liturgy was more likely just the one that Paul here opposes and modifies. Christ's exaltation brought the obeisance of chthonic, earthly, and heavenly powers, according to the hymn that Paul himself quotes in Phil. 2:10. This notion of the submission of the powers to Christ, his triumph over them, is also celebrated in Col. 2:15, as we saw above, but it mixes there with the less militant imagery of reconciliation, peace, and unification (Col. 1:15–20; Eph. 1:10; 3:9–19). Yet the authors of these two letters adapted the cosmic imagery precisely to urge unity and mutual care in the congrega-tions.[62]

Deformity and Transformation
Theissen calls the kinds of symbolism we have discussed so far "socio-morphic," borrowing the classification of Topitsch. The remaining category he calls "physiomorphic transformation symbolism" (enlarging Topitsch's "biomorphic" category).[63] That is, this symbolism derives not from social relations like master and slave, father and son, judge and accused, friend and enemy, but from organic images of growth and decay, life and death, division and union, and from physical or magical notions of changing shapes or of visual transformation by mirrors. This imagery appears sporadically and fragmentarily in the Pauline letters, and its interpretation has been especially

troublesome. Some interpreters posit an elaborate system of myth to which the words of Paul are supposed to allude; others resort to ill-defined categories of mysticism. What Theissen says about the image of union between Christ and the believer, however, applies to the whole complex: "One can call this mysticism, but it is a mysticism of social relations, in which many participate."[64]

We can trace one cluster of images to an interaction between the biblical story of Eden and Adam's creation and sin, elaborated by traditional interpretations, and the specifically Christian understanding of Jesus' death and exaltation. The setting for the development of this cluster was baptism, as shown earlier. Human life is represented as distorted, deprived, and broken. The image of God after which the first human pair was modeled has been lost or defaced, and with it the primordial unity of human life has been fractured. This brokenness was preeminently experienced in the tension and passion between the sexes, but also in the other oppositions of roles and statuses that structure all social existence. Above all, mortality is perceived as unnatural, as a curse or punishment. Salvation, accordingly, is depicted as restoration of the lost image of the Creator, as human reunion by means of union with Christ (himself identified with the Image), and as "being made alive."

In Paul's own use of the transformation symbolism there is a strong eschatological element. The Spirit experienced in the assemblies of Christians is only the "firstfruits" or "down payment" of the future existence, when "we will all be changed" (1 Cor. 15:51) from bodies of flesh and blood to "spiritual bodies" (vs. 44). The real life of the apostle and of all Christians is not the visible one, but a heavenly one, which must be "put on" at death, "that the mortal may be swallowed up by life" (2 Cor. 5:4)—a transformation already represented by the "putting on" of Christ in baptism, when the "down payment" of the Spirit was received (vs. 5). The clearest expression of this expected transformation is in Phil. 3:20f., which alludes to the imagery of the christological hymn in 2:6–11: "From there [heaven] we also expect as savior the Lord Jesus Christ, who will transform our body of humility to conform to his body of glory, by the energy that enables him to subordinate everything to him[self]." Similarly, Paul can climax his picture of the future transformation of the whole creation, in Rom. 8:18–30, with a statement about "those who love God": "Those whom he foreknew, he predestined to conform to the image of his son, so that he would be firstborn among many brothers" (vs. 29). That this accords with the baptismal symbolism is shown by Col. 3:10, "having put on the new (human) who is being renewed in knowledge 'according to the image' of the One who created him." The deutero-Pauline author retained something of Paul's emphasis on the future, however: "For you died and your life is hidden with Christ in God. When Christ is manifested, your life, then you also will be manifested with him in glory" (Col. 3:3f.). Paul, on the other hand, could use this sort of imagery to speak of his own career in the present: "For we, while we live, are always being given up to death on account of Jesus, that also the life of Jesus may be manifested in our mortal flesh." But it is important to note that he does so precisely to make a point about social relations, his authority vis-à-vis the Corinthian Christians: "so that death is working in us, but life in you" (2 Cor. 4:10f., 12).

Context

Among all the negative images used in the Pauline letters, there are few direct references to social or political factors. For example, there is no hint anywhere that Roman imperialism is a cause of the evil state of the present age.[65] Only in the apocalyptic scenario of 2 Thess. 2:3f. is there a hint of political opposition to the divine order. The scale of evil about which the Pauline writers speak is in one sense much smaller than the political realm: personal immorality, weakness, bondage, fear, and suffering, and the peculiar problem of the relation between Jews and gentiles. In another sense the scale is much broader: Satan, the god of this world, cosmic alienation and reconciliation, the end of this age. It is striking that so little is said about solutions or explanations for any of the ordinary evils that plague everybody. Pauline Christianity seems, at least in the extant letters, to offer no general theodicy. Rather, attention is paid only to factors that arise for the first time because the readers have become Christians. Even the reassurances about death in 1 Thess. 4:13–18; 1 Cor. 15; 2 Cor. 5:1–10 speak only to special, intra-Christian problems. It is the continuing solidarity of the Christian community transcending death, or present solidarity of those who must not pretend that death is no longer real, or the right understanding of apostolic power that is addressed, not the general human problem of mortality. But this fact itself points to the social context within which the talk about evil and salvation has its meaning and validity.

Another fact about the Pauline language of evil and good points in the same direction. The context throughout is theological. The Pauline letters do not speak of "natural" evil. Even the apparent exceptions, references to "the corruptible" and "the mortal" (1 Cor. 15:42, 54; 2 Cor. 5:4), are bracketed by God's permission and action (cf. Rom. 8). The theological context is further underlined by the frequent use of forensic and eschatological language. The evil of the world is thus ultimately defined by God's judgment, and it is at the judgment that wrong will be righted. The letters urge the congregations to manifest a paradoxical confidence, endurance, joy, and hope in the face of present experiences of evil and assure them that they can do so because by means of the Spirit they already share the eschatological divine power. This theological and eschatological context has important social implications. Because evil is too mighty for the individual, his hope lies in being transferred from the sphere of power of the evil forces—demons, Satan, sin itself—into the sphere of God's power, "into Christ." The mode of life which corresponds to this picture is not the Stoic autonomy or indifference, but loyal participation in the body of Christ, in which the power of God is at work and to which final vindication is promised.

CORRELATIONS

We have looked from several angles at the patterns of belief and the patterns of socialization that appear, in bits and pieces, in the evidence of the Pauline letters. What we have seen is a highly complex mix of traditional and novel symbols, flexible, ambiguous, constantly changing, yet powerfully centered. We have also seen a social movement, comprising small groups scattered in cities of diverse local character, experiencing conflict within and without, but also strong emotional bonding, and linked with one another and with a highly mobile group of leaders in several complicated ways. From these fragmentary, sometimes confusing pictures we may now list some aspects of the symbol system that seem to match aspects of the social process. Such a list may help us to consider a little more specifically the ways in which sacred symbols affect social reality and social experience affects symbolization.

The Pauline Christians believe in one God, sole creator of the universe and ultimate judge of all human actions. In most respects their monotheism is exactly that of Judaism: they worship not the highest God but the only God and regard the deities of other cults as nonexistent or as antigods, demons. Yet they also accord to the crucified and resurrected Messiah, Jesus, some titles and functions that in the Bible and Jewish tradition were attributed only to God. The social correlate is a network of local groups that wants to be a single "assembly of God" in the whole world. The connections among the local cells are, relative to size, much stronger than those among Jewish communities of the Diaspora. Unity is a powerful and constant concern of the leaders, both in the life of the local assemblies and in the connections among them. The local group is intimate and exclusive; it has strong boundaries. At the same time, its members interact routinely with the larger urban society, and both the local group and the leadership collective are vigorously expansive.

The one God of the Christians, as of the Jews, is personal and active. His spirit or, alternatively, the spirit of his Son, acts in, on, and with individual believers and the whole community. The social correlate is the intimacy of the local household assembly. A high level of commitment is demanded, the degree of direct interpersonal engagement is strong, the authority structure is fluid and charismatic (though not exclusively), and internal boundaries are weak (but not untroublesome).

The Pauline world view is eschatological. The Christians believe that the coming of Jesus, his crucifixion and resurrection, have already set in motion a shift in the order of the world. They expect very soon an end of the present age, the return of Jesus, and the final judgment of both humans and cosmic powers. Corresponding to this change of worlds is the change of social place that each individual has experienced in his or her conversion. Each has transferred allegiance either from the traditional Jewish community or from the looser and more multiplex associations of pagan society to a new, tightly bonded, exclusive cultic community.

The Pauline Christians believe in Jesus the Messiah, son of God, crucified for human sin but raised from the dead and exalted to reign with God
in heaven. They are themselves a community that experiences social contradictions. Their groups include in intimate fellowship persons of a wide mix of
social levels. Mostly, as individuals and as a whole, they are weak in terms of
social power and status, they experience indifference or hostility from neighbors, yet they are exhilarated by experiences of power in their meetings, both
in ordinary forms of leadership, as the groups begin to make their own
institutions, and in the particularly vivid demonstrations of spirit possession.

This last set of observations we can turn about and examine from the
other side. In chapter 2 above we tried to sketch a profile of the social level of
the typical convert to Pauline Christianity and of the mix of levels in the
group. The former turned out to be in effect the profile of the most prominent
members, for they were the ones likely to be mentioned by name or otherwise
identified. We found that their dominant characteristic was status inconsistency or social mobility. Does it seem plausible that the powerful symbols of
change grounded in tradition, symbols of personal and communal transformation, symbols of an evil world encompassed by God's judgment and grace
would be particularly attractive to people who had experienced the hopes and
fears of occupying an ambiguous position in society? Or, contrariwise, would
such experiences among so many leaders of the community tend to reinforce
just those paradoxical and dialectical symbols that we have found so characteristic of Pauline beliefs?

May we further guess that the sorts of status inconsistency we observed—independent women with moderate wealth, Jews with wealth in a
pagan society, freedmen with skill and money but stigmatized by origin, and
so on—brought with them not only anxiety but also loneliness, in a society in
which social position was important and usually rigid? Would, then, the
intimacy of the Christian groups become a welcome refuge, the emotion-
charged language of family and affection and the image of a caring, personal
God powerful antidotes, while the master symbol of the crucified savior
crystallized a believable picture of the way the world seemed really to work?

On the other hand, the sorts of social and physical mobility we observed
in the Pauline prosopography also imply some daring, some self-confidence,
some willingness to break out of the ordinary social structures. And in the
language of Paul and his associates we have vivid images of the new and the
unexpected, of risk and miraculous survival, of a powerful, freedom-giving
Spirit, of a world on the brink of transformation.

The churches, too, were mixtures of social statuses. The kinds of relationships that the members had previously had to one another, and still had
in other settings—between master and slave, rich and poor, freedman and
patron, male and female, and the like—stood in tension with the *communitas*
celebrated in the rituals of baptism and the Lord's Supper. There was tension,
too, between the familiar hierarchy of those roles and the freedom of the
Spirit to confer distinction, by means of some charisma, upon a person of

inferior status. So, too, we find in the letters a stress on symbols of unity, equality, and love, but also correlative symbols of fluidity, diversity, individuation.

Those odd little groups in a dozen or so cities of the Roman East were engaged, though they would not have put it quite this way, in constructing a new world. In time, more time than they thought was left, their ideas, their images of God, their ways of organizing life, their rituals, would become part of a massive transformation, in ways they could not have foreseen, of the culture of the Mediterranean basin and of Europe.

LIST OF ABBREVIATIONS

AJA	*American Journal of Archaeology*
AJT	*American Journal of Theology*
ANRW	*Aufstieg und Niedergang der römischen Welt*
ASR	*American Sociological Review*
b	Babylonian Talmud (followed by name of tractate)
BA	*Biblical Archaeologist*
BAGD	Walter Bauer, William F. Arndt, F. Wilbur Gingrich, and Frederick Danker, eds., *A Greek–English Lexicon of the New Testament and Other Early Christian Literature*
Barn.	The Epistle of Barnabas
BCH	*Bulletin de correspondance hellénistique*
BDF	Friedrich Blass, Albert Debrunner, and Robert W. Funk, eds., *A Greek Grammar of the New Testament and Other Early Christian Literature*
CDC	Cairo Geniza text of the Damascus Covenant
CBQ	*Catholic Biblical Quarterly*
CIG	*Corpus Inscriptionum Graecarum* (Boeckh)
CII	*Corpus Inscriptionum Iudaicarum*
CIL	*Corpus Inscriptionum Latinarum*
CIRB	*Corpus Inscriptionum Regni Bosporani*
Cod. Just.	*Codex Justinianus*
Corinth: Results	*Corinth: Results of Excavations Conducted by the American School of Classical Studies at Athens*
CPJ	*Corpus Papyrorum Judaicarum*
DACL	*Dictionnaire d'archéologie chrétienne et de liturgie*
Did.	Didache (The Teaching of the Twelve Apostles)
EvT	*Evangelische Theologie*
FGH	*Fragmente der griechischen Historiker* (Jacoby)
G. Th.	The Gospel of Thomas
HR	*History of Religions*
HTR	*Harvard Theological Review*
HUCA	*Hebrew Union College Annual*

IDB	*The Interpreter's Dictionary of the Bible*
IDBS	*IDB*, supplementary volume
IESS	*International Encyclopedia of the Social Sciences*
IG	*Inscriptiones Graecae*
IGR	*Inscriptiones Graecae ad Res Romanas Pertinentes*
ILS	*Inscriptiones Latinae Selectae* (Dessau)
Int	*Interpretation*
JAAR	*Journal of the American Academy of Religion*
JAC	*Jahrbuch für Antike und Christentum*
JBL	*Journal of Biblical Literature*
JJS	*Journal of Jewish Studies*
JR	*Journal of Religion*
JRomST	*Journal of Roman Studies*
JSJ	*Journal for the Study of Judaism*
Le Bas– Waddington	Philippe Le Bas and W. H. Waddington, *Voyage archéologique en Grèce et en Asie Mineure*. Vol. 2: *Inscriptions.*
Loeb	The Loeb Classical Library
LSJ	Henry George Liddell, Robert Scott, and Henry Stuart Jones, eds., *A Greek-English Lexicon*
LXX	The Septuagint
M	Mishnah (followed by name of tractate)
Mart. Polyc.	The Martyrdom of Polycarp
MDAI	*Mitteilungen des deutschen archäologischen Instituts* (A) Athens; (I) Istanbul.
NEB	*The New English Bible*
NovT	*Novum Testamentum*
NT	New Testament
NTS	*New Testament Studies*
1QH	*Hodayot* [Hymns] from Qumran Cave 1
1QM	*Serek ha-Milḥāmāh* [War Rule] from Qumran Cave 1
1QS	*Serek ha-Yaḥad* [Rule of the Community] from Qumran Cave 1
1QSa	Appendix A of 1QS
p	Palestinian Talmud (followed by name of tractate)
POxy.	*Oxyrhynchus Papyri*
PRyl.	*Catalogue of the Greek Papyri in the John Rylands Library at Manchester*
PG	*Patrologia Graeca* (Migne)
PW	A. Pauly, G. Wissowa, and W. Kroll, eds., *Real-Encyclopädie der klassischen Altertumswissenschaft*
RAC	*Reallexikon für Antike und Christentum*
RB	*Revue biblique*
REG	*Revue des études grecques*

RGG[3]	*Religion in Geschichte und Gegenwart,* 3d ed.
Rhet. Gr.	*Rhetores Graeci* (Spengel)
RPh	*Revue de philologie*
RSV	Revised Standard Version
SIG	*Sylloge Inscriptionum Graecarum,* 3d ed. (Dittenberger)
Silv.	The Teachings of Silvanus
T	Tosefta (followed by name of tractate)
TAPA	*Transactions of the American Philological Association*
TDNT	*Theological Dictionary of the New Testament*
TLZ	*Theologische Literaturzeitung*
TRu	*Theologische Rundschau*
TWNT	*Theologisches Wörterbuch zum Neuen Testament*
TZ	*Theologische Zeitschrift*
v.l.	varia lectio (a variant reading)
ZNW	*Zeitschrift für die neutestamentliche Wissenschaft*
ZPE	*Zeitschrift für Papyrologie und Epigraphik*
ZTK	*Zeitschrift für Theologie und Kirche*

The usual abbreviations and signs are used for books of the Bible and Apocrypha, manuscripts and versions of the New Testament, and individual works of ancient authors.

NOTES

In the notes I have identified each cited work by its author's name and the date of its first publication in the original language or, if there has been a revised edition significant for the point under discussion, the date of that revision. The reader will thus obtain some information about the sequence of scholarly discussion. However, I have given the page numbers of the most accessible form of each work, that is, in collected essays and English translations, if they exist. In every case the entry in the bibliography specifies the edition to which reference is made, if it differs from the original.

INTRODUCTION

1. See, for example, the complaints by Hengel 1979, vii–viii; Bruce 1976; Malherbe 1977a, 1–4; Kennedy 1978; Meeks 1978; Judge 1972.

2. A number of examples of this renewed interest in sociological or social-historical study are listed in the bibliography and referred to throughout this book. For sketches of the history of such scholarship, see Keck 1974; J. Z. Smith 1975; Scroggs 1980; Theissen 1979, 3–34; Schütz 1982.

3. Recently Averil Cameron (1980, 61f.) quite properly took me to task for slipping into one of those unguarded generalizations about the roles of women "in Greco-Roman society as a whole." It does not help much in my defense that I was paraphrasing certain leading cultural historians, who, I assumed, knew better than I. That only shows how pervasive is the temptation and how wary we ought to be.

4. See Keck 1974.

5. Case 1913, 78.

6. E.g., Kreissig 1967, 1970, and 1977; Ste. Croix 1975; Kippenberg 1978. The review of Soviet and eastern European scholarship on early Christianity by Kowalinski 1972 offers less reason for interest, but Kowalinski is not an unbiased observer. See also Scroggs 1980, 177–79, and Theissen 1979, 25–30. Dupré 1980 provides a useful, brief discussion of the problem of ideology in Marx and in recent Marxists.

7. Cf. Keck 1974, 437.

8. Weber 1922, 98; cf. Geertz 1973, 5 and 22f. Naive trust in a strictly construed scientific method still persists in some quarters (witness the hyperbolic claims of Jewett 1979) but not usually among the natural scientists who were the original paradigm. Cf. Garfinkel 1981, 135 and passim.

9. Geertz 1973, 20f.

10. Ibid., 24.

11. Brown 1970, 17.

12. V. Turner 1974, 23.

13. Geertz 1973, 5.

14. Geertz 1957.

15. Cf. Gellner 1962, who defends "moderate functionalism" against such critics as Peter Winch, but points out that "strong functionalism," which claimed that *every* element in society is functional, has for good reason lost support among social scientists.

16. Here Gellner is helpful. "To understand the *working* of the concepts of a society," he says, "is to understand its institutions." However, contrary to Winch's view, "it is *not* true to say that to understand the concepts of a society (in the way its members do) is to understand the society. Concepts are as liable to mask reality as to reveal it, and masking some of it may be a part of their function" (1962, 115 and 148, n. 1).

17. The proposals are made in a book not yet published, tentatively titled "Theories of Religion and 'Method in Theology': An Encounter with the Thought of Bernard Lonergan." Mr. Lindbeck was kind enough to make the manuscript available for discussion by his students and colleagues.

18. E.g., Koester 1965.

19. See Rensberger 1981 and Lindemann 1979.

20. On the different "socio-ecological factors" operative in the rural and urban settings, see the suggestive proposals by Theissen 1973 and 1975.

21. Beginning in 1973, a research group of the American Academy of Religion and the Society of Biblical Literature met for several years under this rubric. It was suggested by one of the group's founders, John Gager, who used it as the subtitle of his pioneering study (1975).

22. The latter in the sense of Berger and Luckmann 1966.

CHAPTER 1

1. Oscar Broneer (1962, 1971) even thought that Paul must have witnessed the Isthmian games, of which Broneer's excavations have provided a vivid picture. But examples and metaphors from the gymnasium were so common in the Greco-Roman moralists that one can hardly draw that conclusion; see Pfitzner 1967. Further on the relation of Paul's language to that of professional rhetoric and of philosophical schools: Judge 1968; 1972, 29–32; Malherbe 1977a, 29–59.

2. The significance of Paul's work, particularly in the light of the traditional Hellenistic debate about the proper means of support for teachers, is dealt with by Hock 1978 and 1980. Theissen 1975a has connected it with a wide-ranging hypothesis about the "ecology" of the two fundamentally different types of early Christian mission, rural and urban.

3. The expression is peculiar; Luther was perhaps thinking of Acts 5:28, "You have filled (πεπληρώκατε) Jerusalem with your teaching." But in Rom. 15:19 the implied direct object of the verb must be τὸ εὐαγγέλιον, so the verb must mean "finish, bring to completion," as in Col. 1:25.

4. Bietenhard 1977, 256–58. Already asserted by Justin *Dial.* 78.10, as Lightfoot 1880, 88, observed, although even that great exegete succumbed to the romantic

vision of Paul, "like Elijah of old, driven to the desert of Sinai for seclusion from the outer world" in order "to commune with God and his own soul" (88–90).

5. Betz 1979, 73f. The point is nicely made in a manuscript by John A. Bailey, "The City in the Bible," which he kindly showed me.

6. The more elaborate and dramatic account in Acts 9 confirms the centrality of Damascus. The author's insistence on Paul's close connection with Jerusalem probably stems from his use of reports already in circulation in Paul's lifetime and which Paul emphatically rejects in Gal. 1:16–2:10. Evidently the author of Acts did not have access to Galatians—whether he knew any of Paul's letters remains a matter of debate—and the rumors of Paul's dependence on the Jerusalem apostles fitted nicely with his own theological program, which made Jerusalem the pivot in the "growth of the word of God" by addition of gentiles to the People of God. See Haenchen 1959, 283, and 1966, 268; the provocative revision of prevailing views by Jervell 1972, Dahl 1976a, and the important suggestions about the social context and functions of Acts by Adams 1979, 296–305.

7. Besides the standard commentaries on this passage, see Meeks and Wilken 1978, 13–16.

8. No certainty can be attained on the chronology. The fourteen years of Gal. 2:1 may or may not include the "three years" of 1:18, and since ancient reckoning sometimes included the initial and final units of a period as wholes, the total could be as little as slightly more than twelve and two years, respectively. The problems are discussed in all major commentaries and in the works on Pauline chronology, including Schlier 1971 *ad loc.*; Koester 1980, 534–37; Caird 1962. Most recently Jewett 1979 has insisted that only seventeen full years, to the month, could be meant. Lüdemann 1980a disagrees with Jewett but himself proposes a curious inversion of the order of events in Gal. 2:1–10 and 11–14. Neither is persuasive.

9. See the important discussion by Ollrog 1979, 9–13.

10. Early in the second century, Pliny the Younger thought it worthy of notice that Christianity in Bithynia had penetrated "not only the cities but even the villages and farms" (*Ep.* 10.96.9, trans. Radice 1969). By the end of the century, in North Africa, Tertullian boasted, with understandable exaggeration, "Men proclaim aloud that the state is beset with us; in countryside, in villages, in islands, Christians; every sex, age, condition, yes! and rank going over to this name" (*Apol.* 1.7, trans. T. R. Glover in the Loeb ed.); cf. *Apol.* 37.4. The point in both cases is that the unexpected spread of a new cult like Christianity into the country marked it as especially dangerous. That it was preeminently an urban phenomenon after the first beginnings in Palestine is now generally recognized. So far as I can see, only Schille 1967, 69, has denied this for the New Testament period, insisting that we have this impression solely by the accident that the traditions available to the author of Acts were collected in "metropolitan centers." But this depends on his ingenious, entirely hypothetical reconstruction of a uniform, institutionalized pattern of mission by small "colleges" of five or seven evangelists, working in "small towns and villages" not only in Galilee but throughout the area of the Pauline mission. Here one can see what a decisive step forward Theissen 1975a has taken in pointing to the essentially different "ecology" of the mission in Galilee and Judea from that carried out by Paul and other "Gemeindeorganisatoren."

11. See the vivid description in MacMullen 1974, especially 28–56. Compare the remarks by Ste. Croix 1975, 8f., and impressive use of the rural-urban conflict as

an interpretative key in several works by W. H. C. Frend, notably 1952. For a brief survey see Frend 1979.

12. Rostovtzeff 1957, 1:49.

13. Bowersock 1965, 62–72.

14. Magie 1950, 1:472.

15. Rostovtzeff 1957, 1:130–91 and passim.

16. Eubulus, citizen of the free city of Cnidus, appealed to Augustus when it looked as if the city court would convict him of homicide. His appeal, referred to the proconsul of Asia, was successful. *IG* 12.3, 174 (= *IGR* 4.1031b), discussed by Magie 1950, 1:480. The papyri reveal an astonishing amount of litigation even by people of quite low status in Roman Egypt.

17. For all these developments, see the rich evidence in Rostovtzeff 1957, Magie 1950, Levick 1967, and Bowersock 1965.

18. Bowersock 1965, 29. See also Badian 1958.

19. Bowersock 1965, 30–41.

20. Ibid., 42–61; on Herod, 54–57.

21. Josephus, *JW* 1.403–21.

22. Ibid., 422–28.

23. Bruneau 1970, 622–30.

24. Italian associations on Delos, for example, have been much discussed; see the summary of evidence in Bruneau 1970, 585–87. On the *conventus civium Romanorum* and other terms for associations of Romans in eastern provinces, see Magie 1950, 1:162f., and evidence cited in 2:1051f., nn. 6, 7.

25. Levick 1967, 71.

26. Cf. Bowersock 1965, 101–11.

27. Levick 1967, 103–20.

28. Burr 1955; E. G. Turner 1954; Smallwood 1976, 258.

29. See pages 38f.

30. Bruce 1977, 37, quotes a suggestion by Sir William Calder that Paul's father or grandfather might have provided tents for a Roman military campaign. Others have found the Acts report improbable. Citizenship would have to have been conferred by Augustus or Tiberius, and both are known to have been loath to give the *civitas* to *peregrini;* so, e.g., Goodenough 1966, 55f. Even if the claim in Acts should be pious fiction, however, it would indicate that by the end of the first century such a grant of citizenship did not seem grossly implausible.

31. See the discussion later in this chapter.

32. Rostovtzeff 1957 summarizes developments in the first two centuries: 1:343–52. Against Rostovtzeff's anachronism in calling the new situation "capitalistic agriculture," see Polanyi 1968, with the important review by Humphreys 1969, and Finley 1973. But see the criticisms of Finley by Frederiksen 1975.

33. MacMullen 1974, 15f.

34. Ibid., 27.

35. The Horatio Alger story inscribed on a third-century gravestone in Mactar, North Africa, tells of the rise of a hardworking farm laborer to own a house and farm and to be "enrolled among the city senators" (*CIL* 8.11824, cited by MacMullen 1974, 43). The finder of buried treasure, in Thomas's version of Jesus' parable, becomes a moneylender (G. Th. saying 109; 50:31–51:4). Of the villagers who were disciples of Jesus, those about whom we have any reliable information later found their way to the cities. Note that they are not depicted as peasants, however, but

typically as fishermen, who own boats and houses and have hired workers (Mark 1:16–20 and parallels; cf. Wuellner 1967). Nevertheless, Peter when he travels through the cities must be supported by contributions; he is not as free as the artisan Paul (1 Cor. 9:4–6).

36. Acts 14:8–18; cf. Levick 1967, 29–41.

37. MacMullen 1974, 22.

38. Hengel 1971a, 15.

39. Hock 1980, 27; cf. Casson 1974, 128–37.

40. On Phoebe's role see further page 58.

41. On the importance of Romans 16, see the comments by Malherbe 1977a, 64f. Of course this evidence would count differently if Romans 16 were the whole or a fragment of another letter addressed originally to Ephesus, as some critics have urged. See the discussion and references in Kümmel 1973, 317–20. In my judgment Gamble 1977 has convincingly demonstrated the integrity of the sixteen-chapter letter; see also Aland 1979.

42. Friedländer 1901, 268–322.

43. Cf. Hock 1980, 26–31, especially 27f., 30f.

44. MacMullen 1971, 109. Though the sources he cites—principally Vettius Valens, Artemidorus, and Claudius Ptolemy—are all from the second century, the parallels to Paul's catalog of dangers in 2 Cor. 11:23–27 show that the expectations had changed little.

45. *IGR* 4.841.

46. After several previous attempts, beginning in 102 B.C. with Marcus Antonius (grandfather of the like-named triumvir), Pompey cleared the whole Mediterranean of pirates in a campaign begun in 67 B.C. and settled many of them in colonies where they could find alternative employment. Several of these settlements were in Paul's native region, Cilicia, which had been particularly notorious for its buccaneers. Magie 1950, 1:283–300.

47. Magie 1950, 1:41.

48. Ibid., 547.

49. *Or. Rom.* 26.33.

50. For surveys of the road system and the means of travel, see Casson 1974; Charlesworth 1926; Chevallier 1972; Friedländer 1901, 268–322; Herzig 1974 (for Italy only); McCasland 1962; Radke 1973, col. 1666f.; Ramsay 1904. See also the extended bibliographical note in Rostovtzeff 1957, 2:609f., n. 24.

51. Charlesworth 1926, 82f.; Magie 1950, 1:40.

52. Charlesworth 1926, 115f.

53. Collart 1937, 522; see the whole of ch. 5.

54. Friedländer 1901, 282.

55. Charlesworth 1926, 258. However, speed varied widely with direction of travel, season, and type of ship: see Casson 1974, 152, 158.

56. Casson 1974, 182–88.

57. Friedländer 1901, 279f.

58. Casson 1974, 189; Chevallier 1972, 191–95, has a good collection of examples of travel plans, mostly from Livy.

59. Charlesworth 1926, 82f.

60. The classic description of this process of introduction of foreign cults is Nock 1933a, 48–65, but see now MacMullen 1981 for important corrections. See also the observations of J. Z. Smith 1971. Nock discusses the Delian cult of Serapis,

pp. 50–55; see further the full discussion of the archaeological evidence by Bruneau 1970 and Fraser 1960. On Philippi see Collart 1937, 389–486.

61. Scranton-Shaw-Ibrahim 1978, 53–90, and Ibrahim-Scranton-Brill 1976. In the fourth century, after an earthquake had destroyed the shrine, the Christians took it over and erected an imposing basilica. But by then it was a sacred site hallowed by use, and the location tells us nothing about the earlier status of the Christians.

62. *Ant.* 20.34. The translation, from the Loeb ed., is by Louis Feldman, who adds very useful notes throughout the account, which runs from §17 to §53. See also Neusner 1964.

63. Hock 1980, 50–59, sharply distinguishes such patronage seeking by teachers from three other means of support: charging fees, begging, and working. He insists, against Judge, that Paul, by his stress upon working with his own hands, rejected patronage (65). The situation was probably a little more complicated. Ananias took advantage of an opportunity to be elevated from an ἔμπορος to a διδάσκαλος of the king's household; Paul also accepted certain forms of support when they did not compromise his αὐτάρκεια. Hock offers the interesting suggestion that Paul's tent shop itself could have been a center of his evangelistic and catechetical activity, somewhat on the model of the famous cobbler's shop of Simon the Cynic (37–42).

64. *IG* 10.2.1, No. 255 (plate 10); discussed by Merkelbach 1973, 49–54.

65. Both points are well made by Finley 1973. On hierarchical society as excluding individualism, he compares Dumont's study of India (43f.); on the inapplicability of the concept of class, he quotes Georg Lukács (50).

66. Jones 1970, 89; cf. MacMullen 1974, 97–120; Finley 1973, 35–61.

67. The literature on ancient slavery is enormous. Among the more important surveys are Barrow 1928, Buckland 1908, Westermann 1955, Bömer 1957–63; bibliography in Vogt 1971.

68. Flory 1975.

69. Ibid., 112, referring to *CIL* 11. 5400.

70. Ibid., 8f., 59–79.

71. This "minute stratification" is illustrated throughout MacMullen 1974, especially 88–120.

72. Flory 1975, 93–130.

73. MacMullen 1974, 100. For the importance of trade (not just inheritances, as the satirists would have us think) in the rise of the freedmen, see Mrozek 1975.

74. In a detailed study of more than a thousand inscriptions dealing with the lesser aristocracy in Italian towns, Gordon 1931 found Tacitus's claim confirmed (*Ann.* 13.27), that a large proportion of the nobility were descended from freedmen. She found that as many as a third of the officials in great commercial centers like Ostia, Puteoli, and Capua showed signs of being sons of freedmen, and estimated that one-fifth of the aristocracy of Italy as a whole had been. See also the discussion by Finley 1973, 77, who remarks that even if Gordon's figures should be twice too high, her conclusions would still be valid.

75. See Phil. 4:22 and the discussion in chapter 2, Indirect Evidence.

76. The comparison is Friedländer's (1901, 33); see also Westermann 1955, 109–13.

77. Cf. Magie 1950, 1:540f.

78. Boulvert 1970, 1974; Chantraine 1967. The most lucid and suggestive study is Weaver 1972; see also his brief summary 1967.

79. Weaver 1972, 112–61, 179–95.

80. *Ep.* 8.6, trans. Radice 1969; cf. 7.29 and the discussion by Sherwin-White 1967, 84.

81. *Leg.* 166–73 (quotation from 166), trans. F. H. Colson in the Loeb ed.

82. Sherwin-White 1967 points out that Pliny and Tacitus, both of provincial origin, "were of the class that the senators of Claudius' day disliked as newcomers and aliens" (85). "Precisely because they were conscious of their own lack of noble birth, men like Pliny were all the more hostile to any who had risen from yet lower down the social scale" (86). An even more vivid example is Philo, wealthy, sophisticated, superbly educated, a leader of his community, but still a Jew. When he wrote the *Legatio* the crisis of Caligula was past, but Claudius had just firmly rejected the Jews' perennial request to be made full citizens of Alexandria.

83. Reekmans 1971; note especially the table on p. 124.

84. More is said about the problem of status consistency in the following chapter.

85. Pomeroy 1975, 196.

86. Weaver 1972, 193f.; cf. Pomeroy 1975, 195f.

87. Examples are legion; they have been cataloged in a way useful to our study by investigators of the early Christian pattern of paraenesis called by Luther "die Haustafel"; see especially Balch 1981.

88. Diogenes Laertius 6.12.

89. Ibid., 7.175.

90. Text and translation in Lutz 1947, 38–49.

91. ἀρρενωθεῖσα τὸν λογισμόν (*Leg.* 319f.). For Philo's usual misogyny, see Meeks 1974, 176f. and the additional references given there.

92. Pomeroy 1975, 200.

93. Acts 16:14. The author does not tell us that Lydia was a freedwoman, but her name, properly a place name, perhaps is a relic of servile origin.

94. *CIL* 10.810, 811, 812, 813 (Eumachia), and 816 (Mamia), cited by Mac-Mullen 1980, 209, 214. On Eumachia see also Pomeroy 1975, 200.

95. MacMullen 1980, 210, referring to the "hundreds" of responses to women's appeals in *Cod. Just.* "Over a period that begins with Hadrian and runs to Diocletian, women *sui iuris* and over the age of twenty-five make up a fifth of all rescript-addresses. . . ."

96. Ibid.

97. Poland 1909, 289–91.

98. Ibid., 282–89 (for numbers of members) and 289–98 (discussion of the issue). See also his remarks on p. 518.

99. MacMullen 1980, 211.

100. Pomeroy 1975, 200.

101. See, e.g., Poland 1909, 290. On the traditional separation between women's cults and men's, in Greece as well as in Rome, see Bömer 1957–63, 4:217. Pomeroy 1975, 205–26, presents a brief survey of women's roles in the religions of the city of Rome. For the surprising appearance of women occasionally even among Mithraists, see MacMullen 1981, 101 and 193f., n. 31.

102. *Coniug. praec.* 145B–E.

103. Ibid., 140D, trans. F. C. Babbitt in the Loeb edition.

104. Josephus *Ant.* 18.65–84.

105. ἐγώ εἰμι ἡ παρὰ γυναιξὶ θεὸς καλουμένη; the "Memphite archetype" (Harder 1944), line 10 (hereafter cited as M). See Heyob 1975.

106. Cf. Georgi 1976, 37, and especially Becher 1970.

107. So Professor MacMullen informs me, from his own survey of the evidence.

108. Leipoldt 1954, 9. Accepted by, among others, Becher 1970, 85.

109. *POxy.* 1380.145–48; M, lines 17, 18, 19. I owe this observation to my former student, Professor Jouette Bassler.

110. In the popular romance by Xenophon of Ephesus, the *Ephesiaca* (early second century A.D.?), it is Isis who defends the life and chastity of Anthia, a former votary of Ephesian Artemis, against the most improbable series of assaults, in order to reunite her with her equally chaste husband Habrocomes. For the chaste lives demanded of devotees, see Apuleius *Met.* 11.19, which here seems to refer to something more than the temporary abstinence required prior to initiations.

111. Pomeroy 1975, 223, cites only six women out of twenty-six functionaries called *sacerdos* in extant Italian inscriptions; Griffiths 1975, 181f., finds it "strange that Apuleius does not mention a single priestess," and notes that men "assumed the main priestly roles."

112. Examples of such attacks are collected by Balch 1981, 65–80.

113. Balch 1981, 63–116; Malherbe 1977*a*, 50–53.

114. Salamis, 13:5; Pisidian Antioch, 13:14–43; Iconium, 14:1; Philippi, 16:13 (a προσευχή rather than συναγωγή; whether there is a material difference is debated by commentators, but see Hengel 1971*b*); Thessalonica, 17:1–4; Beroea, 17:10–12; Athens, 17:17; Corinth, 18:4; Ephesus, 18:19; 19:8.

115. That seems to be the meaning in Acts of σεβομένη τὸν θεόν and the equivalent term φοβούμενος τὸν θεόν; see especially 17:4, 17. But there are some problems; see n. 175.

116. See chapter 3, n. 44.

117. Cadbury 1926, 321f., proposed translating ἐν ἰδίῳ μισθώματι "on his own earnings," assuming that even under house arrest Paul continued to ply his trade; accepted by Hock 1980, 77, n. 2, with reference to further literature.

118. Lake-Cadbury 1933, 4:212f.

119. See the general remarks earlier in this chapter on the use of Acts as a source. Note, however, that Acts 20:20 depicts Paul as preaching "publicly and from house to house."

120. See Betz 1979, 220–24; I have quoted his translation. On the special importance of hospitality in the development of early Christianity, see Malherbe 1977*b*.

121. See also 1 Cor. 4:12; 9:3–18; 2 Cor. 11:27; 2 Thess. 3:7–9 (if authentic). On the context and significance of 1 Thess. 2, see Malherbe 1970, and on Paul's working, Hock 1980.

122. Judge 1960*b*, 125–37. As Judge has mastered specialized New Testament scholarship, he has imbibed somewhat more of the skepticism that characterizes that discipline.

123. See Downey 1958 and 1961, 582f.; Liebeschuetz 1972, 40f., 92–96.

124. MacMullen 1974, 63.

125. *Flacc.* 25–43.

126. It stands in the first of the famous "we" passages of Acts, but recent critical studies have inclined toward the view that the first-person plural is a stylistic device common in ancient historians, rather than one marking excerpts from a "travel source" or "itinerary." See, e.g., Cadbury 1927, 230; Dibelius 1951, 200–06; Haenchen 1961.

127. Downey 1961, 544, n. 179.

128. *Flacc.* 55.

129. Philo *Leg.* 155; cf. Leon 1960, 135–37.

130. MacMullen 1974, 133, with other examples as well; see the whole of his appendix A, "Subdivisions of the City" (129–37), and pp. 70–73.

131. Cf. Malherbe 1977*a*, 74f.

132. Hock 1980, 37–42.

133. Strobel 1965 undertakes to show that the New Testament preserves the strict legal distinction in which οἶκος = *domus* includes only free adult relatives, but his argument is unconvincing.

134. *De off.* 1.17.58, trans. Walter Miller in the Loeb ed.

135. Cf. Judge 1960*a*, 30–39; Malherbe 1977*a*, 69.

136. For Pompeii: Mau 1904, 276–78, floor plans 245–79; M. Grant 1971, 127f., 193–96; Tanzer 1939, 19, 52. For hotels connected with private houses: Kléberg 1957, 78–80 (evidence mostly from Pompeii); for mixed groups at dinner: Theissen 1974*b*, 293–97.

137. Compare Judge's discussion of *amicitia* and *clientela*, which, he argues, are constitutive of "the social structure of the Roman community" and have their analogies in the Greek-speaking provinces (1960*b*, 6f.).

138. Flory 1975, 17–55.

139. For the whole question of religion among slaves and freedpersons, see the extensive investigation by Bömer 1957–63. Bömer observes that the religious solidarity of the *familia* in old Roman agrarian society gave way under pressures of urbanization, and that under the principate Romans became more laissez faire about slave religion (1:57–78). Moreover, slaves in Rome and in areas under strong Roman influence enjoyed greater freedom for participation in cults than did those in the Greek East (4:61–63; 3:61; and passim).

140. The hundreds of inscriptions they left behind provide the basis for the several modern studies of the phenomenon. For the Latin corporations, the classic work is still Waltzing 1895–1900; for the Greek counterparts Poland 1909 remains indispensable. De Robertis 1973 deals with the legal situation in some depth. For an introduction and overview, see Kornemann 1900.

141. Poland 1909, 272n.

142. "Collegium quod est in domu Sergiae Paullinae," *CIL* 6.9148; see Flory 1975, 22; other examples in Waltzing 1895–1900, 3:222–64.

143. Vogliano 1933. The list of members—nearly four hundred in all—is by office and category, from highest to lowest. At the top is Agrippinilla, priestess, followed by members of her immediate family, also with sacral offices. Further down are other names that occur frequently in senatorial families of the period, although the hierophant has a Greek name and is probably of servile origin. Lower on the list Latin names diminish in number while Greek ones predominate. These facts hardly support Cumont's claim, based on the use of simple *cognomina* in the list, that "les distinctions sociales du monde profane s'effaçaient . . ." (1933, 234); rather the contrary: cf. Bömer 1957–63, 3:135–37. The inscription, on three sides of a statue base that once held a statue of Agrippinilla, is displayed at the Metropolitan Museum in New York.

144. Bömer 1957–63, 4:238–41. Evidence for the trade and artisan guilds, drawn chiefly from Waltzing, is conveniently summarized by Jones 1955. See also Burford 1972, 159–64.

145. *Contra* Préaux 1955, 128f.

146. Jones 1955, 172; cf. MacMullen 1974, 75; see also Rostovtzeff 1957, 1:170f.

147. Robert 1937, 535, n. 3, cited by MacMullen 1974, 135. Other typical names are in Poland 1909 and Waltzing 1895–1900.

148. Poland 1909, 315–25, 517–28.

149. See the discussion by Bruneau 1970, 585–87.

150. These are the practical consequences of the revolutionary work done by Jacob Neusner and his students. However controversial that work has been and however many corrections of detail it will doubtless have to undergo, these results seem to me irreversible. Neusner's investigations are too many even to mention here, but 1970, 1973*b*, 1979*a*, 1979*b*, and 1980 are particularly germane to our project.

151. Philo's figure of one million for Egypt, which would be a seventh of the whole (*Flacc.* 43) is doubtless too high (Smallwood 1976, 222). For Antioch see Meeks-Wilken 1978, 8. The Jewish population of the province Asia may be estimated from the money for the temple tax confiscated by L. Valerius Flaccus in 62 B.C. (Cicero *Pro Fl.* 66–69)—nearly one hundred pounds of gold, which by Smallwood's calculation (1976, 125f. and n. 21) would amount to contributions by nearly fifty thousand adult males. Josephus's report (from Strabo) of 800 talents from the same province seized by Mithridates a quarter-century earlier (*Ant.* 14.112f.) seems much too large (see Marcus's note *ad loc.* in the Loeb ed.; Smallwood 1976, 125, n. 20).

152. He was the younger brother of Marcus Antonius III, the triumvir.

153. *Ant.* 14.235, trans. Ralph Marcus in the Loeb ed.

154. That Jews had been in Sardis "from the earliest times [ἀπ' ἀρχῆς]" is scarcely an exaggeration if the Sefarad of Obad. 20 (sixth century B.C.) is indeed Sardis, as most commentators assume. How continuous their settlement was and how old the institutions here disputed is, of course, another question.

155. *Ant.* 14.259–61, trans. Marcus.

156. The synagogue was discovered in 1962 by the Cornell-Harvard team led by George Hanfmann and has been partially restored. The final excavation report by A. R. Seager has not yet appeared. See Seager 1972; Hanfmann 1962; Kraabel 1968, 1978, 1979; partial publication of inscriptions in Robert 1964, 37–58 and pls. IV–XI.

157. See especially the discussion by Kraabel 1968, 1978; also Wilken 1976.

158. LSJ, s.v.; Poland 1909, 158–63.

159. For this and subsequent exemptions from the laws against clubs, see Smallwood 1976, 133–35.

160. The term συναγωγή, used occasionally by other clubs, recalls the central fact of "gathering" the members. On meals in the synagogue, see Hengel 1966, 167–72; evidence collected with speculative interpretation by Goodenough 1953–68, 2:108f. and vol. 5 passim. On hospitality for visitors and other activities: Krauss 1922, 55f., 182–90.

161. The synagogue of the Augustesians in Rome surely honored the emperor, whether as patron of this particular congregation or for his general favor to Jewish rights; the synagogue of the Agrippesians may have had Marcus Vipsanius Agrippa or King Agrippa I or II as its patron (Leon 1960, 140–42). Capitolina, member of a prominent family in the province Asia and wife or sister of a proconsul, dedicated a mosaic-covered staircase in the synagogue in Tralles (*CIG* 2924; Robert 1937, 409–12, and 1964, 44; Hommel 1975, 175). "Father" and "Mother of the Synagogue": Leon 1960, 186–88; Polycharmus, "Father of the synagogue" in Stobi: *CII* 1.694; Kitzinger 1946, plates 202–04; Hengel 1966, 176–81. The synagogue in Phocae voted προεδρία and a golden wreath for a wealthy, non-Jewish donor, *IGR*

4.1327. In Dura-Europos the elder and priest Samuel was instrumental in having the assembly room decorated with the now-famous paintings; it has been conjectured that the prominent seat immediately below the scene of the biblical Samuel (labeled by name) anointing David was reserved for him: Sivan 1978, 11.

162. *PRyl.* 590 (= *CPJ* no. 138) may refer to a Jewish burial society connected with a synagogue in Alexandria (Tcherikover's note at *CPJ* 1.252); for the Jewish catacombs in Rome, see Leon 1960; Goodenough 1953–68, 2:3–50.

163. ἄρχων is the most frequent; also γραμματεύς; others in Juster 1914, 1:450–56; cf. Applebaum 1974. In Aphrodisias (Asia) a synagogue was headed by a *decania*. (The inscription, not yet published, was kindly described to me by Dr. Joyce Reynolds of Newnham College, Cambridge; see the announcement by Mellink [quoting K. Erim] 1977, 306.) "Priests" were frequently mentioned in Jewish inscriptions, as in those of pagan cult societies, but the title probably had a different significance, particularly after the destruction of the temple in Jerusalem (Kraabel 1981). On evolution of offices from simple to complex, see Hengel 1971*b*, 166f.

164. Smallwood 1976, 133f.

165. Ibid., 134.

166. Philo *Flacc.* 74, 80; Josephus, *JW* 7.412; Tcherikover 1961, 302.

167. Josephus, *JW* 7.47; Libanius *Ep.* 1251 (ed. Foerster), cf. Meeks-Wilken 1978, 6–9, 60.

168. For Rome see the discussion in Leon 1960, 168–70.

169. For Alexandria, the term is used already in the Letter of Aristeas (310), probably second century B.C.; cf. Josephus *Ant.* 12.108. See the general discussion in Tcherikover 1961, 296–332; Smallwood 1976, 139, 141, 224–50, 285, 359–64, 369; Tarn 1952, 210–38.

170. See the discussions by Tcherikover and Smallwood cited in the previous note. They adduce πολιτεύματα of Phrygians, Boeotians, and Lycians in Alexandria, Cretans in the Fayum, Caunians in Sidon, and others (Tcherikover 1961, 505, n. 8; Smallwood 1976, 226, n. 23). On associations of Roman citizens in the new provinces of Asia Minor, see above, n. 24. For various arrangements of parallel πολιτεύματα in colonies, see Levick 1967, 71–83. On the resultant social and economic tensions, see Cracco Ruggini 1980.

171. *C. Ap.* 2.39.

172. *Ant.* 14.235.

173. Ibid., 259; see Marcus's note *ad loc.* and Tarn 1961, 221.

174. *Ant.* 12.126, trans. Marcus. A fuller account, describing Herod's successful intervention with his patron Agrippa and the defense of the Jews by Herod's protégé, Nicolaus of Damascus, is in *Ant.* 16.27–61. See the discussion by Smallwood 1976, 140f. Compare the complaint of Apion quoted by Josephus *C. Ap.* 2.65.

175. On monotheism, see Strabo *Geog.* 16.2.35 (= Stern 1974, no. 115). The success of Jewish proselytism is indicated by the Roman laws and police measures which were taken from time to time to inhibit it, beginning with the expulsion of Jews from Rome by Cornelius Hispalus in 139 B.C., reported by Valerius Maximus (Stern 1974, no. 147a). We still have no completely satisfactory treatment of Jewish proselytism in the late Hellenistic and early Roman periods, but see Kuhn 1959 and Kuhn-Stegemann 1962. The question of "God fearers" as semiproselytes has been much discussed by, e.g., Lake 1933; Feldman 1950; Hommel 1975; Lifshitz 1969, 95f., and 1970; Romaniuk 1964; Siegert 1973; Robert 1964, 39–47. The weight of the evidence seemed until recently to deny such a technical usage. In most cases θεοσεβής

merely means "pious," whether applied to proselytes, sympathizers, or, as in the Miletus theater inscription, the whole Jewish community. However, the newly discovered Aphrodisias synagogue inscription seems to confirm that θεοσεβεῖς could be a formal designation for a group distinct from both proselytes and native Jews, but still enrolled in the membership of a synagogue (see Mellink 1977, 305f.). We need not assume that the same usage prevailed everywhere.

176. Diodor. Sic. *Bibl. hist.* 1.3 (= Stern 1974, no. 63). The best-known version of the leper story was in the anti-Jewish tract by Apion to which Josephus replied. Other examples, beginning with Hecateus of Abdera, are collected by Stern 1974; see also his survey 1976. On anti-Jewish sentiments in antiquity, see Sherwin-White 1967, 86–101; Sevenster 1975.

177. See I. Heinemann 1929–32, 524–28.

178. The degree and kind of Philo's Hellenism has been much debated; one of the surest guides remains the work by Heinemann cited in the previous note.

179. Goodenough 1962, 10.

180. Num. 22:9b LXX.

181. *Mos.* 1.278, trans. F. H. Colson in the Loeb edition.

182. *Migr.* 89–93; quotations from 89, 90 (my translation).

183. Like the Jew reportedly encountered once by Aristotle: Josephus *C. Ap.* 1.180, quoting Clearchus of Soli.

184. Tcherikover 1961, 309.

185. There are many probable allusions to Alexander in Philo's works, e.g., *Mos.* 1.30f. Bassler 1979, 138–43, has argued that Philo's curiously ambivalent portrait of Joseph as a *politicus* is not a model for the Roman prefect of Egypt, as Goodenough 1938, 21–33, proposed, but a warning against just the sort of career Ti. Alexander made, setting himself above "ancestral customs" and passing "from the leadership of the people to the dictatorship over the people" (*Somn.* 2.78f.).

186. Kraabel 1968, 218–21. The Aphrodisias inscription (above, n. 163) when published will add significant new evidence. Caution is needed about the earlier period, however, for Septimius Severus evidently passed laws making it much easier for Jews to serve on city councils (called to my attention by Robert L. Wilken, who cites two inscriptions praising the Severi, *CII* 1.677 and 2.972, in his forthcoming work, *John Chrysostom and the Jews: Rhetoric and Reality in the Fourth Century* [University of California Press], which he showed me in manuscript). See also Levine 1979, 656.

187. Acts 16:37f.; 21:39; 22:3, 25–29.

188. PLond. 1912 in Bell 1924 (= *CPJ* no. 153). The most important sources are conveniently collected in Stern 1974, 1:399–403, and the issues are briefly but incisively discussed by Tcherikover 1961, 305–28.

189. Smallwood 1976, 362f., plausibly argues from *Ant.* 12.120 that the Roman legate Mucianus had intervened sometime between 67 and 69 to restore the Jews' basic rights.

190. Josephus, *JW* 7.40–62, 100–111 (the quotation, in Thackeray's translation, is from 111). See the discussion in Smallwood 1976, 361–64; Meeks-Wilken 1978, 4f.

191. Applebaum 1961, 1979.

192. For good reason Rom. 13:1–7 is now regarded as a traditional piece of paraenesis that was probably formed by the Greek synagogue, then taken over by Christians. See, e.g., Käsemann 1961, Bergmeier 1970.

193. See the survey by Applebaum 1976, 701–27.

194. Ibid., 709–11.

195. These identifications must remain tentative until publication of the inscription. I refer to a handwritten transcription very kindly supplied me by Dr. Joyce Reynolds and quoted by her permission and that of Professor Kenan T. Erim.

196. TSukkah 4:6, also bSukkah 51b, pSukkah 5:1, 55a. See Applebaum 1974, 703, who thinks that the guilds themselves must predate Roman rule, because of Roman hostility to associations, and that they may have been "deliberately incorporated into the synagogue framework in order to avoid suppression by the authorities." But that overstates official opposition to corporations, especially professional ones, which were primarily Roman in inspiration.

197. Hengel 1966, 171f.

198. Josephus *Ant.* 18.160; Applebaum 1976, 705f. Applebaum also thinks the Jewish synagogue on Delos is probably evidence for "maritime trade based on the Alexandria-Delos-Puteoli triangle" (706).

199. Philo *Flacc.* 57.

200. This point has been urged repeatedly and effectively by Kraabel, most recently 1981.

201. Except for 2 Tim. 4:10, which places Titus in Dalmatia.

202. But Prófessor Helmut Koester points out to me that the normal access to Illyria would have been not through Macedonia but from the West.

203. See Kümmel 1973, 252–55; Knox 1950, 74–88; Dupont 1955; Caird 1962, 605–07; Hurd 1976; Jewett 1979; Lüdemann 1980a.

204. Acts 14.22, "reinforcing the souls of the disciples"; 14:23, "appointing elders for them in each church." Acts 20:4 contains a list of persons who accompanied Paul on a later trip from Greece through Macedonia toward Asia. They are from Beroea, Thessalonica, Derbe, and Asia (Ephesus?). Acts 20:7–12 also indicates a Christian group at Troas.

205. See pages 42f.

206. Hans Conzelmann 1965 has even suggested the formation there of a Pauline school in the concrete sense of the word, but see the criticisms cited in chapter 3, n. 45. No reliable inference can be drawn from the insertion of the words ἐν Ἐφέσῳ in the address of "Ephesians," which appears from the better manuscript evidence to have been originally an encyclical of no certain address, probably written pseudonymously. See Dahl 1951 and, for a contrary view, Lindemann 1976.

207. Levick 1967, 34–38; Magie 1950, 1:453–67.

208. Perge, too, which was probably part of the province Galatia as was its neighbor, Side (Levick 1967, 26; Magie 1950, 1:434), is referred to in Acts as "in Pamphylia" (13:13).

209. As Betz 1979, 4, correctly observes. For a partial list of advocates of the so-called south Galatian hypothesis and an outline of arguments on both sides, see Kümmel 1973, 296–98.

210. Levick 1967, 33f. As she points out, they really did not all lie within the old region of Pisidia, either, but given that the military security of Pisidia was one of the principal reasons for the colonies' existence, it would be natural for Augustus to refer to them thus.

211. Magie 1950, 1:6; Jones 1971, 113f.

212. Chevallier 1972, 141f. Somewhat different is the argument of Ollrog 1979, 55f., n. 256, who asserts that Paul intended to head directly for Rome from the time he separated from Barnabas and Antioch, and working in the highlands of Anatolia would have been a diversion. But it can hardly be a trustworthy method that grants to

a hypothesis veto power over evidence that tends against it. For the accessibility of Galatia from another direction (the West), cf. Lucian *Alex.* 10.

213. There was something out of the ordinary about Paul's first arrival in Galatia, which might suggest that the area did not lie on his most natural route. None of the ingenious explanations that have been offered for his δι' ἀσθένειαν τῆς σαρκός (Gal. 4:13) can really relieve our ignorance on this point, however. The fact that the author of Acts refers only to "the Galatian country [χῶρα]" (16:6; 18:23) might imply that he imagines the Pauline mission there to have been limited to rural areas. It is true that urbanization was slow there: "The Gauls were a rustic people and had no taste for town life" (Jones 1971, 117). Yet Pompey had organized them into πόλεις, and in the cities the upper classes rapidly took on Greek ways. Paul's letter is in Greek and presupposes congregations that are able to understand it and appreciate its rhetorical subtleties; in the countryside of Galatia the old tribal languages persisted as late as the fifth century (ibid., 121).

214. Jones 1971, 57–63.

215. Magie 1950, 2:1059, n. 39: 134, 884 sq. km.

216. Ibid., 1:146. The whole of Magie's chapter 5 (119–46) should be consulted, as well as Jones 1971, 28–94.

217. Magie 1950, 1:406f.

218. Ibid., 583f.

219. Col. 1:2; 2:1; 4:13–16; for Laodicea see also Rev. 1:11; 3:14. Philemon was also written to Colossae, though without Col. we would not know that, so we are in the predicament of having to situate a letter almost universally regarded as authentic by information from one most likely pseudonymous.

220. One of the many small ironies of early Christian history is that in the New Testament Colossae looms much larger, by the accident that two letters sent there in Paul's name survive, whereas the one sent at the same time to Laodicea (Col. 4:16) did not.

221. Lightfoot 1879, 16, points out that Strabo had already referred to Colossae as "a small town [πόλισμα]" and that Paul's contemporary, the elder Pliny, does not contradict that claim when he includes Colossae among "the most famous towns of (Phrygia) *besides the ones already mentioned*" (*HN* 5.[41]145), for he had already mentioned Hierapolis, Laodicea, Apameia "and even much less important places than these." Lightfoot's essay, "The Churches of the Lycus" (1–72), is still important.

222. Lightfoot 1879, 4; Jones 1971, 73f.

223. Magie 1950, 1:117.

224. See the survey of the evidence by Kraabel 1968 for Miletus (14–20), Priene (20–25), Smyrna (26–50), Ephesus (51–60), Eumenia (61–69), Acmonia (70–119), Apameia (119–24), Hierapolis (125–35), Laodicea (135–39), Colossae (139–48), Thyatira to Philadelphia (155–97), and Sardis (198–240).

225. *Ant.* 14.223–30, 234, 237–40; see also 16.27–65 and 12.125f. and above, pages 34–36.

226. Kraabel 1968, 74–79.

227. Above, n. 161.

228. Apameia, second only to Ephesus as a market and distribution center (Magie 1950, 1:125f.), lay approximately midway between Pisidian Antioch and Colossae. The strength of its Jewish community is shown by the amount of the temple tax from there seized by M. Flaccus (above, n. 151) and by the possible syncrasis of a local

flood story, the Noah story in the Bible, and the epithet long added to the city's name, Κιβωτός (Kraabel 1968, 119–23).

229. Cf. Elliger 1978, 87–89.

230. Collart 1937, 389–523, discusses the beginnings and the Macedonian period in some detail.

231. Ibid., 227, citing H. Gaebler, *Zeitschrift für Numismatik* 39 (1929): 260–69.

232. Collart 1937, 224–41.

233. Levick 1967, 161; on Antiochene coinage, 132f.

234. Elliger 1978, 22. The forum was excavated by the French School and is now readily accessible by the Kavalla-Drama road, which at this point follows the ancient Via Egnatia. Although the monuments that give the visible forum its character were built between A.D. 161 and 175, the first-century forum was probably similar in plan, though perhaps smaller (see Collart 1937, 329–62).

235. On the rock face of the acropolis scores of relief carvings of various deities and dedicatory inscriptions indicate the variety of cults that flourished in Philippi. Collart classifies them as Latin, indigenous Thracian, and Oriental. Of the third group, the Egyptian gods were the most important (ibid., 389–486).

236. Collart observes that although most of the inscriptions are Latin, the stone-cutters who worked on the forum and the theater made their assembly-marks in Greek (ibid., 305).

237. A great deal of energy has been spent in attempts to pin down the location of the προσευχή mentioned in Acts 16:13, 16. See especially Collart 1937, 323, 459f., who tries to rescue the identification by Renan, Heuzey, and others of the "river" with the Gangites, by making the πυλή not the city gate but the commemorative arch two kilometers west of it. Collart argues that this marked the boundary of the *pomerium,* the sacred margin of a Roman city within which no graves, buildings, or foreign cults were permitted. Elliger 1978, 49f., accepts this despite reservations. Lemerle 1945 refutes it: chance discovery of tombs within the supposed pomerium make it likely that there was a necropolis outside the west gate of the city as there was on the east, rendering impossible the unique deviation proposed by Collart of the western line of the pomerium. Lemerle, pp. 23–27, puts the Jewish meeting place on the banks of the little stream from the springs that gave Philippi its first name. That would have the advantage of lying within the 2,000-cubit limit of a "Sabbath-day's journey" in Mishnaic law, whereas the Gangites was three times that far from the city gate. In the absence of any concrete evidence, all these speculations are of doubtful value.

238. Collart 1937, 274–76.

239. Ibid., 319.

240. Lemerle 1934, 457, 464; Collart 1937, 363, n. 3. The "market" referred to is *macellum,* properly a meatmarket, but often including other groceries; this Genius may have been in charge of only small potatoes. Lemerle 1945, 28, calls attention to one Latin inscription referring to a [*pu*]*purari.*

241. Vickers 1970, who corrects, on the basis of recent evidence, von Schoenebeck 1940. The modern street called ὁδὸς ᾿Εγνάτιας has nothing to do with the route of the ancient Via Egnatia (*pace* Finegan 1962, 629b), which sliced through only the northwest corner of the city: Makaronas 1951.

242. Forum excavations: Petsas 1968. On the Serapeion, briefly reported in *BCH* 45 (1921): 540f., see Vacalopoulos 1963, 8f.; Witt 1970; Edson 1948, 181–88; Salditt-Trappmann 1970, 47–52; Fraser 1960; Merkelbach 1973.

243. *IG* 10.2.1 (1972); cf. Robert 1974.

244. Charlesworth 1926, 126f.; Vacalopoulos 1963, 3, 12.

245. Charlesworth, ibid.

246. Ibid., 126.

247. Cf. Vacalopoulos 1963, 9. However, two sarcophagi painted with seven-branched menorahs have been found in an early Christian cemetery east of the city, and these are undoubtedly Jewish: Pelekanidis 1961, 257, plate 314a,b; J. and L. Robert in *REG* 77 (1964):185, no. 25; and especially Lifshitz and Schiby 1968, 377f. and plate 36.

248. See Moe 1977; Kraabel 1981.

249. Lifshitz and Schiby 1968 (= *IG* 10.2.1, no. 789); on the text, see also Tov 1974.

250. Vacalopoulos 1963, 11.

251. Greek: 1,006; Latin: 14 (*IG* 10.2.1).

252. By Homer, *Il.* 2.570, which Strabo has just quoted. But Strabo is clearly describing also the situation of the new Corinth in his own time, probably toward the end of the first century B.C.

253. *Geog.* 8.6.20, C378, trans. Fowler 1932, 24f.

254. Hence this place was called the διολκός, "haul-across": Strabo *Geog.* 8.2.1, C335; 8.6.4, C369; 8.6.22, C380, who gives the width as forty stadia. Nero undertook to dig a canal across the isthmus but failed (Philostratus *V. Ap.* 4.24; Pausanias 2.1.5); the task was not accomplished until the nineteenth century.

255. Strabo 8.6.23, C381–82; Pausanias 2.1.2. The destruction may not have been so complete as is usually supposed. The archaic temple of Apollo was spared, and apparently some of its priests and servants continued to function, and the South Stoa was left intact: Broneer 1954, 100; Kent 1966, 20, n. 10.

256. Bowersock 1965, 94f.

257. Stillwell in Fowler 1932, 190, 211; Stillwell 1941, 129; 1952, 135.

258. Broneer 1954, 158. The city's wealth had been enhanced during the period A.D. 15–44, when the province Achaia had been placed under the governor of Moesia, a change that diminished Corinth's dignity but also greatly reduced its administrative costs. Restoration of the senatorial province and Corinth as its capital in 44 was probably the occasion when the great βῆμα was erected in the center of the central terrace (cf. Acts 18:12, 16f.), as well as the procurator's office, which has been found in the old south stoa: Scranton 1951, 130; Broneer 1954, 111–14.

259. "Of the 104 texts that are prior to the reign of Hadrian 101 are in Latin and only three are Greek. . ." (Kent 1966, 19).

260. Hayes 1973, 416–70.

261. Kent 1966, 27.

262. Ibid., 18f.

263. Cf. Bowersock 1965, ch. 5, who shows that romanization was not the intended result of Augustus' policy. Many colonists were Greeks returning home, and many of those from Campania likely had Greek ancestors.

264. Crispus, Gaius, Fortunatus, Tertius, Quartus, and Titius Justus. The names of Prisca and Aquila are also Latin, but they are from Pontus via Rome, and their stay in Corinth is temporary (although if we knew more about the rest, we might find such migrations typical). One may count from five to nine Greek names; it is hard to decide which of those who send greetings from Corinth in Rom. 16 are Corinthians and who on the other hand may have been traveling with Paul.

265. Strabo, *Geog.* 8.6.23, C382, says the χώρα was "not very fertile" but rough and uneven. Just before this he describes the high development of αἱ τέχναι αἱ δημιουργικαί in Corinth. Its bronzework was particularly famous (Pliny *Hist. nat.* 34.1, 6–8, 48; 37.49; Pausanias 2.3.3; Strabo 8.6.23, C382), and evidence has been found for bronzework concentrated in and around the forum in the Roman period (Stillwell and Askew 1941, 27–31; Mattusch 1977).

266. Keck 1974, 443, paraphrasing Ernst von Dobschütz.

267. 8.6.23, C381, trans. Horace Leonard Jones in the Loeb edition.

268. West 1931, 107f., quotation from 132. Babbius gave not only the familiar "Babbius Monument," possibly a shrine of Poseidon, whose remains dominate the west end of the excavated lower forum, but also the portico of the Southeast Building and perhaps some part of the Julian Basilica (see inscriptions 2, 3, 98–101, 131, 132, 155, 241, 323, and 364 in West 1931 and Kent 1966). His son was also prominent, contributing to the Southeast Building (Broneer 1954, 27f.; and Kent 1966, no. 327), and another Babbius, who appears in no. 259, from the second half of the second century, was probably a descendant.

269. Inscription 232 in Kent 1966, 99f. and plate 21. Kent comments: "Like his contemporary, Cn. Babbius Philinus, Erastus was probably a Corinthian freedman who had acquired considerable wealth in commercial activities" (100). For identification with the Christian Erastus, see chapter 2.

270. Ibid., no. 62.

271. Ibid., no. 121.

272. Ibid., nos. 124, 125, and 321; see discussion by Kent, p. 127f., and the clarification by Nabers 1969. See also Kent's list of benefactors and gifts, p. 21, and his discussion of the opportunities for advancement, p. 20.

273. Fowler 1932, 16.

274. He names Egypt, Phoenicia, Coelesyria, Pamphylia, Cilicia, "most of Asia up to Bithynia and the corners of Pontus, . . . Europe, Thessaly, Boeotia, Macedonia, Aetolia, Attica, *Argos, Corinth,* and most of the best parts of Peloponnese" (*Leg.* 281f., trans. Colson in the Loeb ed. [my emphasis]).

275. Broneer 1930, 121f. and plate 23 (cat. no. 1511). Broneer says the design on no. 1516 might also be a menorah, but it is more likely a crude tree or palm frond.

276. Inscription 111 in West 1931, first published by Powell 1903, 60f., no. 40. It may now be seen in the courtyard of the museum in Corinth (inv. no. 123). Hengel 1971*b*, 183, suggests that the congregation represented by the inscription may have been an "offshoot" from the Συναγωγὴ Ἑβραίων in Rome, on which see Leon 1960, 147–49. But Leon's explanation of the Roman name, that the first Jewish group in any city would naturally be called Congregation of the Hebrews (= Jews), is equally plausible for Corinth.

277. Malherbe 1977*a*, 75; cf. Powell 1903, 61: "The building was probably not more than a hundred metres from the Propylaea"; but Powell thought the west side of the road, lined with a colonnade and a series of shops nestled under the Apollo temple hill, would not have been a plausible place for a synagogue, so he located it across the street, in what he thought was a "residence quarter."

278. Kent 1966, v.

279. Powell 1903, 61. It is not in fact so very large: 93 cm long, 42 cm wide, 22 cm thick. Powell observes that the inscription is in irregular letters on a secondhand stone, which "may point to the poverty of this foreign cult at Corinth." The date is uncertain but "considerably later than the time of Paul" (Merritt 1931, 79).

280. See above, n. 61.

281. Note, for example, the warning in Claudius's letter, PLond. 1912 (= *CPJ* no. 153), 5,96f. Knox 1964, 11, has suggested that the κύκλῳ of Rom. 15:19 means literally "in a circle," reflecting "Paul's hope and expectation of making a complete circuit of the nations, both north and south of the Sea." But his argument is not very persuasive.

282. As does Dionysius of Halicarnassus, who enjoyed Roman patronage: Bowersock 1965, 131. See also Hengel's comments on Cicero's division of the world into three parts, *Italia, Graecia, omnis barbaria* (1976, 65 and 157, n. 46).

283. On the importance of Rome in Paul's conception of his mission, see Dahl 1941, 241.

CHAPTER 2

1. Origen *C. Cels.* 3.44, trans. Chadwick 1965, 158.

2. *C. Cels.* 3.55, Chadwick 165f.

3. *C. Cels.* 1.62, Chadwick 56f.

4. E.g., Minucius Felix, *Octav.* 36.3–7; *Actus Petri c. Simone* 23 (Lipsius-Bonnet 1891, 1:71.24–25); cf. Justin 2 *Apol.* 10.8; Tatian *Orat. ad Gr.* 32. As late as the last quarter of the fourth century, Libanius could chide those of his own class who had become Christians with having received their doctrines from "your mother, your wife, your housekeeper, your cook" (*Or.* 16.47, trans. A. F. Norman in the Loeb ed.). But contrast Tertullian, *Apol.* 1.7, quoted above, chapter 1, n. 10; cf. *Apol.* 37.4; *Ad Scap.* 5.2. Tertullian's claims recall what Pliny had written to Trajan even earlier: "many of every age, of every estate [*ordo*], of both sexes" (*Ep.* 10.96.9). See also Vogt 1975.

5. See the brief but vivid sketch by Kreissig 1967, 93–96.

6. Deissmann 1911, especially ch. 2 (pp. 27–52).

7. Ibid., 49, 50.

8. Ibid., 50.

9. Ibid., 51.

10. Malherbe 1977*a*, 31. Filson 1939, quotation from p. 111. Compare Eck 1971, 381: "If one takes account of the whole body of sources relevant to this set of questions, and avoids arbitrary generalizations from a few of them, the inference is unavoidable that the adherents to the Christian religion present a virtually exact mirror-image of the general social stratification in the Roman empire. And that was so from the beginnings depicted in the NT documents."

11. Judge 1960*b*, 8; cf. 1960*a*.

12. R. M. Grant 1977, 11. Grant's judgment is not far from the conclusion reached by the Marxist church historian Heinz Kreissig 1967, 99, "that Christianity spread in the first century of our era not so much among 'proletarians' or solitary handworkers of the smallest scale or yet small peasants, but rather in the urban circles of well-situated artisans, merchants, and members of the liberal professions."

13. Malherbe 1977*a*, 29–59.

14. Theissen 1974*b*, 1974*c*, 1975*c*.

15. Scroggs 1980, 169–71, raises several critical questions about this "new consensus," three of which are particularly relevant to an inquiry into the Pauline groups. First, directed especially, I presume, to Judge: "Is the Acts material as historically trustworthy as the proponents assume?" Second, ". . . should the presence of a

few . . . wealthier members be allowed to change, in effect, the social location of the community as a whole? Is this not an elitist definition?" And third, "Should economic alienation be the only alienation considered?" See the response by Judge 1980*b*, 207–09.

16. Finley 1973, 35–61.

17. Lipset 1968, 296–301.

18. Finley 1973, 49f.

19. MacMullen 1974, 88–91.

20. Consequently I do not entirely understand John Gager's remarks in his review of Robert M. Grant, Malherbe, and Theissen (1979, 180). Gager appropriately chides Grant and Malherbe for not distinguishing social class from social status, but then he identifies class with *ordo* and proceeds to argue that "some persons of relatively high social status, but few of high social class were attracted to Christianity in the first two centuries." If I understand his concluding comment correctly, he then infers that such high-status-but-low-class (*ordo*) persons would perceive themselves as *relatively* deprived. That would depend, I think, on their reference group. I am not likely to feel oppressed nor are the people who matter to me likely to snub me because I shall not ever receive a peerage in the British realm. Similarly, I wonder whether Erastus, proudly displaying his new status as aedile of Corinth on the theater pavement, was secretly seething because he could not be a Roman senator as well—though had he lived a century or two later he might well have felt so. Gager is on the right track, and the concept of relative deprivation, which figures largely in his *Kingdom and Community* (1975), is closely related to status inconsistency. But greater precision is needed. We obtain a more useful picture if we treat *ordo* not as the all-important index of prestige, but only as one of the specific dimensions of status—the most formal one, but not the most pervasive. See Cohen 1975.

21. Barber 1968.

22. Lipset 1968, 310; cf. Malewski 1966.

23. Lipset 1968, 312; Pettigrew 1967; Merton and Rossi 1950.

24. Lenski 1954 stimulated a series of responses and further investigations which has probably still not come to an end. Among the many publications the following seem to an outsider representative: Goffman 1957, Lenski 1956, Anderson and Zelditch 1964, Blalock 1967, E. F. Jackson 1962, Jackson and Burke 1965, H. F. Taylor 1973, Hornung 1977. For a recent attempt at quantitative measurement of correlations between status inconsistency and religious commitment, and for some important methodological cautions, see Sasaki 1979.

25. MacMullen 1974, app. B, 138–41; see also ch. 4.

26. The problem would be simpler if, as many commentators have suggested, Romans 16 had not been originally part of the letter. Against that hypothesis, however, see the works cited above, chapter 1, n. 41.

27. If this Sosthenes, joint author of 1 Corinthians, were the ἀρχισυνάγωγος of Corinth (Acts 18:17, apparently successor to Crispus, vs. 8, who had earlier converted to Christianity), we could say something about his wealth, ethnic group, and standing in the Jewish community. However, the name is too common to justify this identification without other evidence.

28. Also the most important figure in the Pastorals. If the information in 2 Tim. 1:5 comes from good tradition, we have the additional clue that not only his father was Greek, but also two generations on his mother's, Jewish, side had had Greek names.

29. With Jason and Sosipater, in Corinth, and Andronicus, Junia(s), and Herodion, in Rome, he is called Paul's συγγενής, which may mean only "fellow Jew" or more narrowly "relative." E. A. Judge recently revived a suggestion by Mommsen that it meant rather "fellow Tarsian" or "Cilician" (lecture at Yale University, 22 October 1980). There is no good reason to identify him with either Lucius of Cyrene (Acts 13:1) or with the person known by the short form of the same name, Lukas (Philem. 24; Col. 4:14; 2 Tim. 4:11).

30. Bowersock 1965, 71. The use of a place name as a cognomen probably indicates servile origins, although that depends on circumstances under which the nickname was given. After all, L. Mummius acquired the honorific "Achaicus" after his destruction of Corinth (Velleius Paterculus 1.13.2; Pliny *Hist. nat.* 35.4.8, §24).

31. Theissen 1974c, 253f., points out that he could be a slave or, on the contrary, could hold a position in the provincial bureaucracy.

32. Ibid., 252–57.

33. Lietzmann 1933, 125f.

34. That is the most likely meaning of συναιχμάλωτος; cf. Philemon 23 (Epaphras) and Col. 4:10 (Aristarchus).

35. Eck 1971, 392. Eck refutes the identification by E. Koestermann of Junia with Junia Lepida, daughter of M. Silanus, consul in A.D. 19. "Julia" is also attested in a few mss., including p46.

36. That a woman should be called, along with her husband, "prominent among the apostles" has seemed unthinkable to most modern commentators, but to Chrysostom only grounds for high praise: "How great is the *philosophia* of this woman that she is held to be worthy of the name of apostle" (*Hom. 31 Rom.* 2; *PG* 60:669f., quoted by Clark 1979, 20). Clark points out elsewhere (16f.) that Chrysostom often uses φιλοσοφία to refer to the celibate life, and that may be his implication here, too. On Junia see also Brooten 1977; Pagels 1979, 61.

37. The most popular deity among the Italian colonists at Philippi; Collart 1937, 402–09. Acts gives him the shortened name Silas, which could represent the Aramaic form of Saul (so BAGD, s.v., and BDF, §125 [2]), but it may just as well be simply the Greek shortened form of Silvanus, like Epaphras for Epaphroditus, or Lukas for Lucius.

38. Cf. Theissen 1974c, 256.

39. Ibid., 235f.; cf. Judge 1960b, 129f.; Meeks-Wilken 1978, 53f., 56.

40. See Malherbe's criticism of Theissen for too easily granting this status by association (1977a, 73, n. 27).

41. Landvogt 1908. See the convenient summaries in Magie 1950, 2:850f., n. 34; and Theissen 1974c, 238–40.

42. Magie 1950, 2:850; Theissen 1974c, 239.

43. The inscription had been in metal letters; only the cuttings for them in the limestone survive. It extended over two paving blocks. A fragment of the left one was found *in situ* in 1929 and matched with another piece found elsewhere the year before. Not until 1947 did part of the right block turn up (Kent 1966, 99f.).

44. [praenomen nomen] ERASTUS PRO AEDILIT[AT]E/(vac) S(ua) P(ecunia) STRAVIT (Kent 1966, no. 232 and plate 21).

45. Ibid., 100.

46. Theissen 1974c, 243.

47. Ibid., 243–45; on municipal (and colonial) *cursus honorum*, see also Gagé 1964, 160.

48. See page 48.

49. Kent 1966, 100.

50. Leon 1960, 93–121. It is not apparent why the author of Acts consistently uses the diminutive Priscilla, whereas Paul never does; we encountered the same phenomenon with Silas/Silvanus.

51. Ollrog 1979 attributes "einen gehobenen Sozialstatus" to Aquila because of his being "Handwerker und damit Geschäftsmann" (26 and n. 105), but that betrays a misconception of ancient society.

52. Judge 1960*b*, 129, reinforced by analogous examples described by Flory 1975, 8f., 59–79, 81–85.

53. Theissen 1974*c*, 245–49.

54. It may be, though, that the absence of the partitive ἐκ (contrast οἱ ἐκ τῶν Ἀριστοβούλου, οἱ ἐκ τῶν Ναρκίσσου οἱ ὄντες ἐν Κυρίῳ, Rom. 16:10f.) implies that the whole of Chloe's household is Christian. In that case Chloe herself would most likely be Christian and thus among the οὐ πολλοὶ . . . δυνατοί of the Corinthian church.

55. This would be borne out if, as Stuhlmacher 1975, 53f., suggests, Col. 4:9 reflects a later, local tradition in Colossae about Onesimus's activity in church service. That hypothesis would require, however, that Colossians be not only pseudonymous but also written considerably later than Philemon. The latter is hard to demonstrate.

56. "Others" is added in several mss., including the Chester Beatty papyrus p46.

57. Cf. Georgi 1964*a*, 31–38.

58. E.g., Leenhardt 1948, 11: "elle servit la communauté en jouant en quelque sort un rôle de tutrice ou d'ange gardien, en mettant à sa disposition ses ressources et son cour. . . ."

59. E.g., Swidler 1979, 310, who observes correctly that "the word . . . always means ruler, leader, *or protector* in all Greek literature" (my emphasis), but insists that it must mean "ruler" here.

60. Magie 1950, 1:59 and 2:842f., n. 28, where a number of examples are given. At Cos προστάται enrolled new citizens, received testimony, estimated the value of a sacrificial bull, provided for expenses of θεωροί sent to Delphi, and so on. At Cos, Cnidus, and elsewhere in Caria and adjacent islands they issue various γνῶμαι. At Iasus, however, where there were both πρυτάνεις and προστάται, the functions of the latter are unclear. Magie guesses they may have been "presidents of the city tribes." See also Schaefer 1962.

61. Poland 1909, 363f.

62. Judge 1960*b*, 128f.; cf. Poland 1909, 364. Josephus describes Herod as σωτὴρ καὶ προστάτης after his success in breaking two Parthian ambuscades (*Ant.* 14.444). On the use of the Latin *patronus* in similar contexts in Greek inscriptions, see Bowersock 1965, 12f. According to Heinrici 1890, 414, Strigel and Bengel already understood Phoebe as patroness of the Cenchreae congregation; so also Lietzmann 1914, 101–07.

63. A point well made by Ollrog 1979, 10–13.

64. Hock 1978.

65. See pages 117f.

66. Consequently I shall not discuss the much-debated question of the history and precise duties of the asiarchs, who appear often in coins and inscriptions, as well as in Strabo 14.1.42; *Digesta* 27.1.6.14; Mart. Polyc. 12:2. See Taylor 1932; Magie 1950, 1:449f.; 2:1298–1301, 1526; Gealy 1962.

67. For the miracle, compare not only Acts 12:6–11, but also Artapanus *apud*

Eusebius *Praep. ev.* 9.27.23–25 = Clement Alex. *Strom.* 1.154.2 (*FGH* 3C.2:684f.);
Euripides *Bacchae* 443–48; Philostratus *V.Ap.* 7.38; 8.5.

68. As for the attempt to connect Paul with Sergius Paulus as a freedman of the
same gens (Kehnscherper 1964), Eck's comment is not unfair: "Kehnscherper . . . hat
aus dem Zusammentreffen des Apostels Paulus mit dem Prokonsul ohne die allge-
meinsten Kenntnisse der römischen Verwaltung, Namengebung und Sozialgeschichte
einen ganzen historischen Roman gesponnen. ." (1971, 391, n. 55). Judge and
Thomas, however, take it seriously (1966, 84).

69. Haenchen 1959, 527, n. 1, suggests that the author may be using a report
about the later Athenian congregation (about which we have very little information),
for as it stands the scene is contradicted by 1 Cor. 16:16. The first convert in Achaia
was not an Athenian but Stephanas's household in Corinth. Haenchen also suspects
that "Areopagite" may be the author's invention, to connect Dionysus with the scene
just described.

70. A number of emendations have been proposed, some already by ancient
copyists, of the list in Acts 20:4, which appears to be a partial list of delegates from
various churches who went with Paul to deliver the collection to Jerusalem. Lake and
Cadbury 1933, 4:254, think the adjective Δερβαῖος originally went with the following name, Timothy, allowing them to identify this Gaius with the Macedonian mentioned with Aristarchus in 19:29. But that would give three delegates from Macedonia. Ollrog 1979, 52–58, removes Timothy as a Lucan addition in order to
reconstruct a pattern in the remaining list, 1/2//1/2, but there hardly seems sufficient
reason to assume such a formal construction. Haenchen 1959, 581, leaves the list as
p74 ℵ B et al. have it, with all except Sopater arranged in pairs.

71. See chapter 1.

72. Haenchen 1959 *ad loc.*; Judge 1960*b*, 128.

73. It is often asserted, usually citing Kuhn and Stegemann 1962, cols. 1266f.,
that "God-fearers" tended to be of higher status than were full converts to Judaism.
The evidence is not very strong, however, and even if the generalization were valid, it
could not be imposed on an individual instance apart from other information.

74. Malherbe 1977*b*, 224 and n. 15.

75. Some mss. have Titus instead of Titius; a few have only Justus. Goodspeed
1950, harmonizing Acts 18:7 with Rom. 16:23, wanted to identify him with Gaius,
thus giving him the full Roman *tria nomina*, C. Titius Justus. "Justus" was properly
an epithet, perhaps given him by the Jews (see the remarks by Lightfoot 1879, 238, on
Jesus Justus), but such an epithet could become a cognomen.

76. For the options, see Kümmel 1973, 324–32.

77. See chapter 1, Mobility. There is also a bare possibility that Paul hints in
Phil. 1:13 of a penetration of the Christian faith into the military establishment, for if
his imprisonment is in Rome, then ἐν ὅλῳ τῷ πραιτωρίῳ must refer to the imperial
guards, the praetorians (see Lightfoot 1913, 99–103). If it is in Ephesus or another
provincial city, the reference may be either to a group of the guards stationed there or
to the governor's palace or court (Dibelius 1937, 64f.). Paul makes no claim that any
of these people or of "all the rest" have become Christians, for "the brothers in the
Lord" are mentioned separately (vs. 14; cf. Dibelius, ibid.). He clearly does believe,
however, that the witness of his imprisonment "in Christ" (vs. 13) has produced a
favorable impression that creates the possibility of conversions among the personnel
of the praetorium.

78. For an exhaustive discussion of the question and of the attitudes toward

slavery in early Christianity, see Gülzow 1969. Bartchy 1973 has much useful information. Among the rather extensive literature on this subject, two others may be singled out: Ste. Croix 1975 and Gayer 1976.

79. Weidinger 1928; Schroeder 1959; Crouch 1973; Balch 1981; Lührmann 1980.

80. I doubt that the stress on obligations of the slaves justifies an inference that Christian eschatological hopes had inspired among them an expectation of improvement of their status, though Bassler 1979, 269–71, has recently argued for that possibility with some acuteness. She points out that the appeal to the impartiality of God—which in the *Haustafel* of Ephesians is, as we would expect, addressed to the masters—is in Col. 3:25 addressed to the slaves. The case of Onesimus, however, can hardly be taken as "historical evidence of actual unrest among the slaves at Colossae." He may be simply one slave who got fed up.

81. See especially Dahl 1951.

82. Best 1972, 176.

83. Van Unnik 1964, 227f.; Dibelius 1937, 23. See the important discussion in Hock 1980, 42–47, who shows that these rules are very similar to those found in Greco-Roman moralists, especially Dio Chrysostom.

84. In quite a different way, Paul's work is made a paradigm in 1 Cor. 9; it is interesting that the principal theme of that passage, the renunciation of ἐξουσία to provide a model for the community, is summed up in 2 Thess. 3:9.

85. μετὰ ἡσυχίας; cf. ἡσυχάζειν 1 Thess. 4:11.

86. BAGD, s.v. εὐοδόω.

87. Conzelmann 1969 *ad loc.*

88. It will not do to interpolate the καθώς of Acts 11:29, however, as do *NEB*, "*in proportion* to his gains," and Orr and Walther 1976, 356, "*commensurate with* the financial gain of the previous week" (my emphasis). These introduce a concept of proportional giving not in the text and anachronistically assume some kind of capitalistic enterprise.

89. These motifs are more reminiscent of 1 Corinthians than of the rest of 2 Corinthians. E.g., compare 2 Cor. 8:7—ὥσπερ ἐν παντὶ περισσεύετε, πίστει καὶ λόγῳ καὶ γνώσει καὶ πάσῃ σπουδῇ καὶ τῇ ἐξ ἡμῶν ἐν ὑμῖν ἀγάπῃ—with 1 Cor. 1:5—ὅτι ἐν παντὶ ἐπλουτίσθητε ἐν αὐτῷ, ἐν παντὶ λόγῳ καὶ πάσῃ γνώσει—and 7—ὥστε ὑμᾶς μὴ ὑστερεῖσθαι ἐν μηδενὶ χαρίσματι. And the teleological pattern statement of 2 Cor. 8:9 recalls the ironic ἤδη ἐπλουτήσατε of 1 Cor. 4:8. On the size of the collection, see Georgi 1965, 88, who points out that the cost of travel for the large delegation bearing the gift would be sensible only if the gift were substantial.

90. See Stählin 1938, especially 354f.

91. Malherbe 1977b, 230, n. 11.

92. For a thorough study of partnership language in the Pauline letters, see Sampley 1980 and 1977. Malherbe points out (in a private communication) that commercial language is frequently used in the topos of friendship, and so it is in Paul.

93. I find myself less persuaded than I once was by the arguments that canonical Philippians is a composite of two or more letter fragments.

94. *De amore divit.* 526A.

95. See Theissen 1975b, especially 40f.

96. E.g., 1 Cor. 9:27; 2 Cor. 10:18; 13:5–7; but not always explicitly eschatological: 2 Cor. 2:9.

97. The καί here is epexegetic; that is, the second clause explicates the first.

98. Theissen 1974*b*.

99. Ibid., 291–92.

100. *Ep.* 2.6, trans. Radice 1969, 63f. From Martial Theissen cites 3.60; 1.20; 4.85; 6.11; 10.49; from Juvenal, *Sat. 5.* On Juvenal's satire, see also Sebesta 1976 and Reekmans 1971.

101. Theissen 1975*c*.

102. Not called that explicitly here, but cf. Rom. 15:1, where Paul draws a general rule from the Corinthian experience.

103. Note Rom. 15:1, "we the strong."

104. See also Theissen 1974*c*.

105. Schütz 1977, now also 1982.

106. Schütz 1977, 7.

107. In brief, he leaves unquestioned the right of women, led by the Spirit, to exercise the same leadership roles in the assembly as men, but insists only that the conventional symbols of sexual difference, in clothing and hair styles, be retained. I discussed this at some length in Meeks 1974. Recent attempts to excise these verses as an interpolation are not persuasive (Walker 1975; Murphy-O'Connor 1976).

108. Because this interrupts the discussion of glossolalia and prophecy, and because it would make nonsense not only of the directives about female prophets and leaders of prayer in 11:2–16 but also of the positive role accorded to single women in chapter 7, a number of scholars have suggested that these verses were added to the letter after Paul's time, by someone of the same views that find even more radical expression in 1 Tim. 2:9–15. That is an attractive solution, although the interpolation would have had to occur before wide circulation of the Pauline letters, for there is no direct manuscript evidence. Some mss. do have v,ss. 34f. in a different place, after vs. 40, but that more likely indicates that some ancient copyist sensed the break in topic than that he had a ms. in which they were absent. Verse 36 would not follow smoothly on vs. 33.

109. On these *Haustafeln* see the literature cited in n. 79 above and further discussion in chapter 3, Models from the Environment.

110. Text in Lipsius-Bonnet 1891, 1:235–72; translated in Hennecke 1959–64, 2:353–64.

111. MacDonald 1979 has argued ingeniously that the Pastoral Epistles were a direct response to the Acts of Paul and Thecla, and to the more widespread movement in Asia Minor which that document represented.

112. The most notable attempt to do so is Georgi 1964*a*. For a sober criticism of the method, see Hickling 1975. See also Barrett 1971 and Holladay 1977, 34–40 and passim.

113. On this ploy, familiar in such speakers as Dio of Prusa, see Judge 1968.

114. Dungan 1971, 3–80, and, more carefully and ingeniously, Theissen 1975*a* have argued that what is at stake is the conflict between two normative styles of missionary support, with the opponents of Paul representing the intrusion into the urban areas of the mendicant, itinerant apostolate described in some of the early sayings of Jesus. The latter was originally at home in Palestinian village culture. I find neither quite convincing. Theissen's suggestion that both styles might have analogies in the contemporary idealized portraits of Cynic philosophers points rather to a different kind of analysis, which has been developed by Hock 1980.

115. Cf. Lee 1971, 132.

CHAPTER 3

1. Homans 1968, 258; cf. Homans 1974, 4 and passim. For an example of too hasty an application of modern small-group theory to our sources, see Schreiber 1977.

2. 1 Cor. 16:19, Aquila and Prisca (in Ephesus); Rom. 16:5, Prisca and Aquila (in Rome); Philem. 2, Philemon (in Colossae); Col. 4:15, Nympha (in Laodicea).

3. Acts 16:15 (Lydia); 16:31–34 (Philippian jailer); 18:8 (Crispus, the archisynagogos of Corinth). Cf. 10:2; 11:14; John 4:53. Stauffer 1949 saw in these passages an Old Testament formula; effectively refuted by Weigandt 1963. Delling 1965 brings useful examples from extrabiblical Greek usage.

4. See chapter 1, Connections. My approach in the following pages may usefully be compared with Banks 1980, which I first saw after finishing this chapter. His aim, however, is somewhat different.

5. See further in this chapter, A Worldwide People.

6. Gülzow 1974, 198.

7. Afanassieff 1974 argues against the existence of separate household groups, insisting that every householder mentioned in connection with a κατ᾽ οἶκον ἐκκλησία was, like Gaius, a "host" of "the whole church" in a given city. His argument is tendentious, however, based too much on an a priori conviction that a single Eucharistic assembly in each city was the theologically necessary "principle of unity" until the monarchical episcopate could develop. Gaius's role was unusual enough for Paul to single it out when mentioning him to the Roman Christians; it may have been unique. The phrase κατ᾽ οἶκον ἐκκλησία, on the other hand, is not used in connection with Gaius. The difficulties with Afanassieff's thesis become acute in the case of Rome, where he is able to avoid the multiplicity of meetings implied by Romans 16 only by banishing Aquila and Prisca, without any evidence, to the suburbs.

8. In time this local stability would manifest itself in the acquisition of all or part of the house for the exclusive use of the Christian group, which, as other cultic groups had done before, would undertake certain modifications for the specific functions of its worship.

9. Schütz 1977, 5. Cf. Malherbe 1977b, on the problems of 3 John; and Corwin 1960, 49, 76f., on the later situation in Antioch.

10. So Acts reports that Jason had to post a bond for the good behavior of Paul and his associates (17:9). See Malherbe 1977b, 230, n. 15.

11. See above, page 64, and the literature cited in chapter 2, n. 79.

12. 1 Tim. 2:1–6:2; Titus 2:1–10; 1 Pet. 5:1–5; Polycarp 4:2–6:1.

13. Brief descriptions of household religion in Greece and Rome may be found in Nilsson 1954; 1961, 187–89, 195, 216f.; Boehm 1924, especially cols. 814–18; Rose 1957 (the last-named dealing mostly with earlier times).

14. Pliny Ep. 10.96—but note that the Christians of Bithynia had modified some of their practices, particularly the communal meals, after the ban against hetaeriae was promulgated. Celsus apud Origen C. Cels. 1.1; cf. Tertullian Apol. 38.1–3. See Wilken 1970, 1971; Frend 1965, 165–68, 191, 243f.

15. Hatch 1892, 26–55; Heinrici 1876 and 1890, 409–17.

16. Besides the remarks of Wilken, cited in n. 14 above, see Judge 1960a, 40–48, and Malherbe 1977a, 87–91, who emphasizes especially the importance of trades and crafts in early Christianity and the possible connections with craft organizations. See also Reicke 1951a, 320–38; de Robertis 1973, 1:338f.; 2:64–89.

17. That is apparently the case with the "collegium quod est in domu Sergiae Paullinae" (*CIL* 6.9148), on which see above, chapter 1, no. 142. The Dionysus association founded by Pompeia Agrippinilla, discussed above, chapter 1, n. 143, is one of the most famous examples. In a Ph.D. dissertation in progress at Yale University, L. Michael White will argue that the cultic association of Agdistis et al. in Philadelphia was another instance of a household-based group.

18. I owe this insight to William Countryman, in a National Endowment for the Humanities seminar for college teachers at Yale University, 1977.

19. Nock 1933*a*, 164–86; see further in this chapter, Philosophic or Rhetorical School.

20. Ironically, the mixing of free males, women, foreigners, slaves, and freedmen was one of the similarities between associations and the early churches cited by Hatch 1892, 31. He based this largely on Foucart 1873, but later investigators have concluded that Foucart exaggerated the mixing of social strata and especially the positions of slaves and women in the collegia. See especially Poland 1909, 277–329, and Bömer 1957–63, 1:17–29, 134–36, 510–14; 2:185 and passim; 3:135–37, 145–53, 173–95, 358; 4:138–205, 238–41.

21. Eusebius, *HE* 10.8; Tertullian *Apol.* 38–39; on the latter, see Wilken 1971, 283f.

22. Poland 1909, ch. 1, has compiled a very extensive list of the Greek terms; for Latin ones, see de Robertis 1973, 1:10–21; and Waltzing 1895–1900, 4:236–42.

23. The assumption frequently made, that he avoids συναγωγή in favor of ἐκκλησία because of Jewish theological connotations of the former, is refuted by K. Berger 1976.

24. Ἐκκλησία was sometimes used of business meetings of clubs, however. Such meetings are rarely mentioned in inscriptions, so this use may have been more common than we know. Poland 1909, 332, cites two, possibly three examples.

25. Linton 1959; K. Berger 1976, 169–83; Schmidt 1938.

26. Poland 1909, 363–66.

27. See above, page 58.

28. Above, chapter 2, n. 62.

29. For examples of διάκονος in inscriptions, see Poland 1909, 391–93.

30. Lietzmann 1914, 96–101.

31. See chapter 1.

32. See Gülzow 1974, 198.

33. Cf. the remarks by Bickerman 1949, 70–73, and the interesting material collected by Davies 1974, 3–158.

34. Linton 1959 and K. Berger 1976. None of the descriptions of the sabbath meetings of the Jews (or the Therapeutae) to hear the scriptures read, cited from Philo and Josephus by Berger (175) in fact uses the term ἐκκλησία.

35. See Hengel 1966, 160–64.

36. *Vit. cont.* 66–90.

37. See chapter 5.

38. 1 Cor. 6:1–11, on which see further in chapter 4. On Jewish judicial proceedings, see, e.g., Josephus *Ant.* 14.235.

39. Hengel 1971*b*, 166f., argues further that the synagogue may have had a more fluid, less differentiated structure at the earlier period than after the disasters of the first- and second-century revolts diminished the importance of the Palestinian center.

40. See Meeks 1974, 174–79, 197–204; despite doubts raised by Cameron 1980.

41. Modern controversy over these ancient debates has flourished since the proposals in the nineteenth century by Ferdinand Christian Baur and shows no sign of abating. The ghost of Baur has been raised again recently by Betz 1973, 1979; Lüdemann 1979; and others. I find their assumption of a single, unified, Jewish Christian, anti-Pauline movement in the first century an unnecessary inference from the sources, and not the most economical way of accounting for what little evidence we have. Moreover, German scholarship's picture of the controversies has been, I believe, too exclusively ideological. The social implications of continuing or abandoning Jewish ritual practices must have been at least as important, both for the various opponents of Paul and for Paul himself, as theological and christological beliefs. For Paul, of course, the pragmatic factors were inseparable from theology and christology. See Dahl 1977, 95–120.

42. Wilken 1971.

43. Conzelmann 1965, 233. Cf. idem 1966, 307f.

44. Conzelmann 1965, 233, n. 7. However, Malherbe 1977a, 89, argues that the σχολή may just as well have been a guild hall, the meeting place of a craft association. For *schola* as a meeting place of a collegium, see Jones 1955, 172; Poland 1909, 462; D. E. Smith 1980, 128f. Cf. Heinrici 1890, 413, n.**.

45. Pearson 1975, 51, has refuted much of the exegetical evidence Conzelmann used to support his thesis, without however entirely rejecting the notion of school activity in Ephesus. A number of scholars have seen evidence for a school of Paul, in some general sense, in the production of pseudonymous letters in his name, including Conzelmann 1966, 307. John Knox 1942, 14f., thought "the continuation into the second century of distinctively Pauline communities . . . the best explanation both of Marcion himself and of the amazingly quick and widespread response to him." Gamble 1977, 115–26, finds evidence for a Pauline school in the "catholicizing" of Paul's letters, that is, revision of the text to remove particularities, such as the fourteen- and fifteen-chapter versions of Romans. Cf. Dahl 1965.

46. Judge 1960b.

47. Ibid., 126.

48. Ibid., 135.

49. See later in this chapter.

50. E.g., the functions of those who "preside" in Thessalonica include "admonishing" the congregations, 1 Thess. 5:12.

51. This has been effectively demonstrated by Malherbe, who has especially emphasized the importance of the several varieties of the Cynic tradition, and by his students; e.g., Malherbe 1968, 1970, 1976, and a forthcoming article in *ANRW*, pt. 2, vol. 28; Balch 1981; Hock 1978, 1980. The work of Hans Dieter Betz and other active participants in the Corpus Hellenisticum ad Novum Testamentum has also shown manifold connections between the letters of Paul and the philosophical and rhetorical issues and practices of the time: Betz 1972, 1975, 1979. See also Judge 1968, 1972; Wuellner 1979.

52. Marrou 1955, 34.

53. These are "The Pythagorean Life" (Περὶ τοῦ Πυθαγορικοῦ βίου), ed. L. Deubner (1937), conveniently available with German translation in Albrecht 1963 and translated into English in Hadas and Smith 1965, 107–28; "Introduction to Philosophy" (Λόγος προτρεπτικὸς εἰς φιλοσοφίαν), ed. H. Pistelli (1888); and three

works on mathematics, edited by N. Festa (1891), H. Pistelli (1894), and V. de Falco (1922).

54. Available in the Loeb edition by F. C. Conybeare (1960). On the vexed problem of sources for the earlier development of the traditions of and about Pythagoras, see Thesleff 1965; Vogel 1966; Burkert 1961, 1962.

55. Discussions of the organization of the Pythagorean school may be found in von Fritz 1960; Minar 1942; Vogel 1966, 150–59; cf. Burkert 1962, 166–208.

56. De Lacy 1948; cf. Cicero De fin. 1.65: ". . . what companies of friends Epicurus held together in one small house, and what affection and sympathy united them! And this still continues among the Epicureans" (trans. Baldry 1965, 149. Cf. Classen 1968.

57. DeWitt 1954a, 93.

58. Sent. Vat. 78; cf. ibid., 52: "Friendship (φιλία) goes dancing round the world proclaiming to us all to awake to the praises of a happy life" (trans. Bailey 1926, 115). Cf. DeWitt 1954a, 101–05, 178f., 307–10; Festugière 1946, 27–50; Baldry 1965, 147–51. See also Diogenes Laertius 10.120b on φιλία and κοινωνία in Epicureanism, and the oft-quoted judgment of Seneca Ep. 6.6, "It was not instruction but fellowship (contubernium) that made great men out of Metrodorus, Hermarchus, and Polyaenus" (trans. DeWitt 1954a, 103). See further DeWitt 1936a.

59. The internal organization of the schools in Roman times is revealed to some extent by the papyrus roll of Philodemus's περὶ παρρησίας, discovered early this century in his Herculaneum villa. I follow DeWitt's analysis (1936b).

60. Apud Eusebius Praep. Ev. 14.5. On the remarkable continuity and conservatism of the Epicureans, see also Malherbe's forthcoming article on "self-definition."

61. Usener 1887, 135f.: πρὸς τοὺς ἐν Αἰγύπτῳ φίλους, πρὸς τοὺς ἐν Ἀσίᾳ φίλους, πρὸς τοὺς ἐν Λαμψάκῳ φίλους. None is extant.

62. The rather undisciplined proposals put forward by DeWitt 1954b may have done more to deter than to encourage serious scholarship in this area, despite the valuable observations scattered through the book. Cf. Malherbe 1977a, 25–28.

63. Olsen 1968, 65–70.

64. Quoted by Schachter 1968, 542, from "Informal Social Communication," Psychological Review 57 (1950):274.

65. B. R. Wilson 1973, especially p. 21.

66. Webber 1971; Olson 1976.

67. See sec. 3 of Malherbe's forthcoming article in ANRW, pt. 2, vol. 28.

68. Malherbe 1970 has shown the similarity of this language, and the whole context in the first part of chapter 2, with that used in the Cynic tradition to distinguish "harsh Cynics" from "mild Cynics."

69. Although the plural continues and Silvanus as joint author may not be entirely forgotten, it is primarily Paul who is speaking here, as 3:1f., 6 indicate.

70. See von Soden 1933.

71. Cf. Malherbe 1970. Addressing readers as "son" or "children" is common in Jewish and other oriental wisdom literature and also in Roman introductory moral or philosophic treatises, but probably neither has directly influenced Paul's style. On the former, see Pearson 1975, 60, n. 7; on the latter, Layton 1979, 38.

72. Since two of the three instances refer to Timothy, and since Phil. 2:20–22 speaks of a uniquely close relation between him and Paul, it is not surprising that the pseudonymous Pastorals pick up the term (1 Tim. 1:2, 18; 2 Tim. 1:2; 2:1) and also use it for Titus (1:4).

73. The term *brother* was rare in clubs. Waltzing 1895–1900, 1:329f., n. 3, cites only one example from a professional association. From religious groups he has a few more examples. For the influence of the Roman concept of brotherhood on Greek usage, see Poland 1909, 54f., 501. Nock 1924b calls attention to the worshipers of Juppiter Dolichenus, who call their fellows *fratres carissimi* (*ILS* 4316; cf. 4296), and to the worshipers of θεὸς ὕψιστος in the Bosporus region, who are referred to as "adoptive brothers" (εἰσποιητοὶ ἀδελφοί). (See later in this chapter.) Nock probably goes too far, however, when he says, "The cult association is primarily a family" (105). Several of the instances he cites of the use of "father" or "mother" by associations are honorifics for patrons and do not imply a family structure. One of the oldest and best known of Roman cultic associations was the priestly college, the *Fratres Arvales*. This quite formal usage should warn us against assuming an intimate association everywhere that such terms appear.

74. Hatch 1892, 44; von Soden 1933, 145.

75. E.g., Exod. 2:11; Lev. 19:17; and especially Deuteronomy. Note especially Deut. 3:18 and 24:7, where ἀδελφοί ὑμῶν (αὐτοῦ) is in apposition with υἱοὶ Ἰσραήλ. 2 Maccabees is a letter from οἱ ἀδελφοὶ οἱ ἐν Ἱεροσολύμοις Ἰουδαῖοι to τοῖς ἀδελφοῖς τοῖς κατ' Αἴγυπτον Ἰουδαίοις.

76. 1QS 6:10,22; 1QSa 1:18; CDC 6:20; 7:1; 20:18; in 1QM 13:1 and 15:4 *'aḥîm* refers to a smaller circle, the priestly leaders of the sect. Cf. CDC 8:6 and 19:18, where the apostate is blamed for acting hatefully "each to his brother."

77. (ε)ἰσποιητοὶ ἀδελφοί: *CIRB* 1281, 1283, 1285, 1286. Discussed briefly by Nock (see n. 73 above) and by Hengel 1971b, 174f. and n. 76. Poland, on the other hand, argued that the associations represented in these inscriptions were probably only temporary, for particular festivals (1909, 72f.). Minns 1913, 620–25, calls attention to *CIRB* 104, in which a deceased member is called the ἴδιος ἀδελφός of the living members. One of the officers is called πατήρ (*CIRB* 105) or πατὴρ συνόδου (ibid.); another, συναγωγός (104).

78. See further, chapter 5.

79. See Meeks 1974, especially pp. 180–89.

80. V. Turner 1969 and 1964.

81. Turner distinguishes "*existential* or *spontaneous* communitas," "*normative* communitas," and "*ideological* communitas" (1969, 132, Turner's emphasis). For the second, he cites particularly "millenarian groups" (111f.), a phenomenon with which early Christianity has often been compared; see, e.g., Gager 1975, 19–65.

82. Meeks 1974, 199–203.

83. The literature on this usage is vast. Among the most sensible treatments remains Best 1955, and J. A. T. Robinson 1952 has also stood up well. Also important are Barrett 1962 and Schweizer 1961a and 1961b.

84. A good many examples are collected by Conzelmann 1969, 211. For Hellenistic Jewish usage, see Philo *Spec. leg.* 3.131.

85. E.g., Tannehill 1967.

86. Cf. Schweizer 1964, 1067. It is hardly fruitful to try to sort out verses in which Paul is using the term in its "proper" (christological) sense from those in the same passage where he is speaking figuratively, as Conzelmann does 1969, 212f.

87. Despite the somewhat abrupt transitions at 12:31 and 14:1, the poem was probably in the original letter. Its relation to the surrounding discussion is much like that of chapter 9 to 8 and 10. Even if it had been added by some editor of the Pauline school, however, that would not much affect my point.

88. Compare the summary use of the figure in Rom. 12:3–8, which is probably suggested by the Corinthian experience, as is much else in the paraenetic section of Rom. 12:1–15:13. Here it reinforces the admonition that no one "think more highly of himself than he ought to think" (RSV).

89. The macrocosmic-reconciliation theme is also presupposed in Ephesians, but the author has transformed it somewhat more thoroughly than has the author of Colossians. See however Eph. 1:3–14 and 2:7–11, 14–16.

90. See Meeks 1977 for more detail.

91. See, e.g., Deutsch 1968 and the literature he cites. He summarizes: ". . . one of the major instrumental functions of interaction [in a small group] is helping to establish 'social reality': the validation of opinions, beliefs, abilities, and emotions in terms of a social consensus" (273). For a theoretical discussion of the emergence of "social reality," see Berger and Luckmann 1966 and, with particular attention to the functions of religious beliefs in the process, P. Berger 1967. The now classic essays by Geertz 1957, 1966 are also pertinent.

92. Hengel 1972.

93. Marcus Aurelius *Medit.* 4.23, who addresses Nature (often equated by late Stoics with Zeus): ἐκ σοῦ πάντα, ἐν σοὶ πάντα, εἰς σὲ πάντα; further examples in Norden 1912, 240–50 and app. 4, 347–54, who calls the form "eine Allmachtsformel."

94. Note, for example, Strabo's description of Moses' doctrine in *Geog.* 16.2.35: "According to him, God is the one thing alone that encompasses us all and encompasses land and sea—the thing which we call heaven, or universe, or the nature of all that exists. What man, then, if he has sense, could be bold enough to fabricate an image of God representing any creature amongst us?" (trans. H. L. Jones in the Loeb ed.; also reproduced by Stern 1974, no. 115, who also collects other examples).

95. See Dahl 1977, 179–91.

96. Cf. ibid., 95–120; Bassler 1979.

97. Note especially 2:11–22.

98. RSV. See Dahl 1954, 30–33.

99. Kramer 1963, 19–64, calls this the "pistis [faith] formula."

100. See the discussion of "sedimentation and tradition" in Berger and Luckmann 1966, 67–79.

101. LSJ, s.v. On the transformation of the Jewish term in Christian usage, see Dahl 1974, especially the title essay (10–36) and "The Messiahship of Jesus in Paul" (37–47).

102. See Bateson 1974.

103. Schubert 1939*a*, 1939*b*. Further literature in Dahl 1976*b*, Doty 1973.

104. Nock 1933*b*; Malherbe 1977*a*, 35–41.

105. For example, J. M. Robinson 1964; Dahl 1951, 262–64.

106. The term ἰδιώτης 1 Cor. 14:23f. is probably equivalent.

107. 1 Cor. 1:20–28; 2:12; 3:19; 5:10; 6:2; 7:31, 33f.; 11:32; Gal. 4:3; 6:14; Eph. 2:2; Col. 2:8, 20. For neutral or even positive use, see, e.g., Rom. 11:12, 15; 2 Cor. 5:19.

108. 1 Cor. 6:6; 7:12–15; 10:27; 14:22–24; 2 Cor. 4:4; 6:14.

109. See chapter 1, Urban Judaism and Pauline Christianity.

110. Gal. 4:8f.; cf. 3:23ff.; Eph. 2:11–22; Rom. 6:17–22; 7:5f.; 11:30; Col. 1:21f.; 1 Pet. 2:10; cf. Gal. 4:3–5; Col. 2:13f.; Eph. 2:1–10; 1 Pet. 1:14f. See Dahl 1954, 33f.

111. Cf. 1 Thess. 4:5; 2 Thess. 1:8. The phrase "those who do not know God" is probably derived from Ps. 78:6 LXX; cf. Jer. 10:25; Isa. 55:5. See Aus 1971, 85–88.

112. Gal. 1:4 belongs to another well-represented type of early Christian preaching, "the teleological pattern" (Dahl 1954, 35f.). The purpose of Christ's self-sacrifice is here said to be "to rescue us from the present, evil age." In the other formulas of this type, such sharp dualism does not appear directly, but those that define the purpose of the salvific action as "purification" or "sanctification" of the believers imply a view of the macrosociety as impure and profane (e.g., Eph. 5:25b–26). But the aim of salvation can also be formulated in more positive terms, probably shaped by the traditional propaganda of the Hellenistic synagogue: the formation of a "new people" or similar expressions, as in Titus 2:14; cf. Barn. 5:7 and Ignatius Smyr. 1:2, which may echo distinctively Pauline tradition, as in NT Eph. 2:12–22.

113. 1 Thess. 5:4–11; Eph. 5:7–14; 2 Cor. 6:14–7:1. The last is commonly regarded as an interpolation. If it is, the original use of the passage, largely consisting of a catena of scriptural quotations, may have been quite different, perhaps to warn against marriage outside the sect. For several quite different assessments of the text see Fitzmyer 1961; Dahl 1977, 62–69; Betz 1973; Rensberger 1978.

114. Cf. Coser 1956, 33–38.

115. Compare the warnings to Jewish proselytes, which probably date from the time of Hadrian, bYeb 47a. Cf. Hill 1976, who takes up and modifies a suggestion by E. Selwyn, that there was a "persecution torah" included in early baptismal instruction.

116. 1 Cor. 4:11–13; 2 Cor. 4:8–12; 6:4–10; 11:23–29. A study of this and related patterns is under way in a Yale dissertation by John Fitzgerald.

117. Pearson 1971 has argued that the whole passage 2:13–16 is a later interpolation, referring to the destruction of the Temple in A.D. 70. Despite his careful argument, I am not convinced of this attractive solution to an old problem. Rather, I am inclined to see in verses 15f. a reinterpretation of Paul's original reference to "the Judeans," understood by the interpolator as the Jews in general. In either case, we would have evidence for the development within the Pauline circle of anti-Jewish sentiment as a reinforcement of group boundaries—a development that is much more obvious in the community that produced the Fourth Gospel.

118. See Aus 1971. We also see in 1 Thess. 4:13–18 how the experience of natural death of members of the group can be turned into an occasion for extending the beliefs in parousia and resurrection, to strengthen the sense of cohesion within the group. Their solidarity is to be eternal: "Thus we shall always be with the Lord" (vs. 17). Note the juxtaposition in 5:1–11 of apocalyptic, dualistic terminology for the same purpose.

119. Douglas 1973, 98.

120. Neusner 1971, 1973a, 1977.

121. *Mos.* 1.278, trans. F. H. Colson in the Loeb edition. See chapter 1, Urban Judaism and Pauline Christianity, and cf. Aristeas 139.

122. The integrity of the argument in these three chapters was conclusively demonstrated by von Soden 1931.

123. See, e.g., Conzelmann 1969 *ad loc.*

124. Theissen 1975c.

125. A number of commentators have recognized traditional elements, e.g., Le Déaut 1965, 320f.; Borgen 1965, 21f., 91f.; Gärtner 1959, 15–18; Ellis 1957. The

structure of the homily, however, has not been satisfactorily explained. I treat this in a forthcoming article in the *Journal for the Study of the New Testament*.

126. See, e.g., the passages cited by Ginzberg 1909–38, 6:51, n. 163.

127. See the "apostolic decree," Acts 15:20, 29; 21:25; further 1 John 5:21; also the rules and the catalogs of vices quoted in the Pauline corpus: Gal. 5:20; 1 Cor. 5:10f.; 6:9; Col. 3:5; Eph. 5:5.

128. Theissen 1975c, 280.

129. This point is well made by Walter 1979, especially pp. 425–36.

130. He shifts from metaphorical to direct speech: instead of "vessel" (σκεῦος), "husband" and "wife," and he makes the rule, utterly androcentric in the form quoted in 1 Thessalonians, reciprocal: husband/wife, wife/husband. This observation, incidentally, confirms the majority opinion about the meaning of σκεῦος in 1 Thess. 4:4. It is the same as in 1 Pet. 3:7 and as its equivalent in later rabbinic texts, such as bPes 112a: "Akiba says: 'The pot in which your fellow did his cooking is not for you to cook in.'"

131. Carrington 1940 argues that the tradition is derived from Lev. 18 and calls it "a Christian Holiness code."

132. 1 Cor. 6:18; Acts 15:20, 29; 21:25; cf. Gal. 5:19; Eph. 5:3; Col. 3:5; 1 Cor. 10:8; 5:9; 6:9; Eph. 5:5.

133. 1 Cor. 6:9; Rom. 1:26f. On the general question see Pope 1976. Illicit sex and idolatry are juxtaposed in the vice catalogs 1 Cor. 6:9 and Gal. 5:19f. and causally connected in Rom. 1:23–27.

134. A rigorous rejection of marriage is a central part of the encratite teaching attributed to Paul in the Acts of Paul and Thecla, a second-century work. For Mac-Donald's interesting proposal about these Acts and the Pastorals, see above, chapter 2, n. 111.

135. In Greek romances of the Roman period, the plot customarily depends upon the chaste devotion of a couple to each other, preserved despite the most bizarre threats. In the *Ephesiaca* of Xenophon of Ephesus, for example, Habrocomes and Anthia vow "that you will abide chaste unto me and never tolerate another man, and I that I shall never consort with another woman" (1.11.3–5, trans. Hadas 1964, 80). That such sentiments were widely cherished is suggested not only by the popularity of such novels, which would hardly have appealed to the well educated, but by the existence of many epitaphs praising women who were μόνανδρος or *univira*. Examples from Jewish tombs in Leon 1960, 129f.

136. See, e.g., Musonius Rufus, "On Sexual Indulgence," "What is the Chief End of Marriage?" and "Is Marriage a Handicap for the Pursuit of Philosophy?" (all readily accessible in Lutz 1947, 84–97). Iamblichus *Vit. Pyth.* 31.209–11 claims that Pythagoras forbade even natural and prudent intercourse except for the conscious purpose of producing lawful children. For additional examples see Preisker 1927, 19f. This attitude was upheld by Jewish writers as well. Josephus not only attributes it to the marrying order of the Essenes, *JW* 2.161, but also asserts that, for all Jews, "The Law recognizes no sexual connexions, except the natural union of man and wife, and that only for the procreation of children" (*C. Ap.* 2.199, trans. Thackeray in the Loeb ed.). Philo entirely agrees; e.g., *Spec. leg.* 3.113 and 3.34–36; *Mos.* 1.28; *Abr.* 137; *Jos.* 43; *Virt.* 107. See the discussion in I. Heinemann 1929–32, 231–329. Note also the prayer of Tobias in Tob. 8:5–8.

137. In the Synoptics, Mark 10:2–12; Luke 16:18; Matt. 5:31f.; 19:3–12. See Dungan 1971, 100f.

138. For a general treatment, see Vööbus 1958–60.

139. Did. 10:6; Bornkamm 1963.

140. Barrett 1968, 397, suggests that even the unbaptized outsider who had been led by prophecy to confess God's presence (14:25) would not be prevented by this formula from participating in the meal.

141. See Theissen 1975c, 281.

142. See Dinkler 1952.

143. Courts within the Jewish congregations to settle internal disputes were among the most important institutions of the diaspora communities. See, e.g., the decree of Lucius Antonius about the Jews of Sardis, Josephus *Ant.* 14.235, quoted above, page 34. For Alexandria see Goodenough 1929. There are also pagan parallels. Poland 1909, 601, cites an Athenian group of Iobacchoi (ca. A.D. 178) who required members to bring disputes (μάχη) and accusations of unseemly behavior before the association's officers (*SIG* 3, no. 1109, lines 72–95). Note especially lines 90–95: "Let the same penalty be (assessed against) one who is injured and does not apply to the priest or the Archibacchos but makes a public accusation." See also D. E. Smith 1980, 149.

144. See the literature cited in n. 91 above.

145. So Barrett 1968, 130.

146. The form of the questions is a trifle awkward, and one might translate them with an opposite sense, expressing skepticism about saving the partner and supporting the resignation to separation by the pagan of verse 15. It is better, however, to take these questions and the preceding clause, "But God has called you to peace," as reverting to the sentiment of verse 14. Cf. Barrett 1968 *ad loc.*

147. See van Unnik 1964.

148. Ibid., 228.

149. See the literature cited in chapter 2, n. 79.

150. See chapter 1, Urban Judaism and Pauline Christianity.

151. For a contrary view see Cullmann 1963, 51f.

152. Meeks 1977.

153. Ibid.

154. Meeks 1972.

155. It has sometimes been suggested, however, that this phrase in 1 Cor. 1:2 was added later, to "catholicize" the collection of Paul's letters, at a point when the Corinthian letters headed the list. See most recently Beker 1980, 26.

156. Harnack 1906, 1:434.

157. Brandis 1905.

158. Cf. Dahl 1941, 240f., who refers to arguments by Erich Peterson.

159. Even more reminiscent of one function of the classical "town meeting" is 1 Cor. 5:4f., where a formal assembly is to be held to expel a member. The word itself does not appear in this context, however. Other examples of ἐκκλησία used of the Christian gathering in a particular city occur in Rom. 16:1 (Cenchreae); 1 Cor. 1:2; 2 Cor. 1:1 (Corinth); Phil. 4:15.

160. Rom. 16:5,19; Philem. 2; Col. 4:15.

161. Poland 1909, 332.

162. Also "ἐκκλησίαι of the saints," 1 Cor. 14:33f.; or simply "every ἐκκλησία," 1 Cor. 4:17; "all the ἐκκλησίαι," 1 Cor. 7:17; 2 Cor. 8:18; 11:28; cf. 12:13.

163. 1 Cor. 6:4; 10:32; 12:28; 14:4,5,12; 15:9; Gal. 1:13; Phil. 3:6; Eph. 1:22; 3:10, 21; 5:23,24,25,27,29,32; Col. 1:18,24. Cf. Linton 1959, col. 912.

164. See also Gal. 1:13 and 1 Cor. 15:9.

165. Note especially Deut. 23:2, 3, 4 and Judg. 20:2: ἐν ἐκκλησίᾳ τοῦ λαοῦ τοῦ θεοῦ; Neh. 13:1: ἐν ἐκκλησίᾳ θεοῦ (v.l. κυρίου); Sir. 24:2: ἐν ἐκκλησίᾳ ὑψίστου; 50:13: ἔναντι πάσης ἐκκλεσίας Ἰσραήλ. See the survey of evidence in Schmidt 1938, 527–29.

166. For Philo as for Deuteronomy, the Sinai assembly was the ἐκκλησία θεοῦ (or κυρίου) par excellence: Virt. 108; Ebr. 213; Som. 2.187; Quis her. 251; Decal. 32. One of the battle standards in the War of the Sons of Light with the Sons of Darkness was to be inscribed qᵉhal ʼel, 1QM 4:10; exclusion of blemished men from the qᵉhal ʼelah (paraphrase of Deut. 23:1–3), 1QSa 2:3; cf. 1QSa 1:25f.; CDC 7:17; 11:22; 12:6. Cf. Linton 1959, cols. 907–11. Note also the use in Heb. 12:23, where the connection with the Sinai assembly is much more direct than in Pauline usage.

167. Since Colossians is probably pseudonymous, the unusually large number of personal greetings in 4:7–15 (more than in any other letter in the Pauline corpus besides Romans) may be partly or wholly fictional (cf. 2 Timothy). If so, it is all the more evident that such personal and group connections were recognized not only by Paul but also by his followers as of first importance in maintaining the interurban fellowship of believers.

168. See Funk 1967.

169. Rom. 16:1f.; 1 Cor. 16:10–12; cf. Phil. 2:25–30; Col. 4:7–9; Eph. 6:21f. Paul can also request hospitality for himself, Philem. 22; Rom. 15:24.

170. See the third- and fourth-century letters collected by Treu 1973.

171. On accommodation for travelers in synagogues, see above, chapter 1, n. 63.

172. Cf. 1 Clem. 1:2; 11:1; 12:1; 35:5. Note also 1 Pet. 4:9. For the requirement that bishops be hospitable, see 1 Tim. 3:2; Titus 1:8; on the whole question, Malherbe 1977a, 65–68, who points out the special interest in hospitality in Luke-Acts.

173. Judge 1980a, 7; cf. Hatch 1892, 44f.

174. 1 Cor. 16:1–4; 2 Cor. 8–9; Rom. 15:25–28; cf. Acts 19:21; 20:1–6.

175. Nickle 1966; Georgi 1965; K. Berger 1977.

176. Berger 1977 argues persuasively that the author of Acts (who avoids any mention of the collection except at 24:17) understood it as an exhibition of piety and loyalty to Israel by someone on the fringes of the Jewish community, like Cornelius (10:2). We have noticed inscriptional evidence that gifts by gentile patrons were sometimes commemorated in diaspora synagogues (chapter 1 above, n. 257). Holmberg 1978, 35–43, accepts Berger's argument, but stresses more the legal obligation from the viewpoint of the Jerusalem group.

177. K. Berger 1977, 198.

178. So Holmberg 1978, 43.

CHAPTER 4

1. See Haenchen 1959, Betz 1979, and the abundant literature they cite.

2. Paul reports the decision to go up to Jerusalem and confer on "the gospel I preach among the gentiles" before he mentions the "false brothers" who force the issue of circumcision, so one could surmise that the latter appeared first at Jerusalem. However, the sequence probably depends on the structure of Paul's argument rather than on the order of events, for the whole context shows that the central issue was circumcision of gentile converts, and Titus was taken along from Antioch as a test case. Cf. Betz 1979 ad loc. In this detail, then, the Acts report is clearer.

3. The style, again, is that of actions by a collegium, imitating decisions by the "council and citizen body" of a city. Compare, e.g., Josephus *Ant.* 14.259–61, discussed above, pages 34f.

4. For the suggestion that Acts incorporates a tradition about the council very similar to the interpretation circulated by Paul's opponents in Galatia, see Linton 1949.

5. Sampley 1980, 21–50. It has been suggested that Paul himself quotes or alludes to some formal document in Gal. 2:7–9, since the name Peter occurs here, whereas elsewhere Paul calls him Cephas, along with the rather un-Pauline phrases "gospel of the uncircumcision . . . of the circumcision" (contrast 1:7–9), but the evidence is inconclusive. See the discussion in Betz 1979 *ad loc.*

6. This shows that the agreement described in Gal. 2:7–9 did not establish two separate missions, as has often been asserted. Nor did Paul think himself thereby forbidden to proselytize fellow Jews (1 Cor. 9:20). The point of the parallel clauses in Gal. 2:7f., 9b is not exclusiveness but equality.

7. See above, pages 41, 103, and, for subsequent developments in Antioch, Meeks-Wilken 1978, 13–52.

8. Holmberg 1978 calls the incident "something of a watershed in Paul's development" (13). See also Ollrog 1979, 11–13.

9. Christian travelers from Philippi helped Paul's work in Achaia by bringing news of the success in Thessalonica (1 Thess. 1:7–10) and, a bit later, brought money to help the Corinthian mission (2 Cor. 11:9) (see above, page 27). Presumably Paul heard of the difficulties in Thessalonica in similar fashion.

10. Notice the wish that forms the transition from the long opening thanksgiving to the rest of the letter (3:11–13) and the παρακαλῶ period that follows (4:1). The latter also takes up again the reminder in 2:12 of the admonitions that formed part of the initial instruction of the new converts. Malherbe has demonstrated that the paraenetic aim stated here belongs to the whole letter, not just to a "paraenetic section" (details in his forthcoming article in *ANRW;* cf. 1970; 1977a, 22–27).

11. Malherbe, forthcoming article in *ANRW.*

12. Koester 1979, 36f.

13. *Pace* Pearson 1971; see above, chapter 3, n. 117.

14. Koester 1979.

15. My understanding of Galatians owes most to Dahl 1973.

16. Compare the discussion in Betz 1979, 30–33.

17. The fullest analysis of the scriptural argument is in Dahl 1973, 52–67; see also Dahl 1969.

18. On this part, see Barrett 1976.

19. For example, δύναμις in First and Second Corinthians twenty-four times, in all the rest of the undoubted letters of Paul, ten; δυνατός, four and six times, respectively; ἐνεργεῖν, four and five times; ἐνέργημα, twice and none; ἐνεργής, one time each; ἔξεστιν, five times and none; ἐξουσία, twelve and five; ἐξουσιάζειν, three times and none, respectively.

20. "Die Christuspartei in der korinthischen Gemeinde, der Gegensatz des petrinischen und paulinischen Christenthums in der ältesten Kirche, der Apostel Petrus in Rom," *Tübinger Zeitschrift für Theologie* 4 (1831):61–206.

21. Dahl 1967.

22. Ibid., 334.

23. Cf. Judge 1968.

24. Hock 1980, 50–65.

25. Schütz 1975 passim.

26. Chapter 2, Indirect Evidence.

27. Not only do those tongue-speakers who are historically related to the Christian tradition assert that it is the same, but Felicitas Goodman's cross-cultural linguistic studies and direct observation have showed a consistent pattern of physical behavior, even in persons of different language families and in those who were apparently uninfluenced by Christian beliefs. She concludes that this consistency has a neurophysiological basis (Goodman 1972).

28. Ibid., 124. Goodman distinguishes the glossolalist's trance, which she calls "hyperarousal" because of the high somatic energy level, from a meditative kind of dissociation, such as that of a yoga, which she terms "hypoarousal" (59f.).

29. Brown 1971.

30. See, e.g., Lewis 1971; S. S. Walker 1972 (bibliography). For applicability to Old Testament prophecy, see R. R. Wilson 1979.

31. Goodman 1972 passim.

32. Lull 1980, 53–95, has tried to overturn this commonly accepted opinion, in my judgment unsuccessfully.

33. More on this in chapter 5.

34. Not only Pauline Christians had this experience at baptism, for Paul expected the Roman Christians to know about it, too: Rom. 8:15f.

35. Compare Goodman 1972 on the lower level of arousal in persons who "interpret" glossolalia and who speak in natural language while still to some degree dissociated (146f., 159).

36. Schütz 1975, 9–14, quotation from p. 14.

37. Friedrich 1958, 35f. Friedrich insists that the potential for "reasoned elaboration" must be present, but Schütz 1975, 13, rightly objects that room must be left for irrational elaboration, as when what is communicated is direct access to power.

38. Stowers 1981.

39. Schütz 1975, 90–112; idem 1974.

40. See Olson 1976. The thematic unity of these chapters makes it hard to accept the solution to their literary unevenness that is often proposed, taking 2:14–7:4 (omitting 6:14–7:1) to belong to a different letter.

41. This central theme in Paul's theology has been very often analyzed, e.g., Güttgemanns 1966. The most fruitful discussion for sociological understanding, however, is that of Schütz 1975, 187–203, 214–21, 226–48. An important criticism of Güttgemanns is found in Adams 1979, 217, along with a limited corrective also to Schütz (209).

42. Schütz 1975, 84–113.

43. Bujard 1973.

44. Ollrog 1979, 219f., and excursus 1, 236–42.

45. Cf. Stuhlmacher 1975, 53f., and above, chapter 2, n. 55.

46. The literature is extensive; the discussion has not reached a satisfying conclusion. For a sample, see Francis and Meeks 1975.

47. See especially Dahl 1951.

48. Bujard 1973, 71–76, 79–100.

49. Ibid., 118f.; Meeks 1977, 209f.

50. Dahl 1947; compare his discussion of Ephesians 1944.

51. Meeks 1977, 210–14.

52. See the literature cited in chapter 2, n. 79.

53. Heinrici 1888, Weiss 1910, Lietzmann 1931, Héring 1959, Conzelmann 1969, Barrett 1968. Barrett is the most useful of them all. For an analysis of the whole case and an attempt to put it into the context of contemporary practice in Jewish sects and early Christianity, see Forkman 1972.

54. But the author of Colossians uses it similarly in 2:18.

55. As Barrett 1968, 124f., seems to suggest.

56. Note that Paul does not even entertain the possibility of the sort of withdrawal practiced by some "pure" groups, notably the Qumran Essenes and the Therapeutae Philo describes in his *Vit. cont.*

57. Barrett 1968, 134.

58. E.g., Lampe 1967*a*.

59. See Barrett 1973, 91.

60. So Barrett argues *ad loc.*

61. Schütz 1975, 133.

62. Cf. Philem. 9, where πρεσβύτης may mean "ambassador" instead of "old man," even if it is not simply a misspelling of πρεσβευτής (Lightfoot 1879, 338f.; Lohse 1968, 199; *contra*, Dibelius-Greeven 1953, 104). See also Jewett 1982.

63. Meeks 1976, 605.

64. So Judge·(see above, chapter 2, n. 29).

65. Ollrog 1979, 79–84, has a good discussion of these delegates, but his insistence that their real function was always to help Paul in missionary work (96–99) requires a tortured and improbable exegesis to avoid the plain sense of 1 Cor. 16:17f. and Phil. 2:29f. On the latter passage, see instead Sampley 1980, 52–60. It is true that the letter to Philemon amounts to an indirect but not overly subtle request that Onesimus be sent back to help Paul. However, the fact that the "assembly in your house" is addressed does not justify Ollrog's inference that the slave is to return as "Gemeindegesandter" and missionary. Ollrog ignores the practical services that were required for the kind of activity that Paul and the "Mitarbeiter" carried on, and he assumes too quickly the existence of institutions and offices.

66. Ollrog 1979, 81.

67. Judge 1960*b*, 131.

68. Theissen 1975*a*, 205f.

69. Ollrog 1979, 9–13, although perhaps this gives too much weight to the Acts picture of Paul's start as a missionary. See Lüdemann 1980*a*, 23f.; and Jewett 1979, 84.

70. Ollrog 1979, 13. Schille 1967, on the other hand, tries to show that *all* early Christian missionary work was organized in local *Arbeitsgemeinschaften* or collegia of five to seven *Mitarbeiter*. His argument is a curious blend of ingenuity and fantasy. Any list of five or seven names, or of objects like loaves, fishes, or baskets, or of different numbers that can be arbitrarily emended to achieve the magic numbers, counts as evidence. And he does not define just what he means by *Kollegien* and *Kollegium*.

71. Ollrog's argument that Titus was independent of Paul, concerned almost entirely with the collection, and had an "altogether different" role from Timothy's (1979, 33–37) requires a peculiar reading of the texts. For a sounder exploration of Titus's role, see Barrett 1969.

72. See the prosopographic remarks above, chapter 2, and the lists and discussions in Redlich 1913, Judge 1960*b*, Ellis 1971, and Ollrog 1979.

73. Ollrog's attempt to show that the great majority of fellow workers were ἀπόστολοι ἐκκλησιῶν, however, is not supported by the evidence (see also n. 65, above). Ellis 1971 tries to use Paul's varied terminology to sort out distinct functional classes that are on their way "from the beginning" to becoming offices. The division is too brittle, as Ollrog shows (74, n. 64). Particularly unpersuasive is Ellis's attempt (13–21) to make "the brothers" a technical term for one kind of staff.

74. Poland 1909, 337–423; Waltzing 1895–1900, 1:357–446; Schultz-Falkenthal 1970.

75. The major modern commentaries (von Dobschütz 1909; Dibelius 1937; Best 1972) support the sense "patron"; cf. Greeven 1952, 346, n. 74. In Rom. 12:8 the same ambiguity exists, but the two parallel terms, μεταδιδούς and ἐλεῶν, make a decision for "protector, patron" easier. The adverbial σπουδῇ would also fit the patron's role; cf. Gal. 2:10, where ἐσπούδασα describes Paul's efforts for the poor. In the Pastoral Epistles the verb is clearly used in the sense "preside" or "govern" (a family: 1 Tim. 3:4, 5, 12; presbyters who govern [προεστῶτες] well get double pay: 1 Tim. 5:17).

76. This ambiguity exists in the divine realm, too. When citizens of Amastris honor Zeus and Hera as οἱ πάτριοι θεοὶ καὶ προεστῶτες τῆς πόλεως, they presumably think of them as "presiding over" as well as "protecting" the city (Le Bas–Waddington 519f., cited by MacMullen 1981, 142, n. 17). MacMullen gives other examples as well: Zeus and Hecate at Panamara, Dionysus in Teos, Artemis in Perge, and the dii patrii et Mauri conservatores in CIL 8.21486.

77. My translation resolves the ambiguity of the Greek by taking the three final examples, which differ sharply in syntax and word choice from the preceding list of four, as parallel in the sense of referring to concrete, practical support by superiors for inferiors. Van Unnik 1974 proposes another, altogether different construction. He takes the three asyndetic examples to sum up the previous four activities under a different perspective. Since the verb μεταδιδόναι alone, as he demonstrates, is not a technical term for "almsgiving" but takes its specific meaning always from an expressed or implied object—wanting altogether in Rom. 12:8—he suggests "he who communicates (the riches of the gospel)" (183).

78. Betz 1979, 304–06, thinks this "may indicate some kind of educational institution as part of the life of the Galatian churches."

79. The evolution of offices in the early church has been the subject of long and vigorous debate. For a good introduction, see the collection of essays edited by Kertelge 1977.

80. Harnack 1906, 1:319–68.

81. See especially Greeven 1952.

82. See above, n. 37.

83. Schütz 1975, 184.

84. Dahl 1954, 32.

85. I have tried to avoid the double anachronism that has clouded modern interpretations. On the one hand, the meaning of "the Law" for Judaism is commonly identified with the ideology of the Torah that came to prevail in the academic circle around R. Judah the Prince toward the end of the second century. We do not know how widely ran the writ of those rabbis in their own time, nor the extent to which their construction was, as Neusner argues, an idealized, utopian world. Above all, it is implausible that, in practical terms, their laws and institutions had been unchanged, in the diaspora cities as well as in Palestinian towns, through two centuries punctuated

by three revolutions and by radical changes in the social and political climate. On the other hand, Paul's revisionism is inevitably distorted by the anti-Judaism that grew up in the church after his time, the anti-Pelagian polemics of Augustine, the medieval penitential system in the West and Luther's revolt against it, modern antisemitism, modern psychological antinomianism, and existentialist theology. Among the most recent attempts to break through to a more historical perspective, Sanders 1977 is important but not altogether successful. For shortcomings in his interpretation of Paul, see Dahl 1978, in his interpretation of Jewish traditions, Neusner 1978. The legal historian B. S. Jackson has made some sane remarks about the issue (1979).

    86. See above, chapter 3.

CHAPTER 5

1. Judge 1980*b*, 212.
2. Ibid.
3. MacMullen 1981, 1–48, with abundant documentation, pp. 141–67.
4. *Ep*. 10.96.8: "Nihil aliud inveni quam superstitionem pravam, immodicam."
5. Tacitus *Ann*. 15.44.3; Suetonius *Nero* 16.3.
6. Celsus, who had made a more thorough investigation of the subject toward the end of the century, accused the Christians not of having no rites, but of performing them in secret (Origen *C. Cels*. 1.3). Morton Smith has argued that the Christians were not only labeled superstitious by outsiders, but often accused of practicing magic (1978, 1980). His argument goes beyond the evidence at many places; e.g., *maleficia* may well have included magic among other kinds of "evildoing," but the word alone can hardly denote that specific accusation in every case. Nevertheless, the accusation was made sometimes, and it would hardly have had any sense if the accusers did not think the Christians performed any rituals at all. On *religio* and *superstitio* in Roman historians, see Momigliano 1972, 4f.
7. Spiro 1966, 96.
8. Ibid., 97.
9. Leach 1968, 524.
10. See the classic discussion of "manifest" and "latent" functions in Merton 1967, 73–138.
11. Goody 1961, 157.
12. Durkheim 1912, 22; Gellner 1962, 119f.
13. Douglas 1973, 42, 78.
14. Berger-Luckmann 1966; Geertz 1957, 1966.
15. Austin 1975. I touch here a philosophic problem more complicated than I have space or competence to pursue. For one thing, ritual, or at least convention, is a necessary condition for a performative utterance to work. Further, Austin showed that one could not absolutely separate "constative" from "performative" speech. Virtually every speech act has "locutionary," "illocutionary," and "perlocutionary" forces—all three.
16. This is implicit in the opening formulas of the letters: τῇ ἐκκλησίᾳ: 1 Thess. 1:1; 2 Thess. 1:1; 1 Cor. 1:2; 2 Cor. 1:1; ταῖς ἐκκλησίαις (in a region): Gal. 1:2; τοῖς ἁγίοις: Phil. 1:1; κλητοῖς ἁγίοις: Rom. 1:7; ἁγίοις καὶ πιστοῖς ἀδελφοῖς: Col. 1:2; ἁγίοις καὶ πιστοῖς: Eph. 1:1.
17. The term ἐκκλησία does not appear in the address, but neither does it in Phil.

1:1, Col. 1:2, or Eph. 1:1. Judge and Thomas 1966 draw some improbable inferences from this fact.

18. Cf. MacMullen's remarks about difficulty finding space for a large dinner party (1981, 36).

19. *Ep.* 10.96.7.

20. *1 Apol.* 67; see also Barn. 15:9, probably earlier but not precisely dated.

21. Besides the standard commentaries, see Bacchiocchi 1977, 90–101, and the literature he cites. Dr. Bacchiocchi, a Seventh-Day Adventist, is happy to expose the tendentiousness of arguments for Sunday observance in 1 Cor. 16:1–3. His reading of Pliny, however, may err in the other direction.

22. Barrett 1968, 327.

23. Dibelius-Greeven 1953 and Lohse 1968 are typical of those who see no clear distinction. Lightfoot 1879 cites Gregory Nyss. *in Psalm.* 100.3. With my discussion below compare now the illuminating remarks by Hengel 1980, an article I was able to obtain only after my manuscript was complete.

24. Lightfoot 1879, 225.

25. E.g., Dodd 1952, Lindars 1961, Hay 1973.

26. Lightfoot 1879, 225, citing Philo's report of hymns of thanksgiving in Alexandria for deliverance from a pogrom (*Flacc.* 121–24), and of the regular practice of the Therapeutae (*Vit. cont.* 80f., 83–89).

27. 1QH. See Vermes 1978, 56–65, and the further literature cited there.

28. See MacMullen 1981, 15–24. Dibelius-Greeven 1953 *ad loc.* call attention to Epictetus *Diss.* 1.15–21, who declares that anyone who recognizes the pervasiveness of providence ought constantly to express thanks, even while digging and plowing and eating, by "a hymn to God." He gives examples, which must have been of a familiar style, such as "Great is God, that he has provided us these instruments." The style is also found in the Greek translation of the biblical Psalms, e.g., 47:2; 88:8; 94:3; 95:4; 98:2; 144:3; 146:5. See below, n. 53.

29. Dahl 1951. Those who have tried to reconstruct a hymn here include Schille 1952, 16–24; 1962, 65f.

30. First to identify Phil. 2:6–11 as a hymn was Lohmeyer 1927, followed by a multitude including Käsemann 1950; Georgi 1964*b*; Braumann 1962, 56–61; and Strecker 1964 to name a small sample. The classicist Eduard Norden 1912, 250–63, had already described Col. 1:12–20 and a number of other passages in the Pauline letters as "liturgical." Lohmeyer 1930 saw in Col. 1:15–20 a hymn. Käsemann's attempt, 1949, to show that a pre-Christian hymn had been worked over into a "baptismal liturgy," beginning with verse 13, has not persuaded many. Other, different analyses include J. M. Robinson 1957; Hegermann 1961; Schweizer 1961*b*; Pöhlmann 1973; Vawter 1971; Meeks 1977, 211f. The most far-reaching attempt to recover "early Christian hymns" from Pauline and other early Christian texts is Schille 1962, but his method is often arbitrary. Other literature on the problem includes Deichgräber 1967, J. M. Robinson 1964, Martin 1967, Wengst 1972, Hengel 1980.

31. Literally "yourselves" in both passages, but the reflexive is here equivalent to the reciprocal, as Col. 3:13 shows; Lightfoot 1879 *ad loc.* and BDF §287.

32. Vielhauer 1939.

33. On the ambiguity of προϊστάμενοι see above, page 134.

34. The reconstruction, by the learned Protestant pastor Paul Billerbeck, of "a synagogue service in the time of Jesus," published posthumously without references to sources (1964), illustrates the danger. It draws together evidence from rabbinic litera-

ture of a wide range of dates and provenances, all later than the New Testament, without any clear principle of selection or attention to the problems of redaction or history of tradition. For a more careful discussion, see Schürer 1973–, 2:447–54.

35. Dahl 1954; cf. Bultmann 1948–53, 1:105f.

36. Rom. 16:25–27; see Gamble 1977.

37. See above, chapter 3, n. 51.

38. On the *berakah,* Audet 1958; Bickerman 1962; J. Heinemann 1964, 77–103; on the shift from third person to second, Towner 1968.

39. Dibelius 1931; Dahl 1947, 1951; Rese 1970; and many others.

40. Schlier 1933.

41. See later in this chapter.

42. *Oxford English Dictionary* s.v. "rite."

43. Goodman 1972.

44. See above, nn. 29, 30, 38, 39. Braumann 1962 undertook to recover the major motifs in the baptismal liturgy presupposed by Paul, but his exegesis is superficial. Schille 1952, 1962 has many imaginative suggestions but no way of testing them. More reliable are the proposals of Dahl 1944, 1947, 1951. Other studies of the baptismal traditions include Dinkler 1962b, Grail 1951, Schlier 1938, Bornkamm 1939, Downing 1964, Fascher 1955. There is besides an enormous literature on the theology of baptism in the New Testament, and another vast array on the antecedents of Christian baptism in the history of religions. For a good review of the latter, see Dahl 1955. Dinkler 1962a and Puniet 1907 provide excellent general surveys.

45. Hippolytus *Trad. apost.* 21; text in Botte 1963, 48–50; Dix 1937, 36f.

46. See Kraeling 1967.

47. Lev. 14:51f.; 15:13; Num. 19:17; and elsewhere.

48. Neusner 1977, 57f., 83–87. I am by no means equating the function of the *tebilah* as a whole with Christian baptism, although the former most likely provided a number of the fundamental procedures for the latter. Neusner's note on p. 87 is apposite: ". . . the Mishnaic conception of the immersion-pool bears no relationship to baptism for the removal of sins. . . ."

49. Perhaps not completely unthinkable, though: the priests of Isis at Cenchreae made use of "the nearest bath" (*ad proximas balneas*) for "the customary ablution" of an initiate, according to Apuleius *Met.* 11.23. Acts 8:36; 16:13–15, 33 imply that any available water could serve.

50. It soon occurred to someone that it would be more appropriate to have the baptized put on new, white garments after immersion. See Klijn 1954 and J. Z. Smith 1965 (with extensive literature). But nothing in the Pauline texts requires us to suppose that that practice was already in use.

51. Already quite elaborate in Hippolytus *Trad. apost.* 21.

52. Lampe 1967b, 61f.

53. Acts 19:28, of Artemis; see the examples cited by Epictetus, cited above, n. 28; Aelius Aristides *Sacr. serm.* 2.7,21 (of Asklepius); Minucius Felix *Octav.* 18.11.

54. E.g., Cullmann 1949; Neufeld 1963; Kramer 1963, 19–128; Campenhausen 1972.

55. There is room for doubt whether the "oath" mentioned by Pliny referred to baptism, but most interpreters have taken it to, for rather good reasons. See, e.g., Nock 1924a; R. M. Grant 1948, 56.

56. So Justin could refer to it quite simply as τὸ . . . λοῦτρον (1 *Apol.* 66.1); Paul had used the cognate verb in 1 Cor. 6:11.

57. Mylonas 1961, 194 and fig. 70; Kerényi 1967, fig. 14.

58. Clement Alex. *Strom.* 4.3.1, cited by Mylonas 1961, 241.

59. Mylonas 1961, 224–85.

60. Apuleius *Met.* 11.23; not to mention the sevenfold washing that Lucius was inspired to undertake before praying to the goddess, while still an ass (11.1).

61. Neusner 1977; cf. idem 1973*a*.

62. Notably Moore 1927, 1:323–53; 3:n. 102; Rowley 1940; Jeremias 1949; Dix 1937, xl; Cullmann 1948, 9, 56, and passim. Criticism: Dahl 1955; Michaelis 1951. It is true that in the late compilation of rules about proselytes, Gerim 2.4, *t*ᵉ*bilah* is treated as one of the indispensable procedures through which a proselyte "enters the covenant," along with circumcision. It has been argued, on the basis of certain statements by Philo, *QE* 2.2, *Virt.* 175–86; remarks by Epictetus, *Diss.* 2.9.19–21; and the debate between R. Eliezer and R. Joshua in the *baraita* of bYeb. 46a, that (male) proselytes were sometimes received by baptism alone, without circumcision. I think in each case that overinterprets what the texts say or, in the case of the Greek sources, do *not* say. Space does not permit me to argue the issue here. The key to a correct understanding of immersion of proselytes (the term *proselyte baptism*, invented by modern Christian scholars, begs the question) is to be found in MPes. 8:8: "The School of Shammai say, 'If a man became a proselyte on the day before Passover, he may immerse himself and consume his Passover-offering in the evening.' And the School of Hillel say, 'He that separates himself from his uncircumcision is as one that separates himself from a grave'" (trans. Danby 1933, 148). This text is very important to Jeremias 1949 but actually rather inauspicious for his interpretation, for it speaks of the ablution of a man who "became a proselyte on the Eve of Passover" [*gr šntgyyr b'rb psḥ*]. That is, the act of becoming a proselyte, far from being identified with baptism, as Jeremias would have it, is explicitly distinguished from it. Beth Shammai and Beth Hillel differ over the question whether one or seven days must lapse before the ritual cleansing that is necessary—not to complete his being made a proselyte, but before eating the Passover. That is also the sense of the sentence, "When he is immersed and comes up, he is an Israelite in all respects" (bYeb. 47b at the beginning). The equation of the proselyte's uncleanness with corpse uncleanness by Beth Hillel seems to me to refute Moore's insistence (1927, 1:334) that the proselyte's bath had nothing to do with purification. The equivalence of different uses of *t*ᵉ*bilah* also underlies the series of rulings in bYeb. 45b.

63. Hippolytus *Trad. apost.* 20.

64. See Dahl 1947.

65. E.g., Odes Sol. 27; Tertullian *De orat.* 14; Minucius Felix *Octav.* 29.8.

66. Dinkler 1954, 125f.; *contra:* Güttgemanns 1966, 126–35; Adams 1979, 221; undecided: Betz 1979, 324f.

67. Much of the evidence is collected in Meeks 1974.

68. E.g., Dio Chrys. *Or.* 60.8; Philostratus *V. Ap.* 4.20; Philo *Som.* 1.224f.; Acts Thom. 58; Silv. 105:13–17; Asterius *in Ps. 8, Hom.* 2 (ed. Richard 1956, 110, 10f.). A variation of this theme is the donning of armor for the struggle of life, found already in Wisd. of Sol. 5:18–20, which also appears in Pauline paraenesis, 1 Thess. 5:8; Rom. 13:12; Eph. 6:10–17, but not connected with baptism.

69. Eph. 2:4–7; cf. 1:3 and Col. 1:5,12; 2:12,20; 3:1–4.

70. For later examples, see the wide-ranging remarks of Widengren 1968; on Mandaean ceremonies of "raising up" that may reflect influence from Syrian Christian rites, see Segelberg 1958, 66f., 89–91. Coronation with wreaths was important in certain Syrian, Armenian, Coptic, and Ethiopic Christian baptismal rites, according to Bernard 1912, 45f.

71. Van Gennep 1909; V. Turner 1969, 94–130.

72. Barrett's skepticism on this point (1968, 264) seems excessive.

73. MacMullen 1981, 36–42 (quotation from p. 36). Broneer 1973, 33–46, describes two interesting subterranean facilities, each with two dining rooms containing altogether eleven couches, under the theater and the Poseidon temple at Isthmia. Dennis Smith 1980 has collected a great deal of evidence of this sort. On the possible influence of club meals on early Christian practice, see Reicke 1951a, 320–38.

74. Trans. Barrett 1968 ad loc.

75. Reicke 1951a, 257. He backs this statement by citing inscriptions from the imperial age, e.g., one from Nicaea in which a certain Aurelius leaves money to the village of the Racelians, "for them to make my memorial" (ποιεῖν αὐτοὺς ἀνά-[μ]νη[σ]ίν μου) (MDAI[A] 12 [1887], 169, quoted by Reicke 1951, 259; other examples pp. 258–60).

76. Reicke 1951a, 257–64; later Christian meals for the dead, 101–49; antecedents in paganism and Judaism, 104–18. Although Reicke thinks the cult of the dead "fundamentally foreign" to "normal Judaism," he admits that there is a good bit of evidence for Jewish memorial meals (263, 104–18). Charles A. Kennedy has also collected valuable evidence for memorial meals in the milieu of early Christianity, in a forthcoming study of the cult of the dead in Corinth which he has kindly let me see in manuscript.

77. Dahl 1947, 21f., and the literature cited in his n. 49.

78. E.g., Rom. 5:6,8; 14:15; 1 Cor. 15:3; 2 Cor. 5:15, 21; Gal. 1:4; 2:20; 3:13; Eph. 5:2,25.

79. Theissen 1974b.

80. Ibid., 309.

81. Ibid., 312.

82. Ibid., 313f.

83. Käsemann 1947, 12f.

84. This view has been forcefully expressed by, among others, Ste. Croix 1975, 19f.

85. Meeks 1974, 180–83.

86. Dahl 1977, 109f.

87. De monog. 10; De cor. 3; Reicke 1951, 120–31. Mart. Polyc. 18:3 shows that at least for martyrs the practice was known earlier.

88. See Jeremias 1954, 900–904, and further literature cited there.

CHAPTER 6

1. MacMullen 1981, 83–94.

2. Ibid.; cf. Vogt 1939, 34–45.

3. Spec. leg. 1.53; Mos. 1.203–05 (based rather on Lev. 24:15f.). Josephus repeats the same interpretation, perhaps depending on Philo, perhaps reflecting a common understanding, C. Ap. 2.237; Ant. 4.207; cf. Tcherikover 1961, 352. Origen has adopted the same position, C. Cels. 8.38.

4. Spec. leg. 1.52, trans. Colson.

5. Nikolaus Walter 1977 argues that this conception of a common life (πο-λιτεύεσθαι) had no real counterpart in Greco-Roman religion except in Judaism: "However much one may characterize the late Hellenistic epoch as a time of uncertainty and religious questing, it still did not experience religion as a binding force that was capable of determining everyday reality by offering support, setting norms, and

forming community. . . . Only in one place could [Hellenistic man] observe such a relationship to one God and a real connectedness through religion—in the whole Mediterranean world—only in the Jews. . ." (427).

6. Pearson 1973, 47–50, has laid this ingenious fantasy to rest.

7. See Reicke 1951b.

8. Cf. Callan 1976.

9. *Sociomorphic* is a term from Topitsch's classification of symbolism, adapted by Theissen 1974a and discussed later in this chapter.

10. Cf. Meeks 1977.

11. Dahl 1977, 178–91; Bassler 1979.

12. For "response to the world" as a means of classifying sects, see B. R. Wilson 1973.

13. Meeks 1972; Bogart 1977.

14. Evans 1969.

15. Goodenough 1928.

16. Schweitzer 1930.

17. Bultmann 1941, 15f.; 1958.

18. Käsemann 1960, 102.

19. Idem 1962.

20. A few examples out of many: Stuhlmacher 1977, reinforcing Käsemann's position; Becker 1970, reconfirming Bultmann's. Baumgarten's major monograph 1975 makes some progress by insisting on attention to the functions of apocalyptic language in its specific contexts—but he means only its theological function; he does not for a moment consider its social functions. He claims to show that the apocalyptic traditions used by Paul include a "cosmology" and that Paul does "anthropologize" them. Yet he insists against Bultmann that this does not entail an "individualist" interpretation. Paul's interpretation of apocalyptic includes a "universal" and especially a strong "ecclesiological" dimension. On the other hand, Beker 1980, in his major work on Paul's theology (especially ch. 8, pp. 135–81), goes even further than Käsemann by insisting that a coherent apocalyptic schema is an essential part of the gospel, and that this means that Christian eschatology is "realistically chronological (but without any real *measure* of time)" and "cosmological" (Beker's emphasis). I confess that I do not know what this means.

21. Baumgarten 1975, 10. For recent attempts to define the genre apocalypse, see Collins 1979 and the essays by Collins, Hartman, Fiorenza, Sanders, Koch, Betz, and Krause in Hellholm 1982.

22. E.g., Wallace 1956; Worsley 1957; Burridge 1969. For an important survey of early work, see Talmon 1962; for problems of relation to classical sociological theory, Kovacs 1976.

23. Cf. Isenberg 1974; Gager 1975, especially pp. 20–37.

24. Aberle 1962.

25. Burridge 1969, 11.

26. I owe this insight to Kovacs 1976, 21f. See also Wallace 1956, 270; Worsley 1957, 36 and passim; Burridge 1969, 141–64; Holmberg 1978, 175–81.

27. For the concept "cognitive dissonance" see Festinger 1957 and Festinger-Riecken-Schachter 1956.

28. The question of the relation between status inconsistency and types of religious commitment has occasionally been raised by sociologists investigating modern societies, but little solid research seems to have been accomplished in this area so far. See Sasaki 1979 and the literature he reviews.

29. I have explored the functions of apocalyptic language in 1 Thessalonians somewhat more fully in Meeks 1982.

30. See above, chapter 4, Reformers in Galatia.

31. Dahl 1973 is the fullest analysis of this argument, too complex to repeat here; cf. Dahl 1969.

32. See chapter 4, Warrants for Authority.

33. The translation of all these passages is from the RSV.

34. Notably Käsemann 1960, 1962; convenient reviews of other literature are in J. H. Wilson 1968 and Boers 1967; see also Koester 1961; Funk 1966, 279–305; Pearson 1973, 27–43; Dahl 1967; Thiselton 1978; Horsley 1978.

35. See chapter 4, Confusion in Corinth.

36. This point has often been made, but by no one more lucidly than Dahl 1960; 1977, 95–120; 1978. Some of Dahl's formulations have recently been taken up and expanded by Beker 1980. For a very compact statement in Paul's own language, see Phil. 3:10f. There the epexegetic phrase, "to know him and the power of his resurrection and the partnership of his sufferings, conformed to the shape of his death, that I might if possible attain to the resurrection from the dead," enlarges on the phrase "the righteousness from God based on faith." This is the climax of the whole passage. The warning against the Judaizers, "Watch out for the mutilation" (vs. 2), is followed by the bold claim, "*We* [ἡμεῖς] are the circumcision, who serve God spiritually" (vs. 3). This radical transfer of terms and reversal of values is illustrated by a succinct autobiographical report (vss. 4–11) leading up to the climax.

37. This states the principal theme not only of the opening doxology of 2 Corinthians, but of the first seven chapters of the present form of the letter. See above and Olson 1976.

38. Chapter 4, Confusion in Corinth.

39. This "conformity pattern" (also in Eph. 5:25,29) is a standard form of early Christian exhortation, not unique to Paul (Dahl 1954, 34).

40. E.g., Dodds 1965, 135; most recently MacMullen 1981, 136f. Both refer to the second- to fourth-century period.

41. MacMullen 1981, 53.

42. Ibid., 57; evidence cited p. 173, n. 30.

43. Ibid., 53–57.

44. On the mysteries, I wonder if MacMullen has not been too skeptical. Apuleius *Met.* 11.6 (Griffiths 1975, 271, 2) presupposes some kind of personal immortality that will be enhanced, though not created, by the initiation. The initiate in the Elysian Fields, in "the subterranean vault," will still be Isis's worshiper and under her protection. So, too, perhaps MacMullen is too cavalier about the Mithraist promise (according to Celsus) of the soul's ascent through the seven planetary spheres ("not to everyone's taste in immortality"; 54). Bousset's description of "die Himmelsreise der Seele" (1901) erred in details and drew too schematic a picture, but this was nevertheless a powerful kind of belief apparently shared by many, not least by the Christian and non-Christian Gnostics now better known through the Nag-Hammadi texts. Teachers of rhetoric recommend that speeches of consolation include reminders of the soul's return to the divine realm as a source of comfort for the bereaved; e.g., Menander Rhet., "On Consolation" and "On the Funeral Speech" (Russell and Wilson 1981, 160–65, 176f. [with translation]; also *Rhet. Gr.* [Spengel] 3:414, 16–25; 421, 15–17). Seneca *Ad Marc. de consol.* 23.2 and Plutarch *Consol. ad ux.* 611D–612B are literary examples of the topos in actual use. All these references I owe to Abraham J. Malherbe, who points out that the rhetorical handbooks are particularly important,

because they do not introduce new ideas, but use popular opinions, expectations, and hopes.

45. See Nickelsburg 1972, Cavallin 1979.

46. Schweizer 1955, 56–67; Hahn 1963, excursus 2 (pp. 129–35); Hay 1973; cf. Schille 1962, 103.

47. So Güttgemanns 1966, who not only exaggerates the frequency and consistency of such paradoxical statements, making them normative for Pauline theology, but also clouds the issue by introducing Käsemann's notion of the apostle's sufferings as "epiphanies" of the crucified Christ. No characteristic of an epiphany appears in any of the texts he cites. See Jervell 1976 and Adams 1979, 209–17, 243.

48. Aus 1971.

49. It is now commonly believed by New Testament scholars that this pattern has its roots in Jewish myths or metaphors about divine Wisdom. See, e.g., Harris 1917; Bultmann 1923; Hegermann 1961; Mack 1973; Feuillet 1966; Hamerton-Kelly 1973.

50. See chapter 4, Confusion in Corinth, and Schütz 1975.

51. Jervell 1976.

52. Meeks 1977.

53. This follows rather loosely the interpretative grid suggested by Theissen 1974a, although the total "field structure of soteriological symbolism" he constructs is, as Beker 1980, 256, says, "too neat." See also Sanders 1977, 463–72.

54. See Schottroff 1979. I have also learned much from an essay by Paul Donahue, not yet published, on the "demonic" character of sin in Romans.

55. It will hardly do to make this *the* central image of Pauline theology, however, as Käsemann 1973 does. Cf. Theissen 1974a, 285, n. 6.

56. Theissen 1974a, 286.

57. Cf. Rom. 15:22, where the same verb appears in the passive, and 1:13, with a synonym; the implied subject is perhaps Satan in both places.

58. Barrett 1957, 72.

59. That Rom. 7:7–25 provides no evidence to the contrary was shown by the now classic work of Kümmel 1929. See Bultmann 1932 and Stendahl 1963. For a timely warning against removing *every* autobiographical element from Romans 7, however, see Beker, 1980, 240f.

60. Dahl 1956.

61. Ps. 110:1 = 109:1 LXX; see Hay 1973.

62. Meeks 1977.

63. Theissen 1974a.

64. Ibid., 300.

65. Schottroff's suggestion (1979, 499f.) that a negative view of the imperium was the source of the metaphor of sin as a world ruler seems farfetched. She insists that the Roman Empire was generally understood by its subjects as the imposition of absolute slavery (502–07), but that is hardly credible, nor will the little evidence she cites support such a view. Fourth Ezra, reflecting on the destruction of Jerusalem, is hardly typical. Philo's philippic against Caligula should not lead us to ignore his encomium on Augustus or even his description of the early years of Gaius under the categories of ideal kingship. And the famous speech put in the mouth of the Scottish warrior Galgacus by Tacitus (*Agric.* 30f.) can hardly be taken as typical of provincial feeling about Rome.

BIBLIOGRAPHY OF SECONDARY WORKS CITED

Standard collections of inscriptions and other sources, such as the *Inscriptiones Graecae,* and reference works, such as the *Reallexikon für Antike und Christentum,* are not included. For some of these, see the list of abbreviations.

Aberle, David. 1962. "A Note on Relative Deprivation Theory as Applied to Millenarian and Other Cult Movements." In *Millennial Dreams in Action: Studies in Revolutionary Religious Movements,* ed. Sylvia L. Thrupp, pp. 209–14. Comparative Studies in Society and History, supp. 2. The Hague: Mouton.

Adams, David. 1979. "The Suffering of Paul and the Dynamics of Luke-Acts." Ph.D. dissertation, Yale University.

Afanassieff, Nicolas. 1974. "L'Assemblée eucharistique unique dans l'église ancienne." *Klēronomia* 6:1–36.

Aland, Kurt. 1979. "Der Schluss und die ursprüngliche Gestalt des Römerbriefes." In *Neutestmentliche Entwürfe.* Theologische Bücherei, Neues . Testament, 63. Munich: Kaiser, pp. 284–301.

Albrecht, Michael von, ed. and trans. 1963. *Iamblichus, Pythagoras: Legende, Lehre, Lebensgestaltung.* Zurich and Stuttgart: Artemis.

Anderson, Bo, and Zelditch, Morris, Jr. 1964. "Rank Equilibration and Political Behavior." *Archives européenes de sociologie* 5:112–25.

Applebaum, Shim'on. 1961. "The Jewish Community of Hellenistic and Roman Teucheira in Cyrenaica." *Scripta Hierosolymitana* 7:27–52.

———. 1974. "The Organization of the Jewish Communities of the Diaspora." In *The Jewish People in the First Century,* ed. Samuel Safrai and Menahem Stern, vol. 1, pp. 464–503. Compendia Rerum Iudaicarum ad Novum Testamentum, 1. Assen: Van Gorcum; Philadelphia: Fortress.

———. 1976. "The Social and Economic Status of the Jews in the Diaspora." In *The Jewish People in the First Century,* ed. Samuel Safrai and Menahem Stern, vol. 2, pp. 701–27. Compendia Rerum Iudaicarum ad Novum Testamentum, 1. Assen: Van Gorcum; Philadelphia: Fortress.

———. 1979. *Jews and Greeks in Ancient Cyrene.* Studies in Judaism in Late Antiquity, 28. Leiden: Brill.

Audet, J. P. 1958. "Esquisse historique du genre littéraire de la 'bénédiction' juive et de l' 'eucharistie' chrétienne." *RB* 65:371–99.

Aus, Roger D. 1971. "Comfort in Judgment: The Use of Day of the Lord and Theophany Traditions in Second Thessalonians 1." Ph.D. dissertation, Yale University.

Austin, J. L. 1975. *How to Do Things with Words.* Edited by J. O. Urmson and Marina Sbisà. 2d ed. Cambridge, Mass.: Harvard University Press.

Bacchiocchi, Samuele. 1977. *From Sabbath to Sunday: A Historical Investigation of the Rise of Sunday Observance in Early Christianity.* Rome: Pontifical Gregorian University Press.

Badian, Ernst. 1958. *Foreign Clientelae (264–70 B.C.).* Oxford: Clarendon.

Bailey, Cyril. 1926. *Epicurus: The Extant Remains.* Reprint. Hildesheim and New York: Olms, 1970.

Balch, David L. 1981. *Let Wives be Submissive: The Domestic Code in 1 Peter.* Society of Biblical Literature Monograph Series, 26. Chico, Calif.: Scholars.

Baldry, Harold C. 1965. *The Unity of Mankind in Greek Thought.* Cambridge: At the University Press.

Banks, Robert. 1980. *Paul's Idea of Community: The Early House Churches in Their Historical Setting.* Grand Rapids: Eerdmans.

Barber, Bernard. 1968. Introduction to "Social Stratification." *IESS,* vol. 15, pp. 288–96.

Barrett, Charles Kingsley. 1957. *A Commentary on the Epistle to the Romans.* Harper/Black New Testament Commentaries. London: Black; New York: Harper & Row.

_____. 1962. *From First Adam to Last: A Study in Pauline Theology.* London: Black; New York: Scribner's.

_____. 1968. *A Commentary on the First Epistle to the Corinthians.* Harper/Black New Testament Commentaries. London: Black; New York: Harper & Row.

_____. 1969. "Titus." In *Neotestamentica et Semitica: Studies in Honour of Matthew Black,* ed. E. Earle Willis and Max Wilcox, pp. 1–14. Edinburgh: Clark.

_____. 1971. "Paul's Opponents in II Corinthians." *NTS* 17:233–54.

_____. 1973. *A Commentary on the Second Epistle to the Corinthians.* Harper/Black New Testament Commentaries. London: Black; New York: Harper & Row.

_____. 1976. "The Allegory of Abraham, Sarah, and Hagar in the Argument of Galatians." In *Rechtfertigung: Festschrift für Ernst Käsemann zum 70. Geburtstag,* ed. Johannes Friedrich, Wolfgang Pöhlmann, and Peter Stuhlmacher, pp. 1–16. Tübingen: Mohr (Siebeck); Göttingen: Vandenhoeck & Ruprecht.

Barrow, Reginald H. 1928. *Slavery in the Roman Empire.* Reprint. New York: Barnes & Noble, 1964.

Bartchy, S. Scott. 1973. *Mallon Chrēsai: First-Century Slavery and the In-*

terpretation of 1 Corinthians 7:21. Society of Biblical Literature Dissertation Series, 11. Missoula, Mont.: Scholars.

Bassler, Jouette M. 1979. "The Impartiality of God: Paul's Use of a Theological Axiom." Ph.D. dissertation, Yale University.

Bateson, Mary Catherine. 1974. "Ritualization: A Study in Texture and Texture Change." In *Religious Movements in Contemporary America,* ed. Irving I. Zaretsky and Mark P. Leone, pp. 150–65. Princeton: Princeton University Press.

Baumgarten, Jörg. 1975. *Paulus und die Apokalyptik: Die Auslegung apokalyptischer Überlieferungen in den echten Paulusbriefen.* Wissenschaftliche Monographien zum Alten und Neuen Testament, 44. Neukirchen: Erziehungsverein.

Becher, Ilse. 1970. "Der Isiskult in Rom—ein Kult der Halbwelt?" *Zeitschrift für ägyptische Sprache und Altertumskunde* 96:81–90.

Becker, Jürgen. 1970. "Erwägungen zur apokalyptischen Tradition in der paulinischen Theologie." *EvT* 30:593–609.

Beker, J. Christiaan. 1980. *Paul the Apostle: The Triumph of God in Life and Thought.* Philadelphia: Fortress.

Bell, Harold Idris. 1924. *Jews and Christians in Egypt: The Jewish Troubles in Alexandria and the Athanasian Controversy, Illustrated by Texts from Greek Papyri.* London: British Museum.

Berger, Klaus. 1976. "Volksversammlung und Gemeinde Gottes: Zu den Anfängen der christlichen Verwendung von 'ekklesia.'" *ZTK* 73:167–207.

——. 1977. "Almosen für Israel: Zum historischen Kontext der paulinischen Kollekte." *NTS* 23:180–204.

Berger, Peter L. 1967. *The Sacred Canopy: Elements of a Sociological Theory of Religion.* Garden City, N.Y.: Doubleday.

Berger, Peter L., and Luckmann, Thomas. 1966. *The Social Construction of Reality: A Treatise in the Sociology of Knowledge.* Garden City, N.Y.: Doubleday.

Bergmeier, Roland. 1970. "Loyalität als Gegenstand paulinischer Paraklese: Eine religionsgeschichtlicher Untersuchung zu Röm. 13:1ff. und Jos. B.J. 2.140." *Theokratia: Jahrbuch des Institutum Judaicum Delitzschianum* 1:51–63.

Bernard, J. H. 1912. *The Odes of Solomon.* Texts and Studies, vol. 8, pt. 3. Cambridge: At the University Press.

Best, Ernest. 1955. *One Body in Christ: A Study in the Relationship of the Church to Christ in the Epistles of the Apostle Paul.* London: S.P.C.K.

——. 1972. *A Commentary on the First and Second Epistles to the Thessalonians.* Harper/Black New Testament Commentaries. London: Black; New York: Harper & Row.

Betz, Hans Dieter. 1972. *Der Apostel Paulus und die sokratische Tradition: Eine exegetische Untersuchung zu seiner "Apologie" 2 Korinther 10–13.* Beiträge zur historischen Theologie, 45. Tübingen: Mohr (Siebeck).

_____. 1973. "2 Cor. 6:14–7:1: An Anti-Pauline Fragment?" *JBL* 92:88–108.

_____. 1975. "The Literary Composition and Function of Paul's Letter to the Galatians." *NTS* 21:353–79.

_____. 1979. *Galatians: A Commentary on Paul's Letter to the Churches in Galatia.* Hermeneia. Philadelphia: Fortress.

Bickerman, Elias J. 1949. "Historical Foundations of Post-Biblical Judaism." In *The Jews: Their History, Culture, and Religion,* ed. Louis Finkelstein, vol. 1, pp. 70–114. Philadelphia: Jewish Publication Society.

_____. 1962. "Bénédiction et prière." *RB* 69:524–32.

Bietenhard, Hans. 1977. "Die syrische Dekapolis von Pompeius bis Traian." *ANRW,* pt. 2, vol. 8:220–61.

Billerbeck, Paul. 1964. "Ein Synagogengottesdienst in Jesu Tagen." *ZNW* 55:143–61.

Blalock, Herbert M., Jr. 1967. "Status Inconsistency, Social Mobility, Status Integration, and Structural Effects." *ASR* 32:790–801.

Boehm, Fritz. 1924. "Lares." PW, vol. 12. 1:cols. 806–33.

Bömer, Franz. 1957–63. *Untersuchungen über die Religion der Sklaven in Griechenland und Rom.* Akademie der Wissenschaften . . . Mainz . . . Abhandlungen der geistes- und sozialwissenschaftlichen Klasse. 4 vols. Mainz: Steiner.

Boers, Hendrick W. 1967. "Apocalyptic Eschatology in 1 Corinthians 15." *Int* 21:50–65.

Bogart, John. 1977. *Orthodox and Heretical Perfectionism in the Johannine Community as Evident in the First Epistle of John.* Society of Biblical Literature Dissertation Series, 33. Missoula, Mont.: Scholars.

Borgen, Peder. 1965. *Bread from Heaven: An Exegetical Study of the Concept of Manna in the Gospel of John and the Writings of Philo.* Supplements to Novum Testamentum, 10. Leiden: Brill.

Bornkamm, Günther. 1939. "Taufe und neues Leben bei Paulus." *Theologische Blätter* 18:233–42. References are to the reprint in *Das Ende des Gesetzes: Paulusstudien.* 4th ed. Munich: Kaiser, 1963, pp. 34–50.

_____. 1963. "Das Anathema in die urchristlichen Abendmahlsliturgie." In *Das Ende des Gesetzes: Paulusstudien.* 4th ed. Munich: Kaiser, pp. 123–32. References are to the translation by Paul L. Hammer in *Early Christian Experience.* London: SCM; New York: Harper & Row, 1969, pp. 169–79.

Botte, Bernard. 1963. *La Tradition apostolique de Saint Hippolyte: Essai de reconstruction.* Liturgiewissenschaftliche Quellen und Forschungen, 39. Münster: Aschendorff.

Boulvert, Gérard. 1970. *Esclaves et affranchis impériaux sous le haut-empire romain: Rôle politique et administratif.* Naples: Jovene.

_____. 1974. *Domestique et fonctionnaire sous le haut-empire romain: La Condition de l'affranchi et de l'esclave du prince.* Paris: Belles Lettres.

Bousset, Wilhelm. 1901. "Die Himmelsreise der Seele." *Archiv für Re-*

ligionswissenschaft 4:136–69, 229–73. References are to the separate reprint, Darmstadt: Wissenschaftliche Buchgesellschaft, 1960.

Bowersock, Glen W. 1965. *Augustus and the Greek World.* Oxford: Clarendon Press.

Brandis, C. G. 1905. "Ekklēsia." *PW,* vol. 5:cols. 2163–2200.

Braumann, Georg. 1962. *Vorpaulinische christliche Taufverkündigung bei Paulus.* Beiträge zur Wissenschaft vom Alten und Neuen Testament, 82. Stuttgart: Kohlhammer.

Broneer, Oscar. 1930. *Terracotta Lamps. Corinth: Results,* no. 4, pt. 2. Cambridge, Mass.: Harvard University Press.

_____. 1954. *The South Stoa and Its Roman Successors. Corinth: Results,* vol. 1, pt. 4. Princeton: Princeton University Press.

_____. 1962. "The Apostle Paul and the Isthmian Games." *BA* 25:1–31.

_____. 1971. "Paul and the Pagan Cults at Isthmia." *HTR* 64:169–87.

_____, ed. 1973. *Isthmia.* Vol. 2: *Topography and Architecture.* Princeton: American School of Classical Studies, Athens.

Brooten, Bernadette. 1977. "'Junia . . . outstanding among the Apostles' (Rom. 16:7)." In *Women Priests: A Catholic Commentary on the Vatican Declaration,* ed. Leonard Swidler and Arlene Swidler, pp. 141–44. New York: Paulist.

Brown, Peter R. L. 1970. "Sorcery, Demons, and the Rise of Christianity: From Late Antiquity into the Middle Ages." In *Witchcraft Confessions and Accusations,* ed. Mary Douglas, pp. 17–45. Association of Social Anthropologists Monographs, 9. London: Tavistock. References are to the reprint in *Religion and Society in the Age of St. Augustine.* London: Faber & Faber, 1972, pp. 119–46.

_____. 1971. "The Rise and Function of the Holy Man in Late Antiquity." *JRomSt* 61:80–101.

Bruce, Frederick F. 1976. "The New Testament and Classical Studies." *NTS* 22:229–42.

_____. 1977. *Paul, Apostle of the Heart Set Free.* Grand Rapids: Eerdmans.

Bruneau, Philippe. 1970. *Recherches sur les cultes de Délos à l'époque hellénistique et à l'époque impériale.* Bibliothèque des Écoles françaises d'Athènes et de Rome, 217. Paris: Boccard.

Buckland, W. W. 1908. *The Roman Law of Slavery: The Condition of the Slave in Private Law from Augustus to Justinian.* Cambridge: At the University Press.

Bujard, Walter. 1973. *Stilanalytische Untersuchungen zum Kolosserbrief als Beitrag zur Methodik von Sprachvergleichen.* Studien zur Umwelt des Neuen Testaments, 11. Göttingen: Vandenhoeck & Ruprecht.

Bultmann, Rudolf K. 1923. "Der religionsgeschichtliche Hintergrund des Prologs zum Johannes-Evangelium." In *Eucharisterion: Festschrift für Hermann Gunkel,* ed. Hans Schmidt, pt. 2, pp. 1–26. Forschungen zur Religion und Literatur des Alten und Neuen Testamentes, n.s., 19. Göttingen: Vandenhoeck & Ruprecht.

_____. 1932. "Römer 7 und die Anthropologie des Paulus." In *Imago Dei: Festschrift für Gustav Krüger,* ed. Hans Bornkamm, pp. 53–62. Giessen: Töpelmann. Translated as "Romans 7 and the Anthropology of Paul." In *Existence and Faith: Shorter Writings of Rudolf Bultmann,* ed. Schubert M. Ogden, pp. 147–57. New York: Meridian, 1960.

_____. 1941. "Neues Testament und Mythologie." In idem, ed., *Offenbarung und Heilsgeschehen.* Beiträge zur evangelischen Theologie, 7. Munich: Lempp. References are to the translation by Reginald Fuller, "The New Testament and Mythology." In *Kerygma and Myth: A Theological Debate,* ed. Hans Werner Bartsch, vol. 1, pp. 1–44. 2d ed. London: S.P.C.K., 1964.

_____. 1948–53. *Theologie des Neuen Testaments.* 2 vols. Neue theologische Grundrisse. Tübingen: Mohr (Siebeck). References are to the translation by Kendrick Grobel, *Theology of the New Testament.* 2 vols. New York: Scribner's, 1951–55.

_____. 1958. *Jesus Christ and Mythology.* New York: Scribner's.

Burford, Alison. 1972. *Craftsmen in Greek and Roman Society.* Aspects of Greek and Roman Life. London: Thames and Hudson; Ithaca, N.Y.: Cornell University Press.

Burkert, Walter. 1961. "Hellenistische Pseudopythagorica." *Philologus* 105:16–42, 226–46.

_____. 1962. *Weisheit und Wissenschaft: Studien zu Pythagoras, Philolaos und Platon.* Nuremberg: H. Carl. References are to the translation by E. L. Minar, Jr., *Lore and Science in Ancient Pythagoreanism.* Cambridge, Mass.: Harvard University Press, 1972.

Burr, Viktor. 1955. *Tiberius Iulius Alexander.* Antiquitas, series 1. Abhandlungen zur alten Geschichte, 1. Bonn: Habelt.

Burridge, Kenelm. 1969. *New Heaven, New Earth: A Study of Millennarian Activities.* London and New York: Schocken.

Cadbury, Henry J. 1926. "Lexical Notes on Luke-Acts III: Luke's Interest in Lodging." *JBL* 45:305–22.

_____. 1927. *The Making of Luke-Acts.* Reprint. London: S.P.C.K., 1958.

Caird, George B. 1962. "The Chronology of the NT." *IDB,* vol. 1, pp. 599–607.

Callan, Terrance. 1976. "The Law and the Mediator: Gal. 3:19b–20." Ph.D. dissertation, Yale University.

Cameron, Averil. 1980. "Neither Male nor Female." *Greece and Rome,* 2d ser. 27:60–68.

Campenhausen, Hans von. 1972. "Das Bekenntnis in Urchristentum." *ZNW* 63:210–53.

Carrington, Philip. 1940. *The Primitive Christian Catechism: A Study in the Epistles.* Cambridge: At the University Press.

Case, Shirley Jackson. 1913. "The Nature of Primitive Christianity." *AJT* 17:63–79.

Casson, Lionel. 1974. *Travel in the Ancient World.* London: Allen and Unwin.

Cavallin, Hans C. 1979. "Leben nach dem Tode in Spätjudentum und im frühen Christentum. I. Spätjudentum." *ANRW*, pt. 2, vol. 19.1: 240–345.

Chadwick, Henry. 1965. *Origen, Contra Celsum*. Cambridge: At the University Press.

Chantraine, Heinrich. 1967. *Freigelassene und Sklaven im Dienst des römischen Kaiser: Studien zu ihrer Nomenklatur*. Forschungen zur antiken Sklaverei, 1. Wiesbaden: Steiner.

Charlesworth, M. P. 1926. *Trade Routes and Commerce in the Roman Empire*. 2d ed. Cambridge: At the University Press.

Chevallier, Raymond. 1972. *Les Voies romaines*. Paris: Armand Colin. References are to the translation by N. H. Field, *Roman Roads*. Berkeley: University of California Press, 1976.

Clark, Elizabeth, A. 1979. *Jerome, Chrysostom, and Friends: Essays and Translations*. Studies in Women and Religion, 1. New York and Toronto: Mellen.

Classen, C. Joachim. 1968. "Poetry and Rhetoric in Lucretius." *TAPA* 99:77–118.

Cohen, Benjamin. 1975. "La Notion d'‘ordo' dans la Rome antique." *Bullétin de l'Association G. Budé* 1975:259–82.

Collart, Paul. 1937. *Philippes: Ville de Macédoine depuis ses origines jusqu'à la fin de l'époque romaine*. École française d'Athènes travaux et mémoires, 5. Paris: Boccard.

Collins, John J., ed. 1979. *Apocalypse: The Morphology of a Genre*. Semeia, 14. Chico, Calif.: Scholars.

Conzelmann, Hans. 1965. "Paulus und die Weisheit." *NTS* 12:231–44.

——. 1966. "Luke's Place in the Development of Early Christianity." In *Studies in Luke-Acts: Essays Presented in Honor of Paul Schubert*, ed. Leander E. Keck and J. Louis Martin, pp. 298–316. Nashville and New York: Abingdon.

——. 1969. *Der erste Brief an die Korinther*. 11th ed. Kritisch-exegetischer Kommentar über das Neue Testament, 5. Göttingen: Vandenhoeck & Ruprecht. References are to the translation by James W. Leitch, *1 Corinthians: A Commentary on the First Epistle to the Corinthians*. Hermeneia. Philadelphia: Fortress, 1975.

Corwin, Virginia. 1960. *St. Ignatius and Christianity in Antioch*. Yale Studies in Religion, 1. New Haven and London: Yale University Press.

Coser, Lewis. 1956. *The Functions of Social Conflict*. New York: Free Press.

Cracco Ruggini, Lellia. 1980. "Nuclei immigrati e forze indigene in tre grande centri commerciali dell'impero." *Memoirs of the American Academy in Rome* 36:55–76.

Crouch, James E. 1973. *The Origin and Intention of the Colossian Haustafel*. Forschungen zur Religion und Literatur des Alten und Neuen Testamentes, 109. Göttingen: Vandenhoeck & Ruprecht.

Cullmann, Oscar. 1948. *Die Tauflehre des Neuen Testaments: Erwachsenen-*

und Kindertaufe. Zurich: Zwingli. References are to the translation by J. K. S. Reid, *Baptism in the New Testament.* Studies in Biblical Theology, 1. London: SCM; Chicago: Regnery, 1950.

————. 1949. *Die ersten christlichen Glaubensbekenntnisse.* Theologische Studien, 15. Zollikon-Zurich: Evangelischer Verlag. References are to the translation by J. K. S. Reid, *The Earliest Christian Confessions.* London: Lutterworth, 1949.

————. 1963. *The State in the New Testament.* Rev. ed. London: SCM.

Cumont, Franz. 1933. "La Grande Inscription Bachique du Metropolitan Museum, II: Commentaire religieuse de l'inscription." *AJA,* 2d ser. 37:215–31.

Dahl, Nils Alstrup. 1941. *Das Volk Gottes: Eine Untersuchung zum Kirchenbewusstsein des Urchristentums.* Reprint. Darmstadt: Wissenschaftliche Buchgesellschaft, 1963.

————. 1944. "Dopet i Efesierbrevet." *Svensk teologisk kvartalskrift* 21: 85–103.

————. 1947. "Anamnesis: Mémoire et commémoration dans le christianisme primitif." *Studia Theologica* 1:69–95. References are to the translation, "Anamnesis: Memory and Commemoration in Early Christianity." In *Jesus in the Memory of the Early Church.* Minneapolis: Augsburg, 1976, pp. 11–29.

————. 1951. "Adresse und Proömium des Epheserbriefs." *TZ* 7:241–64.

————. 1954. "Formgeschichtliche Beobachtungen zur Christusverkündigung in der Gemeindepredigt." In *Neutestamentliche Studien für Rudolf Bultmann,* ed. Walter Eltester, pp. 3–9. Beihefte zur *ZNW* 21. Berlin: De Gruyter. References are to the translation, "Form-critical Observations on Early Christian Preaching." In *Jesus in the Memory of the Early Church.* Minneapolis: Augsburg, 1976, pp. 30–36.

————. 1955. "The Origin of Baptism." In *Interpretationes ad Vetus Testamentum Pertinentes Sigmundo Mowinckel Septuagenario Missae,* ed. Nils A. Dahl and A. S. Kapelrud, pp. 36–52. Oslo: Land og Kirke.

————. 1956. "Misjonsteologien i Romerbrevet." *Norsk Tidsskrift for Misjon* 10:44–60. References are to the translation, "The Missionary Theology in the Epistle to the Romans." In Dahl 1977, 70–94.

————. 1960. "Der gekreuzigte Messias." In *Der historische Jesus und der kerygmatische Christus,* ed. Helmut Ristow and Karl Matthiae, pp. 149–69. Berlin: Evangelische Verlagsanstalt. Translated as "The Crucified Messiah." In Dahl 1974, 10–36.

————. 1965. "The Particularity of the Pauline Epistles as a Problem in the Ancient Church." In *Neotestamentica et Patristica: Freundesgabe Oscar Cullmann.* Supplements to Novum Testamentum, 6. Leiden: Brill, pp. 261–71.

————. 1967. "Paul and the Church at Corinth according to 1 Corinthians 1:10–4:21." In *Christian History and Interpretation: Studies Presented to John Knox,* ed. William R. Farmer, C. F. D. Moule, and Richard R. Niebuhr, pp. 313–35. Cambridge: At the University Press.

_____. 1969. "Motsigelser i Skriften—et gammelt hermeneutiskt problem." *Svensk teologisk kvartalskrift* 45:22–36. References are to the translation, "Contradictions in Scripture." In Dahl 1977, 155–77.

_____. 1973. "Paul's Letter to the Galatians; Epistolary Genre, Content, and Structure." Paper presented at the annual meeting of the Society of Biblical Literature, Chicago 1973.

_____. 1974. *The Crucified Messiah and Other Essays.* Minneapolis: Augsburg.

_____. 1976a. "The Purpose of Luke-Acts." In *Jesus in the Memory of the Early Church.* Minneapolis: Augsburg, pp. 87–98.

_____. 1976b. "Letter." *IDBS*, pp. 538–41.

_____. 1977. *Studies in Paul: Theology for the Early Christian Mission.* Minneapolis: Augsburg.

_____. 1978. Review of Sanders 1977. *Religious Studies Review* 4:153–58.

Danby, Herbert, ed. and trans. 1933. *The Mishnah: Translated from the Hebrew with Introduction and Brief Explanatory Notes.* Oxford: Oxford University Press.

Davies, W. D. 1974. *The Gospel and the Land: Early Christianity and Jewish Territorial Doctrine.* Berkeley, Los Angeles, and London: University of California Press.

Deichgräber, Reinhard. 1967. *Gotteshymnus und Christushymnus in der frühen Christenheit.* Göttingen: Vandenhoeck & Ruprecht.

Deissmann, Gustav Adolf. 1911. *Paulus: Eine kultur- und religionsgeschichtliche Skizze.* Tübingen: Mohr (Siebeck). References are to the translation by William E. Wilson, *Paul: A Study in Social and Religious History.* 2d ed. New York: Harper & Row, 1957.

De Lacy, P. H. 1948. "Lucretius and the History of Epicureanism." *TAPA* 79:12–23.

Delling, Gerhard. 1965. "Zur Taufe von 'Häusern' im Urchristentum." *NovT* 7:285–311.

Deutsch, Morton. 1968. "Group Behavior." *IESS*, vol. 6, pp. 265–76.

DeWitt, Norman. 1936a. "Epicurean Contubernium." *TAPA* 67:59–60.

_____. 1936b. "Organization and Structure of Epicurean Groups." *Classical Philology* 31:205–11.

_____. 1954a. *Epicurus and His Philosophy.* Reprint. Cleveland and New York: Meridian, 1967.

_____. 1954b. *St. Paul and Epicurus.* Minneapolis: University of Minnesota.

Dibelius, Martin. 1931. "Zur Formgeschichte des Neuen Testaments (ausserhalb der Evangelien)." *TRu*, n.s. 3:207–42.

_____. 1937. *An die Thessalonicher I, II; An die Philipper.* Handbuch zum Neuen Testament, 11. Tübingen: Mohr (Siebeck).

_____. 1951. *Aufsätze zur Apostelgeschichte.* Edited by Heinrich Greeven. Forschungen zur Religion und Literatur des Alten und Neuen Testamentes, n.s., 42. Göttingen: Vandenhoeck & Ruprecht. References are to the translation by Mary Ling, *Studies in the Acts of the Apostles.* London: SCM, 1956.

Dibelius, Martin, and Greeven, Heinrich. 1953. *An die Kolosser, Epheser, an Philemon.* 3d ed. Handbuch zum Neuen Testament, 12. Tübingen: Mohr (Siebeck).

Dinkler, Erich. 1952. "Zum Problem der Ethik bei Paulus." *ZTK* 49: 167–200.

_____. 1954. "Jesu Wort vom Kreuztragen." In *Neutestamentliche Studien für Rudolf Bultmann,* ed. Walter Eltester, pp. 110–29. Beihefte zur *ZNW* 21. Berlin: De Gruyter.

_____. 1962a. "Taufe, II. Im Urchristentum." *RGG*³ vol. 6,cols. 627–37.

_____. 1962b. "Die Taufterminologie in 2 Kor. 1:21f." In *Neotestamentica et Patristica: Freundesgabe Oscar Cullmann.* Supplements to Novum Testamentum, 6. Leiden: Brill, pp. 173–91.

Dix, Gregory. 1937. *The Treatise on the Apostolic Tradition of St. Hippolytus of Rome.* London: S.P.C.K.

Dobschütz, Ernst von. 1909. *Die Thessalonicher-Briefe.* 7th ed. Kritisch-exegetischer Kommentar über das Neue Testament, 10. Göttingen: Vandenhoeck & Ruprecht.

Dodd, Charles Harold. 1952. *According to the Scriptures: The Substructure of New Testament Theology.* London: Nisbet.

Dodds, E. R. 1965. *Pagan and Christian in an Age of Anxiety: Some Aspects of Religious Experience from Marcus Aurelius to Constantine.* References are to the Norton Library edition, New York: Norton, 1970.

Doty, William G. 1973. *Letters in Primitive Christianity.* Philadelphia: Fortress.

Douglas, Mary. 1973. *Natural Symbols: Explorations in Cosmology.* 2d ed. London: Barrie & Jenkins.

Downey, Glanville. 1958. "The Size of the Population of Antioch." *TAPA* 89:84–91.

_____. 1961. *A History of Antioch in Syria.* Princeton: Princeton University Press.

Downing, J. D. H. 1964. "Possible Baptismal References in Galatians." In *Studia Evangelica,* ed. Frank L. Cross, pt. 1, pp. 551–56. Papers presented to the Second International Congress on New Testament Studies held at Christ Church, Oxford, 1961. Texte und Untersuchungen, 87. Berlin: Akademie.

Dungan, David. 1971. *The Sayings of Jesus in the Churches of Paul.* Philadelphia: Fortress.

Dupont, Jacques. 1955. "Chronologie paulinienne." *RB* 62:55–59.

Dupré, Louis. 1980. "Marx's Critique of Culture and Its Interpretations." *Review of Metaphysics* 24:91–121.

Durkheim, Emile. 1912. *Les Formes élémentaires de la vie religieuse: Le Système totémique en Australie.* Paris: Alcan. References are to the translation by J. W. Swain, *The Elementary Forms of the Religious Life.* 1915. Reprint. New York: Free Press, 1965.

Eck, Werner. 1971. "Das Eindringen des Christentums in den Senatorenstand bis zu Konstantin d. Gr." *Chiron* 1:381–406.

Edson, Charles. 1948. "Cults of Thessalonica." *HTR* 41:153–204.

Elliger, Winfried. 1978. *Paulus in Griechenland: Philippi, Thessaloniki, Athen, Korinth.* Stuttgarter Bibelstudien, 92/92. Stuttgart: Katholisches Bibelwerk.

Ellis, E. Earle. 1957. "A Note on First Corinthians 10:4." *JBL* 76:53–56.

———. 1971. "Paul and his Co-workers." *NTS* 17:437–52. References are to the reprint in *Prophecy and Hermeneutic in Early Christianity,* pp. 3–22. Wissenschaftliche Untersuchungen zum Neuen Testament, 18. Tübingen: Mohr (Siebeck); Grand Rapids: Eerdmans, 1978.

Evans, Donald. 1969. *The Logic of Self-Involvement.* New York: Herder.

Fascher, Erich. 1955. "Zur Taufe des Paulus." *TLZ* 80:cols. 643–48.

Feldman, Louis. 1950. "Jewish 'Sympathizers' in Classical Literature and Inscriptions." *TAPA* 81:200–208.

Festinger, Leon. 1957. *A Theory of Cognitive Dissonance.* Stanford: Stanford University Press.

Festinger, Leon; Riecken, Henry W.; and Schachter, Stanley. 1956. *When Prophecy Fails: A Social and Psychological Study of a Modern Group That Predicted the Destruction of the World.* Reprint. New York: Harper & Row, 1964.

Festugière, André Marie Jean. 1946. *Épicure et ses dieux.* Paris: Presses universitaires de France. References are to the translation by C. W. Chilton, *Epicurus and His Gods.* Cambridge, Mass.: Harvard University Press, 1956.

Feuillet, André. 1966. *Le Christ Sagesse de Dieu d'après les épîtres pauliniennes.* Études bibliques. Paris: Gabalda.

Filson, Floyd V. 1939. "The Significance of the Early House Churches." *JBL* 58:109–12.

Finegan, Jack. 1962. "Thessalonica." *IDB,* vol. 4, p. 629.

Finley, Moses I. 1973. *The Ancient Economy.* Sather Classical Lectures, 43. Berkeley: University of California Press.

Fitzmyer, Joseph A., S.J. 1961. "Qumran and the Interpolated Paragraph in 2 Cor. 6:14–7:1." *CBQ* 23:271–80. Reprinted in *Essays on the Semitic Background of the New Testament,* pp. 205–17. London: Chapman, 1971; Missoula, Mont.: Scholars, 1974.

Flory, Marleen B. 1975. "Family and 'Familia': A Study of Social Relations in Slavery." Ph.D. dissertation, Yale University.

Forkman, Göran. 1972. *The Limits of the Religious Community: Expulsion from the Religious Community within the Qumran Sect, within Rabbinic Judaism, and within Primitive Christianity.* Coniectanea Biblica, New Testament Series, 5. Lund: Gleerup.

Foucart, Paul. 1873. *Des associations religieuses chez les Grecs: Thiases, éranes, orgéons, avec le texte des inscriptions rélatives à ces associations.* Paris: Klincksieck.

Fowler, H. N., ed. 1932. *Introduction, Topography, Architecture. Corinth: Results,* vol. 1, pt. 1. Cambridge, Mass.: Harvard University Press.

Francis, Fred O., and Meeks, Wayne A. 1975. *Conflict at Colossae: A Problem in the Interpretation of Early Christianity Illustrated by Selected Modern Studies.* Rev. ed. Sources for Biblical Study, 4. Missoula, Mont.: Scholars.

Fraser, P. M. 1960. "Two Studies on the Cult of Sarapis in the Hellenistic World." *Opuscula Atheniensa* 3:1–54.

Frederiksen, M. W. 1975. "Theory, Evidence, and the Ancient Economy." *JRomSt* 65:164–71.

Frend, William H. C. 1952. *The Donatist Church: A Movement of Protest in Roman North Africa.* Oxford: Clarendon Press.

_____. 1965. *Martyrdom and Persecution in the Early Church: A Study of a Conflict from the Maccabees to Donatus.* Reprint. New York: New York University Press, 1967.

_____. 1979. "Town and Countryside in Early Christianity." In *The Church in Town and Countryside,* ed. Derek Baker, pp. 25–42. Studies in Church History, 16. Oxford: Blackwell.

Friedländer, Ludwig. 1901. *Darstellungen aus der Sittengeschichte Roms in der Zeit von August bis zum Ausgang der Antonine.* 7th ed. rev. 2 vols. Leipzig: Hirzel. References are to the translation by L. A. Magnus and J. Freese, *Roman Life and Manners under the Early Empire.* 4 vols. Reprint. New York: Barnes & Noble, 1968.

Friedrich, Carl J. 1958. "Authority, Reason and Discretion." In *Authority.* Nomos, 1. Cambridge, Mass.: Harvard University Press, pp. 28–48.

Fritz, Kurt von. 1960. "Mathematiker und Akusmatiker bei den alten Pythagoreern." *Sitzungsberichte der bayerischen Akademie der Wissenschaften, philosophisch-historische Klasse* 11.

Funk, Robert W. 1966. *Language, Hermeneutic, and Word of God: The Problem of Language in the New Testament and Contemporary Theology.* New York: Harper & Row.

_____. 1967. "The Apostolic *Parousia:* Form and Significance." In *Christian History and Interpretation: Studies Presented to John Knox,* ed. William R. Farmer, C. F. D. Moule, and Richard R. Niebuhr, pp. 249–68. Cambridge: At the University Press.

Gärtner, Bertil. 1959. *John 6 and the Jewish Passover.* Coniectanea Neotestamentica, 17. Lund: Gleerup.

Gagé, Jean. 1964. *Les Classes sociales dans l'empire romain.* Bibliothèque historique. Paris: Payot.

Gager, John G. 1975. *Kingdom and Community: The Social World of Early Christianity.* Englewood Cliffs, N.J.: Prentice-Hall.

_____. 1979. Review of R. M. Grant 1977, Malherbe 1977a, and Theissen 1979. *Religious Studies Review* 5:174–80.

Gamble, Harry A., Jr. 1977. *The Textual History of the Letter to the Romans: A Study in Textual and Literary Criticism.* Grand Rapids: Eerdmans.

Garfinkel, Alan. 1981. *Forms of Explanation: Rethinking the Questions of Social Theory.* New Haven and London: Yale University Press.

Gayer, Roland. 1976. *Die Stellung des Sklaven in den paulinischen Gemeinden und bei Paulus: Zugleich ein sozialgeschichtlich vergleichender Beitrag zur Wertung des Sklaven in der Antike.* Europäische Hochschulschriften, series 23, Theologie, 78. Bern: Lang.

Gealy, Fred D. 1962. "Asiarch." *IDB,* vol. 1, p. 259.

Geertz, Clifford. 1957. "Ethos, World View, and the Analysis of Sacred Symbols." *Antioch Review* 17:421–37. Reprinted in Geertz 1973, 126–41.

_____. 1966. "Religion as a Cultural System." In *Anthropological Approaches to the Study of Religion,* ed. Michael Barton, pp. 1–46. Association of Social Anthropologists Monographs, 3. London: Tavistock.

_____. 1973. *The Interpretation of Cultures: Selected Essays.* New York: Basic Books.

Gellner, Ernest. 1962. "Concepts and Society." In *Transactions of the Fifth World Congress of Sociology* 1:153–83. References are to the reprint in *Sociological Theory and Philosophical Analysis,* ed. Dorothy Emmet and Alasdair MacIntyre, pp. 115–49. London and New York: Macmillan, 1970.

Gennep, Arnold van. 1909. *Les Rites de passage: Étude systématique des rites de la porte.* . . . Paris: Nourry. Translated by M. B. Vizedom and G. L. Caffee, *The Rites of Passage.* London: Routledge and Kegan Paul; Chicago: University of Chicago Press, 1960.

Georgi, Dieter. 1964a. *Die Gegner des Paulus im 2. Korintherbrief: Studien zur religiösen Propaganda in der Spätantike.* Wissenschaftliche Monographien zum Alten und Neuen Testament, 11. Neukirchen: Neukirchener Verlag.

_____. 1964b. "Der vorpaulinische Hymnus Phil. 2:6–11." In *Zeit und Geschichte: Dankesgabe an Rudolf Bultmann zum 80. Geburtstag,* ed. Erich Dinkler, pp. 263–93. Tübingen: Mohr (Siebeck).

_____. 1965. *Die Geschichte der Kollekte des Paulus für Jerusalem.* Theologische Forschung, 38. Hamburg-Bergstedt: Evangelischer Verlag.

_____. 1976. "Socioeconomic Reasons for the 'Divine Man' as a Propagandistic Pattern." In *Aspects of Religious Propaganda in Judaism and Early Christianity,* ed. Elisabeth Schüssler Fiorenza, pp. 27–42. Notre Dame: University of Notre Dame Press.

Ginzberg, Louis. 1909–38. *The Legends of the Jews.* 7 vols. Philadelphia: Jewish Publication Society.

Goffman, Irwin. 1957. "Status Consistency and Preference for Change in Power Distribution." *ASR* 22:275–81.

Goodenough, Erwin Ramsdell. 1928. "The Political Philosophy of Hellenistic Kingship." *Yale Classical Studies* 1:55–102.

_____. 1929. *The Jurisprudence of the Jewish Courts in Egypt: Legal Administration by the Jews under the Early Roman Empire as Described by Philo Judaeus.* New Haven and London: Yale University Press.

_____. 1938. *The Politics of Philo Judaeus: Practice and Theory.* New Haven and London: Yale University Press.

_____. 1953–68. *Jewish Symbols in the Greco-Roman Period*. 13 vols. Bollingen Series, 37. New York: Pantheon; Princeton: Princeton University Press.

_____. 1962. *An Introduction to Philo Judaeus*. 2d ed. Oxford: Blackwell.

_____. 1966. "The Perspective of Acts." In *Studies in Luke-Acts*, ed. Leander E. Keck and J. Louis Martyn, pp. 51–59. Nashville and New York: Abingdon.

Goodman, Felicitas D. 1972. *Speaking in Tongues: A Cross-Cultural Study of Glossolalia*. Chicago and London: University of Chicago Press.

Goodspeed, Edgar J. 1950. "Gaius Titius Justus." *JBL* 69:382–83.

Goody, Jack. 1961. "Religion and Ritual: The Definitional Problem." *British Journal of Sociology* 12:142–64.

Gordon, Mary. 1931. "The Freedman's Son in Municipal Life." *JRomSt* 21:65–77.

Grail, Augustin, O. P. 1951. "Le baptême dans l'Épître aux Galates." *RB* 58:503–20.

Grant, Michael. 1971. *Cities of Vesuvius: Pompeii and Herculaneum*. London: Weidenfeld and Nicholson.

Grant, Robert M. 1948. "Pliny and the Christians." *HTR* 41:273–74. References are to the reprint in *After the New Testament: Studies in Early Christian Literature and Theology*. Philadelphia: Fortress, 1967, pp. 55–56.

_____. 1977. *Early Christianity and Society: Seven Studies*. New York: Harper & Row.

Greeven, Heinrich. 1952. "Propheten, Lehrer, Vorsteher bei Paulus." *ZNW* 44:1–43. References are to the reprint in Kertelge 1977, 305–61.

Griffiths, J. Gwyn. 1975. *Apuleius of Madauros, The Isis Book (Metamorphoses, Book XI)*. Études préliminaires aux religions orientales dans l'empire romain, 39. Leiden: Brill.

Gülzow, Henneke. 1969. *Christentum und Sklaverei in den ersten drei Jahrhunderten*. Bonn: Habelt.

_____. 1974. "Die sozialen Gegebenheiten der altchristlichen Mission." In *Kirchengeschichte als Missionsgeschichte*, ed. Heinzgünther Frohnes and Uwe W. Knorr, vol. 1, pp. 189–226. Munich: Kaiser.

Güttgemanns, Erhardt. 1966. *Der leidende Apostel und sein Herr*. Göttingen: Vandenhoeck & Ruprecht.

Hadas, Moses, ed. and trans. 1964. *Three Greek Romances*. The Library of Liberal Arts. Indianapolis: Bobbs-Merrill.

Hadas, Moses, and Smith, Morton. 1965. *Heroes and Gods: Spiritual Biographies in Antiquity*. Religious Perspectives, 13. New York: Harper & Row.

Haenchen, Ernst. 1959. *Die Apostelgeschichte*. 12th ed. Kritisch-exegetischer Kommentar über das Neue Testament, 3. Göttingen: Vandenhoeck & Ruprecht. References are to the translation by Bernard Noble and Gerald Shinn, *The Acts of the Apostles: A Commentary*. Philadelphia: Westminster; Oxford: Blackwell, 1971.

_____. 1961. "Das 'Wir' in der Apostelgeschichte und das Itinerar." *ZTK*

58:329–66. References are to the reprint in *Gott und Mensch: Gesammelte Aufsätze.* Tübingen: Mohr (Siebeck), 1965, pp. 227–64.

———. 1966. "The Book of Acts as Source Material for the History of Earliest Christianity." In *Studies in Luke-Acts: Essays Presented in Honor of Paul Schubert,* ed. Leander E. Keck and J. Louis Martyn, pp. 258–78. Nashville and New York: Abingdon.

Hahn, Ferdinand. 1963. *Christologische Hoheitstitel: Ihre Geschichte im frühen Christentum.* Forschungen zur Religion und Literatur des Alten und Neuen Testamentes, 83. Göttingen: Vandenhoeck & Ruprecht. References are to the translation by Harold Knight and George Ogg, *The Titles of Jesus in Christology: Their History in Early Christianity.* London: Lutterworth, 1969.

Hamerton-Kelly, Robert G. 1973. *Pre-Existence, Wisdom, and the Son of Man: A Study of the Idea of Pre-Existence in the New Testament.* Society for New Testament Studies Monograph Series, 21. Cambridge: At the University Press.

Hanfmann, George M. A. 1962. *Letters from Sardis.* Cambridge, Mass.: Harvard University Press.

Harder, Richard. 1944. "Karpocrates von Chalkis und die memphitische Isispropaganda." *Abhandlungen der Preussischen Akademie der Wissenschaften* 14:1–63.

Harnack, Adolf von. 1906. *Die Mission und Ausbreitung des Christentums in den ersten drei Jahrhunderten.* 2d rev. ed. Leipzig: Hinrichs. References are to the translation by James Moffatt, *The Mission and Expansion of Christianity in the First Three Centuries.* 2 vols. London: Williams & Norgate, 1908. Reprint, vol. 1. New York: Harper & Row, 1962.

Harris, J. Rendel. 1917. *The Origin of the Prologue to St. John's Gospel.* Cambridge: At the University Press.

Hatch, Edwin. 1892. *The Organization of the Early Christian Churches.* 4th ed. Bampton Lectures for 1880. London: Longmans, Green.

Hay, David M. 1973. *Glory at the Right Hand: Psalm 110 in Early Christianity.* Society of Biblical Literature Monograph Series, 18. Nashville and New York: Abingdon.

Hayes, John W. 1973. "Roman Pottery from the South Stoa at Corinth." *Hesperia* 42:416–70.

Hegermann, Harald. 1961. *Die Vorstellung vom Schöpfungsmittler im hellenistischen Judentum und Urchristentum.* Texte und Untersuchungen, 82. Berlin: Akademie.

Heinemann, Isaac. 1929–32. *Philons griechische und jüdische Bildung: Kulturvergleichende Untersuchungen zu Philons Darstellung der jüdischen Gesetze.* Reprint. Darmstadt: Wissenschaftliche Buchgesellschaft, 1962.

Heinemann, Joseph. 1964. *Prayer in the Period of the Tannai'm and the Amora'im* [in Hebrew]. References are to the translation *Prayer in the Talmud: Forms and Patterns.* Studia Judaica, 9. Berlin: De Gruyter, 1977.

Heinrici, [C. F.] Georg. 1876. "Die Christengemeinde Korinths und die religiösen Genossenschaften der Griechen." *Zeitschrift für Wissenschaftliche Theologie* 19:464–526.

———. 1888. *Kritisch-Exegetisches Handbuch über den ersten Brief an die Korinther.* 7th ed. Kritisch-exegetischer Kommentar über das Neue Testament, 5. Göttingen: Vandenhoeck & Ruprecht.

———. 1890. *Der Zweite Brief an die Korinther.* 7th ed. Kritisch-exegetischer Kommentar über das Neue Testament, 6. Göttingen: Vandenhoeck & Ruprecht.

Hellholm, David, ed. 1982. *Apocalypticism in the Mediterranean World and the Near East: Proceedings of the International Colloquium on Apocalypticism, Uppsala, August 12–17, 1979.* Tübingen: Mohr (Siebeck).

Hengel, Martin. 1966. "Die Synagogeninschrift von Stobi." *ZNW* 57: 145–83.

———. 1971*a*. "Die Ursprünge der christlichen Mission." *NTS* 18:15–38.

———. 1971*b*. "Proseuche und Synagoge: Jüdische Gemeinde, Gotteshaus und Gottesdienst in der Diaspora und in Palästina." In *Tradition und Glaube: Das frühe Christentum in seiner Umwelt: Festgabe für Karl Georg Kuhn,* ed. Gert Jeremias, Heinz-Wolfgang Kuhn, and Hartmut Stegemann, pp. 157–83. Göttingen: Vandenhoeck & Ruprecht.

———. 1972. "Christologie und neutestamentliche Chronologie: Zu einer Aporie in der Geschichte des Urchristentums." In *Neues Testament und Geschichte: Historisches Geschehen und Deutung im Neuen Testament: Oscar Cullmann zum 70. Geburtstag,* ed. Heinrich Baltensweiler and Bo Reicke, pp. 43–67. Zurich: Theologischer Verlag; Tübingen: Mohr (Siebeck).

———. 1976. *Juden, Griechen, und Barbaren: Aspekte der Hellenisierung des Judentums in vorchristlicher Zeit.* Stuttgarter Bibelstudien, 76. Stuttgart: Katholisches Bibelwerk. References are to the translation by John Bowden, *Jews, Greeks, and Barbarians: Aspects of the Hellenization of Judaism in the Pre-Christian Period.* London: SCM; Philadelphia: Fortress, 1980.

———. 1979. *Zur urchristlichen Geschichtsschreibung.* Stuttgart: Calver. References are to the translation by John Bowden, *Acts and the History of Earliest Christianity.* London: SCM; Philadelphia: Fortress, 1980.

———. 1980. "Hymnus und Christologie." In *Wort in der Zeit: Neutestamentliche Studien: Festgabe für Karl Heinrich Rengstorf zum 75. Geburtstag,* ed. Wilfrid Haubeck and Michael Bachmann, pp. 1–23. Leiden: Brill.

Hennecke, Edgar, ed. 1959–64. *Neutestamentliche Apokryphen.* 3d ed., revised by Wilhelm Schneemelcher. 2 vols. Tübingen: Mohr (Siebeck). References are to the translation, *New Testament Apocrypha,* ed. R. McL. Wilson. 2 vols. Philadelphia: Westminster; London: Lutterworth, 1963–65.

Héring, Jean. 1959. *La Première Épître de Saint Paul aux Corinthiens.* 2d ed. Commentaire au Nouveau Testament, 7. Neuchâtel: Delachaux et Niestle. References are to the translation by A. W. Heathcote and P. J. Allcock, *The First Epistle of Saint Paul to the Corinthians*. London: Epworth, 1962.

Herzig, Heinz E. 1974. "Probleme des römischen Strassenwesens: Untersuchungen zur Geschichte und Recht." *ANRW*, pt. 2, vol. 1:593–648.

Heyob, Sharon Kelly. 1975. *The Cult of Isis among Women in the Graeco-Roman World*. Études préliminaires aux religions orientales dans l'empire romain, 51. Leiden: Brill.

Hickling, Colin J. A. 1975. "Is the Second Epistle to the Corinthians a Source for Early Church History?" *ZNW* 66:284–87.

Hill, David. 1976. "On Suffering and Baptism in 1 Peter." *NovT* 18:181–89.

Hock, Ronald F. 1978. "Paul's Tentmaking and the Problem of His Social Class." *JBL* 97:555–64.

_____. 1980. *The Social Context of Paul's Ministry: Tentmaking and Apostleship*. Philadelphia: Fortress.

Holladay, Carl H. 1977. *Theios Aner in Hellenistic Judaism*. Society of Biblical Literature Dissertation Series, 40. Missoula, Mont.: Scholars.

Holmberg, Bengt. 1978. *Paul and Power: The Structure of Authority in the Primitive Church as Reflected in the Pauline Epistles*. Coniectanea Biblica, New Testament, 11. Lund: Gleerup. American ed. Philadelphia: Fortress, 1980.

Homans, George C. 1968. "The Study of Groups." *IESS*, vol. 6, pp. 258–65.

_____. 1974. *Social Behavior: Its Elementary Forms*. Rev. ed. New York: Harcourt Brace Jovanovich.

Hommel, Hildebrecht. 1975. "Juden und Christen im kaiserzeitlichen Milet: Überlegungen zur Theaterinschrift." *MDAI* (I) 25:157–95.

Hornung, Carlton A. 1977. "Social Status, Status Inconsistency, and Psychological Stress." *ASR* 42:623–38.

Horsley, Richard A. 1978. "'How can some of you say that there is no resurrection of the dead?' Spiritual Elitism in Corinth." *NovT* 20:203–31.

Humphreys, Sally C. 1969. "History, Economics, and Anthropology: The Work of Karl Polanyi." *History and Theory* 8:165–212.

Hurd, John C. 1976. "Chronology, Pauline." *IDBS*, pp. 166–67.

Ibrahim, Leila; Scranton, Robert; and Brill, Robert. 1976. *Kenchreai, Eastern Port of Corinth. Results of Investigations by the University of Chicago and Indiana University for the American School of Classical Studies at Athens*, vol. 2: *The Panels of Opus Sectile in Glass*. Leiden: Brill.

Isenberg, Sheldon. 1974. "Millenarism in Greco-Roman Palestine." *Religion* 4:26–46.

Jackson, Bernard. 1979. "Legalism." *JJS* 30:1–22.

Jackson, Elton F. 1962. "Status Consistency and Symptoms of Stress." *ASR* 27:469–80.

Jackson, Elton F., and Burke, Peter J. 1965. "Status and Symptoms of Stress: Additive and Interaction Effects." *ASR* 30:556–64.

Jeremias, Joachim. 1949. "Proselytentaufe und NT." *TZ* 5:418–28.

_____. 1954. "πάσχα." *TWNT* 5:895–903. References are to the translation in *TDNT* 5 (1967):896–904.

Jervell, Jacob. 1972. *Luke and the People of God*. Minneapolis: Augsburg.

_____. 1976. "Der schwache Charismatiker." In *Rechtfertigung: Festschrift für Ernst Käsemann zum 70. Geburtstag*, ed. Johannes Friedrich, Wolfgang Pöhlmann, and Peter Stuhlmacher, pp. 185–98. Tübingen: Mohr (Siebeck).

Jewett, Robert. 1979. *A Chronology of Paul's Life*. Philadelphia: Fortress.

_____. 1982. "Romans as an Ambassadorial Letter." *Int* 36:5–20.

Jones, A. H. M. 1955. "The Economic Life of the Towns of the Roman Empire." In *La Ville*, ed. Jean Firenne, pt. 1, pp. 171–85. Recueils de la Société Jean Bodin, 6. Brussels: Libraire encyclopédique.

_____. 1970. "The Caste System in the Later Roman Empire." *Eirene* 8:79–96.

_____. 1971. *The Cities of the Eastern Roman Provinces*. 2d ed., revised by Michael Avi-Yonah et al. Oxford: Clarendon Press.

Judge, Edwin A. 1960a. *The Social Pattern of Christian Groups in the First Century*. London: Tyndale.

_____. 1960b. "The Early Christians as a Scholastic Community." *Journal of Religious History* 1:4–15, 125–37.

_____. 1968. "Paul's Boasting in Relation to Contemporary Professional Practice." *Australian Biblical Review* 16:37–50.

_____. 1972. "St. Paul and Classical Society." *JAC* 15:19–36.

_____. 1979. " 'Antike und Christentum': Towards a Definition of the Field. A Bibliographical Survey." *ANRW*, pt. 2, vol. 23.1:3–58.

_____. 1980a. *The Conversion of Rome: Ancient Sources of Modern Social Tensions*. North Ryde, Australia: Macquarrie Ancient History Association.

_____. 1980b. "The Social Identity of the First Christians: A Question of Method in Religious History." *Journal of Religious History* 11:201–17.

Judge, Edwin A., and Thomas, G. S. R. 1966. "The Origin of the Church at Rome: A New Solution?" *Reformed Theological Review* 25:81–94.

Juster, Jean. 1914. *Les Juifs dans l'empire romain: Leur Condition juridique, économique, et sociale*. 2 vols. Reprint. New York: Franklin, n.d.

Käsemann, Ernst. 1947. "Anliegen und Eigenart der paulinischen Abendmahlslehre." *EvT* 7:263–83. References are to the reprint in *Exegetische Versuche und Besinnungen*, vol. 2, pp. 11–34. 3d ed. Göttingen: Vandenhoeck & Ruprecht, 1964.

_____. 1949. "Eine urchristliche Taufliturgie." In *Festschrift Rudolf Bultmann zum 65. Geburtstag überreicht*. Stuttgart: Kohlhammer, pp. 133–48. References are to the translation by W. J. Montague, "A Primitive Christian Baptismal Liturgy." In *Essays on New Testament Themes*. London: SCM, 1964, pp. 149–68.

_____. 1950. "Kritische Analyse von Phil. 2, 5–11." *ZTK* 47:313–50.

Reprinted in *Exegetische Versuche und Besinnungen,* vol. 1, pp. 51–95. 3d ed. Göttingen: Vandenhoeck & Ruprecht, 1964.

———. 1960. "Die Anfänge christlicher Theologie." *ZTK* 57: 162–85. References are to the translation by W. J. Montague, "The Beginnings of Christian Theology." In *New Testament Questions of Today.* London: SCM; Philadelphia: Fortress, 1969, pp. 82–107.

———. 1961. "Grundsätzliches zur Interpretation von Römer 13." In *Unter der Herrschaft Christi.* Beiträge zur evangelischen Theologie 32. Munich: Kaiser, pp. 37–55. References are to the translation by W. J. Montague, "Principles of the Interpretation of Romans 13." In *New Testament Questions of Today.* London: SCM; Philadelphia: Fortress, 1969, pp. 196–216.

———. 1962. "Zum Thema der urchristlichen Apokalyptik." *ZTK* 59:257–84. References are to the translation by W. J. Montague, "On the Subject of Primitive Christian Apocalyptic." In *New Testament Questions of Today.* London: SCM; Philadelphia: Fortress, 1969, pp. 108–38.

———. 1973. *An die Römer.* Handbuch zum Neuen Testament, 8a. Tübingen: Mohr (Siebeck). References are to the translation by G. W. Bromiley, *Commentary on Romans.* Grand Rapids: Eerdmans, 1980.

Keck, Leander E. 1974. "On the Ethos of Early Christians." *JAAR* 42:435–52.

Kehnscherper, Gerhard. 1964. "Der Apostel Paulus als römischer Bürger." In *Studia Evangelica,* ed. Frank L. Cross, pt. 1, pp. 411–40. Papers presented to the Second International Congress on New Testament Studies at Christ Church, Oxford, 1961. Texte und Untersuchungen, 87. Berlin: Akademie.

Kennedy, George. 1978. "Classical and Christian Source Criticism." In *The Relationships among the Gospels: An Interdisciplinary Dialogue,* ed. William O. Walker, pp. 125–55. San Antonio: Trinity University Press.

Kent, J. H. 1966. *Inscriptions 1926–1960. Corinth: Results,* vol. 8, pt. 3. Princeton: Princeton University Press.

Kerényi, C. [Károly]. 1967. *Eleusis: Archetypal Image of Mother and Daughter.* Reprint. New York: Schocken, 1977.

Kertelge, Karl, ed. 1977. *Das kirchliche Amt im Neuen Testament.* Wege der Forschung, 439. Darmstadt: Wissenschaftliche Buchgesellschaft.

Kippenberg, Hans G. 1978. *Religion und Klassenbildung im antiken Judäa: Eine religionssoziologische Studie zum Verhältnis von Tradition und gesellschaftlicher Entwicklung.* Göttingen: Vandenhoeck & Ruprecht.

Kitzinger, Ernst. 1946. "The Town of Stobi." *Dumbarton Oaks Papers* 3:81–162 and plates 124–216.

Kleberg, Tönnes. 1957. *Hôtels, restaurants, et cabarets dans l'antiquité romaine: Études historiques et philologiques.* Bibliotheca Ekmaniana Universitatis Regiae Upsaliensis, 61. Uppsala: Almqvist & Wiksells.

Klijn, A. F. J. 1954. "An Early Christian Baptismal Liturgy." In *Charis kai*

Sophia: Festschrift Karl Heinrich Rengstorf, ed. Ulrich Luck, pp. 216–28. Leiden: Brill.

Knox, John. 1942. *Marcion and the New Testament.* Chicago: University of Chicago Press.

————. 1950. *Chapters in a Life of Paul.* Nashville and New York: Abingdon.

————. 1964. "Romans 15:14–33 and Paul's Conception of His Apostolic Mission." *JBL* 83:1–11.

Koester, Helmut. 1961. Review of Ulrich Wilckens, *Weisheit und Torheit. Gnomon* 33:590–95.

————. 1965. "Gnomai Diaphoroi: The Origin and Nature of Diversification in the History of Early Christianity." *HTR* 58:279–319. References are to the reprint in James M. Robinson and Helmut Koester, *Trajectories through Early Christianity.* Philadelphia: Fortress, 1971, pp. 114–57.

————. 1979. "I Thessalonians—Experiment in Christian Writing." In *Continuity and Discontinuity in Church History: Essays Presented to George H. Williams,* ed. F. Forrester Church and Timothy George, pp. 33–44. Leiden: Brill.

————. 1980. *Einführung in das Neue Testament im Rahmen der Religionsgeschichte und Kulturgeschichte der hellenistischen und römischen Zeit.* Berlin and New York: De Gruyter.

Kornemann, Ernst. 1900. "Collegium." PW, vol. 4.1:cols. 380–479.

Kovacs, Brian. 1976. "Contributions of Sociology to the Study of the Development of Apocalypticism: A Theoretical Survey." Paper presented at the annual meeting of the Society of Biblical Literature, St. Louis, October 1976.

Kowaliński, P. 1972. "The Genesis of Christianity in the Views of Contemporary Marxist Specialists of Religion." *Antonianum* 47:541–75.

Kraabel, Alf Thomas. 1968. "Judaism in Western Asia Minor under the Roman Empire, with a Preliminary Study of the Jewish Community at Sardis, Lydia." Th.D. dissertation, Harvard University.

————. 1978. "Paganism and Judaism: The Sardis Evidence." In *Paganisme, Judaïsme, Christianisme: Influences et affrontements dans le monde antique: Mélanges offerts à Marcel Simon,* ed. André Benoit, Marc Philonenko, and Cyrille Vogel, pp. 13–33. Paris: Boccard.

————. 1979. "The Diaspora Synagogue: Archaeological and Epigraphical Evidence since Sukenik." *ANRW,* pt. 2, vol. 19.1:477–510.

————. 1981. "Social Systems of Six Diaspora Synagogues." In *Ancient Synagogues: The State of Research,* ed. Joseph Gutmann, pp. 79–121. Chico, Calif.: Scholars.

Kraeling, Carl H. 1967. *The Christian Building. The Excavations at Dura-Europos: Final Reports,* vol. 8, pt. 2. New Haven and London: Yale University Press.

Kramer, Werner. 1963. *Christos Kyrios Gottessohn.* Abhandlungen zur Theologie des Alten und Neuen Testaments, 44. Zurich: Zwingli. References are to the translation by Brian Hardy, *Christ, Lord, Son of God.* Studies in Biblical Theology, 50. London: SCM, 1966.

Krauss, Salomo. 1922. *Synagogale Altertümer*. Berlin and Vienna: Harz.

Kreissig, Heinz. 1967. "Zur sozialen Zusammensetzung der frühchristlichen Gemeinden im ersten Jahrhundert u.Z." *Eirene* 6:91–100.

———. 1970. *Die sozialen Zusammenhänge des jüdischen Krieges: Klassen und Klassenkampf im Palästina des 1. Jh. v. u.Z.* Berlin: Akademie.

———. 1977. "Das Frühchristentum in der Sozialgeschichte des Altertums." In *Das Korpus der griechischen christlichen Schriftsteller: Historie, Gegenwart, Zukunft*, ed. Johannes Irmscher and Kurt Treu, pp. 15–19. Texte und Untersuchungen, 120. Berlin: Akademie.

Kümmel, Werner Georg. 1929. *Römer 7 und die Bekehrung des Paulus*. Untersuchungen zum Neuen Testament, 17. Leipzig: Hinrichs. Reprinted in *Römer 7 und Das Bild des Menschen im Neuen Testament: Zwei Studien*. Theologische Bücherei, 53. Munich: Kaiser, 1974.

———. 1973. *Einleitung in das Neue Testament*. 17th ed. Heidelberg: Quelle & Meyer. References are to the translation by Howard C. Kee, *Introduction to the New Testament*. Nashville and New York: Abingdon, 1975.

Kuhn, Karl Georg. 1959. "προσήλυτος." *TWNT* 6:727–45. References are to the translation in *TDNT* 6:727–44.

Kuhn, Karl Georg, and Stegemann, Hartmut. 1962. "Proselyten." PW, supp. vol. 9:cols. 1248–83.

Lake, Kirsopp. 1933. "Proselytes and God-fearers." In Lake and Cadbury 1933, 5:74–96.

Lake, Kirsopp, and Cadbury, Henry J., eds. 1933. *The Acts of the Apostles*. Edited by F. J. Foakes Jackson and Kirsopp Lake. Vol. 4: *English Translation and Commentary*. Vol. 5: *Additional Notes*. Reprint. Grand Rapids: Baker, 1979.

Lampe, G. W. H. 1967a. "Church Discipline and the Interpretation of the Epistles to the Corinthians." In *Christian History and Interpretation: Studies Presented to John Knox,* ed. William R. Farmer, C. F. D. Moule, and Richard R. Niebuhr, pp. 337–61. Cambridge: At the University Press.

———. 1967b. *The Seal of the Spirit: A Study in the Doctrine of Baptism and Confirmation in the New Testament and the Fathers*. 2d ed. London: S.P.C.K.

Landvogt, Peter. 1908. *Epigraphische Untersuchungen über den* oikonomos: *Ein Beitrag zum hellenistischen Beamtenwesen*. Strasbourg: Schauberg.

Layton, Bentley. 1979. *The Gnostic Treatise on Resurrection from Nag Hammadi*. Harvard Dissertations in Religion, 12. Missoula, Mont.: Scholars.

Leach, Edmund. 1968. "Ritual." *IESS*, vol. 13, pp. 520–26.

Le Déaut, Roger. 1965. *La Nuit pascale*. Rome: Biblical Institute Press.

Lee, Clarence L. 1971. "Social Unrest and Primitive Christianity." In *The Catacombs and the Colosseum: The Roman Empire as the Setting of Primitive Christianity*, ed. Stephen Benko and John J. O'Rourke, pp. 121–38. Valley Forge: Judson.

Leenhardt, F. J. 1948. "La Place de la femme dans l'Église d'après le Nouveau Testament." *Études théologiques et religieuses* 23:3–50.

Leipoldt, Johannes. 1954. *Die Frau in der antiken Welt und im Urchristentum.* Leipzig: Koehler & Amelang.

Lemerle, Paul. 1934. "Inscriptions latines et grecques de Philippes." *BCH* 58:448–83.

———. 1945. *Philippes et la Macédoine orientale à l'époque chrétienne et byzantine.* Recherches à l'histoire et d'archéologie. Paris: Boccard.

Lenski, Gerhard E. 1954. "Status Crystallization: A Non-vertical Dimension of Social Status." *ASR* 19:405–13. Reprinted in *Sociology: The Progress of a Decade,* ed. Seymour Martin Lipset and Neil J. Smelser, pp. 485–94. Engelwood Cliffs, N.J.: Prentice-Hall, 1961.

———. 1956. "Social Participation and Status Crystallization." *ASR* 21:458–64.

Leon, Harry J. 1960. *The Jews of Ancient Rome.* Philadelphia: Jewish Publication Society.

Levick, Barbara M. 1967. *Roman Colonies in Southern Asia Minor.* Oxford: Clarendon Press.

Levine, Lee I. 1975. *Caesarea under Roman Rule.* Studies in Judaism in Late Antiquity, 7. Leiden: Brill.

———. 1979. "The Jewish Patriarch (Nasi) in Third Century Palestine." *ANRW,* pt. 2, vol. 9.2:649–88.

Lewis, Ioan M. 1971. *Ecstatic Religion: An Anthropological Study of Spirit Possession and Shamanism.* Baltimore: Penguin.

Liebeschuetz, J. H. W. G. 1972. *Antioch: City and Imperial Administration in the Later Roman Empire.* Oxford: Oxford University Press.

Lietzmann, Hans. 1914. "Zur altchristlichen Verfassungsgeschichte." *Zeitschrift für Wissenschaftliche Theologie* 55:97–153. References are to the reprint in Kertelge 1977, 93–143.

———. 1931. *An die Korinther I, II.* 3d ed. Handbuch zum Neuen Testament, 9. Tübingen: Mohr (Siebeck).

———. 1933. *An die Römer.* 4th ed. Handbuch zum Neuen Testament, 8. Tübingen: Mohr (Siebeck).

Lifshitz, Baruch. 1969. "Notes d'épigraphie grecque." *RB* 76:92–98.

———. 1970. "Du nouveau sur les 'Sympathisants'." *JSJ* 1:77–84.

Lifshitz, Baruch, and Schiby, J. 1968. "Une Synagogue samaritaine à Thessalonique." *RB* 75:368–78.

Lightfoot, Joseph Barber. 1879. *Saint Paul's Epistles to the Colossians and to Philemon.* Reprint. Grand Rapids: Zondervan, 1959.

———. 1880. *The Epistle of St. Paul to the Galatians.* 6th ed. Reprint. Grand Rapids: Zondervan, 1978.

———. 1913. *Saint Paul's Epistle to the Philippians.* Reprint. Grand Rapids: Zondervan, 1953.

Lindars, Barnabas, S. S. F. 1961. *New Testament Apologetic: The Doctrinal Significance of the Old Testament Quotations.* London: SCM; Philadelphia: Fortress.

Lindemann, Andreas. 1976. "Bemerkungen zu den Adressaten und zum Anlass des Epheserbriefes." *ZNW* 67:235–51.

———. 1979. *Paulus im ältesten Christentum: Das Bild des Apostels in der frühchristlichen Literatur bis Marcion.* Beiträge zur historischen Theologie, 58. Tübingen: Mohr (Siebeck).

Linton, Olof. 1949. "The Third Aspect: A Neglected Point of View: A Study in Gal. i–ii and Acts ix and xv." *Studia Theologica* 3:79–95.

———. 1959. "Ekklesia I: Bedeutungsgeschichtlich." *RAC* 4:Cols. 905–21.

Lipset, Seymour Martin. 1968. "Social Class." *IESS,* vol. 15, pp. 296–316.

Lipsius, Richard Adelbert, and Bonnet, Maximilian, eds. 1891. *Acta Apostolorum Apocrypha.* 3 vols. Reprint. Darmstadt: Wissenschaftliche Buchgesellschaft, 1959.

Lohmeyer, Ernst. 1927. "Kyrios Jesus. Eine Untersuchung zu Phil. 2:5–11." *Sitzungsberichte der Heidelberger Akademie der Wissenschaften, Philosophisch-historische Klasse* 4 (1927–28). References are to separate reprint, Darmstadt: Wissenschaftliche Buchgesellschaft, 1961.

———. 1930. *Die Briefe an die Philipper, an die Kolosser und an Philemon.* Kritisch-exegetischer Kommentar über das Neue Testament, 9. Göttingen: Vandenhoeck & Ruprecht.

Lohse, Eduard. 1968. *Die Briefe an die Kolosser und an Philemon.* 14th ed. Kritisch-exegetischer Kommentar über das Neue Testament, 9.2. Göttingen: Vandenhoeck & Ruprecht. References are to the translation by William R. Poehlmann and Robert J. Karris, *Colossians and Philemon: A Commentary on the Epistles to the Colossians and to Philemon.* Hermeneia. Philadelphia: Fortress, 1971.

Lüdemann, Gerd. 1979. "Antipaulinism in the First Two Centuries: A Contribution to the History and Theology of Jewish Christianity." Paper presented to the Studiorum Novi Testamenti Societas Seminar on Jewish Christianity, Durham, England, 22 August 1979.

———. 1980a. *Paulus, der Heidenapostel.* Vol. 1: *Studien zur Chronologie.* Forschungen zur Religion und Literatur des Alten und Neuen Testamentes, 123. Göttingen: Vandenhoeck & Ruprecht.

———. 1980b. "Zum Antipaulinismus im frühen Christentum." *EvT* 40: 437–55.

Lührmann, Dieter. 1980. "Neutestamentliche Haustafeln und antike Ökonomie." *NTS* 27:83–97.

Lull, David J. 1980. *"Pneuma" in Paul's Letter to the Churches of Galatia: An Interpretation of the Spirit in Light of Early Christian Experience in Galatia, Paul's Message to the Galatians, and Theology Today.* Society of Biblical Literature Dissertation Series, 49. Chico, Calif.: Scholars.

Lutz, Cora. 1947. "Musonius Rufus: 'The Roman Socrates.'" *Yale Classical Studies* 10:3–147.

MacDonald, Dennis. 1979. "Virgins, Widows, and Paul in Second-Century Asia Minor." In *Society of Biblical Literature 1979 Seminar Papers,* ed. Paul J. Achtemeier, pp. 169–84. Missoula, Mont.: Scholars.

Mack, Burton. 1973. *Logos und Sophia: Untersuchungen zur Weisheits-*

theologie im hellenistischen Judentum. Studien zur Umwelt des Neuen Testaments, 10. Göttingen: Vandenhoeck & Ruprecht.

MacMullen, Ramsay. 1971. "Social History in Astrology." *Ancient Society* 2:105–16.

_____. 1974. *Roman Social Relations.* New Haven and London: Yale University Press.

_____. 1980. "Women in Public in the Roman Empire." *Historia* (Baden-Baden) 29:208–18.

_____. 1981. *Paganism in the Roman Empire.* New Haven and London: Yale University Press.

Magie, David. 1950. *Roman Rule in Asia Minor to the End of the Third Century after Christ.* 2 vols. Reprint. New York: Arno, 1975.

Makaronas, Ch. I. 1951. "Via Egnatia and Thessalonike." In *Studies Presented to D. M. Robinson,* ed. George E. Mylonas, vol. 1, pp. 380–88 and plate 21. St. Louis: Washington University Press.

Malewski, Andrzej. 1966. "The Degree of Status Incongruence and Its Effects." In *Class, Status, and Power: Social Stratification in Comparative Perspective,* ed. Reinhard Bendix and Seymour M. Lipset, pp. 303–08. 2d ed. New York: Free Press; London: Macmillan.

Malherbe, Abraham J. 1968. "The Beasts at Ephesus." *JBL* 87:71–80.

_____. 1970. "'Gentle as a Nurse': The Cynic Background of I Thess ii." *NovT* 12:203–17.

_____. 1976. "Cynics." *IDBS,* pp. 201–03.

_____. 1977a. *Social Aspects of Early Christianity.* Rockwell Lectures of 1975. Baton Rouge and London: Louisiana State University Press.

_____. 1977b. "The Inhospitality of Diotrephes." In *God's Christ and His People: Studies in Honour of Nils Alstrup Dahl,* ed. Jacob Jervell and Wayne A. Meeks, pp. 222–32. Oslo, Bergen, and Tromsö: Universitetsforlaget.

_____. forthcoming. "Hellenistic Moralists and the New Testament." *ANRW,* pt. 2, vol. 28.

_____. forthcoming. "Self-definition among Epicureans and Cynics." In *Jewish and Christian Self-Definition,* ed. E. P. Sanders, vol. 3. London: SCM; Philadelphia: Fortress.

Marrou, Henri. 1955. *Histoire de l'éducation dans l'antiquité.* 3d ed., rev. Paris: Éditions du Seuil. References are to the translation by George Lamb, *A History of Education in Antiquity.* New York: Sheed and Ward, 1956.

Martin, Ralph P. 1967. *Carmen Christi: Philippians in Recent Interpretation and in the Setting of Early Christian Worship.* Cambridge: At the University Press.

Mattusch, Carol C. 1977. "Corinthian Metalworking: The Forum Area." *Hesperia* 46:380–89.

Mau, August. 1904. *Pompeii: Its Life and Art.* Translated by F. W. Kelsey. Rev. ed. New York: Macmillan.

McCasland, S. Vernon, 1962. "Travel and Communication in the NT." *IDB*, vol. 4, pp. 690–93.

Meeks, Wayne A. 1972. "The Stranger from Heaven in Johannine Sectarianism." *JBL* 91:44–72.

_____. 1974. "The Image of the Androgyne: Some Uses of a Symbol in Earliest Christianity." *HR* 13:165–208.

_____. 1976. "Moses in the NT." *IDBS*, pp. 605–07.

_____. 1977. "In One Body: The Unity of Humankind in Colossians and Ephesians." In *God's Christ and His People: Studies in Honour of Nils Alstrup Dahl*, ed. Jacob Jervell and Wayne A. Meeks, pp. 209–21. Oslo, Bergen, and Tromsö: Universitetsforlaget.

_____. 1978. "Hypomnēmata from an Untamed Sceptic: A Response to George Kennedy." In *The Relationships among the Gospels: An Interdisciplinary Dialogue*, ed. William O. Walker, pp. 157–72. San Antonio: Trinity University Press.

_____. 1982. "Social Functions of Apocalyptic Language in Pauline Christianity." In Hellholm 1982.

Meeks, Wayne A., and Wilken, Robert L. 1978. *Jews and Christians in Antioch in the First Four Centuries of the Common Era*. Society of Biblical Literature Sources for Biblical Study, 13. Missoula, Mont.: Scholars.

Mellink, Machfeld J. 1977. "Archaeology in Asia Minor." *AJA*, 2d ser. 81:281–321.

Merkelbach, Reinhold. 1973. "Zwei Texte aus dem Serapeum zu Thessalonike." *ZPE* 10:49–54.

Merritt, Benjamin Dean. 1931. *Greek Inscriptions 1896–1927. Corinth: Results*, vol. 8, pt. 1. Cambridge, Mass.: Harvard University Press.

Merton, Robert K. 1967. *Social Theory and Social Structure: Five Essays, Old and New*. New York: Free Press.

Merton, Robert K., and Rossi, Alice Kitt. 1950. "Reference Group Theory and Social Mobility." In *Continuities in Social Research*, ed. Robert K. Merton and Paul F. Lazarsfeld, pp. 40–105. Glencoe, Ill.: Free Press.

Michaelis, Wilhelm. 1951. "Zum jüdischen Hintergrund der Johannestaufe." *Judaica* 7:81–120.

Minar, Edwin L., Jr. 1942. *Early Pythagorean Politics in Practice and Theory*. Connecticut College Monographs, 2. Baltimore: Waverly.

Minns, Ellis H. 1913. *Scythians and Greeks: A Survey of Ancient History and Archaeology on the North Coast of the Euxine from the Danube to the Caucasus*. Cambridge: At the University Press.

Moe, Dean. 1977. "The Cross and the Menorah." *Archaeology* 30:148–57.

Momigliano, Arnaldo. 1972. "Popular Religious Beliefs and the Late Roman Historians." In *Popular Belief and Practice*, ed. C. J. Cuming and Derek Baker, pp. 1–18. Studies in Church History, 8. Cambridge: At the University Press.

Moore, George Foot. 1927. *Judaism in the First Centuries of the Christian Era:*

The Age of the Tannaim. 3 vols. Cambridge, Mass.: Harvard University Press.

Mrozek, Stanislaw. 1975. "Wirtschaftliche Grundlagen des Aufstiegs der Freigelassenen im römischen Reich." *Chiron* 5:311–17.

Murphy-O'Connor, Jerome, O. P. 1976. "The Non-Pauline Character of 1 Corinthians 11:2–16?" *JBL* 95:615–21.

Mylonas, George F. 1961. *Eleusis and the Eleusinian Mysteries.* Princeton: Princeton University Press.

Nabers, Ned. 1969. "A Note on *Corinth* VIII,2,125." *AJA*, 2d ser. 73:73–74.

Neufeld, Vernon H. 1963. *The Earliest Christian Confessions.* New Testament Tools and Studies, 5. Leiden: Brill; Grand Rapids: Eerdmans.

Neusner, Jacob. 1964. "The Conversion of Adiabene to Judaism: A New Perspective." *JBL* 83:60–66.

_____. 1970. *Development of a Legend: Studies on the Traditions Concerning Yohanan ben Zakkai.* Studia Post-Biblica, 16. Leiden: Brill.

_____. 1971. *The Rabbinic Traditions about the Pharisees before 70.* 3 parts. Leiden: Brill.

_____. 1973a. *The Idea of Purity in Ancient Judaism.* Studies in Judaism in Late Antiquity, 1. Leiden: Brill.

_____. 1973b. " 'Pharisaic-Rabbinic' Judaism: A Clarification." *HR* 12: 250–70.

_____. 1977. *A History of the Mishnaic Law of Purities.* Studies in Judaism in Late Antiquity 6. Part 22: *The Mishnaic System of Uncleanness.* Leiden: Brill.

_____. 1978. "Comparing Judaism." *HR* 18:177–91. Reprinted, with revisions, as "The Use of the Later Rabbinic Evidence for the Study of Paul." In *Approaches to Ancient Judaism,* ed. William S. Green, vol. 2, pp. 43–63. Brown Judaic Studies, 9. Chico, Calif.: Scholars.

_____. 1979a. "The Formation of Rabbinic Judaism: Yavneh (Jamnia) from A.D. 70 to 100." *ANRW,* pt. 2, vol. 19.2:3–42.

_____. 1979b. "Map without Territory: Mishnah's System of Sacrifice and Sanctuary." *HR* 19:103–27.

_____. 1980. "The Use of the Mishnah for the History of Judaism prior to the Time of the Mishnah." *JSJ* 11:1–9.

Nickelsburg, George W. E., Jr. 1972. *Resurrection, Immortality, and Eternal Life in Intertestamental Judaism.* Harvard Theological Studies, 26. Cambridge, Mass.: Harvard University Press.

Nickle, Keith. 1966. *The Collection: A Study in Paul's Strategy.* Studies in Biblical Theology, 48. London: SCM.

Nilsson, Martin P. 1954. "Roman and Greek Domestic Cult." *Opuscula Romana* 18:77–85.

_____. 1961. *Geschichte der griechischen Religion.* 2d ed. Vol. 2. Handbuch der Altertumswissenschaft, sec. 5, pt. 2. Munich: Beck.

Nock, Arthur Darby. 1924a. "The Christian *Sacramentum* in Pliny and a Pagan Counterpart." *Classical Review* 38:58–59.

———. 1924*b*. "The Historical Importance of Cult-Associations." *Classical Review* 38:105–09.

———. 1933*a*. *Conversion: The Old and the New in Religion from Alexander the Great to Augustine of Hippo.* Reprint. Oxford: Oxford University Press (Oxford Paperbacks), 1961.

———. 1933*b*. "The Vocabulary of the New Testament." *JBL* 52:131–39. Reprinted in *Essays on Religion and the Ancient World,* ed. Zeph Stewart, pp. 341–47. Cambridge, Mass.: Harvard University Press, 1972.

Norden, Eduard. 1912. *Agnostos Theos: Untersuchungen zur Formengeschichte religiöser Rede.* Reprint. Darmstadt: Wissenschaftliche Buchgesellschaft, 1956.

Ollrog, Wolf-Henning. 1979. *Paulus und seine Mitarbeiter: Untersuchungen zu Theorie und Praxis der paulinischen Mission.* Wissenschaftliche Monographien zum Alten und Neuen Testament, 50. Neukirchen: Erziehungsverein.

Olsen, Marvin E. 1968. *The Process of Social Organization.* New York: Holt, Rinehart.

Olson, Stanley N. 1976. "Confidence Expressions in Paul: Epistolary Conventions and the Purpose of 2 Corinthians." Ph.D. dissertation, Yale University.

Orr, William F., and Walther, James Arthur. 1976. *I Corinthians: A New Translation.* Anchor Bible, 32. Garden City, N.Y.: Doubleday.

Pagels, Elaine H. 1979. *The Gnostic Gospels.* New York: Random House.

Pearson, Birger A. 1971. "1 Thessalonians 2:13–16: A Deutero-Pauline Interpolation." *HTR* 64:79–94.

———. 1973. *The Pneumatikos-Psychikos Terminology in 1 Corinthians.* Society of Biblical Literature Dissertation Series, 12. Missoula, Mont.: Scholars.

———. 1975. "Hellenistic-Jewish Wisdom Speculation and Paul." In *Aspects of Wisdom in Judaism and Early Christianity,* ed. Robert L. Wilken, pp. 43–66. Notre Dame and London: University of Notre Dame Press.

Pelekanidis, Stratis. 1961. "Παλαιοχριστιανικοὶ τάφοι." *Archaiologikon Deltion* 17:257 and plate 314a,b.

Petsas, Photios M. 1968. "Ἡ ἀγορὰ τῆς Θεσσαλονίκης." *Athens Annals of Archaeology* 1:156–62.

Pettigrew, Thomas F. 1967. "Social Evaluation Theory: Convergences and Applications." In *Nebraska Symposium on Motivation 1967,* ed. David Levine, pp. 241–311. Lincoln: University of Nebraska Press.

Pfitzner, Victor C. 1967. *Paul and the Agon Motif.* Supplements to Novum Testamentum, 16. Leiden: Brill.

Pöhlmann, Wolfgang. 1973. "Die hymnische All-Prädikationen in Kol. 1:15–20." *ZNW* 64:53–74.

Poland, Franz. 1909. *Geschichte des griechischen Vereinswesens.* Preisschriften . . . der fürstlich Jablonowskischen Gesellschaft, 38. Leipzig: Teubner.

Polanyi, Karl. 1968. *Primitive, Archaic, and Modern Economics.* Edited by George Dalton. Garden City, N.Y.: Doubleday (Anchor).

Pomeroy, Sarah B. 1975. *Goddesses, Whores, Wives, and Slaves: Women in Classical Antiquity.* New York: Schocken.

Pope, Marvin. 1976. "Homosexuality." *IDBS,* pp. 415–17.

Powell, Benjamin. 1903. "Inscriptions from Corinth." *AJA,* 2d ser. 7:26–71.

Préaux, Claire. 1955. "Institutions économiques et sociales des villes hellénistiques." In *La Ville,* ed. Jean Firenne, pt. 1, pp. 89–135. Recueils de la Société Jean Bodin, 6. Brussels: Libraire encyclopédique.

Preisker, Herbert. 1927. *Christentum und Ehe in den ersten drei Jahrhunderten: Eine Studie zur Kulturgeschichte der alten Welt.* Berlin: Trowitsch.

Puniet, P. de. 1907. "Baptême." *DACL,* vol. 2:cols. 251–346.

Radice, Betty, trans. 1969. *The Letters of the Younger Pliny.* Harmondsorth: Penguin.

Radke, Gerhard. 1973. "Viae publicae Romanae." PW, supp. 13:cols. 1417–1686.

Ramsay, William M. 1904. "Roads and Travel." In *A Dictionary of the Bible,* ed. James Hastings, supp. vol. pp. 375–402. Edinburgh and New York: Clark.

Redlich, E. Basil. 1913. *St. Paul and His Companions.* London: Macmillan.

Reekmans, Tony. 1971. "Juvenal's Views on Social Change." *Ancient Society* 2:117–61.

Reicke, Bo. 1951. *Diakonie, Festfreude, und Zelos in Verbindung mit der altchristlichen Agapenfeier.* Uppsala Universitets Årsskrift 1951, 5. Uppsala: Lundequist; Wiesbaden: Harrassowitz.

———. 1951b. "The Law and This World according to Paul." *JBL* 70:259–76.

Rensberger, David. 1978. "2 Corinthians 6:14–7:1—A Fresh Examination." *Studia Biblica et Theologica* 8, no. 2:25–49.

———. 1981. "As the Apostle Teaches: The Development of the Use of Paul's Letters in Second-Century Christianity." Ph.D. dissertation, Yale University.

Rese, Martin. 1970. "Formeln und Lieder im Neuen Testament: Einige notwendige Anmerkungen." *Verkündigung und Forschung* 15, no. 2:75–95.

Richard, Marcel. 1956. *Asterii sophistae. Commentariorum in Psalmos quae supersunt, accedunt aliquot homiliae anonymae.* Oslo: Brøgge.

Robert, Louis. 1937. *Études anatoliennes: Recherches sur les inscriptions grecques de l'Asie Mineure.* Paris: Boccard.

———. 1964. *Nouvelles Inscriptions de Sardes.* Vol. 1. Paris: Librairie d'Amerique et d'Orient A. Maisonneuve.

———. 1974. "Les Inscriptions de Thessalonique." *RPh* 48:180–246.

Robertis, Francesco M. de. 1973. *Storia delle corporazioni e del regime associativo nel mondo romano.* 2 vols. Bari: Adriatica editrice.

Robinson, James M. 1957. "A Formal Analysis of Col. 1:15–20." *JBL* 76:270–87.

_____. 1964. "Die Hodajot-Formel in Gebet und Hymnus des Frühchristentums." In *Apophoreta: Festschrift für Ernst Haenchen,* ed. Walther Eltester, pp. 194–235. Beihefte zur ZNW 30. Berlin: Töpelmann.

Robinson, John A. T. 1952. *The Body: A Study in Pauline Theology.* Studies in Biblical Theology, 5. London: SCM.

Romaniuk, Kazimierz. 1964. "Die 'Gottesfürchtigen' im Neuen Testament." *Aegyptus* 44:66–91.

Rose, H. J. 1957. "The Religion of a Greek Household." *Euphrosyne* 1:95–116.

Rostovtzeff, Mihail. 1957. *The Social and Economic History of the Roman Empire.* 2 vols. 2d ed., revised by P. M. Fraser. Oxford: Clarendon Press.

Rowley, H. H. 1940. "Jewish Proselyte Baptism and the Baptism of John." *HUCA* 15:313–34.

Russell, D. A., and Wilson, N. G., ed. and trans. 1981. *Menander Rhetor.* Oxford: Clarendon Press; New York: Oxford University Press.

Ste. Croix, G. E. M. de. 1975. "Early Christian Attitudes to Property and Slavery." In *Church, Society, and Politics,* ed. Derek Baker, pp. 1–38. Studies in Church History, 12. Oxford: Blackwell.

Salditt-Trappmann, Regina. 1970. *Tempel der ägyptischen Götter in Griechenland und an der Westküste Kleinasiens.* Études préliminaires aux religions orientales dans l'empire romain, 15. Leiden: Brill.

Sampley, J. Paul. 1977. "*Societas Christi:* Roman Law and Paul's Conception of the Christian Community." In *God's Christ and His People: Studies in Honour of Nils Alstrup Dahl,* ed. Jacob Jervell and Wayne A. Meeks, pp. 158–74. Oslo, Bergen, and Tromsö: Universitetsforlaget.

_____. 1980. *Pauline Partnership in Christ: Christian Community and Commitment in Light of Roman Law.* Philadelphia: Fortress.

Sanders, E. P. 1977. *Paul and Palestinian Judaism: A Comparison of Patterns of Religion.* Philadelphia: Fortress; London: SCM.

Sasaki, M. S. 1979. "Status Inconsistency and Religious Commitment." In *The Religious Dimension: New Directions in Quantitative Research,* ed. Robert Wuthnow, pp. 135–56. New York, San Francisco, and London: Academic.

Schachter, Stanley. 1968. "Social Cohesion." *IESS,* vol. 2, pp. 542–46.

Schaefer, Hans. 1962. "Prostatēs." PW, supp. vol. 9:cols. 1288–1304.

Schille, Gottfried. 1952. "Liturgisches Gut im Epheserbrief." D. Theol. dissertation, Göttingen.

_____. 1962. *Frühchristliche Hymnen.* Berlin: Evangelische Verlagsanstalt.

_____. 1967. *Die urchristliche Kollegialmission.* Abhandlungen zur Theologie des Alten und Neuen Testaments, 48. Zurich and Stuttgart: Zwingli.

Schlier, Heinrich. 1933. "ἀμήν." *TWNT* 1:339–42. References are to the translation in *TDNT* 1:335–38.

_____. 1938. "Die Taufe nach dem 6. Kap. des Röm." *EvT* 5:335–47. Reprinted in *Die Zeit der Kirche.* Freiburg: Herder, 1956, pp. 47–56.

_____. 1971. *Der Brief an die Galater.* 14th ed. Kritisch-exegetischer Kommentar über das Neue Testament, 7. Göttingen: Vandenhoeck & Ruprecht.

Schmidt, Karl Ludwig. 1938. "ἐκκλησία." *TWNT* 3:502–39. References are to the translation in *TDNT* 3:501–36.

Schoenebeck, Hans von. 1940. "Die Stadtplannung des römischen Thessalonike." In *Bericht über den 6. Internationalen Kongress für Archäologie,* ed. Max Wenger, pp. 478–82. Berlin: De Gruyter.

Schottroff, Luise. 1979. "Die Schreckensherrschaft der Sünde und die Befreiung durch Christus nach dem Römerbrief des Paulus." *EvT* 39:497–510.

Schreiber, Alfred. 1977. *Die Gemeinde in Korinth: Versuch einer gruppendynamischen Betrachtung der Entwicklung der Gemeinde von Korinth auf der Basis des ersten Korintherbriefes.* Neutestamentliche Abhandlungen, n.s., 12. Münster: Aschendorff.

Schroeder, David. 1959. "Die Haustafeln des Neuen Testaments: Ihre Herkunft und ihr theologischer Sinn." D. Theol. dissertation, Hamburg.

Schubert, Paul. 1939a. *Form and Function of the Pauline Thanksgivings.* Beihefte zur *ZNW* 20. Berlin: Töpelmann.

_____. 1939b. "Form and Function of the Pauline Letters." *JR* 19:365–77.

Schürer, Emil. 1973–. *The History of the Jewish People in the Age of Jesus Christ (175 B.C.–A.D. 135).* Edited and revised by Geza Vermes, Fergus Millar, and Matthew Black. Edinburgh: Clark. 2 vols. to date.

Schütz, John Howard. 1975. *Paul and the Anatomy of Apostolic Authority.* Society for New Testament Studies Monograph Series, 26. Cambridge: At the University Press.

_____. 1977. "Steps toward a Sociology of Primitive Christianity: A Critique of the Work of Gerd Theissen." Paper presented to the Social World of Early Christianity Group of the American Academy of Religion/Society of Biblical Literature, 27–31 December 1977.

_____. 1982. Introduction to Theissen 1982.

Schultz-Falkenthal, Heinz. 1970. "Zur Frage der organisatorischen Vorbilder für den korporativen Zusammenschluss in den *collegia opificium* u. ihre Verhältnis zu den mittelalterlichen Zünften." *Wissenschaftliche Zeitschrift der Martin-Luther-Universität Halle-Wittenberg* 19, no. 2:41–50.

Schweitzer, Albert. 1930. *Die Mystik des Apostels Paulus.* Tübingen: Mohr (Siebeck). Translated by William Montgomery, *The Mysticism of Paul the Apostle.* 1931. Reprint. New York: Seabury, 1968.

Schweizer, Eduard. 1955. *Erniedrigung und Erhöhung bei Jesus und seinen Nachfolgern.* Zurich: Zwingli. References are to the translation, *Lordship and Discipleship.* Studies in Biblical Theology, 28. London: SCM, 1960.

_____. 1961a. "Die Kirche als Leib Christi in den paulinischen Homologoumena." *TLZ* 86:161–74. References are to the reprint in *Neotesta-*

mentica: Deutsche und englische Aufsätze. Zurich and Stuttgart: Zwingli, 1963, pp. 272–92.

_____. 1961*b*. "Die Kirche als Leib Christi in den paulinischen Antilegomena." *TLZ* 86:241–56. References are to the reprint in *Neotestamentica: Deutsche und englische Aufsätze.* Zurich and Stuttgart: Zwingli, 1963, pp. 293–316.

_____. 1964. "σῶμα, κτλ." *TWNT* 7:1024–91. References are to the translation in *TDNT* 7:1024–94.

Scranton, Robert L. 1951. *Monuments in the Lower Agora and North of the Archaic Temple. Corinth: Results,* vol. 1, pt. 3. Princeton: Princeton University Press.

Scranton, Robert L.; Shaw, Joseph W.; and Ibrahim, Leila. 1978. *Topography and Architecture. Kenchreai, Eastern Port of Corinth: Results of Investigations by the University of Chicago and Indiana University for the American School of Classical Studies at Athens,* vol. 1. Leiden: Brill.

Scroggs, Robin. 1980. "The Sociological Interpretation of the New Testament: The Present State of Research." *NTS* 26:164–79.

Seager, Andrew R. 1972. "The Building History of the Sardis Synagogue." *AJA* 76:425–35.

Sebesta, Judith Lynn. 1976. "Dine with Us as an Equal." *Classical Bulletin* 53:23–26.

Segelberg, Eric. 1958. *Maṣbūtā: Studies in the Ritual of the Mandaean Baptism.* Uppsala: Almqvist & Wiksells.

Sevenster, J. N. 1975. *The Roots of Pagan Anti-Semitism in the Ancient World.* Supplements to Novum Testamentum, 41. Leiden: Brill.

Sherwin-White, A. N. 1967. *Racial Prejudice in Imperial Rome.* Cambridge: At the University Press.

Sivan, Hagith S. 1978. *The Painting of the Dura-Europos Synagogue: A Guidebook to the Exhibition* [sponsored by the New Haven Jewish Federation and the New Haven Jewish Community Center, 13 April–15 May, 1978].

Siegert, Folker. 1973. "Gottesfürchtige und Sympathisanten." *JSJ* 4:109–64.

Smallwood, E. Mary. 1976. *The Jews under Roman Rule: From Pompey to Diocletian.* Studies in Judaism in Late Antiquity, 20. Leiden: Brill.

Smith, Dennis E. 1980. "Social Obligation in the Context of Communal Meals: A Study of the Christian Meal in 1 Corinthians in Comparison with Graeco-Roman Communal Meals." Th.D. dissertation, Harvard University.

Smith, Jonathan Z. 1965. "The Garments of Shame." *HR* 5:224–30.

_____. 1971. "Native Cults in the Hellenistic Period." *HR* 11:236–39.

_____. 1975. "The Social Description of Early Christianity." *Religious Studies Review* 1:19–25.

Smith, Morton. 1978. *Jesus the Magician.* New York: Harper & Row.

_____. 1980. "Pauline Worship as Seen by Pagans." *HTR* 73:241–49.

Soden, Hans von. 1931. "Sakrament und Ethik bei Paulus." In *Marburger*

Theologische Studien (Rudolf Otto-Festgruss). Vol. 1. Reprinted in *Urchristentum und Geschichte.* Tübingen: Mohr (Siebeck), 1951, pp. 239–75. Abridged translation in *The Writings of St. Paul,* ed. Wayne A. Meeks, pp. 257–68. New York: Norton, 1972.

———. 1933. "ἀδελφός, κτλ." *TWNT* 1:144–46. References are to the translation in *TDNT* 1:144–46.

Spiro, Melford E. 1966. "Religion: Problems of Definition and Explanation." In *Anthropological Approaches to the Study of Religion,* ed. Michael Banton, pp. 85–126. Association of Social Anthropologists Monographs, 3. London: Tavistock.

Stählin, Gustav. 1938. "ἴσος, κτλ." *TWNT* 3:343–56. References are to the translation in *TDNT* 3:343–55.

Stauffer, Ethelbert. 1949. "Zur Kindertaufe in der Urkirche." *Deutscher Pfarrerblatt* 49:152–54.

Stendahl, Krister. 1963. "The Apostle Paul and the Introspective Conscience of the West." *HTR* 56:199–215. Reprinted in *Paul among Jews and Gentiles and Other Essays.* Philadelphia: Fortress, 1976, pp. 78–96.

Stern, Menahem. 1974. *Greek and Latin Authors on Jews and Judaism.* Part 1: *From Herodotus to Plutarch.* Leiden: Brill.

———. 1976. "The Jews in Greek and Latin Literature." In *The Jewish People in the First Century,* ed. Samuel Safrai and Menahem Stern, 2:1101–59. Compendia Rerum Iudaicarum ad Novum Testamentum, 1. Assen: Van Gorcum; Philadelphia: Fortress.

Stillwell, Richard, ed. 1941. *Architecture. Corinth: Results,* vol. 1, pt. 2. Cambridge, Mass.: Harvard University Press.

———. 1952. *The Theater. Corinth: Results,* vol. 2. Princeton: Princeton University Press.

Stillwell, Richard, and Askew, H. Ess. 1941. "The Peribolos of Apollo." In Stillwell 1941, 1–54.

Stowers, Stanley K. 1981. *The Diatribe and Paul's Letter to the Romans.* Society of Biblical Literature Dissertation Series, 57. Chico, Calif.: Scholars.

Strecker, Georg. 1964. "Redaktion und Tradition im Christushymnus Phil. 2,6–11." *ZNW* 55:63–78.

Strobel, August. 1965. "Der Begriff des Hauses im griechischen und römischen Privatrecht." *ZNW* 56:91–100.

Stuhlmacher, Peter. 1975. *Der Brief an Philemon.* Evangelisch-Katholischer Kommentar zum Neuen Testament, 1. Zurich: Einsiedeln; Cologne: Benziger; Neukirchen: Erziehungsverein.

———. 1977. "Zur paulinischen Christologie." *ZTK* 74:449–63.

Swidler, Leonard. 1979. *Biblical Affirmations of Women.* Philadelphia: Westminster.

Talmon, Yonina. 1962. "Pursuit of the Millennium: The Relation between Religious and Social Change." *Archives européenes de sociologie* 3:125–48. Reprinted in *Reader in Comparative Religion: An An-*

thropological Approach, ed. W. A. Lessa and E. Z. Vogt, 2d ed., pp. 522–37. New York: Harper & Row, 1965.

Tannehill, Robert C. 1967. *Dying and Rising with Christ: A Study in Pauline Theology.* Beihefte zur ZNW 32. Berlin: Töpelmann.

Tanzer, Helen H. 1939. *The Common People of Pompeii: A Study of the Graffiti.* Johns Hopkins University Studies in Archaeology, 29. Baltimore: Johns Hopkins University Press.

Tarn, William W. 1952. *Hellenistic Civilization.* 3d ed., revised by the author and G. T. Griffith. Reprint. Cleveland and New York: World (Meridian), 1961.

Taylor, Howard F. 1973. "Linear Models of Consistency: Some Extensions of Blalock's Strategy." *AJS* 78:1192–1215.

Taylor, L. R. 1933. "The Asiarchs." In Lake and Cadbury 1933, 5:256–62.

Tcherikover, Victor. 1961. *Hellenistic Civilization and the Jews.* Philadelphia: Jewish Publication Society.

Theissen, Gerd. 1973. "Wanderradikalismus: Literatursoziologische Aspekte der Überlieferung von Worten Jesu im Urchristentum." *ZTK* 70:245–71. Reprinted in Theissen 1979, 79–105. Translated by Anne C. Wire in *Radical Religion* 2, nos. 2–3 (1975):84–93.

_____. 1974*a.* "Soteriologische Symbolik in den paulinischen Schriften: Ein strukturalistischer Beitrag." *Kerygma und Dogma* 20:282–304.

_____. 1974*b.* "Soziale Integration und sakramentales Handeln: Eine Analyse von 1 Cor. XI 17–34." *NovT* 24:179–205. References are to the reprint in Theissen 1979, 290–317.

_____. 1974*c.* "Soziale Schichtung in der korinthischen Gemeinde." *ZNW* 65:232–72. References are to the reprint in Theissen 1979, 231–71.

_____. 1975*a.* "Legitimation und Lebensunterhalt. Ein Beitrag zur Soziologie urchristlicher Missionare." *NTS* 21:192–221. References are to the reprint in Theissen 1979, 201–30.

_____. 1975*b.* "Die soziologische Auswertung religiöser Überlieferungen." *Kairos* 17:284–99. References are to the reprint in Theissen 1979, 35–54.

_____. 1975*c.* "Die Starken und Schwachen in Korinth: Soziologische Analyse eines theologischen Streites." *EvT* 35:155–72. References are to the reprint in Theissen 1979, 272–89.

_____. 1979. *Studien zur Soziologie des Urchristentums.* Wissenschaftliche Untersuchungen zum Neuen Testament, 19. Tübingen: Mohr (Siebeck).

_____. 1982. *The Social Setting of Pauline Christianity: Essays on Corinth.* Edited and translated by John H. Schütz. Philadelphia: Fortress.

Thesleff, Holger. 1965. *The Pythagorean Texts of the Hellenistic Period.* Acta Academiae Aboensis, Humaniora, no. 30, pt. 1. Åbo: Åbo Akademi.

Thiselton, Anthony C. 1978. "Realized Eschatology at Corinth." *NTS* 24:510–26.

Tov, Emmanuel. 1974. "Une Inscription grecque d'origine samaritaine trouvé à Thessalonique." *RB* 81:394–99.

Towner, W. Sibley. 1968. "'Blessed be YHWH' and 'Blessed Art Thou, YHWH': The Modulation of a Biblical Formula." *CBQ* 30:386–99.

Treu, Kurt. 1973. "Christliche Empfehlungs-Schemabriefe auf Papyrus." In *Zetesis: Album amicorum door vrieden en collega's aangeboden aan Prof. Dr. E. de Stryker.* . . . Antwerp: Nederlandsche Boekhandel, pp. 629–36.

Turner, E. G. 1954. "Tiberius Iulius Alexander." *JRomSt* 44:54–64.

Turner, Victor. 1964. "Betwixt and Between: The Liminal Period in *Rites de Passage.*" In *Proceedings of the American Ethnological Society, 1964.* References are to the reprint in idem, ed., *The Forest of Symbols: Aspects of Ndembu Ritual.* Ithaca, N.Y.: Cornell University Press, 1977, pp. 93–111.

_____. 1969. *The Ritual Process: Structure and Anti-Structure.* Reprint. Ithaca, N.Y.: Cornell University Press, 1977.

_____. 1974. *Dramas, Fields, and Metaphors: Symbolic Action in Human Society.* Ithaca, N.Y.: Cornell University Press.

Unnik, Willem C. van. 1964. "Die Rücksicht auf die Reaktion der Nicht-Christen als Motiv in der altchristlichen Paränese." In *Judentum, Urchristentum, Kirche: Festschrift für Joachim Jeremias,* ed. Walther Eltester, pp. 221–33. Beihefte zur *ZNW,* 26. Berlin: Akademie.

_____. 1974. "The Interpretation of Romans 12:8 "ὁ μεταδιδοὺς ἐν ἁπλότητι." In *On Language, Culture, and Religion: In Honor of Eugene A. Nida,* ed. Matthew Black and William A. Smalley, pp. 169–83. The Hague and Paris: Mouton.

Usener, Hermann Karl. 1887. *Epicurea.* Reprint. Stuttgart: Teubner, 1966.

Vacalopoulos, Apostolos E. 1963. *A History of Thessaloniki.* Thessalonica: Institute for Balkan Studies.

Vawter, Bruce. 1971. "The Colossians Hymn and the Principle of Redaction." *CBQ* 33:62–81.

Vermes, Geza. 1978. *The Dead Sea Scrolls: Qumran in Perspective.* Cleveland: Collins-World.

Vickers, Michael J. 1970. "Towards Reconstruction of the Town Planning of Roman Thessaloniki." In *Ancient Macedonia,* ed. Basileios Lourdas and Ch. I. Makaronas, pp. 239–51. Thessalonica: Institute for Balkan Studies.

Vielhauer, Philipp. 1939. "*Oikodomē:* Das Bild vom Bau in der christlichen Literatur vom Neuen Testament bis Clemens Alexandrinus." D.Theol. dissertation, Heidelberg. References are to the reprint in *Oikodome: Aufsätze zum Neuen Testament,* ed. Günter Klein, vol. 2, pp. 1–168. Theologische Bücherei, 65. Munich: Kaiser.

Vogel, C. J. de. 1966. *Pythagoras and Early Pythagoreanism: An Interpretation of Neglected Evidence on the Philosopher Pythagoras.* Assen: Van Gorcum.

Vogliano, Achille. 1933. "La grande iscrizione Bacchia del Metropolitan Museum: I." *AJA,* 2d ser., 37:215–31.

Vogt, Joseph. 1939. *Kaiser Julian und das Judentum: Studien zum*

Weltanschauungskampf der Spätantike. Morgenland, 30. Leipzig: Morgenland.

_____. 1971. *Bibliographie zur antiken Sklaverei.* Bochum: Brockmeyer.

_____. 1975. "Der Vorwurf der sozialen Niedrigkeit des frühen Christentums." *Gymnasium* 82:401–11.

Vööbus, Arthur. 1958–60. *History of Asceticism in the Syrian Orient.* 2 vols. Corpus Scriptorum Christianorum Orientalium, 184 and 197. Louvain: CSCO.

Walker, Sheila S. 1972. *Ceremonial Spirit Possession in Africa and Afro-America: Forms, Meanings, and Functional Significance for Individuals and Social Groups.* Supplements to Numen, 2d ser. 4. Leiden: Brill.

Walker, William O., Jr. 1975. "1 Corinthians and Paul's Views Regarding Women." *JBL* 94:94–110.

Wallace, Anthony F. C. 1956. "Revitalization Movements." *American Anthropologist* 58:264–81.

Walter, Nikolaus. 1977. "Die Philipper und das Leiden." In *Die Kirche des Anfangs: Festschrift für Heinz Schürmann,* ed Rudolf Schnackenburg, Josef Ernst, and Joachim Wanke, pp. 417–34. Leipzig: St. Benno.

_____. 1979. "Christusglaube und heidnische Religiosität in paulinischen Gemeinden." *NTS* 25:422–42.

Waltzing, Jean. 1895–1900. *Étude historique sur les corporations professionelles chez les Romains.* 4 vols. Louvain: Peeters.

Weaver, P. R. C. 1967. "Social Mobility in the Early Roman Empire: The Evidence of the Imperial Freedmen and Slaves." *Past and Present* 37:3–20. Reprinted in *Studies in Ancient Society,* ed. Moses I. Finley, pp. 121–40. London: Routledge and Kegan Paul, 1974.

_____. 1972. *Familia Caesaris: A Social Study of the Emperor's Freedmen and Slaves.* Cambridge: At the University Press.

Webber, Robert D. 1971. "The Concept of Rejoicing in Paul." Ph.D. dissertation, Yale University.

Weber, Max. 1922. *Grundriss der Sozialökonomik. Wirtschaft und Gesellschaft,* pt. 1, sec. 3. Tübingen: Mohr (Siebeck). References are to the translation by A. M. Henderson and Talcott Parsons, *The Theory of Social and Economic Organization.* New York: Free Press; London: Macmillan, 1947.

Weidinger, Karl. 1928. *Die Haustafeln: Ein Stück urchristlicher Paränese.* Untersuchungen zum Neuen Testament, 14. Leipzig: Hinrichs.

Weigandt, Peter. 1963. "Zur sogenannten 'Oikosformel.'" *NovT* 6:49–74.

Weiss, Johannes. 1910. *Der erste Korintherbrief.* 9th ed. Kritisch-exegetischer Kommentar über das Neue Testament, 5. Göttingen: Vandenhoeck & Ruprecht.

Wengst, Klaus. 1972. *Christologische Formeln und Lieder des Urchristentums.* Studien zum Neuen Testament, 7. Gütersloh: Mohn.

West, Allen Brown. 1931. *Latin Inscriptions, 1896–1926. Corinth: Results,* vol. 8, pt. 2. Cambridge, Mass.: Harvard University Press.

Westermann, William L. 1955. *Slave Systems of Greek and Roman Antiquity.* Memoirs of the American Philosophical Society, 40. Philadelphia: American Philosophical Society.

Widengren, Geo. 1968. "Heavenly Enthronement and Baptism: Studies in Mandaean Baptism." In *Religions in Antiquity: Essays in Memory of Erwin Ramsdell Goodenough,* ed. Jacob Neusner, pp. 551–89. Studies in the History of Religion, 14. Leiden: Brill.

Wilken, Robert L. 1970. "Toward a Social Interpretation of Early Christian Apologetics." *Church History* 39, no. 1:1–22.

_____. 1971. "Collegia, Philosophical Schools, and Theology." In *The Catacombs and the Colosseum,* ed. Stephen Benko and John J. O'Rourke, pp. 268–91. Valley Forge: Judson.

_____. 1976. "Melito, the Jewish Community at Sardis, and the Sacrifice of Isaac." *Theological Studies* 37:53–69.

Wilson, Brian R. 1973. *Magic and the Millennium: A Sociological Study of Religious Movements of Protest among Tribal and Third-World Peoples.* London: Heinemann.

Wilson, Jack H. 1968. "The Corinthians Who Say There Is No Resurrection of the Dead." *ZNW* 59:90–107.

Wilson, Robert R. 1979. "Prophecy and Ecstasy: A Reexamination." *JBL* 98:321–37.

Witt, Rex. 1970. "The Egyptian Cults in Ancient Macedonia." In *Ancient Macedonia,* ed. Basileios Lourdas and Ch. I. Makaronas, pp. 324–33. Thessalonica: Institute for Balkan Studies.

Worsley, Peter. 1957. *The Trumpet Shall Sound: A Study of 'Cargo' Cults in Melanesia.* References are to the 2d ed. New York: Schocken, 1968.

Wuellner, Wilhelm. 1967. *The Meaning of "Fishers of Men."* Philadelphia: Westminster.

_____. 1979. "Greek Rhetoric and Pauline Argumentation." In *Early Christian Literature and the Classical Intellectual Tradition: In honorem Robert M. Grant,* ed. William Schoedel and Robert L. Wilken, pp. 177–88. Théologie historique, 53. Paris: Beauchesne.

INDEX OF BIBLICAL REFERENCES

INDEX OF MODERN AUTHORS

SUBJECT INDEX

Achaia, 47; Pauline mission at, 42, 114, 231*n*9; first converts, 57, 75, 119, 218*n*69; history, 212*n*258. *See also* Athens; Cenchreae; Corinth

Achaicus, 16, 56, 58, 119, 133

Acts of the Apostles: authorship, 7; reliability of accounts, 26, 61–62, 200*n*30, 230*n*2, 231*n*4; portrayal of Paul and his mission, 28, 41, 168, 199*n*6; sources, 40, 112, 148, 204*n*126

Acts of the Apostles, apocryphal, 102

Aelius Aristides, 17

Africa, 49

Agrippa, King, 26, 61

Alexandria, 29, 34, 35, 38, 39, 203*n*82, 229*n*143

Ampliatus, 57

Ancyra, 43

Andronicus, 57, 132, 216*n*29

Antioch by Pisidia, 41, 42, 43, 49

Antioch-on-the-Orontes, 28, 38, 39

—church: controversy over Gentiles, 10, 81, 110, 111–13, 132, 168, 230*n*2; Paul's relation with, 10, 133, 209–10*n*212; leaders, 61, 62; conflict over table fellowship, 103, 116, 134, 161

Apameia, 45, 50, 210*nn*221, 224, and 228

Apelles, 56

Apocalyptic, Christian: characteristics of, 96, 177; debate about importance of, for Paul, 171–72, 240*n*20; functions of, 172, 173–75, 179; Paul's use of, 174–75, 175–76, 177–79, 182–83, 189, 227*n*118. *See also* Millenarian movements

Apocalyptic, Jewish, 92, 96, 171, 174, 177, 185

Apollos, 61, 67, 82, 117–18, 133, 134

Apostles, office and function of, 131–33

Apostolic council, 40–41. *See also* Antioch on-the-Orontes; Jerusalem

Apphia, 60, 63, 143

Apuleius, *Metamorphoses,* 49

Aquila, 217*n*51. *See also* Prisca and Aquila

Archippus of Colossae, 56

Aristarchus, 47, 56, 218*n*70

Aristobulus, 16, 56, 75, 217*n*54

Artisans and manual workers, 17, 64–65. *See also* Paul

Asia, 41, 42, 43, 57, 108, 113, 209*n*204

Associates of Paul. *See* Paul, associates of

Asyncritus, 56, 75

Athens, 26, 41, 61, 114, 133, 218*n*69

Authority structure of Christian group, 90, 190. *See also* Offices in churches

Banquets, 68, 159

Baptism: images connected with, 87, 107, 169, 179, 185, 187; traditions connected with, 88, 115, 126–27; pattern of dying and rising, 89, 93, 150, 152, 154–57, 158, 182, 188; symbolized by Red Sea crossing, 99; connection with paraenesis, 100, 147, 154, 157, 166–67, 227*n*115; functions of, 102, 107, 139, 153–54, 191; in Corinth, 117, 119, 121; connection with Spirit, 121; modern study of, 142, 237*n*44; actions of ritual, 150–52, 237*n*50; relation to Jewish washings, 237*n*48. *See also* Initiation; Jesus, death and resurrection of; Ritual, definition and functions of

Barnabas: and Paul, 10–11, 62, 133–34; cousin of Mark, 60; church leader in Antioch, 61; celibate, 102; break with Paul, 103, 161, 209–10*n*212; with Paul in Jerusalem, 110–12

Benefactors, role in churches, 135, 137. *See also* Patrons of churches

Beroea, 28, 41, 47, 209*n*204

Body of Christ, as metaphor, 89

Boundaries, between Christians and outsiders, 85, 97, 169, 190. *See also* Purity, of community; Ritual boundaries, Jewish

Caesar, household of (*familia caesaris*), 21–22, 63, 73, 75, 76

Caesarea, 63